Migration, Transnationalization, and Race in a Changing New York

Migration, Transnationalization, and Race in a Changing New York

EDITED BY

Héctor R. Cordero-Guzmán,
Robert C. Smith, and
Ramón Grosfoguel

TEMPLE UNIVERSITY PRESS

PHILADELPHIA

Temple University Press, Philadelphia 19122
Copyright © 2001 by Temple University
All rights reserved
Published 2001
Printed in the United States of America

Library of Congress Cataloging-in-Publication Data

Migration, transnationalization, and race in a changing New York / edited by
Héctor R. Cordero-Guzmán, Robert C. Smith, and Ramón Grosfoguel.
    p. cm.
   Includes bibliographical references.
    ISBN 1-56639-887-8 (cloth : alk. paper) — ISBN 1-56639-888-6 (pbk. : alk. paper)
    1. Immigrants—New York (State)—New York. 2. New York (N.Y.)—Emigration
and immigration. I. Cordero-Guzmán, Héctor R. II. Smith, Robert C., 1964– .
III. Grosfoguel, Ramón.
F128.9.A1 M54 2001
305.8'009747'109045—dc21   00-053675

To our parents, our partners, and our children: Alexandra Cordero-Villafuerte, Héctor Joaquin Cordero-Villafuerte, Owen Daly-Smith, Liam Daly-Smith, and Nadia Grosfoguel

Contents

Acknowledgments

Working in a collective enterprise is a very rewarding challenge. Once we decided we wanted to prepare an edited volume that presented some new research on the changing dynamics of migration, race, and ethnicity in New York City, we organized a small conference to discuss our work and the drafts of the various chapters. Several colleagues participated in the conference and helped us with the project. They include: Cesar Ayala, Jorge Ayala, Francios Avenas, Peter Benda, Frank Bonilla, Mehdi Bozorgmehr, Gerard Bushell, Eric Canales, Josh DeWind, Greta Gilbertson, Sherri Grasmuck, Ben Harrison, David Howell, Tarry Hum, Dae Young Kim, Jack Krauskopf, David Kyle, Peter Kwong, Douglas S. Massey, John Mollenkopf, Liz Mueller, Arturo Sanchez, Livio Sansone, Saskia Sassen, Roger Waldinger, and Aristide Zolberg. We would also like to thank Joe Behalo, Maureen Burnley, Catherina Villafuerte Cordero, Janice Dunmore, Jean Charles, Rose Diaz, Laura Elerbee, Eric Feliciano, Anita Fletcher, Linda Freeman, Alejandra Vicco, and Kevin Wedan from the Milano Graduate School at the New School University for their support in organizing the meeting and managing the project. Michael Ames, Doris Braendel, Deborah Stuart Smith, David Updike, and two anonymous reviewers from Temple were very helpful with their comments and suggestions as they steered us through the rigorous publication process. Our deepest gratitude goes to Dr. Melvin Oliver and his staff at the Ford Foundation for their kind support and for giving us a grant to do the project.

Migration, Transnationalization, and Race in a Changing New York

CHAPTER 1

Introduction: Migration, Transnationalization, and Ethnic and Racial Dynamics in a Changing New York

Robert C. Smith, Héctor R. Cordero-Guzmán, and Ramón Grosfoguel

This is a book about the meaning and experience of contemporary immigration to the United States, focusing specifically on New York City. The chapters provide insights into both the particular historical juncture in which New York finds itself and the current state of studies of immigration. We seek to understand the complex processes of assimilation, incorporation, transnationalization, and ethnic and racial formation in the context of the city's changing political economy. And we focus on the social dynamics of New York City's racial, ethnic, and national diversities as these three elements interact with a changing political economy to place groups in particular positions in economic and social hierarchies and structures.

Following the Introduction, the book is divided into two parts, with the first focusing on transnational processes and the second on immigrant incorporation. Part I has six chapters. Its main analytical work is to add a historical dimension to the study of transnational life and processes among immigrants in New York, and to contextualize these processes through case studies that examine the local effects of global, national, and local policies and stratification patterns (see also Morales and Bonilla 1993; Sassen 1988, 1991). Part II also has six chapters and focuses on immigrant incorporation, examining such issues as racialization, ethnicity, and economic structures.

Three Social Facts About Transnationalization, Immigrant Incorporation, and the Changing Ethnic Structure and Political Economy of New York City

Three social facts related to New York and immigration frame this book. First, New York continues to be a major center of immigration with changing racial and ethnic dynamics. Second, racial, ethnic, and gender processes are interrelated with change in the local and global economies. Third, New York is an important site of transnational action and a node in the global economy. Our discussion includes new analyses of some established research topics, such as poverty among Puerto Ricans, as well as among new groups, such as Peruvians, and new themes, such as the creation of social capital in the context of interminority relations. This approach underlines the importance of specifying the structural and historical context of the analysis, no matter what its theoretical stripe (Tilly 1981). We discuss each of these themes briefly, before moving onto a critical engagement with the literature on migration.

Compositional Change

New York has undergone profound changes in its political economy and its ethnic and racial composition over the past half century and especially in the past twenty-five years. The first change has been from an economy based in manufacturing and related industries to one based in services and related industries, and it has been ably analyzed (see, e.g., Mollenkopf and Castells 1991; Sassen 1988, 1991; Waldinger 1996;). One statistic suffices to illustrate the change. In 1950 manufacturing accounted for 42.8 percent of the city's 3.47 million jobs; in 1997 it accounted for only 15.8 percent of the city's 3.41 million jobs (Mollenkopf 1999, 414). The major sectors of growth have been in services, producing both high and low income jobs. The end result has been an "hourglass economy," with many good jobs at the top for those in highly skilled "information jobs" requiring high levels of education and many jobs at the bottom in the non-union, unstable labor markets populated by the city's poor, including increasing numbers of immigrants. Middle-class jobs offering stable employment and a ladder out of poverty—especially those not requiring college educations—are declining relative to the growth in high and low skilled, and paid, jobs. Many analysts, Saskia Sassen (1988, 1991) in particular, link this hourglass economy with larger processes of globalization and New York's growing importance in this global economy. Profound transformations in economics, social relations, and relations of governance have accompanied New York's engagement with such global systems (see also Cordero Guzmán and Grosfoguel 2000; Mollenkopf 1999; Sassen 1996; Waldinger 1996). Alex Julca's analysis in Chapter 11 of Peruvian immigrants' incorporation into and adaptation to New York's unsteady labor markets offers one case of such dynamics.

Simultaneously, the city has undergone tremendous demographic change. In 1950 New York was a largely white, native-born, working-class city whose main jobs were in manufacturing. Now whites are a numerical minority (though still the largest minority, and a much larger proportion of voters), 85 percent of jobs are not in manufacturing, and interethnic and interracial dynamics have become even more complicated by the influx of many new, nonwhite immigrants. In 1997, non-Hispanic whites constituted 36 percent of the city's population, while non-Hispanic blacks were 29 percent, non-Hispanic Asians were 8 percent, and Hispanics were 26 percent. Moreover, immigrants and their children—"foreign stock"—constitute significant percentages of the population in all these groups: 55 percent of the black population, 59 percent of Latinos (excluding Puerto Ricans), 98 percent of Asians, and, surprisingly, 52 percent of whites in the city (Mollenkopf 1999). New York received more than 1.5 million immigrants between 1980 and 1996 (Rivera-Batiz 1996), the largest number since the beginning of this century. Also, New York receives the most diverse immigrant population of any city in the country, and perhaps the world. The New York City Emergency Immigrant Education Census of 1996 indicates that there were children from 204 countries in its schools, and 23 different countries had more than 7,000 new immigrant children enter within the previous three years (Rivera-Batiz 1996). Moreover, this immigrant influx has changed the greater New York region; Reynolds Farley (1998) estimates that 48 percent of the region's population is of foreign stock.

These two large-scale changes are affecting other major cities with large immigrant populations, such as Los Angeles (Waldinger and Bozorgmehr 1996), and doing so in broadly similar ways that include a cutback in public services and fiscal retrenchment that can be traced to the dynamics of globalization and global cities (Sassen 1988, 1991, 1998). But several characteristics make New York different from Los Angeles. New York is the oldest immigrant city in the United States and one of the country's original and certainly historically its most important port of entry for the immigrants during previous waves of immigration. As a result, New York's politics are much more pro-immigrant than those of Los Angeles and other cities, not because New Yorkers are more enlightened on the topic of immigration, but because the city's political institutions and population dynamics have evolved in ways that require greater collaboration among ethnic groups. John Mollenkopf (1999) cites three factors that make New York's politics more pro-immigrant than Los Angeles's. Whites in New York, he points out, must form majority voting coalitions to govern, while whites in Los Angeles do not. Also, the population of New York is more evenly balanced between blacks, whites, and Latinos than is the population in Los Angeles, and there are more immigrants and their children in each group in New York than in Los Angeles, thus constraining anti-immigrant sentiment. Furthermore, New York's political institutions are more broadly representative than are those of Los Angeles in the sense that New York's power is more decentralized and provides more outlets for representation and the negotiation of conflict. Cordero-Guzmán and Navarro (2000; see also Cordero-Guzmán 2001) analyze another factor that makes New York different from most other cities—its large number of long-term community-based organizations (CBOs) serving immigrants. These CBOs and other service institutions are politically well connected, have been in existence for many years, and can advocate on behalf of their clients in ways that similar organizations in Los Angeles have not and cannot.

These differences manifest themselves in the pro-immigrant stances of the current mayor, Rudy Giuliani, a moderate-to-conservative Republican. While New York's multicultural history has not inured it to the dangers of anti-immigrant sentiments or racism, New York's current immigration politics reflect its historical multiculturalism and the conflicts inherent in it. The comparison with Los Angeles is ironic and telling. The irony lies in the fact that whereas much of the population boom in California since 1900 has been whites fleeing the East Coast and Midwest when immigrants and minorities entered, seeking greener pastures, less crowded cities, and whiter neighborhoods, their descendants now live in a state with a huge influx of immigrants (Mollenkopf 1999). The effects of the historical differences in political culture and institutions between New York and California can be seen by contrasting political leadership on immigration issues in the two states. California governor Pete Wilson led the political fight to pass the anti-immigrant Proposition 187 in his state in 1994—which denied all but emergency aid to undocumented immigrants and placed an affirmative obligation on public employees, such as doctors and teachers, to report those they suspected of being undocumented—and Propositions 209 and 227 later, and Los Angeles Mayor Riordan adopted largely neutral positions toward such anti-immigrant legislation (Mollenkopf 1999). In New York, Giuliani sued the federal government to stop enforcement of municipal regulations that forbid city employees from sharing information on a person's legal status except in the context of a criminal investigation, and to challenge the legality of stopping food stamp distribution to elderly and disabled legal immigrants. There are two points. First, in New York, even a Republican mayor whose support comes strongly from white, U.S.–born citizens in the outer boroughs, must support immigrants, even if he deviates from his party's line. This difference marks one way that New York is particularly interesting, and perhaps distinct. There are some signs that things are changing. Governor Wilson's anti-immigrant policies actually helped make more Latino immigrants into U.S. citizens in California by pushing them to defend themselves with citizenship and the vote, and Latinos have entered California politics as never before. For example, in 1999–2000, both the Speaker of the California House and the Minority leader were minorities, and both Democrats and Republicans have actively been courting the Latino vote (see Mollenkopf, Olson, and Ross 1998). The second point is that Giuliani's pro-immigrant stance did not stop him from adopting a variety of positions that hurt these same immigrants, including cutting spending on, and restricting access to, social services (Cordero-Guzmán and Navarro 2000).

Ethnic and Racial Dynamics

Having more enlightened racial and ethnic politics than Los Angeles, however, is a standard to which few should be content to aspire, and New York has plenty of room for improvement in its racial and ethnic dynamics. In particular, New York's relative success in the sphere of formal politics, in which blacks and Puerto Ricans are somewhat included in the liberal establishment, does not negate its particular history with racialization processes in other aspects of life. This leads us to a larger analytical point, that racialization processes can proceed differently at different levels of social life. In politics, they can work in one way and in the labor market in another and in schools, or social arenas, in another. New York and its environs also have the distinction of being the primary initial destination for Puerto Ricans, West Indians, and other black and Latino immigrants, and a main destination for African Americans migrating from the south. While this diversity has increased awareness of the presence and experiences of other groups, it has also made New York the site for the development of a sophisticated stratification system where racial phenotype, immigrant status, and ethnicity and nationality all figured into creating racializing hierarchies, which evolved as the definitions of whiteness and blackness, and other categories, have changed. These categories matter because once they are established, they influence life chances and future trajectories. Immigrants identified as black experienced a segregation and discrimination that stratified their incorporation and subsequent economic, geographical, and social mobility (Massey and Denton 1993; Torres 1995).

Understanding racializing dynamics helps put the "immigrant analogy" and related processes in context (see Omi and Winant 1986). In its standard form, the immigrant analogy compares the socioeconomic fates of African Americans and non-black immigrants and uses the greater historical success of the latter group to infer the moral culpability of native minorities and exonerate the larger society of any responsibility for structuring those different trajectories (Lieberson 1980; Model 1990; Roediger 1991; Waldinger 1996). This analogy traces its intellectual roots back to W.E.B. Du Bois's argument that poor whites received a "public psychological wage" by being "not black" in the United States, which proved their fitness for membership in a free community (Roediger 1991, 25; see also Du Bois 1977, 700–701; Ignatiev 1995). While Du Bois attempted to explain why poor whites in the postbellum South ignored their common class interests to ally with the white aristocracy in exploiting and demonizing blacks, David Roediger (1991) insightfully applies this analysis to the white working class, including immigrants, during the last wave of migration. Italian and Irish immigrants of the last wave were not seen as being white when they came into the United States. They demonstrated their whiteness, however, in large part by embracing anti-black racism and thus received advantages in the labor market, in housing, and in other spheres of life. This reasoning is still used to explain the different outcomes among descendants of African Americans and white immigrants: My ancestors endured discrimination when they came to this country, but they prospered through hard work. If other groups—such as African Americans—do not prosper, then it must be their fault.

This logic both absolves the larger society of any responsibility and upholds the image of a level playing field. It also provides what seems to many descendants of these immigrants a plausible narrative to explain the fate of these two groups. The problem, though, lies in the failure to consider the effects of racial segregation in housing and the devastating and persistent effects such segregation and differences in resources can have, as convincingly shown in the work of Douglas Massey and Nancy Denton (1993). Furthermore, this logic does not consider racial and ethnic dynamics in the allocation of opportunities in jobs (Model 1990), or in the structuring of political power. In fact, it denies what could be argued is a foundational social premise of the U.S. republic, which immigrants learn quickly when they come to the United States: Only whites are fit for citizenship, for full membership in the polity and society, so make sure that when your group's ethnicity and race are defined, they fall on the "white ethnic" and not "native minority" side of the color line (Ignatiev 1995; Roediger 1991). What then occurs among many of these groups is a process of "whitening." The Irish, Jews, Italians, and before them the Bohemians, Magyars, Slavs, and other "races" were seen in the twentieth century—and for some in the postwar period—as non-white, as a different race from the white Protestants who defined the "mainstream" ideals for many years—witness Milton Gordon's account, published in 1964—and the white Roman Catholics who came to the fore later (see also Perlmann and Waldinger 1997; Portes and Rumbaut 1990). In particular, as groups have improved their position in politics, in the economy, and in the neighborhoods they lived in, and they have become "whiter"; hence, the Jews, Irish, and Italians are now considered white. Groups that did not have "success in" all three of these categories did not become "white."

These racializing dynamics are repeating themselves in New York and throughout the United States today under somewhat new and different conditions. First, most newcomers are immigrants "of color," meaning non-white, and come from continents other than Europe. We put "of color" in quotation marks because the Italians, Jews, and Irish, among others, were also considered non-white when they arrived, and it is not certain what category some of these new immigrants will ultimately fall into. Moreover, the experience of racialization will likely also vary not just by the four main racial categories of Asian, Latino, black, and white but also by particular ethnic and national groups, and according to levels of socioeconomic success, and even by gender. Second, the racialization process in New York City includes also Puerto Ricans in the most stigmatized minority category with native-born blacks because of their colonial status, cultural differences, and experience of discrimination. Third, the immigrant status of the first generation and the ethnic identity of much of the second and subsequent generations can partially (but will not necessarily) insulate some of them from the vagaries of American racism, as discussed by Vilna Bashi Bobb (Chapter 10, this volume), and others (e.g., M. Waters 1994, 1996, 1999). Many immigrants and their descendants, especially Latinos (but also Asians), have an "in-between" status, in which they are "not Black but not White" (Perlmann and Waldinger 1997, 905) or "native born, and not black" (Smith 1995, 1996). In this state, the meaning of their Latino identity, and its relationship to the U.S. color line, is not clear and is still being determined.

Taken together, these three conditions have made for interesting distinctions in social identities and outcomes for many new immigrants and their children. For example, some West Indian youth who are seen by mainstream U.S. society as "black" might end up identifying themselves, depending on factors such as education, family social class, and parents' affiliation with ethnic organizations, as "ethnics" and hence not black in the same ways native-born blacks are black and not affected by U.S.

racism in the same way native blacks are. Other such West Indian youth might end up as (racialized) native minorities whose lives are much like native blacks and whose life chances are similarly limited, or as immigrants who are outside the U.S. racial dichotomy altogether (M. Waters 1994, 1999), and who perceive but are not much affected by racist limits. In an explicit statement of the immigrant analogy, Mexican gang and religious youth group leaders told Robert Smith (1995, 1996) that Mexicans, and all members of the "Hispanic race"—which they said includes Mexicans, Central Americans, South Americans, and Puerto Ricans born on the island—were better than native-born minorities, which include blacks and Puerto Ricans born in New York. The difference, they argued, lay in the positive effect of their immigrant culture as against the deleterious effect of the cultures of native minorities, thus explicitly elaborating a racialized schema to explain their own difference and success (Smith 1995, 1996, 2001). These same people, however, lament the turn that young Mexican immigrants and Mexican Americans in New York have taken since those statements were made in the early 1990s. National studies demonstrate that, with important exceptions, Mexicans with lighter skins, especially those growing up in Spanish-speaking neighborhoods, do better in school and have higher self-esteem than do Mexicans with darker skins (Murgia and Telles 1996). One could argue that in certain arenas, New York City is becoming more of what the notable Caribbeanist Gordon Lewis calls a "multilayered pigmentocracy" (1983; see also Grosfoguel 1996) where pigmented hierarchy greatly affects life chances. Analyzing how this pigmentocracy emerges and is reproduced is an important analytical task.

The interplay between racializing processes, the immigrant analogy, and economic changes and social hierarchies is playing out in interesting and different ways for Asians and Latinos. Puerto Ricans represent perhaps the paradigmatic case of how these racializing dynamics can combine with economic change and discrimination to create enduring poverty. Moreover, the version of the immigrant analogy aimed at Puerto Ricans has a twist because they are both migrants and citizens. There is a perception that citizenship has advantages; but second-class citizenship does not. As discussed, Puerto Ricans were subjected to racial segregation and discrimination in schools and neighborhoods that concentrated the negative effects of poverty (Massey and Denton 1993; Torres 1995). They migrated in large numbers to New York during the 1940s through the 1970s when other immigration was at historic lows, but vacancies for entrepreneurship were also low. Furthermore, they were discriminated against in the labor market and their employment was concentrated in the declining manufacturing and garment industry. This meant that better employment and economic mobility were limited (Waldinger 1996). In addition, when the previous generation of Jews and Italians left the industry and vacancies in entrepreneurial activities did open up, Puerto Ricans faced new competition in the form of better financed and more experienced immigrants from Asia and Latin America. At the same time, "second-generation" Puerto Ricans—those born in New York—were not entering this industry but pursuing employment in other sectors instead, with some, especially women, emphasizing education and professional employment as a route to upward mobility. Here the problem was that as this mainland-raised and -educated second generation came of age in the 1970s through 1990s, they faced an hourglass economy. Many found employment in the professional sector, but others found that their educational attainment was too high to allow them to compete effectively for the lower- and middle-income jobs but considered too low for the better jobs (Rodriguez 1989; Torres 1995). The Puerto Rican experience in New York City illustrates the development and maintenance of a sophisticated stratification system based on social-class background, but where the allocation and distribution of material resources is also driven by the dynamics of race, ethnicity, and national origin.

The experience of Dominicans provides another example of how race and political economy combine to produce particular outcomes. Dominican entrepreneurs have shown an impressive capacity to mobilize social capital and circumvent their exclusion from mainstream institutions in trying to achieve upward mobility, and some have used this dynamism to make a case that immigrant success is due to an abundance of, and native minority distress due to a lack of, work ethic (Chavez 1991). Others argue that we can deepen our understanding of these differences through a focus on community-level variables, which articulate a community's economic and social energies and are often neglected for purely structural or cultural explanations (Portes and Zhou 1992, 1993). Yet the larger Dominican population is coming to look more and more like the larger Puerto Rican population in terms of its low income and educational levels, its use of public assistance, and its rate of single-headed households, as well as other indicators of social inequality (Hernandez, Rivera-Batiz, and Agodini. 1995; Lobo, Salvo, and Virgin 1996, 1998). These similarities push the analysis toward structural causation, especially racial segregation and the resulting concentration in poverty (Massey and Denton 1993), as key in determining Dominican life chances in New York.

Asians as a group have a very different relationship to racialization than do many Latinos, particularly those with more "African" features and darker skin. One way this relationship manifests itself is in differential access to entrepreneurial training and resources, as analyzed by Jennifer Lee in Chapter 12. Lee asks why African Americans have much lower rates of self-employment than Koreans and Jews, and what are the consequences. She starts by noting the importance of entrepreneurship for upward mobility among some immigrant groups and its clear importance in our thinking about such matters. She then explicates the reasons for lower rates of entrepreneurship she gleaned from fieldwork and interviews with Korean, Jewish, and African American entrepreneurs. In contrast to the Koreans and Jews, who were able to secure capital for their businesses through family and friends even when they had little credit, almost all African Americans had to use formal institutions, such as banks, to get credit to start their businesses. Moreover, when problems emerged, African Americans had less help in overcoming obstacles, such as fires and robberies, than did Koreans and Jews. She shows clear racial patterns in social processes supporting entrepreneurship, which is one important avenue to upward mobility.

Another way these racializing dynamics manifest themselves is in the decreasing "social distance" between Asians and whites; Asians have become less "socially distant" from whites than Latinos and blacks (Alba and Nee 1999, 144–45). On the whole and over several generations, Asians and their children tend to achieve parity with or surpass their white non-Hispanic counterparts in terms of income and, especially, education. As with Jews in the past, the limited mobility available in the ethnic niche helps push the second and subsequent generations toward education and mainstream employment, a tendency made stronger by the greater rewards of education in an hourglass economy (Alba and Nee 1999; Nee, Sanders, and Sernau 1994). Moreover, Asians, especially women, increasingly marry "out," most often with whites. David Lopez (1999) compares rates of endogamy among two cohorts of Asian women in Los Angeles aged 55–64 years and aged 25–34 years. The younger women married out at higher rates than the older ones, with endogamy rates of 86 percent for the older ones and 44 percent for the younger ones. The Japanese endogamy rate for older women was 89 percent, compared with 32 percent for the younger women, a rate that approached the 24 percent among Jews. The disproportionate representation of Asians at America's elite universities also signals a decrease in the social distance and a possible whitening of Asians in certain spheres of social life.

Another example involves the dynamics of the 1991 redistricting on the Lower East Side of New York City (Woo 1997). In the redistricting process, one intent was to increase the chances of electing an Asian to the city council from Chinatown. The question was raised whether to draw the district to include the Lower East Side, which would put Asians in a district with more blacks and Latinos, or whether to go west toward Greenwich Village so that it would include more whites. The latter course was chosen, apparently on the belief that Asians would be more likely to be elected in a "white" district than in a black and Latino one. In the black and Latino district, many Asian leaders feared either that they would be treated as the newest minorities who would not be given a chance to get power or that Asians' middle-class status would be held against them were the district drawn to include more lower income people on the east side. The "in-between" status of Asians seems to be tipping toward a whitening process that is very reminiscent of the course taken by Jews—from high levels of niche concentration in self-employment, through universities and into more mainstream employment, and out to suburbs to increasingly intermarry with whites.

A final example is analyzed in Johanna Lessinger's discussion in Chapter 8 of Indian immigrants and their children as they "confront the American Dream." Lessinger insightfully analyzes how Indian immigrants have constructed their social location and self-identification as members of the professional middle class, who, despite their dark skin, are not racial but rather neutrally ethnic—"honorary whites" in her phrase. Part of this neutrality has been a cultivated absence, as a group, from politics, broadly defined. This homogenized picture of an upwardly mobile group incorporating to the right side of America's racial divide and the immigrant analogy is complicated by the internal stratification within the Indian population, and the resulting contradictions. Many Indians are not professionals but shopkeepers or small entrepreneurs, whose success depends, like that of other immigrants, on their being able to exploit their worse-off coethnics as cheap labor. Moreover, the Indians' embrace of a kind of racial neutrality leaning toward whiteness is not completely accepted by many, including U.S. natives, some of whom have violently attacked Indians. Among the U.S.-born second generation, it is harder to maintain their race-neutral position as other natives try to fit them into black, white, or Latino categories or reject them for not being able to fit.

As these examples show, the relationship to the racialization process will differ for various nationality groups listed under the label "Asian" and will depend on their place in the economy, what neighborhoods they live in, and their reception by institutions—corporate, governmental, and social—now dominated by whites, especially in the suburbs, or by earlier minorities. Moreover, while Asians have certainly achieved significant upward mobility, through ethnic solidarity and through education and geographical mobility and decreased social distance with whites, Asian ethnicity can also function as a screen, hiding coethnic exploitation from scrutiny (see Chin 1996; Kwong 1987, 1997).

This brief discussion has generated more questions than answers about the current racialization process. Will Asians become "ethnics" as the Jews, Irish, Italians, and Eastern Europeans did and hence "whiter," or at least "ethnic, but not black"? Will we continue to have four racial categories—whites, Asians, blacks, Latinos—with the former two seen as falling on the "right" side of America's color line, and the latter two on the "wrong" side? Will or have light-skinned Latinos—such as Colombians—become "whiter," particularly if they are economically more successful? How will educational, geographical, and work mobility affect each group's relationship to racialization? How will different kinds of Latino groups negotiate their "in-between" status as being not black and not white? How will the fact of different kinds of pigmentation and physical appearance among Caribbean Latinos—who are more likely to have African ancestry, appearance, and cultural traits—differ from those of meso-American and South American Latinos—who are more likely to have Spanish and indigenous ancestry, appearance, and cultural traits? (See Smith forthcoming b, for speculation on this question with Mexicans, and Cordero-Guzmán and Navarro 2000 on immigrant youth service providers.) What is clear is that these Latino immigrants and their descendants will have to negotiate their in-between status, and that the outcome of their engagement with these racialized structures in not certain. These are important areas for future research.

New York as a Site of Transnational Action and Processes

As a center of transnational migrant activity, New York is a site for practices and discourses that link sending communities and countries with emigrants and migrants abroad. As a central node in the global economy, New York also manifests in particularly virulent forms the contradictions and exigencies of global capitalist development (Torres 1995; Torres and Bonilla 1993). Hence, New York City has adjacent postal ZIP codes in the Upper East Side and East Harlem that have among the highest and lowest per capita incomes in the country. Many of the former's inhabitants are linked by their investments and other activities into global markets while the latter may barely have links outside their immediate neighborhood. Sassen has written (1988) with particular eloquence about how global cities like New York have experienced further social and economic polarization because of globalization. Polarization helps explain, for example, why so many immigrants would come to a place with such high rates of unemployment in the 1980s. It also examines how the lives of such globally engaged elite become so disengaged from the rest of the city, with their fates having very little to do with one another (Sassen 1998).

New York has also been a historically important site of home country and diasporic politics. Transnational life is not new among immigrants, who have waged many nationalist and other struggles in New York as well as on their native turf. As Michael Hanagan (1998) points out, struggles for the formation of an Irish nation and state were carried out the United States, especially in New York and Boston. Indeed, Eamon de Valera, Ireland's first president, was a U.S. citizen whose life was spared after his participation in the 1916 Easter Rising because of his American citizenship. De Valera used the United States as a place to organize support free from the coercion of the British state and also to raise funds for the revolt. Similarly, New York and the United States became important in helping to forge Italian nationalism. Many migrants from villages learned that they were "Italian" only upon arriving in the United States and being treated as such and then were enlisted in the nationalist cause (Gabaccia 2000; Portes and Rumbaut 1990; Wyman 1993). Intense, simultaneous debate over remittances and exploitation by the *banchisti* (brokers and money remitters, like Sarah Mahler's *"viajeros"* in Chapter 5) raged in New York and Italy, resulting in transnational mobilization by immigrants, the *banchisti,* and their respective advocates in both places (Cinel 1991; Smith 1998b).

Today, history repeats itself: Leonel Fernandez, former president of the Dominican Republic, holds a U.S. green card and is a product of the New York City public schools. New York is also the site of extraterritorial domestic and transnational politics by Colombians, Dominicans, Mexicans, Israelis, Central Americans, West Indians, Indians and Pakistanis, Poles, and others (Glick Schiller and Fouron, Chapter 3; Guarnizo, Sanchez, and Roach 1999; Lessinger 1998; Pienkos 1991; Smith 1998b). Some of these mobilizations, such as those by Colombians, began as grass-roots efforts later engineered by the sending state for its own foreign policy objectives, while others, such as those by extreme nationalists among Indian immigrants, involved organizing outside the home state's coercive capacity. Moreover, as Pamela Graham documents in Chapter 4, these processes of political incorporation in New York and the Dominican Republic are not disjointed but take place simultaneously and reinforce each other.

While much transnational activity is a form of extraterritorially conducted national politics, most of it is quotidian. Sarah Mahler, in Chapter 5, and Nancy Foner, in Chapter 2, analyze some of the everyday activities that go into the emergence of transnational life, or limiting its ability to emerge. Mahler analyzes how the daily routine of life is and is not transnational, and how it differs at the sites of origin and destination. Foner analyzes the ways in which transnational life during the last great wave of migration and today are similar and different, comparing the effects of technology, social and political environment, and other factors.

The Literature

This volume reflects the editors' belief that contemporary studies of immigrant incorporation and transnationalization must demonstrate cognizance of the pervasive influence of gender, ethnicity and, especially, race in determining life chances, as well as cognizance of the emergence of transnational forms of migrant life and how these change social and political forms and create new forms, including forms of political community and membership. Such studies must ground these analyses within the political economy that shapes other processes, on the local and the global level, and must acknowledge the importance of considering the geo-strategic linkages and (neo)colonial relations in analyzing the development of contemporary social processes. The authors in this volume arrive at these conclusions from different perspectives but agree broadly on the importance of including these elements in contemporary analyses of migration. The authors also illustrate the diversity and complexity of current work on immigration to New York City.

We identify four schools of thought, which have evolved around the concepts of assimilation, social capital, transnationalization, and world systems. In this section, we examine each perspective's theoretical utility and explore its limitations in helping us understand contemporary migration and related processes.

Assimilation

Assimilationism was the dominant approach in the study of immigration for many decades, from the 1920s to the late 1960s, but has become a favorite theoretical "other" against which many scholars working on ethnicity and related topics today define their own work. This is both understandable and lamentable. It is understandable because there are many weaknesses in the assimilationist paradigm. First, its proponents were unaware of their "domain assumptions." They posited that the progress of immigrants in their new societies would stem from the inherent characteristics of the immigrant groups themselves and their ability to conform to mainstream values, norms, and expectations. The problem was not so much that their schemes did not describe social reality—they often did— but that they did so uncritically. Hence, W. Lloyd Warner and Leo Srole's (1945) now infamous descriptions of the slower assimilation and upward mobility of blacks, non-English speakers, and non-Christians did accurately reflect much of the social reality that existed in America in the mid-1940s. But to simply describe this reality without offering a normative critique, and without imputing causal responsibility to the larger structures that shaped these different rates and paths of assimilation, was to collude with this oppression. The presumption that assimilation to the mainstream was desirable, that such a white mainstream existed, and that adherence to its norms would automatically benefit newcomers plagued research in the assimilation paradigm. Like most social scientists of the day, these early assimilationists believed that joining the mainstream and surrendering one's own past were prerequisites to success in the United States.

Yet despite its weaknesses, the assimilationist theoretical paradigm and especially its normative political project, still informs much current scholarship because it deals with the fundamental question of how immigrants become part of the larger U.S. society. Moreover, early scholars studying assimilation made theoretical contributions that remain useful today, such as Milton Gordon's (1964) distinction between cultural and structural assimilation, the former referring to such changes as immigrants and their descendants learning English or adopting American cultural norms (or an "overly homogenized and reified conception of it" [Gans 1999, 162]) and the latter referring to their integration into social institutions with the dominant (white) population, including such measures as rates of intermarriage or entry into universities, corporate power centers, or neighborhood integration, which imply leaving their own ethnic institutions (see Gans 1999). Richard Alba and Victor Nee's (1999) interesting and in some ways successful attempt to rehabilitate assimilation redefines the concept by recontextualizing it (Morawska 1994). While defining assimilation as "the decline, and at its endpoint the disappearance, of an ethnic and racial distinction and the cultural and social differences that express it" (Alba and Nee 1999, 159), they purposefully omit comment on whether the changes will be one-sided or mutual on the part of the majority or minority, and whether the assimilation will be to a majority (e.g., white) or minority (e.g., African American) group. Theirs is a useful effort to retool a concept that is often dismissed out of hand. For example, assimilationist approaches identify different arenas—social, economic, institutional—in which processes of assimilation may or may not take place, and thus they help us understand the dynamics of intergroup relations in the United States. Moreover, immigrants today confront many of the same problems earlier generations of immigrants confronted, such as identity, opportunity, and generational change. And there is evidence that assimilation, as defined above, is proceeding apace for many immigrant groups, even low-income ones. For example, by the third generation most grandchildren of immigrants, including Mexicans, are monolingual English speakers who hold political and cultural beliefs (and even experience forms of bad health) much like those of most other Americans (de la Garza and DeSipio 1998; Rumbaut 1998, forthcoming). Moreover, suburbanization tends to speed assimilation in that it usually accompanies increasing socioeconomic status, the decreasing importance of ethnic institutions, and the retention of a symbolic ethnicity (Gans 1979).

Part of the problem with this concept in general is that by focusing on whether or not a group ends up conforming to native norms, be they white or black, it fails to fully identify and sufficiently critique what we consider to be a central process in immigrant incorporation, the racialization process. Even in Alba and Nee's cogently argued resuscitation of the concept (1999), there is strong evidence that some engagement with racialization is a central part of the experience of immigrants and their children in the United States. For example, they argue that the most "impassable racist barriers" for immigrants and their children in the United States are not just dark skin—witness the mobility of dark-skinned Indians—but rather a "connection to the African American group" (149). They also note that the disadvantages of low educational level last through generations, especially for Hispanics. Finally, they speculate that Asians and some light-skinned Latinos may jump the racial divide and become "whiter," following Jews and Italians and others before them. We think that given this kind of pervasive racial dynamic in the processes of incorporation, racialization merits inclusion as an important theory in social science tool kit for studying immigration today.

Social Capital

An important and valuable line of inquiry has emerged around the concept of "social capital." Growing out of the work of Pierre Bourdieu (e.g., 1977), James Coleman (1988), and others, the concept has often been used to explain different outcomes between groups, focusing on the relations between the group members—including such factors as group expectations and norms—as an important cause of these different outcomes. The concept of social capital produced a boom of scholarship in the 1980s and 1990s in studies of immigration. These studies examine such questions as why and how immigrants that appear to have characteristics similar to those of native minorities (such as low educational levels, low incomes, and residence in poor neighborhoods) seem to do better in school and at work (see Gibson 1988; Kao and Tienda 1995; Portes and Zhou 1993; Zhou and Bankston 1998; and Lee, Chapter 12, and Chin, Chapter 13, this volume). Many, including those who have skillfully developed the concept, have lamented that "social capital" as a concept has been too quickly and too randomly applied (Portes 1998).

The work of Portes and Zhou, writing together (1993) and apart (Portes 1998), has set the parameters for much of the debate with the concept of "segmented assimilation." Portes and Zhou (1993:82) argue against a single model of assimilation to the mainstream, instead positing three different possibilities: "[The first] replicates the time honored portrayal of growing acculturation and parallel integration into the white middle-class; a second leads straight in the opposite direction to permanent poverty and assimilation to the underclass; still a third associates rapid economic advancement with deliberate preservation of the immigrant community's values and tight solidarity." This last choice is segmented assimilation and represents a kind of delayed, "ethnic" assimilation: immigrants take the road to upward mobility by maintaining their culture during the transition. The other two choices recall John Ogbu's (1978, 1987) concepts of voluntary and involuntary immigrants. The former are immigrant groups who have come to the United States of their own volition, and the latter have come through slavery (African Americans), conquest (e.g., American Indians or Mexican Americans in the southwest), or colonialism (e.g., Puerto Ricans). The "choice" presented to the children of immigrants is a stark and forbidding dilemma: one leads to self-perpetuating upward mobility but requires surrendering one's own identity; the other enables one to retain one's identity in opposition but in so doing takes a path of "doomed resistance" (Willis 1977) and self-perpetuating poverty. Alejandro Portes and Alex Stepick (1993) portray the contest between assimilation to the mainstream, largely white, middle-class and minority underclass as a "race": immigrant parents try desperately to help their children succeed and get them on the ethnic upward path before they "Americanize" to a dangerous and oppositional inner-city minority model in a sort of contagion effect.

This formulation is backed up by some empirical research (Fordham 1996; Gibson 1988; Portes and MacLeod 1996; Portes and Rumbaut 1990; Portes and Stepick 1993; Rumbaut 1996; Zhou and Bankston 1998) and provides a picture of reality quite similar to that perceived by and acted upon by many immigrant parents and their children. It also describes an important racial and cultural dynamic in the processes of immigrant incorporation in contemporary America, laying out a template for other analyses. Moreover, ethnic effects on academic achievement persist even when controlling for parents' education, socioeconomic status, length of residency in the United States, and child's hours spent on homework. Moreover, the "negative effect of disadvantaged group membership among immigrant children was reinforced rather than reduced in suburban schools, but that the positive effect of advantaged group membership remained significant even in inner-city schools" (Zhou 1999, 206; see also Kao and Tienda 1995; Portes and MacLeod 1996; Portes and Rumbaut 1996; Rumbaut 1996, forthcoming). Recent research on education makes good use of the concept of social capital to argue the importance of generational difference within the same ethnic group (Stanton-Salazar and Dornbusch 1995; see the excellent ethnography in Valenzuela 1999). Zhou (1999) usefully emphasizes ways that the segmented assimilation framework should focus on the interaction of macro- and micro-level factors, thus contextualizing community-level analysis.

Yet in its initial incarnation the concept of segmented assimilation also overlooked important variations and incorporation processes that affect both the perceptions that lead immigrants to frame their options in particular ways and concrete models that may point to alternative paths. The concept would have benefited from a stronger appreciation of the racialization process with which immigrants must engage in the United States. Immigrants choose and are forced to define themselves in juxtaposition to negative images of African Americans, usually with the result that the juxtaposition affirms explanations of differential progress positing different work ethics among immigrants and African Americans. The second generation has a more complex relationship to the immigrant analogy, with some in the second generation accepting it and seeing themselves as different from native minorities, and others seeing their futures as more similar to those of same natives. An appreciation of the racialization process is not inconsistent with the concepts of social capital and segmented assimilation, but we attempt to more explicitly analyze the relationship between these processes and the effects of the transmission of behaviors, of being subject to similar discriminatory processes, and of interaction between different levels of analysis.

Also, segmented assimilation curiously leaves out the possibility of what Kathryn Neckerman, Prudence Carter, and Jennifer Lee (1999) call a "minority culture of mobility." According to Neckerman and colleagues, a minority culture of mobility describes, not an "entire culture, but a set of cultural 'tools' relevant to problems of economic mobility." Moreover, this culture orients group-specific beliefs and habits and "emerges in response to distinctive problems that middle class and upwardly mobile minorities face" (947). A minority culture of mobility can also co-exist with an oppositional minority culture (posited in segmented assimilation), both being responses to the conditions within which different segments of a minority population find themselves. Finally, a minority culture of opposition is not a newcomer culture but rather one that emerges through a group's continual experiences with exclusion and discrimination. Neckerman and colleagues' analysis (1999) is consistent with the attention to racialization processes we call for.

Gender is another important factor not initially given an important role in the literature on segmented assimilation or in most theories of immigrant incorporation (Hondagneu-Sotelo 1994). Experiences in school, at home, and in the labor market are very different for minority men than for minority women. For example, minority women are more likely to experience upward mobility and employment in the "pink-collar" labor market than are their male counterparts because employers feel that minority women, and not men, possess the interpersonal, "soft skills" necessary to get work in these sectors (Myers and Cranford 1998; Moss and Tilly 1996). Moreover, gender roles at home, gendered involvement with representing parents to U.S. institutions, and differential gender roles in school and among peers all lead to different kinds of ethnic identity and oppositional and incorporational stances among men and women (see Fordham 1996; Smith forthcoming e; Valenzuela 1998; M. Waters 1999). This creates a very different reality for minority men and women to confront and tends to have important consequences for the kind of incorporation and ethnic and racial identity that each will experience.

Recent work by Smith (forthcoming d, e) uses and critiques the segmented assimilation model. Smith finds that second-generation Mexican Americans in New York experience their ethnicity in at least three ways, with corresponding effects on academics and work. First, as segmented assimilation predicts, a plurality of Smith's sample understands their ethnicity as being an important resource that helps increase ethnic pride and emphasize difference from native minorities, which in turn provides ethnically understood practices fostering school and work success. Second, and partly consistent with segmented assimilation, alarmingly increasing numbers adopt an oppositional stance that defines "Mexicanness," especially for men, with cutting school, making money, and joining gangs, in a repetition of classic working-class rebellion (Perlmann and Waldinger 1997; Willis 1977). This process is related to both different gender roles for Mexican American men and women in school, at home, in the street, and in the labor market and to larger changes caused by the great influx of large numbers of teen immigrants, especially men who are not with their parents, in the early 1990s (T. Waters 1999). The emerging youth culture includes large numbers of early adolescent immigrants (what one might call "1.3 generation" immigrants), young men who come to the United States at a younger age than did their predecessors and with little supervision, go to U.S. schools, and experience a partial second socialization here (see also Rumbaut 1998). Fascinatingly, these teen immigrants and their second-generation friends reject both mainstream white assimilation and native minority assimilation (black, Puerto Rican, Dominican). They see themselves as better than natives by virtue of being immigrants and Mexican, though most do so without the academic or work success segmented assimilation posits. The result is a kind of downwardly mobile segmented (or ethnic) assimilation, especially for men. The empirical question remains whether this ethnic downward mobility will be racialized in the future, moving it closer to what both segmented assimilation and a racialization argument predict. Third, a small but growing and very academically successful group is adopting upwardly mobile identities that are black, "neutral," or "multicultural geekish" in school and in public (see also Fordham 1996; M. Waters 1999), while remaining Mexican at home, in private. The common theme here is a conscious attempt to dissociate themselves from the pervasive educational failure of their Mexican peers, and to actively integrate themselves into the orbit of what Neckerman, Carter and Lee (1999) call "minority culture of mobility." This research uses the segmented assimilation framework to map out the possibilities of current incorporation, including explaining ethnically understood, Mexican American upward mobility, while attempting to integrate gender more fully into the framework, and envisioning possibilities for native minority youth culture other than racialized downward mobility. These include an upwardly mobile native minority youth subculture as well as a downwardly mobile Mexican ethnic subculture.

Like Lee (Chapter 12), Vilna Bashi, Philip Kasinitz and Milton Vickerman, and Margaret Chin make important contributions in their chapters to the use and development of social capital analyses. A key finding in Bashi's study (Chapter 10) is that membership in an immigrant social network can provide "insulation" from the effects of racism. It may limit one's interactions with whites because of the sector of the economy one works in; it may offer financial rewards and a style of living higher than that of comparable people in the native black population, hence offering "socio-economic separation" from them; and it may thus provide one with status and accomplishments that belie racial stereotypes about blacks. In contrast, those in Bashi's sample outside such a network did not have such insulation and suffered and experienced the effects of racial discrimination more severely. The networks, then, help determine the meaning of race and its circumstantial relationship to social conditions (see Kasinitz 1992).

Kasinitz and Vickerman (Chapter 9) also take up these themes of racialization and social capital among West Indians. Their message, in sum, is: not all ethnic niches are equal, and not across generations. Engaging the literature on ethnic enclaves and niches as modes of upward mobility, Kasinitz and Vickerman sound a cautionary note about the West Indian niches for the first and second generations, a point consistent with Waldinger's insight (1996) that niches can shrink as well as grow, affecting future opportunity in them accordingly. They argue that while West Indians have done better on average than Latino immigrants—in large part because of higher education and English language ability—holding them up as a model of ethnic upward mobility is premature. Indeed, they argue that the West Indians niches are low paying and, because they are public, do not lend themselves as readily to the kind of mutual support the private sector makes possible. Moreover, they argue that the realities of racialization and discrimination for the second generation, including their segregation into very poor neighborhoods and schools, makes it even harder for many West Indians to help their children get ahead. They experience racial discrimination in the same way native black youth do and adopt similarly negative attitudes toward the larger society, as posited by oppositional theories and segmented assimilation. Kasinitz and Vickerman fear that the niches of the parents—poor as they may be—may be better than what is in store for their racialized and excluded U.S.–born children.

Chin (Chapter 13) treads new and exciting intellectual and empirical ground by examining how social capital does or does not get generated in the garment industry. A main point in her analysis is that Chinese immigrants who work on piece-rate, whole-garment production bring in coethnics, while Latino immigrant workers who work on sections of garments at an hourly rate for Korean employers do not. Why the difference? Work in the Chinese factories is organized differently than in the Korean factories. The Chinese factories have a union, long training that is eased by having a coethnic sponsor, and longer-term employment, whereas the Korean factories have a large turnover, little training, and no union and non-coethnic employees. What is particularly impressive in Chin's work is not only that she identifies that ethnic social capital is generated in one case and not the other but she traces it to different organizations of the workplace and their coincidence with different ethnicities of the employers.

Transnationalization and Globalization

Transnationalization

Two related but distinct approaches to contemporary immigration are the transnationalization and globalization or world systems approaches. For the purposes of this chapter, we can consider transnational those works that tend to focus on social processes relating to particular migrant populations and nation-states, while globalization tends to analyze how economic, institutional, cultural, and other changes at a global level reconfigure power, including the places of states, in our world (see Glick Schiller 1999; Mato 1997; Sassen 1998; Smith forthcoming b). In this section we draw on and critique both perspectives.

The transnational perspective on migration issues has gone through at least two stages of theoretical and empirical development. The first widely recognized work to lay out a transnational perspective on migration was that of Nina Glick Schiller and colleagues (Basch, Glick Schiller, and Szanton Blanc 1994; Glick Schiller, Basch, and Blanc-Szanton 1992; see also Massey et al. 1987; Sutton 1987). In what came to be its standard form, this perspective argues that the practices and discourses among "transmigrants" and their states are new or fundamentally different than in the past;

the nation-state has been transcended as the main structure organizing political, social, and economic life; and global capitalism is the main force driving transnationalism (Basch, Glick Schiller, and Szanton Blanc 1994). Linda Basch and colleagues (1994) posit that migrants create a "transnational social field" between their countries of origin and destination that results in a "deterritorialized nation-state" in which "the nation's people may live anywhere in the world and still not live outside the state" (269; see also Baubock 1994; Kearney 1991, 1995).

This formulation has three major problems. The first involves its treatment of the state. The use of "global capitalism" as the theoretical prime mover leads its proponents to overlook the role of an active state in creating transnational public life (see Goldring 1998; Guarnizo 1998; Levitt forthcoming a, b; Smith 1997, 1998; Smith and Guarnizo 1998). Moreover, the concept of "deterritorialized nation-state" fails to appreciate that territoriality is a defining dimension of the nation-state, in part because it holds a monopoly on the use of violence and also on the use of resources extracted from the collectivity in that territory (Smith 1996, 1998b; see Smith forthcoming a; Smith and Guarnizo 1998; Zolberg and Smith 1996; also see Ruggie 1993, on territoriality). Finally, issues of citizenship and membership are not explicitly discussed, and the concept of community is rejected. These elisions are puzzling given the prevalence of these concepts in migrant and sending-state discourse and action, and the proliferation of sending states' attempts to cultivate and institutionalize relations with their diasporas. The second problem is that the implicit or explicit claims by early proponents of transnationalism about the newness or larger impact of transnational life were not properly contextualized in history, were not comparative, and did not take account of how gender and class, for example, structured transnational life. (Notable exceptions on gender include Goldring 1995 and Levitt 1995; Hondogneu-Sotelo and Avila 1997.) Gender was neglected in part because these early studies focused mainly on the conduct of public life between the sending and receiving states and communities, which are in practice still mainly men's worlds. The third problem is that the focus on how migrants create social fields that transcend nation-states has obscured the focus on cases showing transnational activity that are occurring at a different level of social reality from that engaged so fully with the nation-state, particularly those with past or present colonial relations with a global center, as seen for example, in the concepts of metropoles (Grosfoguel 1997a, b; Grosfoguel and Cordero-Guzmán 1998; Grosfoguel and Georas 1996) and world cities (Sassen 1991, 1998).

Many of these problems have been identified and there is much good work being done on them (Glick Schiller 1999; Guarnizo and Smith 1998; Kyle 2001; Perez Godoy 1998; Portes, Guarnizo, and Landolt 1999; Vertovec 1999). A spate of work has been excavating the past, showing how a transnational perspective can help us gain insight into past migrant experiences, and delineating more precisely what is and is not new about this phenomenon and why it matters. As Nancy Foner details in Chapter 2 (and Foner 1997), the short answers to these questions are that transnational life among migrants is not new but has been significantly changed in its pace and potential impact by the possibilities for collapsing time and space and creating simultaneity raised by current technology and other factors, such as the U.S. encouragement of ethnic identity (Foner 1999 and Chapter 2; Glick Schiller 1999; Morawska 1989; Portes, Guarnizo, and Landolt 1999; Smith 1998b, forthcoming a, f; Vertovec 1999; Wyman 1993). Recent work on gender has helped illuminate the ways that gender structures transnational life and has brought a focus onto new arenas of life beyond those more public ones initially considered, including work on the changing dynamics within transnational families (Foner 1999; Hondagneu-Sotelo and Avila 1997; see also Mahler, Chapter 5, this volume; Levitt forthcoming a, b). The term "community," which has been both too broadly applied and too narrowly rejected, has undergone more critical scrutiny and development (Anderson 1991; Goldring 1996a; Hagan 1994; Smith 1995, 1998c). Finally, more systematic comparisons across cases have enabled scholars to identify broader similarities and differences in the processes of transnational life, to identify how networks help create transnational communities, and how transnational life relates to larger processes of racialization, nationalism, community, and nation building, and others (Foner 1999 and Chapter 2, this volume; Glick Schiller 1999; Portes, Guarnizo, and Landolt 1999; Smith and Guarnizo 1998).

Further research is needed to establish the existence of the phenomenon of transnationalization in a migrant context, both empirically and in terms of its being accepted as theoretically important to the mainstream disciplines (Portes 1999). This will involve demonstrating important effects of transnational life in the sending and receiving societies, and perhaps in other arenas too, such as international relations or global politics. Another area that requires further research is the sending-states' increasingly deep and complex relationships with their diasporas in the United States and elsewhere, and the ultimate importance of their diasporas for both home and host-state politics and related processes of incorporation and mobility (Guarnizo 1998; Goldring 1999; Guarnizo, Sanchez, and Roach 1999; Portes 1999; Roberts, Frank, and Lozano-Ascencio 1999; Smith 1998b, forthcoming b).

A third area that needs further research is the nature and extent of participation by the second generation in transnational life. If the children of immigrants do not participate at all in transnational activity or are not significantly affected by it, then it is mainly a first-generation issue. This would mean that transnational life did not really affect second-generation assimilation and incorporation in the United States, or that the second generation did not really affect the continued relationship with the sending country—two key dimensions of transnational life (see Rumbaut 1994, 1997). Current research on this issue shows interesting variation in the degree and nature of transnational activities, both contemporarily and historically (Foner 1999 and Chapter 2, this volume; Glick Schiller and Fouron, Chapter 3, this volume; Pienkos 1991; Portes, Guarnizo, and Landolt 1999; Smith 1998b, forthcoming a, f). Peggy Levitt and Mary Waters' edited book (forthcoming) comparing transnational life in the second generation across cases from different continents should make an important contribution to this literature.

Glick Schiller and Fouron stake out a new position on transnationalism. They define second-generation transnationals as those youth whose lives or identities have been significantly structured by this transnational field, be they born in the United States of Haitian parents or born in Haiti. Children of Haitian immigrants become "long-distance nationalists" when they embrace a Haitian identity as they confront racialization in the United States, when some of them actually return to Haiti, and when they cultivate a Haitian identity to sate their desire to belong in a Haitian nation that might never have existed in the form they imagine. For Haitian youth in Haiti, the diaspora looms like a mountainous landscape behind many political and economic changes in Haiti and in their imaginations. For Glick Schiller and Fouron, both Haitian youth in Haiti and Haitian youth in the United States are transnational because they become part of the same "imagined community"; both use their identification with the Haitian nation as vital parts of their sense of self. Most definitions of second-generation transnational life are narrower than theirs (Levitt forthcoming a, b; Portes, Guarnizo, and Landolt 1999; Smith forthcoming b). Their research, which pushes the frontiers of theory and knowledge in a growing field they helped to found, asks, Which children of immigrants and which of their children are transnationally active and how? And of what significance are these activities, and for whom?

Sarah Mahler (Chapter 5) adds another dimension to the transnational perspective. Mahler uses her case of Salvadoran migrants on Long Island to ask insightful questions about the nature and durability of transnational ties, and how they are influenced by their context. She asks how transnational ties and actions are shaped by a context that is very different than those often assumed in transnational research. Unlike most others, her Salvadoran migrants are almost all poor, have little chance to return to their home country because of violence and poverty born first of the civil war and then of its aftermath, and are located in the culturally dissipating context of suburban Long Island. She also cleverly contrasts the daily life and transnational practices of Salvadorans living on Long Island with those living in the hometowns in El Salvador, showing how transnational practices are differently lived. For example, a particularly important development in the Salvadoran case is the pervasiveness of *viajeros* (travelers), who serve as brokers to deliver goods paid for in New York to relatives in El Salvador. *Viajeros* arrive daily in Salvadoran towns but are seen only every few weeks by those remitting the money or goods in New York, illustrating Mahler's argument that transnational practices pervade life in the hometowns but only "punctuate" it for those on Long Island. The difficulties for Salvadorans are heightened by the legal limbo they live in the United States. The Salvadoran state's action and interest in developing a program for Salvadorans abroad introduces another contextual element in Mahler's analysis. She argues, insightfully, that the state's heightened interest in Salvadorans abroad stems from, among other causes, its recognition of the Salvadoran economy's dependence on remittances, a significant shift away from El Salvador's dependence on U.S. aid during the civil war.

Pamela Graham (Chapter 4) analyzes simultaneous political incorporation in the United States and the Dominican Republic among Dominican migrants. She argues, persuasively, that ignoring or even playing down the role of the state and national identity weakens any study of transnational processes. Indeed, she nicely captures the simultaneous and synergistic processes of political mobilization in New York and in the Dominican Republic, highlighting the role that the United States and Dominican states have played in creating opportunities for mobilization. A main strength of her work is that it solidly grounds the analysis of transnational life in the particular contexts in New York and in the Dominican Republic: the process of redistricting in New York City creates the opportunity for faster political mobilization among Dominicans in New York, at the same time that their increasing influence in the Dominican Republic is converted into political power that secures them the right to vote (see Guarnizo 1994). The end result of this simultaneous political incorporation has not been the lessening of Dominicans' commitment to their life in the United States but their increasing engagement with both political systems. While the precise conditions that led to this positive outcome for Dominicans are not likely to be repeated for other immigrant groups, similar ones are likely to recur. Mexicans for example, have used their organizations for political mobilization relative to the Mexican state to also mobilize for local politics in Los Angeles and elsewhere (Goldring 1998; Guarnizo 1998; Smith 1998c). Moreover, this kind of simultaneous mobilization around national or local politics is not a new pattern (Foner 1999, this volume; Glick Schiller 1999; Smith forthcoming b; Wyman 1993).

Globalization, or World Systems, Approach

When the globalization, or world systems, approach is well deployed, it is intrinsically historical and comparative. It analyzes how systems such as capitalism, nationalism, and the sovereign state system have evolved in relationship to one another. Moreover, because it traces the historical evolution of large structures of power, it enables scholars to discern patterns and variations in this evolution that may affect how these structures operate or how they may be transcended by changes in the very processes that have produced them.

With regard to migration, this approach has yielded interesting insights. Ramón Grosfoguel (1995), for example, has analyzed transnational systems that have emerged out of colonial relationships between the Caribbean and Europe and has mapped out how current theories fail to appreciate those differences, an analysis expanded by Grosfoguel and Cordero-Guzmán (1998). Sassen (1991, 1998) argues that the conditions within which states are sovereign are changing and that cities and global corporations are now negotiating some of the same kinds of citizenship-like relationships that were earlier worked out between citizens and states. John Meyer and colleagues (1997) argue that global processes have been largely responsible for the creation and maintenance of global norms and structures, such as the nation-state and human rights. With respect to migration, and along the lines of the work of Meyer and colleagues, Yasmin Soysal (1994) argues that we are in a period of "post-national membership" in which migrants have rights without being citizens (e.g., members of the nation-state). She suggests that the basis of this and other claims, including human rights claims, now lies not in nation-states but in a universally respected notion of the rights of the "modern person" enforced by international agreements and norms. Arjun Appadurai (1996, 8) goes further, however, arguing for the current or imminent demise of the nation-state. She says that global, cultural, economic and other processes have made the state so irrelevant that it is "on its last legs."

Other theorists, like Appadurai, go too far in diminishing the continuing role of the nation-state. As work in this volume (Graham, Chapter 4) and others (Goldring 1998; Guarnizo 1998; 1998b, c) has shown, while the state is indeed transcended by transnational or global processes, it most decidedly is not dead. It continues to structure most political life throughout the world (see Smith and Guarnizo 1998), and its extension is important in creating certain types of transnational life (Smith 1997, 1998b, forthcoming a, b, d). There are other, important types of transnational life that circumvent the state, but these too are "engaged" with the state, though not in activities directed by it. For example, much of the transnational political activity seen among migrants from Mexico, the Dominican Republic, Colombia, Italy, India, and other countries revolves around gaining access to home-state power through the transnational implementation of the right to vote in home-state national or even local elections. While the notion of a right to vote and to representation may be the manifestation of a global human rights norm, it also sets in motion very state-centered transnational activity, with nationalistic and state-centered goals. Similarly, the efforts of sending states to cultivate ties with their communities of origin should not be seen as attempts to colonize receiving states (e.g., Brimelow 1995) but rather as attempts by the sending states to reassert control over the extra-territorial conduct of their national politics (Goldring 1998, 2000; Gonzalez-Gutierrez 1993; Guarnizo 1998; Martinez 1998; Miller 1981; Smith 1998c, 1999). What seems to be happening today is that sending states are attempting to create diasporas, rather than that diasporas or other global structures are transcending the state to the point of being liberated from and posing an alternative to it (Smith 1998c). The "Israeli lobby" is often cited as a model of a diaspora created by the state. Perhaps the most important point here is that more than one structure of power can co-exist in the same place. This is not to say that the state has not been profoundly affected by globalization—it has. The state is still arguably the most important actor in shaping political and economic life, in creating social closure, and in determining the evolution of citizenship and membership, even within supranational institutions such as the European Union (Brubaker 1989; Hanagan 1998, 1999; Soysal 1997; Weiner 1997).

In a recent paper, Héctor Cordero-Guzmán and Ramón Grosfoguel (2000; see also Grosfoguel and Cordero-Guzmán 1998) argue that in order to understand differences in selectivity, location in the socioeconomic structure, and patterns of social and economic mobility among immigrant groups it is necessary to analyze in detail the socio-politico-economic history of the given country of origin with the receiving country, the location of the sending country in the global political economy, and the particular migratory history between the sending country and the receiving country. (Their example of a receiving country is the United States.) The historical specificities of the political and economic relation between a particular sending country and the United States (or any other receiving country) have a central role in explaining the class selectivity and the particular location of members of that national origin group in the receiving country's socioeconomic structure. Transnational factors continue to impact the group (particularly if there is a continuous immigrant flow) even after it has settled in the receiving country, but national, host-country class forces, labor market structures, racial dynamics, and political processes begin exert an increased influence on a given community's rate of socioeconomic integration, mobility, and rewards in the receiving society.

This volume has two chapters that make these broad linkages. Zai Liang (Chapter 6) analyzes the relationship between U.S. asylum policy and undocumented Chinese immigration, arguing that U.S. asylum policy and its effects have been transnationalized within this global context. He examines these links, lamenting the exploitation and danger that accompanies Chinese immigrants' clandestine passage to the United States and analyzing how smugglers have incorporated asylum policy into their strategies for getting their clients into the United States. He describes how U.S. asylum policy and its effects have been transnationalized. First, smugglers are the transnational agents. They have connections with both sending and receiving communities and they have good knowledge of the asylum system. Second, the link between U.S. asylum policy, Chinese domestic politics, and smugglers' strategies implicates larger dimensions of U.S.–China relations. Third, the "game of the rules" is also transnational in the sense that the large influx of Fujianese into New York's Chinatown has transformed and transnationalized politics there. In arguing that U.S. asylum policy has become an unwitting encouragement for this migration, he also acknowledges the dilemma for U.S. policy: how to have an open asylum policy while minimizing such abuse by smugglers and aliens. Dennis Conway, Adrian Bailey, and Mark Ellis (Chapter 7) discuss circular migration, employment, and poverty among Puerto Rican women. They analyze processes intimately tied into globalization and the enduring impacts of colonial relationships, explicating the link between a colonial past on the island and an impoverished present on the mainland. In particular, they focus on how migration between the mainland and the island of poor Puerto Rican women—their "circularity"—is a strategy deployed to manage their material condition in the United States and on Puerto Rico and reflects the connection that exists between the global and the local, the national and the transnational.

References

Alba, Richard, and Victor Nee. 1999. "Rethinking Assimilation Theory for a New Era of Immigration." In *Handbook of Immigration: The American Experience*, edited by Charles Hirschman, Philip Kasinitz, and Josh DeWind. New York: Russell Sage Foundation.

Anderson, Benedict. 1991. *Imagined Communities: Reflections on the Growth and Spread of Nationalism*. 2d ed. New York: Verso.

Appadurai, Arjun. 1996. *Modernity at Large: Cultural Dimensions of Globalization*. Minneapolis: University of Minnesota Press.

Basch, Linda, Nina Glick Schiller, and Cristina Szanton Blanc. 1994. *Nations Unbound: Transna-*

tional Projects, Postcolonial Predicaments, and Deterritorialized Nation States. Langhorne, Pa.: Gordon and Breach.

Baubock, Rainer. 1994. *Transnational Citizenship: Membership and Rights in International Migration.* Aldershot: Edward Elgar.

Bourdieu, Pierre. 1977. *Outline of a Theory of Practice.* New York: Cambridge University Press.

Brimelow, Peter. 1995. *Alien Nation.* New York: Harper Perennial.

Brubaker, William Rogers, ed. 1989. *Immigration and the Politics of Citizenship in Europe and North America.* Lanham, Md.: University Press of America.

Chavez, Linda. 1991. *Out of the Barrio: A New Politics of Hispanic Assimilation.* New York: Basic Books.

Chin, John. 1998. "The Construction of Chineseness: The Overseas Chinese Business Class and Implications for Social Control in Chinatown." Paper prepared for Columbia University Ph.D. Program in Urban Planning.

Cinel, Dino. 1991. *The National Integration of Italian Return Migration, 1870–1929.* New York: Cambridge University Press.

Coleman, James. 1988. "Social Capital in the Creation of Human Capital." *American Journal of Sociology* 94 (supplement).

Cordero-Guzmán, Héctor. 2001. "Integrative and Counter Integrative Forces in Host Society: The United States." Paper prepared for Robert J. Milano Graduate School of Management and Urban Policy, New School University.

Cordero-Guzmán, Héctor, and Ramón Grosfoguel. 2000. "The Demographic and Socio-Economic Characteristics of Post-1965 Immigrants to New York City: A Comparative Analysis by National Origin." *International Migration* 38 (4): 41–79.

Cordero-Guzmán, Héctor, and Jose Navarro. 2000. "What Do Immigrant Groups, Organizations, and Service Providers Say About the Impacts of Recent Changes in Immigration and Welfare Laws?" *Migration World* 28 (4): 20–28.

de la Garza, Rodolfo O., and Louis DeSipio. 1998. "Interests Not Passions: Mexican American Attitudes Toward Mexico and Issues Shaping U.S.–Mexico Relations." *International Migration Review* 32 (summer): 401–22.

Farley, Reynolds. 1998. "First and Second Generation Immigrants in New York: Their Numbers and Characteristics." Paper presented at the annual meeting of the Eastern Sociological Association, Philadelphia, March.

Foner, Nancy. 1997. "What's So New About Transnationalism? New York Immigrants Today and at the End of the Century." *Diaspora* 6 (3): 354–75.

———. 1999. "Immigrant Women and Work in New York, Then and Now." *Journal of American Ethnic History* 18 (3): 95–113.

Fordham, Signithia. 1996. *Blacked Out: Dilemmas of Race, Identity, and Success at Capital High.* Chicago: University of Chicago Press.

Gabaccia, Donna. 2000. *Italy's Many Diasporas.* Seattle: University of Washington Press.

Gans, Herbert. 1979. "Symbolic Ethnicity: The Future of Ethnic Groups and Cultures in America." *Ethnic and Racial Studies* 2 (1): 1–20.

———. 1999. "Toward a Reconciliation of 'Assimilation' and 'Pluralism': The Interplay of Acculturation and Ethnic Retention." Pp. 161–71 in *Handbook of Immigration: The American Experience,* edited by Charles Hirshman, Philip Kasinitz, and Josh DeWind. New York: Russell Sage Foundation.

Gibson, Margaret. 1988. *Accommodation Without Assimilation.* Ithaca: Cornell University Press.

Glick Schiller, Nina. 1999. "Transmigrants and Nation-States: Something Old and Something New in the Immigrant Experience." Pp. 94–119 in *The Handbook of International Migration: The American Experience*, edited by Charles Hirshman, Philip Kasinitz, and Josh DeWind. New York: Russell Sage Foundation.

Glick Schiller, Nina, Linda Basch, and Cristina Blanc-Szanton. 1992. *Towards a Transnational Perspective on Migration*. New York: New York Academy of Sciences.

Goldring, Luin. 1996a. "Blurring Borders: Reflections on Transnational Community." Pp. 69–104 in *Research in Community Sociology*, vol.6, edited by Daniel Chekki. Greenwich, Conn.: JAI Press.

———. 1996b. "Gendered Memory: Reconstructions of the Village by Mexican Transnational Migrants." Pp. 303–29 in *Creating the Countryside: The Politics of Rural and Environmental Discourse*, edited by E. Melanie DuPuis and Peter Vandergeest. Philadelphia: Temple University Press.

———. 1998. "From Market Membership to Transnational Citizenship?" The Changing Politization of Transnational Social Spaces." *L'Ordinaire Latino-Americain* 173–74 (July–December): 167–72.

———. 2000. "El Estado Mexicano y las Organizaciones Transmigrantes: Reconfigurando a Nacion, Ciudadania, y Relaciones entre Estado y Sociedad Civil?" In *Fronteras Fragmentadas*, edited by Gail Mummert. Zamora, Michoacan: El Colegio de Michoacan.

Gonzalez-Gutierrez, Carlos. 1993. "The Mexican Diaspora in California: The Limits and Possibilities of the Mexican Government." Pp. 221–35 in *The California–Mexico Connection*, edited by Katrina Burgess and Abraham Lowenthal. Berkeley: University of California Press.

Gordon, Milton. 1964. *Assimilation in American Life*. New York: Oxford University Press.

Grosfoguel, Ramón. 1997a. "Colonial Caribbean Migrations to France, The Netherlands, Great Britain, and the United States." *Ethnic and Racial Studies* 20 (3): 594–612.

———. 1997b. "Migration and Geopolitics in the Greater Antilles: From the Cold War to the Post–Cold War." *Review* 20 (1): 115–45.

Grosfoguel, Ramón, and Héctor Cordero-Guzmán. 1998. "Social Capital, Context of Reception, and Transnationalsim: Recent Approaches to International Migration." *Diaspora* 7 (3): 351–68.

Grosfoguel, Ramón, and Chloe S. Georas. 1996. "The Racialization of Latino Caribbean Migrants in the New York Metropolitan Area." *CENTRO Journal of the Center for Puerto Rican Studies* 8 (1 and 2): 191–201.

Guarnizo, Luis E. 1994. "*Los Dominicanyorks:* The Making of a Binational Society." *Annals of the Academy of Political and Social Sciences* 553:70–86.

———. 1998. "The Rise of Transnational Social Formations: Mexican and Dominican State Responses to Transnational Migration." *Political Power and Social Theory* 12:45–94.

Guarnizo, Luis, Arturo Sanchez, and Elizabeth Roach. 1999. "Mistrust, Fragmented Solidarity, and Transnational Migration: Colombians in New York City and Los Angeles." *Ethnic and Racial Studies* 22 (2): 367–97.

Guarnizo, Luis E., and M. P. Smith. 1998. "The Locations of Transnationalism." Pp. 3–34 in *Transnationalism from Below*, edited by M. P. Smith and Luis Guarnizo. New Brunswick, N.J.: Transaction Press.

Hagan, J. 1994. *Deciding to Be Legal*. Philadelphia: Temple University Press.

Hanagan, Michael. 1998. "Irish Transnationalism, Social Movements, Deterritorialized Migrants, and the State System: The Last One Hundred and Forty Years." *Mobilization: An International Journal* 3 (1): 107–26.

———. 1999. "Introduction." In *Expanding Citizenship, Reconfiguring States*, edited by Michael Hanagan and Charles Tilly. Lanham, Md.: Rowman and Littlefield.

Hernandez, Ramona, Francisco Rivera-Batiz, and Roberto Agodini. 1995. *Dominican New Yorkers: A Socio-Economic Profile*. Dominican Research Monographs. New York: CUNY Dominican Studies Institute.

Hondagneu-Sotelo, Pierrette. 1994. *Gendered Transitions: Mexican Experiences of Migration*. Berkeley: University of California Press.

Hondagneu-Sotelo, Pierrette, and Ernestine Avila. 1997 " 'I'm Here but I'm There': The Meanings of Transnational Latina Motherhood." *Gender and Society* 11 (5): 548–69.

Ignatiev, Noel. 1995. *How the Irish Became White*. New York: Routledge.

Kao, Grace, and Marta Tienda. 1995. "Optimism and Achievement: Educational Performance of Immigrant Youth." *Social Science Quarterly* 76 (1): 1–19.

Kasinitz, Philip. 1992. *Caribbean New York*. Ithaca: Cornell University Press.

Kearney, Michael. 1991. "Borders and Boundaries of State and Self at the End of Empire." *Journal of Historical Sociology* 4 (1): 52–74.

———. 1995. "The Local and the Global: The Anthropology of Globalization and Transnationalism." *Annual Review of Anthropology* 24:547–66.

Kwong, Peter. 1987. *The New Chinatown*. New York: Hill and Wang.

———. 1997. *Forbidden Workers: Illegal Chinese Immigrants and American Labor*. New York: New Press.

Kyle, David. 2001. *Transnational Peasants: Migrations, Networks, and Ethnicity in Andean Ecuador*. Baltimore: Johns Hopkins University Press.

Lessinger, Johanna. 1998. "Indian Transnationalism: The Politics of Opposition from the Diaspora." Paper presented at the conference States and Diaspora, Casa Italiana, Columbia University, New York, May.

Levitt, Peggy. 1995. "Migration and Development: Changes in Organization of Political, Religious and Associational Life in Boston and the Dominican Republic." Ph.D. diss., Massachusetts Institute of Technology.

———. Forthcoming a. "Forms of Transnational Community and Their Impact on the Second Generation." In *Second Generation Transnationalism*, edited by Peggy Levitt and Mary Waters. New York: Russell Sage Foundation.

———. Forthcoming b. *The Transnational Villagers*. Berkeley: University of California Press.

Levitt, Peggy, and Mary Waters. Forthcoming. *Second Generation Transnationalism*. New York: Russell Sage Foundation.

Lewis, Gordon K. 1983. *Main Currents in Caribbean Thought*. Baltimore: Johns Hopkins University Press.

Lieberson, Stanley. 1980. *A Piece of the Pie: Black and White Immigrants Since 1880*. Berkeley: University of California Press.

Lobo, Arun Peter, Joseph Salvo, and Vicky Virgin. 1996. *The Newest New Yorkers, 1990–1994*. New York: Department of City Planning.

———. 1998. *The Newest New Yorkers, 1995–96*. New York: New York: Department of City Planning.

Lopez, David E. 1999. "Social and Linguistic Aspects of Assimilation Today." In *The Handbook of International Migration: The American Experience*, edited by Charles Hirschman, Philip Kasinitz, and Josh DeWind. New York: Russell Sage Foundation.

Mahler, Sarah. 1998. "Theoretical and Empirical Contributions Toward a Research Agenda for

Transnationalism." Pp. 64–102 in *Transnationalism from Below,* edited by Michael Peter Smith and Luis Eduardo Guarnizo. New Brunswick, N.J.: Transaction Press.

Martinez, Jesus. 1998. "In Search of Our Lost Citizenship: Mexican Immigrants, the Right to Vote, and the Transition to Democracy in Mexico." Paper presented at the conference States and Diaspora, Casa Italiana, Columbia University, May.

Massey, Douglas, and Rafael Alarcon, Jorge Durand, and Humberto Gonzalez. 1987. *Return to Aztlan: The Social Process of Transnational Migration from Western Mexico.* Berkeley: University of California Press.

Massey, Douglas, and Nancy Denton. 1993. *American Apartheid.* Cambridge: Harvard University Press.

Mato, Daniel. 1997. "On Global and Local Agents and the Social Making of Transnational Identities and Related Agendas." *Identities: Global Studies in Culture and Power* 4 (2): 167–212.

Meyer, J., J. Boli, G. Thomas, and F. Ramirez. 1997. "World Society and the Nation State." *American Journal of Sociology* 103 (July): 144–81.

Miller, Mark J. 1981. *Immigrants in Europe: An Emerging Political Force.* New York: Praeger Press.

Model, Suzanne. 1990. "Blacks and Immigrants from South and East Europe." In *Immigration Reconsidered,* edited by Virginia Yans-McLaughlin. New York: Oxford University Press.

Mollenkopf, John H. 1999. "Urban Political Conflicts and Alliances: New York and Los Angles Compared." Pp: 390–412 in *Handbook of Immigration: The American Experience,* edited by Charles Hirshman, Philip Kasinitz, and Josh DeWind. New York: Russell Sage Foundation.

Mollenkopf, John, and Manuel Castells, eds. 1991. *Dual City.* New York: Russell Sage Foundation.

Mollenkopf, John, David Olson, and Tim Ross. 1998. "Immigrant Political Participation in New York and Los Angeles." Working paper, International Center for Migration, Ethnicity, and Citizenship, New School for Social Research, New York.

Morales, Rebecca, and Frank Bonilla, eds. 1993. *Latinos in a Changing U.S. Economy.* Newbury Park, Calif.: Sage.

Morawska, Eva. 1989. "Labor Migrations of Poles in the Atlantic World Economy, 1880–1914." *Comparative Studies in Society and History* 31 (2): 237–70.

———. 1994. "In Defense of the Ethnic Assimilation Model." *Journal of American Ethnic History* 13 (2): 76–87.

Moss, Philip, and Chris Tilly. 1996. "'Soft' Skills and Race: An Investigation of Black Men's Employment Problems." *Work and Occupations* 23 (3).

Murgia, Edward, and Edward Telles. 1996. "Phenotype and Schooling Among Mexican Americans." *Sociology of Education* 69 (October): 276–89.

Myers, Dowell, and Cynthia Cranford. 1998. "Temporal Differentiation in the Occupational Mobility of Immigrant and Native-Born Latino Workers." *American Sociological Review* 63 (February): 68–93.

Neckerman, Kathyrn, Prudence Carter, and Jennifer Lee. 1999. "Segmented Assimilation and Minority Cultures of Mobility." *Ethnic and Racial Studies* 22 (6): 945–65.

Nee, Victor, Jimy Sanders, and Scott Sernau. 1994. "Job Transitions in an Immigrant Metropolis: Ethnic Boundaries and the Mixed Economy." *American Sociological Review* 59: 849–72.

Ogbu, John. 1978. *Minority Education and Caste: The American System in Cross-Cultural Perspective.* New York: Academic Press.

———. 1987. "Variability in Minority School Performance: Problem in Search of an Explanation." *Anthropology and Education Quarterly* 18 (4): 312–34.

Omi, Michael, and Howard Winant. 1986. *Racial Formation in the United States.* New York: Routledge.

Perez Godoy, Mara. 1998. "Social Movements and International Migration: The Mexican Diaspora Seeks Inclusion in Mexico's Political Affairs, 1968–1998." Ph.D. diss., University of Chicago.

Perlmann, Joel, and Roger Waldinger. 1997. "Second Generation Decline? Children of Immigrants, Past and Present—A Reconsideration." *International Migration Review* 31 (4): 893–922.

Pienkos, Donald E. 1991. *For Your Freedom Through Ours: Polish American Efforts on Poland's Behalf, 1863–1991*. East European Monographs. New York: Columbia University Press.

———. 1999. "Conclusion." *Ethnic and Racial Studies* 22 (2): 463–77.

Portes, Alejandro. 1996. "Transnational Communities: Their Emergence and Significance in the Contemporary World System." Pp. 151–69 in *Latin America in the World Economy*, edited by R. P. Korzeniewicz and W. C. Smith. Westport, Conn.: Greenwood Press.

———. 1998. "Social Capital: Its Origins and Applications in Modern Sociology." *Annual Review of Sociology* 24:1–24.

———, ed. 1995. *The Economic Sociology of Immigration: Essays on Networks, Ethnicity and Entrepreneurship*. New York: Russell Sage Foundation.

Portes, Alejandro, Luis E. Guarnizo, and Patricia Landolt. 1999. "Introduction: Pitfalls and Promise of an Emergent Research Field." *Ethnic and Racial Studies* 22 (2): 217–38.

Portes, Alejandro, and Dag MacLeod. 1996. "Educational Progress of Children of Immigrants: The Roles of Class, Ethnicity, and School Context." *Sociology of Education* 69 (4): 255–75.

Portes, Alejandro, and Rubén Rumbaut. 1990. *Immigrant America*. Berkeley: University of California Press.

Portes, Alejandro, and Alex Stepick. 1993. *City on the Edge: The Transformation of Miami*. Berkeley: University of California Press.

Portes, Alejandro, and Min Zhou. 1992. "Gaining the Upper Hand: Economic Mobility Among Immigrant and Domestic Minorities." *Ethnic and Racial Studies* 15:491–522.

———. 1993. "The New Second Generation: Segmented Assimilation and Its Variants." *Annals of the American Academy of Political and Social Science* 530:74–93.

Rivera-Batiz, Francisco. 1996. "The Education of Immigrant Children: The Case of New York City." Immigrant New York Series, International Center for the Study of Migration, Ethnicity and Citizenship, New School for Social Research.

Roberts, Bryan, and Reanne Frank, and Fernando Lozano-Ascencio. 1999. "Transnational Migrant Communities and Mexican Migration to the U.S." *Ethnic and Racial Studies* 22 (2): 238–66.

Rodriguez, Clara. 1989. *Puerto Ricans: Born in the USA*. Boston: Unwin Hyman.

Roediger, David. 1991. *The Wages of Whiteness*. New York: Verso.

Ruggie, John G. 1993. "Territoriality and Beyond: Problematizing Modernity in International Relations." *International Organizations* 47 (winter): 139–74.

Rumbaut, Rubén. 1994. "The Crucible Within: Ethnic Identity, Self-Esteem, and Segmented Assimilation Among Children of Immigrants." *International Migration Review* 28 (4): 748–94.

———. 1996. "Unraveling a Public Health Enigma: Why Do Immigrants Experience Superior Perinatal Health Outcomes?" *Research in the Sociology of Health Care* 13:335–88.

———. 1997. "Assimilation and Its Discontents: Between Rhetoric and Reality." *International Migration Review* 31 (4): 923–60.

———. 1998. "Children of Immigrants: Is 'Americanization' Hazardous to Infant Health?" Pp. 159–83 in *Children of Color: Research, Health, and Public Policy Issues*, edited by Hiram Fitzgerald, Barry Lester, and Barry Zuckerman. New York: Garland.

———. Forthcoming. "Severed or Sustained Attachments? Language, Identity, and Imagined

Communities in the Post-Immigration Generation." In *Second Generation Transnationalism*, edited by Peggy Levitt and Mary Waters. New York: Russell Sage Foundation.

Sassen, Saskia. 1988. *The Mobility of Capital and Labor.* New York: Cambridge University Press.

———. 1991. *The Global City: New York, London, Tokyo.* Princeton: Princeton University Press.

———. 1996. *Losing Control? Sovereignty in an Age of Globalization.* The 1995 Columbia University Leonard Hastings Schoff Memorial Lectures. New York: Columbia University Press.

———. 1998. *Globalization and Its Discontents.* New York: New Press.

Smith, Michael Peter, and Luis Eduardo Guarnizo, eds. 1998. *Transnationalism from Below.* New Brunswick, N.J.: Transaction Press.

Smith, Robert C. 1995. " 'Los Ausentes Siempre Presentes': The Imagining, Making, and Politics of a Transnational Migrant Community Between New York City and Ticuani, Puebla, Mexico." Ph.D. diss., Columbia University.

———. 1996. "Mexicans in New York City: Membership and Incorporation of New Immigrant Group." Pp. 57–103 in *Latinos in New York,* edited by S. Baver and G. Haslip Viera. Notre Dame, Ind.: University of Notre Dame Press.

———. 1997. "Transnational Migration, Assimilation, and Political Community." In *The City and the World,* edited by Margaret Crahan and Alberto Vourvoulias-Bush. New York: Council on Foreign Relations.

———. 1998a. "The Changing Nature of Citizenship, Membership, and Nation: Comparative Insights from Mexico and Italy." Paper presented at Transnational Communities Program, Manchester, England.

———. 1998b. "Reflections on the State, Migration, and the Durability and Newness of Transnational Life: Comparative Insights from the Mexican and Italian Cases." *Socziale Welt* 12:197–220.

———. 1998c. "Transnational Localities: Technology, Community, and the Politics of Membership Within the Context of Mexico–U.S. Migration." In *Transnationalism from Below,* edited by Michael Peter Smith and Luis Eduardo Guarnizo. New Brunswick, N.J.: Transaction Press.

———. 2001. "Migration, Settlement, and Transnational Life: Generation, Gender and the Politics of Community Among Mexican Migrants and their U.S. Born Children in Mexico and the U.S." Unpublished manuscript.

———. Forthcoming a. "Current Dilemmas and Future Prospects of the Inter-American Migration System." In *Migration Systems and Public Policy: Comparative Insights from the Inter-American and European Migration Experiences,* edited by Aristide Zolberg and Robert Smith. New York: Routledge.

———. Forthcoming b. "Gendered Ethnicity at Three Strategic Sites." In *Latinos in the 21st Century,* edited by Marcelo Suárez-Orozco. Berkeley: University of California Press.

———. Forthcoming c. "How Durable and New Is Transnational Life? Historical Retrieval Through Local Comparison." *Diaspora: A Journal of Transnational Affairs.*

———. Forthcoming d. "Local Level Transnational Life in Rattvik, Sweden, and Ticuani, Mexico: An Essay in Historical Retrieval." In *Transnational Social Spaces,* edited by Ludger Pries. New York: Routledge.

———. Forthcoming e. "Mexicans: Social, Educational, Economic, and Political Problems and Prospects in New York." In *New Immigrants in New York,* edited by Nancy Foner. New York: Columbia University Press.

———. Forthcoming f. "Social Location, Generation, and Life Course as Social Processes Shaping Second Generation Transnational Life." In *Second Generation Transnationalism,* edited by Peggy Levitt and Mary Waters. New York: Russell Sage Foundation.

Soysal, Yasmin N. 1994. *Limits to Citizenship: Migrants and Postnational Membership in Europe.* Chicago: University of Chicago Press.

———. 1997. "Changing Parameters of Citizenship and Claims-Making: Organized Islam in European Public Spheres." *Theory and Society* 26:511–28.

Stanton-Salazar, Ricardo, and Sanford Dornbusch. 1995. "Social Capital and the Social Reproduction of Inequality: The Formation of Informational Networks Among Mexican Origin High School Students." *Sociology of Education* 68 (2): 116–35.

Sutton, Constance. 1987. "The Caribbeanization of New York City and the Emergence of Transnational Socio-Cultural System." In *Caribbean Life in New York City: Socio-Cultural Dimensions,* edited by Constance Sutton and Elsa Chaney. New York: Center for Migration Studies.

Tilly, Charles. 1981. *As Sociology Meets History.* New York: Academic Press.

———. 1999. "Why Worry About Citizenship?" In *Expanding Citizenship, Reconfiguring States,* edited by Michael Hanagan and Charles Tilly. Lanham, Md.: Rowman and Littlefield.

———, ed. 1996. *Citizenship, Identity, and Social History.* Cambridge: Cambridge University Press.

Torres, Andres. 1995. *Between the Melting Pot and the Mosaic: African Americans and Puerto Ricans in the New York Political Economy.* Philadelphia: Temple University Press.

Torres, Andres, and Frank Bonilla. 1993. "Decline Within Decline. The New York Perspective." In *Latinos in a Changing U.S. Economy,* edited by Rebecca Morales and Frank Bonilla. Newbury Park, Calif.: Sage.

Valenzuela, Abel, Jr. 1998. "Gender Roles and Settlement Activities Among Children and Their Immigrant Families." *American Behavioral Scientist,* August, 720–42.

Valenzuela, Angela. 1999. *Subtractive Schooling: U.S.–Mexican Youth and the Politics of Caring.* Albany: State University of New York Press.

Vertovec, Steven. 1999. "Conceiving and Researching Transnationalism." *Ethnic and Racial Studies* 22 (2): 447–62.

Waldinger, Roger. 1996. *Still the Promised City? African-Americans and New Immigrants in Postindustrial New York.* Cambridge: Harvard University Press.

Waldinger, Roger, and Mehdi Bozorgmehr, eds. 1996. *Ethnic Los Angeles.* New York: Russell Sage Foundation.

Warner, W. Lloyd, and Leo Srole. 1945. *The Social Systems of American Ethnic Groups.* New Haven: Yale University Press.

Waters, Mary C. 1994 "Ethnic and Racial Identities of Second Generation Black Immigrants in New York City." *International Migration Review* 27 (4): 795–820.

———. 1996 "The Intersection of Gender, Race, and Ethnicity in Identity Development of Caribbean American Teens." In *Urban Girls,* edited by Bonnie Leadbeater and Niobe Way. New York: New York University Press.

———. 1999. *Black Identities: West Indian Dreams and American Realities.* New York: Russell Sage Foundation; Berkeley: Harvard University Press.

Waters, Tony. 1999. *Immigrant Youth and Crime.* Boulder, Colo.: Westview Press.

Weiner, Antje. 1997. "Making Sense of the New Geography of Citizenship: Fragmented Citizenship in the European Union." *Theory and Society* 26:531–59.

Willis, Paul. 1977. *Learning to Labor: How Working Class Kids Get Working Class Jobs.* New York: Columbia University Press.

Woo, Jan (Jung Ah). 1997. "Electoral Participation and Representation of Asian Americans in New York City." Senior thesis, Barnard College.

Wyman, Mark. 1993. *Round-Trip to America: The Immigrants Return to Europe, 1880–1930.* Ithaca: Cornell University Press.

Zhou, Min. 1999. "Segmented Assimilation: Issues, Controversies, and Recent Research on the New Second Generation." In *Handbook of Immigration: The American Experience,* edited by Charles Hirshman, Philip Kasinitz, and Josh DeWind. New York: Russell Sage Foundation.

Zhou, Min, and Carl Bankston. 1998. *Growing Up American.* New York: Russell Sage.

Zolberg, Aristide, and Robert Smith. 1996. "Migration Systems in Comparative Perspective: An Analysis of the Inter-American Migration System with Comparative Reference to the Mediterranean-European System." Report to U.S. Department of State, Bureau of Population, Refugees and Migration.

Zolberg, Aristide, Astri Suhrke, and Sergio Aguayo. 1989. *Escape from Violence: Conflict and the Refugee Crisis in the Developing World.* New York: Oxford University Press.

Part I

Migration and Transnational Processes

CHAPTER 2

Transnationalism Then and Now: New York Immigrants Today and at the Turn of the Twentieth Century

Nancy Foner

> The conception of citizenship itself is rapidly changing and we may have to recognize a sort of world or international citizenship as more logical than the present peripatetic kind, which makes a man an American while here, and an Italian while in Italy. International conferences are not so rare nowadays. Health, the apprehension or exclusion of criminals, financial standards, postage, telegraphs and shipping are today to a great extent, regulated by international action. . . . The old barriers are everywhere breaking down. We may even bring ourselves to the point of recognizing foreign "colonies" in our midst, on our own soil, as entitled to partake in the parliamentary life of their mother country.

Sound familiar? This reflection on the globalizing world and the possibility of electoral representation for Italians abroad describes issues that immigration scholars are debating and discussing today. The words were written, however, in 1906 by Gino Speranza ([1906] 1974, 310), secretary of the Society for the Protection of Italian Immigrants. They are a powerful reminder that processes scholars now call transnational have a long history. Contemporary immigrant New Yorkers are not the first newcomers to live transnational lives. While there are many new dynamics to immigrants' transnational connections and communities today, there are also significant continuities with the past.

The term *transnationalism*, as developed in the influential work of anthropologist Linda Basch and colleagues, refers to processes by which immigrants "forge and sus-

Revised and expanded from Nancy Foner, "What's New About Transnationalism? New York Immigrants Today and at the Turn of the Century," *Diaspora* 6 (3) 1997. Reprinted by permission of University of Toronto Press Incorporated.

tain multi-stranded social relations that link together their societies of origin and set-tlement. . . . An essential element . . . is the multiplicity of involvements that transmi-grants' sustain in both home and host societies." It is not just a question of political ties that span borders of the kind that Gino Speranza had in mind. In a transnational per-spective, contemporary migrants are seen as maintaining familial, economic, cultural, and political ties across international borders, in effect, making the home and host soci-ety a single arena of social action (Basch, Glick Schiller, and Szanton Blanc 1994, 7). Migrants may be living in New York, but, at the same time, they maintain strong involvements in their societies of origin, which, tellingly, they continue to call home.

In developing conceptual frameworks to understand and guide research on transna-tionalism, scholars of the subject often make an analytic distinction between transna-tionalism or transnational migration, on one hand, and globalism and cultural diffusion, on the other. Michael Kearney, for example, argues that transnational processes are anchored and transcend one or more nation-states while global processes are "largely decentered from specific national territories and take place in a global space" (1995, 548; cf. Glick Schiller 1999; Mato 1997). Alejandro Portes and colleagues (1999, 223) observe that some of the activities that fall under the transnationalism label have been examined from alternative conceptual focuses such as economic globalization, international rela-tions, and cultural diffusion (e.g., Sassen 1991, 1995), yet they also note that the "emer-gent literature on transnationalism" has generally focused on the "less institutionalized initiatives of ordinary immigrants and their home country counterparts" at the grass-roots level.

My concern here is that in much of what is written on the subject, transnationalism is treated as if it were a new invention; a common assumption is that earlier European immigration cannot be described in transnational terms that apply today. Perhaps, as Nina Glick Schiller (1996, 4) notes, the excitement over the "first flurry of the transna-tional aspects of contemporary migration" led to a "tendency to declare . . . transnational migration . . . a completely new phenomenon." A few years earlier, she and her col-leagues argued that transnationalism was a new type of migrant experience—that a new conceptualization, indeed a new term, *transmigrant,* was needed to understand the immigrants of today (Glick Schiller, Basch, and Szanton Blanc 1992; Basch, Glick Schiller, and Szanton Blanc 1994). Comments like Elsa Chaney's (1979, 209)—that new Caribbean immigrants "apparently differ from the settler immigrants of another era who left their homelands permanently"—are typical, Glick Schiller (1996) says, of the way many ethnographers of the post-1965 migration have viewed the past. For example, the anthro-pologist Constance Sutton (1992) suggests that, unlike earlier European arrivals, recent third-world immigrants forge social practices and ethnic identities that have a transna-tional character; rather than becoming hyphenated Americans, they operate with a transnational dual-place identity. Recently, Alejandro Portes has argued that present-day transnational communities—dense networks across political borders created by immigrants in their quest for economic advancement and social recognition—possess a distinctive character that justifies coining a new concept to refer to them (1997, 812–13).[1]

There are of course hints in the current literature that modern-day transnationalism is not altogether new—suggestions, for example, that it differs in "range and depth" (Goldberg 1992) or "density and significance" (Jones 1992) from patterns in earlier eras or that contemporary connections with home societies are of "a different order" than in the past (Glick Schiller, Basch, and Szanton Blanc 1995; cf. Portes, Guarnizo, and Landolt 1999). Glick Schiller (1996) marks an important step forward by beginning to systematically compare current transnational migration to the United States with past patterns (see also Glick Schiller 1999). Following this lead, Luis Guarnizo analyzes differences in the meanings, implications, and effects of transnational political practices among contemporary and turn-of-the-century immigrants (1997, 1998; see also R. Smith 1998b).

This chapter offers a closer look at transnationalism past and present.[2] By narrowing the field of analysis to one context—New York City—and comparing contemporary immigration with one period—the turn of the twentieth century—we can begin to specify the kinds of social, economic, and political relationships immigrants have established and maintained with their home societies in different eras. Many transnational patterns said to be new actually have a long history—and some of the sources of transnationalism seen as unique today also operated in the past. At the same time, much is distinctive about transnationalism today not only because earlier patterns have been intensified or become more common but because new processes and dynamics are involved.

This analysis is part of a larger project that compares immigrants in New York today with immigrants at the beginning of the twentieth century—the two peak periods in the city's immigration history (see Foner 2000). Between 1880 and 1920, over one million immigrants arrived and settled in New York City—so that by 1910, fully 41 percent of all New Yorkers were foreign born. In this earlier period, the focus is on Eastern European Jews and Italians; they were the vast bulk of the new arrivals at the time and defined what was then thought of as the "new immigration." Today, no two groups predominate in this way, and New York's immigrants now include sizable numbers from a variety of Asian, West Indian, and Latin American nations and European countries as well. For this reason, the discussion of the present draws on material on a larger number of groups. Since the 1960s, immigrants have been streaming into New York City at what is now a rate of over 100,000 a year.[3] Altogether, the 1990 Census counted 2.1 million foreign-born New Yorkers, who represented 28 percent of the city's population; by 1998, census estimates put the proportion at over a third.

The bulk of this chapter discusses the similarities and differences between transnationalism among today's immigrant New Yorkers and those at the turn of the twentieth century. In the conclusion, I consider some additional issues, including whether transnationalism is a first-generation phenomenon or whether it persists among the children of immigrants born and raised in this country.

Transnationalism: Continuities Between Past and Present

Like contemporary immigrants, Russian Jews and Italians in early twentieth-century New York established and sustained familial, economic, political, and cultural links to their home societies at the same time as they developed ties and connections in their new land. They did so for many of the same reasons that have been advanced to explain transnationalism today. There were relatives left behind and ties of sentiment to home communities and countries. Many immigrants came to the United States with the notion that they would eventually return. If, as one anthropologist notes, labor-exporting nations now acknowledge "that members of their diaspora communities are resources that should not and need not be lost to the home country" (Pessar 1995, 76), this was also true of the Italian government in the past. Moreover, lack of economic security and full acceptance also plagued these earlier immigrants and may have fostered their continued involvement in and allegiance to their home societies. Of the two groups, Italians best fit the ideal type of transmigrant described in the contemporary literature; many led the kind of dual lives said to characterize transmigrants today.

Russian Jews and Italian immigrants in New York's past, like their modern-day counterparts, continued to be engaged with those they left behind. What social scientists now call "transnational households," with members scattered across borders, were not uncommon a century ago. Most Italian men—from 1870 to 1910 nearly 80 percent of Italian immigrants to the United States were men—left behind wives, children, and parents; Jewish men, too, were often pioneers who later sent money to pay for the passage of other family members. Those who came to New York sent letters to relatives and friends in the Old World—and significant amounts of money. Jake, the young Jewish immigrant in Abraham Cahan's story *Yekl*, was following a common pattern when he regularly sent money to his wife in Russia. Whenever he got a letter from his wife, Jake would hold onto his reply "until he had spare United States money enough to convert to ten rubles, and then he would betake himself to the draft office and have the amount, together with the well-crumpled epistle, forwarded to Poveodye" (Cahan [1896] 1970, 27). The New York Post Office sent 12.3 million individual money orders to foreign lands in 1900–1906, with half of the dollar amount going to Italy, Hungary, and Slavic countries (Wyman 1993, 61). Gino Speranza claimed that "it was quite probable that 'Little Italy' in New York contributes more to the tax roll of Italy than some of the poorer provinces in Sicily or Calabria" ([1906] 1974, 309).4

There were organized kinds of aid, too. New York's Jewish *landsmanshaftn,* or home town associations, sent millions of dollars to their war-ravaged home communities between 1914 and 1924. The societies' traditional activities—concerts, balls, banquets, regular meetings, and Sabbath services—all became occasions for raising money. Special mass meetings were held as well. In one week in December 1914 more than twenty rallies took place in New York, raising between seventy-five and fifteen hundred dollars each for the war victims of various towns (Soyer 1997, 172). After the war, many Jewish immigrant associations sent delegates who actually delivered the money. A writer in one Yiddish daily write: "The 'delegate' has become, so to speak, an institution in the Jewish community. There is not a single landsmanshaft here in America . . . which has not sent, is not sending, or will not send a delegate with money and letters to the landslayt on the other side of the ocean" (177).

Putting away money in New York to buy land or houses in the home country is another long-term habit among immigrants who intend to return. In the last great wave, Italian immigrants were most likely to invest in projects back home. "He who crosses the ocean can buy a house" was a popular refrain celebrating one goal of emigration (Cinel 1982, 71). An inspector for the port of New York quizzed fifteen entering Italians who had previously been to the United States. "When I asked them what they did with the money they carried over, I think about two-thirds told me they had bought a little place in Italy, a little house and a plot of ground; that they had paid a certain sum; that there was a mortgage on it; that they were returning to this country for the purpose of making enough money to pay that mortgage off" (Wyman 1993, 131). It was not unusual for Italians in New York to send funds home with instructions about land purchases. An Italian told of his five years of backbreaking construction work in New York. Each day, he recalled, "I dreamed of the land I would one day buy with my savings. Land anywhere else has no value to me" (130).

Many did not just dream of going back—they actually returned. Nationwide, return migration rates are actually lower now than they were in the past. In the first two decades of the twentieth century, for every one hundred immigrants who entered the United States, thirty-six left; between 1971 and 1990, the number had fallen to twenty-three (Jones-Correa 1998, 96). Return migration, as Glick Schiller (1996) observes, should be viewed as part of a broader pattern of transnational connection. Those who have come to America with the notion of going back truly have their "feet in two societies." To organize return, Glick Schiller argues, necessitates the maintenance of home ties. And plans to return entail a continuing commitment to the norms, values, and aspirations of the home society.

Russian Jews in New York were unusual for their time in the degree to which they were permanent settlers. Having fled political repression and virulent anti-Semitism, the vast majority came to the New World to stay. Even then, there was more return migration than is generally assumed. Between 1880 and 1900 perhaps as many as 15 to 20 percent who came to the United States returned to Europe (Sarna 1981).

Many Russian Jewish migrants planned to return only temporarily in order to visit their old home towns, although "not a few turned out to be one-way visits." Some had aged relatives whom they longed to see; others sought brides, young Jewish women being in short supply in the United States; still others went home merely to show off, to demonstrate that they had somehow made good; and in a few cases immigrants returned home to study. Some Russian Jews went back, savings in hand, to found businesses. Jonathan Sarna tells us that a few "enterprising immigrants employed their knowledge of English and Russian to engage in commerce. In 1903, according to Alexander Hume Ford, there was 'a Russian American Hebrew in each of the large Manchurian cities securing in Russia the cream of the contracts for American material used in Manchuria'" (Sarna 1981, 264). Altogether, Russian statistics indicate that 12,313 more U.S. citizens entered Russian territory from 1881 to 1914 than left. According to U.S. government investigators, "plenty of Jews living in Russia held United States passports, the most famous being Cantor Pinchas Minkowsky of Odessa, formerly of New York" (264).

After 1900, however, events in Russia led immigrants in New York to abandon the notion of return. With revolutionary upheaval and the increasing intensity of pogroms, the return migration rate among Russian Jews fell off to about 5 percent (Wyman 1993). In the post-1900 period there were also few repeat crossers. Of the Jews who entered the United States between 1899 and 1910, only 2 percent had been in the country before, the lowest rate of any immigrant group in the United States in this period (Joseph 1967).

Many more Italians came with the expectation of returning home. Italians were the quintessential transnational New Yorkers of their time, as much commuters as many contemporary immigrants. Many were "birds of passage" who went back to their villages seasonally or after a few years in the United States. Italians called the United States "the workshop"; many arrived in the spring and returned to Italy in the winter when layoffs were most numerous (Wyman 1993, 79). They flitted "back and forth," writes Mark Wyman (1993, 131), "always trying to get enough for that additional plot, to pay off previous purchases, or to remove the load of debt from their backs." By the end of the nineteenth century, steamships were bigger, faster, and safer than before; tickets for the sixteen- or seventeen-day passage in steerage from Naples to New York cost fifteen dollars in 1880 and twenty-five dollars in 1907 and could be paid for in installments. Prefiguring terms used today, one early twentieth-century observer of Italian migration wrote of how improved methods of transportation were leading to the "annihilation of time and space" (Speranza [1906] 1974). Overall, between the 1880s and World War I, of every ten Italians who left for the United States, five returned. Many of these returnees—*ritornati* as the Italians called them— remigrated to the United States. According to reports of the U.S. Immigration Commission, about 15 percent of all Italian immigrants between 1899 and 1910 had been in the United States before.[5]

If economic insecurity, both at home and abroad, now leads many migrants to hedge their bets by participating in two economies, it was also a factor motivating Italians to travel back and forth across the Atlantic. The work Italian men found in New York's docks and construction sites was physically strenuous and often dangerous: the pay was low and the hours long; and the seasonal nature of the building trades meant that laborers had many weeks without work at all. During economic downturns, work was scarcer and, not surprisingly, Italian rates of return went up during the financial depression of 1894 and the panic years of 1904 and 1907 (Wyman 1993, 79). Many Jews in the late nineteenth century, according to Sarna (1981, 266), returned to Russia because they could not find decent work in America—because of "the boom-bust cycle, the miserable working conditions, the loneliness, the insecurity." Fannie Shapiro remembers crying when her father returned from a three-month stay in America since she had wanted to join him. (She later emigrated on her own in 1906.) In Russia, she explained, her father "put people to work; . . . he was the boss," but in New York "they put him in a coal cellar" (Kramer and Masur 1976, 2).

Lack of acceptance in America then, as now, probably contributed to a desire to return. Certainly, it fostered a continued identification with the home country or, among Jews, a sense of belonging to a large diaspora population. Because most current immigrants are people of color, it is argued that modern-day racism is an important underpinning of transnationalism; nonwhite immigrants, denied full acceptance in the United States, maintain and build home ties to have a place they feel they can call home (Glick Schiller 1996). Unfortunately, rejection of immigrants on the grounds of race has a long history. At the beginning of the twentieth century, the white population was seen as divided into many sharply distinguishable races. In the days before "white ethnics," Italians and Jews were thought of as racially distinct in physiognomy, intelligence, and character.[6] Many Americans recoiled in horror from eastern and southern Europeans who were thought to belong to inferior, "mongrel" races that were polluting the country's Anglo-Saxon or Nordic stock. In fact, negative images of Italians partly fastened on their darker appearance; many Americans doubted that Italians were white, calling them "swarthy" or referring, like sociologist Edward A. Ross (1914), to "the Italian dusk."

Whether because they felt marginalized and insecure in the United States or because they maintained ethnic allegiances for other reasons, Italians and Jews then, like many immigrants today, avidly followed news of and remained actively involved in home-country politics. As Matthew Jacobson (1995, 2) puts it in his study of "the diasporic imagination" of Irish, Polish, and Jewish immigrants, the homelands did not lose their centrality in "migrants' ideological geographies." Life in the diaspora, he writes, remained in many ways oriented to the politics of the old center. Although the immigrant press was a force for Americanization, equally striking, says Jacobson, "is the tenacity with which many of these journals positioned their readers within the envisaged 'nation' and its worldwide diaspora. . . . In its front-page devotion to Old World news, in its focus upon the ethnic enclave as the locus of U.S. news, in its regular features on the groups' history and literature, in its ethnocentric frame on American affairs, the immigrant journal located the reader in an ideological universe whose very center was Poland, Ireland, or Zion" (62). Continued connections to the homeland influenced immigrants' political orientations and involvements in other ways. According to Michael Topp (1997), the ideas, activities, and strategies of Italian American radicals in the years just before and just after World War I were shaped, at least in part, by communications with unionists and other activists in Italy, their reactions to events in Italy, and their physical movement back and forth between countries.

New York immigrants have also long been tapped by home-country politicians and political parties as a source of financial support. Today, Caribbean politicians regularly come to New York to campaign and raise money; earlier in the twentieth century, Irish nationalist politicians made similar pilgrimages to the city. Irish immigrants, who arrived in large numbers in the mid-1800s, were deeply involved in the Irish nationalist cause in the early decades of the twentieth century. In 1918, the Friends of Irish Freedom sponsored a rally in Madison Square Garden attended by fifteen thousand people, and street orators for Irish freedom spoke "every night of the week" in Irish neighborhoods around the city. In 1920, Eamon de Valera traveled to New York seeking support for Sinn Fein and an independent Irish Republic, raising $10 million for his cause (Doyle 1996; McNickle 1996).

Moreover, homeland governments were involved with their citizens abroad. The enormous exodus to the United States and return wave brought a reaction from the Italian government, which, like many immigrant-sending states today, was concerned about the treatment of its dispersed populations—and also saw them as a global resource.[7] The Italian government offered subsidies to several organizations in the United States that provided social services to Italian immigrants and set up an emigration office on Ellis Island to provide the newly arrived with information on employment opportunities in the United States. The current of remigration, an Italian senator said in 1910, "represents an economic force of the first order for us. It will be an enormous benefit for us if we can increase this flow of force in and out of our country." In 1907, the Italian government started to require shipping lines to bring remigrants back from North and South America at a third of the normal price; in 1901, it empowered the Banco di Napoli to open branches or deputize intermediaries overseas to receive emigrant savings that could be used for Italian development. Beyond wanting to ensure the flow of remittances and savings homeward, Italy tried to retain the loyalty of emigrants overseas as part of its own nation-building project. A 1913 law addressed the citizenship issue: returnees who had taken foreign citizenship could regain Italian citizenship simply by living two years in Italy; their children were considered Italian citizens even if born elsewhere (Wyman 1993, 93–94, 199). Although it never came to pass, there was even discussion in Italy of allowing the colonies abroad to have political representation in Italy.

Transnationalism: What's New

Clearly, transnationalism was alive and well a hundred years ago. But if there are continuities with the past, there is also much that is new. Technological changes have made it possible for immigrants to maintain more frequent and closer contact with their home societies and, in a real sense, have changed the very nature of transnational connections. Today's global economy encourages international business operations; the large number of professional and prosperous immigrants in contemporary America are well-positioned to operate in a transnational field. Dual nationality provisions by homeland governments have, in conjunction with other changes, added new dimensions to transnational political involvements. Moreover, greater tolerance for ethnic pluralism and multiculturalism in late twentieth-century America, and changed perspectives of immigration scholars themselves, have put transnational connections in a new, more positive, light.

Transformations in the technologies of transportation and communication have increased the density, multiplicity, and importance of transnational interconnections (Glick Schiller, Basch, and Szanton Blanc 1995) and made it possible for the first time for immigrants to operate more or less simultaneously in a variety of places (Rouse 1995). A century ago, the trip back to Italy took about two weeks, and more than a month elapsed between sending a letter home and receiving a reply. Today, immigrants can hop on a plane or make a telephone call to check out how things are going at home. Or, as Patricia Pessar (1995, 69) observes for New York Dominicans: "It merely requires a walk to the corner newsstand, a flick of the radio or television dial to a Spanish-language station, or the placement of an overseas call" to learn about news in the Dominican Republic.

In the jet age, inexpensive air fares mean that immigrants, especially from nearby places in the Caribbean and Central America, can fly home for emergencies, such as funerals, or celebrations, such as weddings; go back to visit their friends and relatives; and sometimes move back and forth, in the manner of commuters, between New York and their home community. Among the immigrant workers I studied in a New York nursing home (Foner 1994), some routinely spent their annual vacation in their home community in the Caribbean; others visited every few years. A study of New York's Asian Indians notes that despite the distance and cost, they usually take their families back to visit India every year or two (Lessinger 1992). Inexpensive air travel means that relatives from home also often come to New York to visit. In the warmer months, Johanna Lessinger (1995, 42) reports, when relatives from India make return visits to the United States, "a family's young men are often assigned to what is laughingly called 'airport duty,' going repeatedly to greet the flights of arriving grandparents, aunts and uncles, cousins and family friends." Thanks to modern communications and air travel, a group of Mexicans in New York involved in raising money to improve their home community's water supply was able to conduct meetings with the municipio via conference call and to fly back to the community for the weekend to confer with contractors and authorities when they learned the new tubing had been delivered (R. Smith 1998c).

Now that telephones reach into the far corners of most sending societies, immigrants can hear about news and people from home right away and participate immediately in family discussions on major decisions. Rates have become cheap—in 1998, a three-minute call to the Dominican Republic cost as little as $1.71 and to India $3.66; phone parlors, ubiquitous in New York, and pre-paid phone calls are even cheaper.[8] Cristina Szanton Blanc describes how a Filipino couple in New York maintained a key role in childrearing decisions although several of their children remained in Manila. On the telephone, they could give advice and orders and respond to day-to-day problems. When their only daughter in Manila had an unfortunate romance, they dispatched a friend visiting the Philippines to investigate the situation. Adela, the mother of the family, had herself been back to visit the Philippines three times in six years (Basch, Glick Schiller, and Szanton Blanc 1994, 237). Asian Indian New Yorkers typically telephone relatives in India weekly or biweekly, and Johanna Lessinger reports that one rich young woman called her mother in Delhi every day (Lessinger l992; see Min 1998 on Koreans' telephone contact with family members back home). Some Mexicans in New York have even purchased cellular phones for relatives in their home village so they can call easily (R. Smith 1998c). Most Brazilians whom Maxine Margolis (1998) interviewed in New York City ran up telephone bills of between $80 and $150 a month while a few admitted that they typically spent $200 a month or more. She offers an illustration of how readily Brazilians call home: "When I was in a home furnishing store in Manhattan and asked the Brazilian owner, a long time resident of New York City, how to say 'wine rack' in Portuguese, he was disturbed when he could not recall the phrase. As quickly as one might consult a dictionary, he dialed Brazil to ask a friend" (115).

Faxes and videotapes also allow immigrants to keep in close touch with those they left behind. Some Brazilians in New York, Margolis (1998) tells us, regularly record or videotape sixty-to-ninety-minute messages to send family and friends back home. Like other immigrant New Yorkers, they can participate vicariously, through videotape, in important family events. Johanna Lessinger (1995) recounts how Indians in Queens gather to watch full-length videos of weddings of widely scattered relatives, able to admire the dress and jewelry of the bride and calculate the value of pictured wedding gifts. The better-off and better-educated may use e-mail as well. An Irish journalist in New York explains: "My grandfather, who came here in the late 1800s, . . . he was an immigrant. . . . We don't have the finality of the old days. I can send E-mail. I can phone. I can be in Bantry in twelve hours" (Mathieu 1998, 140). Immigrant cable-television channels, moreover, allow an immediate, and up-close, view of homeland news for many groups; Koreans in Queens can watch the news from Seoul on the twenty-four-hour Korean channel, while Russian émigrés can view live performances from a Moscow concert hall (Sontag and Dugger 1998).

Modern forms of transportation and communications, in combination with new international forms of economic activity in the new global economy, have meant that more immigrants today are involved in economic endeavors that span national borders. Certainly, it is much easier today than a hundred years ago for immigrants to manage businesses thousands of miles away given, among other things, modern telecommunications, information technologies, and instantaneous money transfers. Alejandro Portes and Luis Guarnizo describe how Dominican entrepreneurs in New York reap rewards by using their time in New York to build a base of property, bank accounts, and business contacts and then travel back and forth to take advantage of economic opportunities in both countries (Portes 1996). A few years after a Dominican man Patricia Pessar (1995) knew bought a garment factory in New York, he expanded his operations by purchasing (with his father and brother) a garment factory in the Dominican Republic's export processing zone. He and his wife and children continue to live in New York, where he has become a U.S. citizen, though he has also built a large house in the Dominican Republic.

Many Asian Indian New Yorkers, encouraged by the Indian government's attempt to capture immigrant capital for development, invest in profit-making ventures in India, including buying urban real estate and constructing factories, for-profit hospitals, and medical centers. Often, relatives in India provide on-the-spot help in managing the business there (Lessinger 1992, 1995). After receiving a graduate degree in engineering in the United States. Dr. S. Vadivelu founded a factory in New Jersey that makes electrolytic capacitors. He later opened two factories in his home state of Andhra Pradesh, where he manufactures ceramic capacitors for sale to Indian electronics manufacturers. His father and brothers manage both plants daily; Dr. Vadivelu travels back and forth several times a year to check on the factories (Lessinger 1995, 91).

The Indian example points to something else that's new about transnationalism today. Compared with the past, a much higher proportion of newcomers today come with advanced education, professional skills, and sometimes substantial amounts of financial capital that facilitate transnational connections—and allow some immigrants to participate, in the manner of modern-day cosmopolitans, in high-level institutions and enterprises here and in their home society. The affluence of Indian New Yorkers, Lessinger (1995) argues, makes them one of the most consistently transnational immigrants in behavior and outlook. Indeed, within the Asian Indian community, it is the wealthiest and most successful professionals and business people who maintain the closest links with India and for whom "extensive transnationalism is a way of life." They are the ones able to afford many phone calls, to invest in India, to frequently fly home where they mix business with pleasure, and who have "a certain influence and standing wherever they go" (89). The Chinese "astronauts" who shuttle back and forth by air between Taiwan or Hong Kong and the United States are typically well-educated and well-off professionals, executives, and entrepreneurs who move easily in financial, scientific, and business worlds around the globe (see Wong 1998). Pyong Gap Min (1998) describes international commuter marriages involving high-level Korean professionals and business executives who have returned to Korea for better jobs while their wives and children remain in New York for educational opportunities. The couples talk on the telephone several times a week; the husbands fly to New York two to five times a year while the wives visit Korea once or twice a year.

Technological advances also play a role in transnational political involvements. The newest New Yorkers can hop on a plane to vote in national elections in their home countries, as thousands did in a recent Dominican presidential election. Politicians from home, in turn, can make quick trips to New York to campaign and raise funds. Candidates for U.S. electoral positions have been known to return to their country of origin for the same reason. Guillermo Linares, for example, briefly visited the Dominican Republic during his 1991 campaign for New York's City Council, where rallies held in support of his candidacy generated campaign funds and afforded opportunities for photographs that were featured in New York newspapers (Pessar 1995).

Apart from technological advances, there are other new aspects to transnational political practices today. A hundred years ago, Russian Jews brought with them a notion of belonging to a broader Jewish diaspora community, but they had no interest in being part of the oppressive Russian state they left behind. Italians, coming from a country in the midst of nation-state consolidation, did not arrive with a modern "national identity." Except for a tiny group of political exiles, migrants did not care much about building an Italian state that "would welcome them back, protect them from the need to migrate further, or represent the character and glories of the Italian people" (Gabaccia 1998). Among other groups in the past, like the Irish, migration became part of their continuing struggle for national liberation. What is different today is that immigrants are arriving from sovereign countries, with established nationalist ideologies and institutions, and are a potential basis of support for government pro-jects, policies, and leaders in the homeland. As a new way of building support among migrants abroad, former president Jean-Bertrand Aristide of Haiti popularized the concept of overseas Haitians as the Tenth Department in a country that is divided into nine geographical and political departments, and he set up the Ministry of Haitians Living Abroad within the Haitian Cabinet (Glick Schiller and Fouron 1998).[9]

Moreover, today, when the United States plays such a dominant role in the global political system and development strategies depend heavily on U.S. economic and political support, many sending states view their migrant populations as potential lobbies to influence U.S. policy. It has been argued that one reason that some nations are encouraging their nationals to become U.S. citizens is their desire to nurture a group of advocates to serve the home country's interests in the American political arena (DeSipio 1998; Guarnizo 1998; R. Smith 1998b).

Of enormous importance are the dual nationality provisions that now cover a growing number of New York's immigrants. Although the United States still requires naturalizing citizens to renounce prior citizenships, more and more states of origin permit their citizens to retain nationality despite naturalization elsewhere (Aleinikoff 2000, 139–40). As of December 1996, seven of the ten largest immigrant groups in New York City had the right to be dual nationals (Sengupta 1996). Since 1998 legislation in Mexico, Mexican Americans, one of the fastest-growing immigrant groups in the city, are allowed to hold Mexican nationality as well as U.S. citizenship although, as of this writing, dual nationals cannot vote in Mexican elections or hold high office there (J. Smith 1998).

The details of dual nationality policies vary from country to country. In Trinidad and Tobago, for example, dual nationals can vote only if they have lived there for a year prior to elections, whereas Colombian nationals can vote at the Colombian Con-sulate or polling sites in Queens and run for office in their homeland even after they become U.S. citizens. In 1994 the Dominican Republic recognized the right to dual nationality; three years later, as part of an electoral reform package, the government adopted a proposal to give naturalized U.S. citizens of Dominican descent the right to vote in Dominican elections and run for office while living in New York. When implemented, the recent voting reforms will make the Dominican community in New York City the second largest concentration of voters in any Dominican election, exceeded only by Santo Domingo (Sontag and Rohter 1997).

A powerful economic incentive is involved in the recognition of dual nationality by various sending countries. In the Dominican Republic, for example, immigrant remit-tances are the most important source of foreign exchange and there, as elsewhere, the government wants to ensure the flow of money and business investment homeward (Guarnizo 1997). The record-breaking naturalization rates in the United States in recent years may have increased concern about losing the allegiance—and dollars—of emi-grants. On his first visit to New York City as president of the Dominican Republic, Lionel Fernandez Reyna (who grew up in New York City, where he attended elemen-tary and high school on the Upper West Side) publicly urged Dominicans to feel free to pursue dual citizenship. "If you, young mother, or you, elderly gentleman, or you, young student, feel the need to adopt the nationality of the United States in order to confront the vicissitudes of that society stemming from the end of the welfare era, do not feel tormented by this," he said in a speech televised on New York's Channel 41. "Do it with a peaceful conscience, for you will continue being Dominicans, and we will welcome you as such when you set foot on the soil of our republic" (Rohter 1996). Political calculations come into play, too. Extending dual citizenship provisions may be a way of trying to secure the role of overseas nationals as "advocates of *la patria*'s interests in the United States, the new global hegemon" (Guarnizo 1998, 79). And though the migrant community's economic clout is an important reason why, as in the case of the Dominican Republic, migrant lobbying efforts for dual citizenship were successful, political developments and conflicts in the home country are also involved.[10]

Although some scholars and public figures worry about the trend toward dual nationality—it makes citizenship akin to bigamy, the newspaper columnist Georgie Anne Geyer (1996) complains in her book on the "death of American citizenship"—by and large transnational connections are viewed in a more favorable light today than they were in the past. Early in the twentieth century, return migration inflamed popular opinion. "Immigrants were expected to stay once they arrived," writes Walter Nugent (1992, 159). "To leave again implied that the migrant came only for money; was too crass to appreciate America as a noble experiment in democracy; and spurned American good will and helping hands." Another historian notes: "After 1907, there was tremendous hostility . . . toward temporary or return migrants. . . . The inference frequently drawn was that [they] considered the United States good enough to plunder but not to adopt. The result was a high degree of antipathy" (Shumsky quoted in Nugent 1992, 159; see Shumsky 1992). Indeed, Randolph Bourne's classic essay, "Trans-national America," published in 1916, responded to rising anti-immigrant sentiment, arguing that the nation should "accept . . . free and mobile passage of the immigrant between America and his native land. . . . To stigmatize the alien who works in America for a few years and returns to his own land, only perhaps to seek American fortune again, is to think in narrow nationalistic terms" (quoted in Goldberg 1992, 212).

At the time, a common concern was that the new arrivals were not making serious efforts to become citizens and real Americans. Schools, settlement houses, and progressive reformers put pressure on immigrants to abandon their old-fashioned customs and languages. A popular guide on becoming American advised immigrant Jews to "forget your past, your customs, and your ideals." The Americanization movement's "melting pot" pageants, inspired by Israel Zangwill's play, depicted strangely attired foreigners stepping into a huge pot and emerging as immaculate, well-dressed, accent-free "American-looking" Americans (Schwartz 1995). Expressions of ethnicity were suffocated in the schools where, in the words of New York City's Superintendent William Maxwell, the goal was "to train the immigrant child . . . to become a good American citizen" (Brumberg 1986). Much of the scholarship concerning the earlier immigration emphasized the way immigrants were assimilating and becoming American; ties to the home society were often interpreted as "evidence for, or against, Americanization" (Glick Schiller 1996) and, in many accounts, were seen as impeding the assimilation process.

Today, when there is an official commitment to cultural pluralism and cultural diversity, transnational ties are more visible and acceptable—and sometimes even celebrated in public settings. Anti-immigrant sentiment is still with us, and immigrant loyalties are still often questioned, but rates of return are not, as in the past, a key part of immigration debates. In an era of significant international money flows, and huge U.S. corporate operations abroad, there is also less concern that immigrants are looting the United States by sending remittances home. Indeed, as Luis Guarnizo (1997) observes, U.S. corporations unintentionally reinforce and encourage transnationalism by developing marketing incentives to promote migrants' monetary transfers, long-distance communications, and frequent visits to their countries of origin. Increasingly today, the message is that there is nothing un-American about expressing one's ethnicity. In New York, officials and social service agencies actively promote festivals and events to foster ethnic pride and glorify the city's multiethnic character. Practically every ethnic group has its own festival or parade, the largest being the West Indian American Day parade on Brooklyn's Eastern Parkway, which attracts between one and two million people every Labor Day. Exhibits in local museums and libraries highlight the cultural background of diverse immigrant groups; special school events feature the foods, music, and costumes of various homelands; and school curricula include material on different ethnic heritages. In the quest for votes, established New York politicians of all stripes recognize the value of visits to immigrant homelands. As part of her mayoral campaign, for example, Democratic candidate Ruth Messenger traveled to the Dominican Republic and Haiti for four days of official meetings, news conferences, and honorary dinners that led to coverage in newspapers and radio and television stations reaching Dominicans and Haitians in New York (Nagourney 1996). This kind of campaigning across borders, Luis Guarnizo (1997) argues, lends legitimacy, status, and a sense of empowerment to groups like Dominicans who maintain intense transnational relations.

As this volume makes clear, scholars are now more interested in transnational ties and see them in a more positive way than in the past. In emerging transnational perspectives, the maintenance of multiple identities and loyalties is seen as a normal feature of immigrant life; ties to the home society complement—rather than necessarily detract from—commitments in this country. At the same time as immigrants buy property, build houses, start businesses, make marriages, and influence political developments in their home societies, they are also shown to be deeply involved in building lives in New York where they buy homes, work on block associations and community boards, join unions, run school boards, and set up businesses (Basch, Glick Schiller, and Szanton Blanc 1994; see also Foner 2001). And while financial obligations to relatives left behind have been pictured as a drain on resources needed for projects in New York (Mahler 1995), generally the literature on transnationalism stresses the way transnational relationships and connections benefit immigrants.[11] In an era when globalization is a major subject of scholarly study, it is perhaps not surprising that immigrants are seen as actors who operate in a transnational framework, or that commentators in the media are following suit. "Today," writes the journalist Roger Rosenblatt (1993), "when every major business enterprise is international, when money is international, when instant international experiences are pictured on T.V., more people think of themselves as world citizens. Why should not immigrants do likewise?"

Conclusion

Modern technology, the new global economy and culture, and new laws and political arrangements have all combined to produce transnational connections that differ in fundamental ways from those maintained by immigrants a century ago. Once ignored or reviled, transnational ties are now a favorite topic at conferences and sometimes are even celebrated in today's multicultural age. Yet the novelty of contemporary conditions should not be exaggerated. Immigrants who move from one country to another seldom cut off ties and allegiances to those left behind, and immigrant New Yorkers a century ago were no exception. It may have been harder to maintain contacts across the ocean than it is today, but many immigrants in the last great wave maintained extensive, and intensive, transnational ties and operated in what social scientists now call a transnational social field.

A comparison of transnationalism then and now raises some additional issues that need to be addressed. If academic observers who studied earlier immigrants were guilty of overlooking transnational ties in the quest to document assimilation, now there is a risk of overemphasizing the centrality of transnationalism and minimizing the extent to which contemporary immigrants "become American" and undergo changes in behavior and outlook in response to circumstances in this country. Indeed, as David Hollinger (1995, 154) observes, today's immigrants "are more prepared for a measure of assimilation by the worldwide influence of American popular culture; most are more culturally attuned to the United States before they arrive here than were their counterparts a century ago." Moreover, as a recent study of Mexican and Central American migrants points out, transnationalism tends to put too much stress on ephemeral migration circuits and understates the permanency of migrant settlement (Hondagneu-Sotelo and Avila 1997). Although many, perhaps most, immigrants come with the idea of improving their lot and returning home, as they extend their stay and as more family members join them, they become increasingly involved with life and people in the United States. Ties to the homeland seldom disappear, but they often gradually become fewer and thinner.

Perhaps because studies using a transnational approach are in their infancy, we still know little about how pervasive and extensive various transnational ties actually are for different groups. Or, for that matter, how transnationalism affects immigrants—from their family lives to their political involvements—and the communities in which they live. The new immigration, like the old, to quote Hollinger (1995, 153) again, is behaviorally mixed. "It displays a variety of degrees of engagement with the United States and with prior homelands, and it yields some strong assimilationist impulses alongside vivid expressions of diasporic consciousness." In the past, Italians were more transnational in behavior and outlook than Russian Jews mainly because Jews came to stay, whereas large numbers of Italians were labor migrants, who aimed to— and often did—go back home after a spell of work in New York.

Today, as well, some groups are likely to maintain more intense, more regular, and denser transnational connections than others—and we need research that explores and explains the differences. Peggy Levitt (1998) suggests several factors that help explain why the groups she is studying in Boston differ in type, intensity, and durability of transnational ties. She lists geography, including the home country's distance from the United States and the extent of residential clustering here; institutional completeness or the degree to which the group creates institutions enabling migrants to satisfy most of their needs within their own ethnic community, particularly transnational institutions, such as churches, that extend across borders; and the role of the state, both the home government's role in reinforcing and encouraging migrants' ties with people back home and the U.S. government's history of political and economic involvement in the homeland. She also mentions socioeconomic factors, including high levels of social parity between migrants and those in the home community that make it easier for members to stay attached to one another and to sanction those who do not. Additional factors are also likely to be important: the nature of social organization and cultural patterns in the home community that may encourage the maintenance of transnational connections as well as the particularities of homeland political movements, leaders, and organizations that may lead them to actively recruit support abroad.

There is also variation within groups in the frequency, depth, and range of transnational ties. Just as well-off Asian Indian immigrants have more resources to maintain transnational connections than do their poorer compatriots, so, too, this may be true in other immigrant groups. Legal status is likely to affect the types and extent of transnational connections maintained; undocumented immigrants cannot easily go back and forth, for example. Whether migrants came on their own or with their families also must be considered. And there are bound to be differences in the nature and impact of transnational ties between men and women and among the old, young, and middle-aged. Furthermore, transnational connections may well lose force with the length of stay in the United States, as suggested by research showing that remittances tend to taper off over time.

These observations lead to the question whether transnational ties persist among the second generation. As one scholar speculates, we may be currently witnessing a first-generation phenomenon and the culture and political economy of the transnational migrant experience may wither (Goldberg 1992). Basically, this is what happened in the past. Connections with their parents' homelands became extremely attenuated among the children of Jewish and Italian immigrants. To be sure, "some hyphenated Americans," as Mary Waters and colleagues note, "continued to play an important role in sending society politics or international political movements, such as Zionism and the struggles for Irish independence. But by and large they did so as ethnic *Americans,* not as 'transmigrants' " (Waters, Kasinitz, and Mollenkopf 1998, 5).

Continued day-to-day involvement in the communal life of the sending societies fell off sharply after the first generation. Many second- and third-generation Jews have identified with and given financial support to Israel, but most do not have close relatives in Israel or ongoing contact with people there. In the 1990s, an Italian-based tourist agency was tapping into a growing market of affluent Italian Americans as it offered tours to ancestral villages as part of its "Progetto Ritorno," since, as the brochure states, "only a fraction have ever visited Italy."

What undercut transnationalism among the second generation in the past? Born and bred in the United States, and socialized in a variety of U.S. institutions, the children of the earlier immigrants became thoroughly engaged with life in this country. Many managed to climb the socioeconomic ladder, if only in small steps. Also, their ethnic communities received few fresh recruits after the 1920s in the wake of legislated immigration restrictions and the Great Depression. Without replenishment, the number of Italians and Jews with fresh memories of and connections to the homeland became steadily smaller. The economies of Italy and eastern Europe, moreover, had little to offer the children of immigrant parents. And political events—World War II and the Holocaust—cut off connections there and heightened their patriotic embrace of America.

As for the future, different circumstances today and in the years ahead are likely to support and sustain transnational connections for at least some of the current second generation. Even if there is some move toward restrictionism, the United States, as Roger Waldinger (1996) predicts, is likely to remain an immigration country, allowing five or six hundred thousand persons to enter each year. Continued inflows will bring new recruits who will enrich and replenish ethnic communities—and include substantial numbers of people, of all ages, with close ties to their homelands. The ethos of ethnic pluralism in the United States is also, as I note, quite different from the environment of Americanization that prevailed earlier in the century (cf. R. Smith 1998b). Transnational ties are more visible and more acceptable in today's multicultural America, so that the second generation often feel pride—not shame—in connections to their parents' homelands.

Where dual nationality provisions extend to the second generation—as is the case for Dominican New Yorkers—this may foster continued political involvement in the "home country" among the second generation. When recent electoral reforms go into effect, adult children of Dominican parents born in the United States will have the right to vote from abroad in Dominican elections. Some of them, in addition, may have spent part of their childhood or teenage years in the Dominican Republic, and that experience, among other things, is likely to reinforce and create ties to relatives and friends there. In the late 1990s, Dominican educators and government officials estimated that as many as ten thousand students from schools in the United States, mainly from the New York area, were enrolled in the country's schools, typically sent back by parents who wanted to protect their children from drugs, gangs, and violence in New York (Rohter 1998). Many Mexican parents send their children back to their villages during summer vacations so they will not get into trouble in New York (R. Smith 1998a). At the other end of the life course, parental retirement patterns may also strengthen transnational ties. Some of the first generation will end up retiring to their birthplaces, ensuring that their children will make regular trips to see them and keeping children and grandchildren connected, however tenuously, to the sending country.

At the same time, scholars predict that the economic restructuring of the U.S. economy and the declining demand for less-educated labor will threaten the ability of the second generation to advance occupationally.[12] This change may make it more appealing for them to try their hand at ventures (including illegal ones) that involve transnational connections. In today's global economy, the more successful may take up this tack as well. That some sending nations have robust and prosperous economies means that they may attract a number of educated and well-trained descendants of the current immigrants, who will find it profitable to invest in their parents' homeland, return there for a time to work, or end up commuting back and forth. Cheap air travel and increased global tourism in the modern era are also likely to increase the first-hand contact that members of the second generation have with their homeland, although caution is needed in evaluating whether short vacations or special tours to the homeland are evidence of or lead to significant transnationalism.

Predictions about the future are of course always risky. Most members of the present second generation are too young to permit definitive conclusions about the kinds of ties they will develop or maintain with their parents' homelands. What is clear is that transnational practices of the first generation are very much part of the modern scene and have far-reaching effects for the lives of immigrants as well as for their children. This chapter shows that in trying to understand transnationalism among the latest arrivals it is useful to revisit the past to begin to sort out the continuities as well as contrasts between then and now. As David Kennedy (1996) writes, "the only way we can know with certainty as we move along time's path that we have come to a genuinely new place is to know something of where we have been." Transnationalism has been with us for a long time, and a comparison with the past allows us to assess just what is new about the patterns and processes involved in transnational ties today.

Notes

1. In a further refinement of the term, Portes and colleagues (Portes, Guarnizo, and Landolt 1999) now limit the concept of transnationalism to "occupations and activities that require regular and sustained social contacts over time across national borders for their implementation." What constitutes "truly original phenomena and, hence, a justifiable new topic of investigation are the high intensity of exchanges, the new modes of transacting, and the multiplication of activities that require cross-border travel and contacts on a sustained basis" (219).

2. This chapter is not an analysis of the evolution of the concept of transnationalism, a fascinating and important topic that deserves full treatment elsewhere. Rather, my goal is to broaden our understanding of transnationalism, as the concept has been developed by migration scholars in recent years, by exploring just what is new about transnational practices among contemporary immigrant New Yorkers.

3. In the 1970s, the annual rate of immigration to New York was about 78,000; in the 1980s, about 85,000; and in the early 1990s, about 112,000 (Lobo, Salvo, and Virgin 1996, 7).

4. According to the Italian Bureau of Emigration, a total of 23 million lire arrived in Italy from abroad (about $7.75 million) in 1903, 18 million from the United States. Except in 1906 and 1907, the remittances from overseas increased every year, passing 150 million lire in 1916 and reaching an all-time high of 1 billion lire in 1920 (Cinel 1982b, 75).

5. On Italian "birds of passage" and return migration see Archdeacon 1983; Cinel 1982a, b; Foerster 1924; Tomasi 1975; and Wyman 1993. For a general discussion of return migration to Europe also see Morawska 1991.

6. Historians use phrases such as "not-yet-white ethnics" and "in-between peoples" to describe Italians' and Jews' ambiguous racial status, sometimes white, sometimes not (Barrett and Roediger 1997; Gerstle 1997, Jacobson 1995, Roediger 1991).

7. For an interesting comparison of the involvement of the Italian and Mexican states in their emigrant populations see R. Smith 1998b.

8. It was not possible to make a transatlantic telephone call until 1927, and then it was pro-hibitively expensive—$200 in present-day currency for a three-minute call to London. These days, phone parlors and card businesses buy telephone minutes in bulk from long-distance carriers and sell them at sharply discounted rates (see Sontag and Dugger 1998).

9. Aristide's successor, Rene Preval, distanced himself from Aristide on many points, including the use of the term the Tenth Department, although he retained the Ministry of Haitians Living Abroad (Glick Schiller and Fouron 1998, 148–49).

10. On the politics of dual-nationality legislation in the Colombian and Dominican cases, see Sanchez 1997; Graham, Chapter 4, this volume; and Guarnizo 1997. Also see Jones-Correa 1998 (160–68) on lobbying efforts for dual citizenship among Colombians, Ecuadorians, and Domini-cans in New York.

11. An important but understudied question is the consequences of transnational connec-tions for migrants' lives (Foner 2000, 186–87). On the costs of transnationalism, see Hondagneu-Sotelo and Avila 1997, in which the authors argue that "transnational motherhood" among Latina immigrant domestic workers in California brings enormous personal strain. The women worry about the care the children they have left behind are receiving and whether their children will get into trouble during adolescence and will transfer their allegiance and affection to the "other mother." Jones-Correa 1998 points to the way Latin American men's involvement in political and organizational affairs of the home country draws energies and interests away from political engagement and activism on behalf of the New York immigrant community.

12. For differing views of the socioeconomic prospects of today's second generation see Alba and Nee 1997; Gans 1992; and Perlmann and Waldinger 1997.

References

Alba, Richard, and Victor Nee. 1997. "Rethinking Assimilation for a New Era of Immigration." *International Migration Review* 31:826–74.

Aleinikoff, T. Alexander. 2000. "Between Principles and Politics: U.S. Citizenship Policy." In *From Migrants to Citizens*, edited by T. Alexander Aleinikoff and Douglas Klusmeyer. Wash-ington, D.C.: Carnegie Endowment for International Peace.

Archdeacon, Thomas. 1983. *Becoming American.* New York: Free Press.

Barrett, James, and David Roediger. 1997. "Inbetween Peoples: Race, Nationality, and the 'New Immigrant' Working Class." *Journal of American Ethnic History* 16:3–44.

Basch, Linda, Nina Glick Schiller, and Cristina Szanton Blanc. 1994. *Nations Unbound: Transnational Projects, Postcolonial Predicaments, and Deterritorialized Nation-States.* Langhorne, Pa.: Gordon and Breach.

Brumberg, Stephan. 1986. *Going to America, Going to School: The Jewish Immigrant Public School Encounter in Turn-of-the-Century New York City.* New York: Praeger.

Cahan, Abraham. [1896] 1970. *Yekl and Other Stories of Yiddish New York.* New York: Dover.

Chaney, Elsa. 1979. "The World Economy and Contemporary Migration." *International Migration Review* 13:204–12.

Cinel, Dino. 1982a. "The Seasonal Emigration of Italians in the Nineteenth Century: From Internal to International Migration." *Journal of Ethnic Studies* 10:43–68.

———. 1982b. *From Italy to San Francisco: The Immigrant Experience.* Stanford: Stanford University Press.

DeSipio, Louis. 1998. "Building a New Foreign Policy Among Friends: National Efforts to Construct Long-Term Relationships with Latin American Emigres in the United States." Paper presented at the conference States and Diasporas, Casa Italiana, Columbia University, May.

Doyle, Joe. 1996. "Striking for Ireland on the New York Docks." In *The New York Irish,* edited by Ronald Bayor and Thomas Meagher. Baltimore: Johns Hopkins University Press.

Foerster, Robert. 1924. *The Italian Emigration of Our Times.* Cambridge: Harvard University Press.

Foner, Nancy. 1994. *The Caregiving Dilemma: Work in an American Nursing Home.* Berkeley: University of California Press.

———. 2000. *From Ellis Island to JFK: New York's Two Great Waves of Immigration.* New Haven: Yale University Press.

———. 2001. "Immigrant Commitment to America, Then and Now: Myths and Realities." *Citizenship Studies* 5:27–40.

Gabaccia, Donna. 1998. "Italians and Their Diasporas: Cosmopolitans, Exiles, and Workers of the World." Paper presented at the conference States and Diasporas, Casa Italiana, Columbia University, May.

Gans, Herbert. 1992. "Second Generation Decline: Scenarios for the Economic and Ethnic Futures of Post-1965 American Immigrants." *Ethnic and Racial Studies* 15:173–92.

Gerstle, Gary. 1997. "Liberty, Coercion, and the Making of Americans." *Journal of American History* 84:524–58.

Geyer, Georgie Anne. 1996. *Americans No More: The Death of American Citizenship.* New York: Atlantic Monthly Press.

Glick Schiller, Nina. 1996. "Who Are Those Guys? A Transnational Reading of the U.S. Immigrant Experience." Paper presented at Social Science Research Council conference Becoming American/America Becoming: International Migration to the United States, Sanibel Island, Fla.

———. 1999. "Transmigrants and Nation-States: Something Old and Something New in the U.S. Immigrant Experience." In *The Handbook of International Migration: The American Experience,* edited by Charles Hirschman, Philip Kasinitz, and Josh DeWind. New York: Russell Sage Foundation.

Glick Schiller, Nina, Linda Basch, and Cristina Szanton Blanc. 1992. "Transnationalism: A New Analytic Framework for Understanding Migration." In *Towards a Transnational Perspective on*

Migration, edited by Nina Glick Schiller, Linda Basch, and Cristina Blanc-Szanton. New York: New York Academy of Sciences.

———. 1995. "From Immigrant to Transmigrant: Theorizing Transnational Migration." *Anthropological Quarterly* 68 (1): 48–63.

Glick Schiller, Nina, and Georges Fouron. 1998. "Transnational Lives and National Identities: The Identity Politics of Haitian Immigrants." In *Transnationalism from Below,* edited by Michael P. Smith and Luis Guarnizo. New Brunswick, N.J.: Transaction Press.

Goldberg, Barry, 1992. "Historical Reflections on Transnationalism, Race, and the American Immigrants Saga." In *Towards a Transnational Perspective on Migration,* edited by Nina Glick Schiller, Linda Basch, and Cristina Blanc-Szanton. New York: New York Academy of Sciences.

Guarnizo, Luis Eduardo. 1997. "On the Political Participation of Transnational Migrants: Old Practices and New Trends." Paper presented at Social Science Research Council workshop, Immigrants, Civic Culture, and Modes of Political Incorporation: A Contemporary and Historical Comparison, Santa Fe, N.M.

———. 1998. "The Rise of Transnational Social Formations: Mexican and Dominican State Responses to Transnational Migration." *Political Power and Social Theory* 12:45–94.

Hondagneu-Sotelo, Pierrette, and Ernestine Avila. 1997. " 'I'm Here, but I'm There:' The Meanings of Transnational Latina Motherhood." *Gender and Society* 11 (5): 548–69.

Hollinger, David. 1995. *Postethnic America.* New York: BasicBooks.

Hood, Clifton. 1993. *722 Miles: The Building of the Subways and How They Transformed New York.* New York: Simon and Schuster.

Jacobson, Matthew. 1995. *Special Sorrows.* Cambridge: Harvard University Press.

Jones, Delmos. 1992. "Which Migrant? Temporary or Permanent?" In *Towards a Transnational Perspective on Migration,* edited by Nina Glick Schiller, Linda Basch, and Cristina Blanc-Szanton. New York: New York Academy of Sciences.

Jones-Correa, Michael. 1998. *Between Two Nations: The Political Predicament of Latinos in New York City.* Ithaca: Cornell University Press.

Joseph, Samuel. 1967. *Jewish Immigration to the United States: From 1881–1910.* New York: AMS Press.

Kearney, Michael. 1995. "The Local and the Global: The Anthropology of Globalization and Transnationalism." *Annual Review of Anthropology* 24:547–66.

Kennedy, David. 1996. "Can We Still Afford to Be a Nation of Immigrants?" *Atlantic Monthly,* November, 52–68.

Kramer, Sydelle, and Jenny Masur, eds. 1976. *Jewish Grandmothers.* Boston: Beacon Press.

Lessinger, Johanna. 1992. "Investing or Going Home? A Transnational Strategy Among Indian Immigrants in the United States" In *Towards a Transnational Perspective on Migration,* edited by Nina Glick Schiller, Linda Basch, and Cristina Blanc-Szanton. New York: New York Academy of Sciences.

———. 1995. *From the Ganges to the Hudson.* Boston: Allyn and Bacon.

Levitt, Peggy. 1998. "Forms of Transnational Community and Their Impact on the Second Generation: Preliminary Findings." Paper presented at the conference Transnationalism and the Second Generation, Harvard University, April 3–4.

Lobo, Arun Peter, Joseph Salvo, and Vicky Virgin. 1996. *The Newest New Yorkers, 1990–1994.* New York: Department of City Planning.

Mahler, Sarah. 1995. *American Dreaming: Immigrant Life on the Margins.* Princeton: Princeton University Press.

Margolis, Maxine. 1998. *An Invisible Minority: Brazilians in New York City*. Boston: Allyn and Bacon.

Mathieu, Joan. 1998. *Zulu: An Irish Journey*. New York: Farrar, Straus, and Giroux.

Mato, Daniel. 1997. "On Global Agents, Transnational Relations, and the Social Making of Transnational Identities and Associated Agendas in Latin America." *Identities* 4:167–212.

McNickle, Chris. 1996. "When New York Was Irish, and After." In *The New York Irish*, edited by Ronald Bayor and Thomas Meagher. Baltimore: Johns Hopkins University Press.

Min, Pyong Gap. 1998. *Changes and Conflicts: Korean Immigrant Families in New York*. Boston: Allyn and Bacon.

Morawska, Eva. 1997. "On New-Old Transmigrations and Transnationalism Qua Ethnicization." Paper presented at Social Science Research Council workshop, Immigrants, Civic Culture, and Modes of Political Incorporation: A Contemporary and Historical Comparison, Santa Fe, N.M.

———. 1991. "Return Migration: Theoretical and Research Agenda." In *A Century of European Migrations, 1830–1930*, edited by Rudolph Vecoli and Suzanne Sinke. Urbana: University of Illinois Press.

Nagourney, Adam. 1996. "Long Roads to City Hall Get Longer." *New York Times*, December 4.

Nugent, Walter. 1992. *Crossings: The Great Transatlantic Migrations, 1870–1914*. Bloomington: Indiana University Press.

Perlmann, Joel, and Roger Waldinger. 1997. "Second Generation Decline? The Children of Immigrants Past and Present—A Reconsideration." *International Migration Review* 31 (4): 893–922.

Pessar, Patricia. 1995. *A Visa for a Dream*. Boston: Allyn and Bacon.

Portes, Alejandro. 1996. "Global Villagers: The Rise of Transnational Communities." *American Prospect* (March–April): 74–78.

———. 1997. "Immigration Theory for a New Century: Some Problems and Opportunities." *International Migration Review* 31:799–825.

Portes, Alejandro, Luis Guarnizo, and Patricia Landolt. 1999. "The Study of Transnationalism: Pitfalls and Promise of an Emergent Research Field." *Ethnic and Racial Studies* 22:218–37.

Roediger, David. 1991. *The Wages of Whiteness: Race and the Making of the American Working Class*. London: Verso.

Rohter, Larry. 1996. "U.S. Benefits Go; Allure to Dominicans Doesn't." *New York Times*, October 12.

———. 1998. "Island Life Not Idyllic for Youths from U.S." *New York Times*, February 20.

Ross, Edward A. 1914. *The Old World in the New*. New York: Century.

Rouse, Roger. 1995. "Thinking Through Transnationalism: Notes on the Cultural Politics of Class Relations in the Contemporary United States." *Public Culture* 7:353–402.

Rosenblatt, Roger. 1993. "Sunset, Sunrise." *New Republic*, December 27, 20–23.

Sanchez, Arturo. 1997. "Transnational Political Agency and Identity Formation among Colombian Immigrants." Paper presented at the conference Transnational Communities and the Political Economy of New York City in the 1990s, New School for Social Research.

Sarna, Jonathan. 1981. "The Myth of No Return: Jewish Return Migration to Eastern Europe, 1881–1914." *American Jewish History* 71:256–68.

Sassen, Saskia. 1988. *The Mobility of Capital and Labor: A Study of International Investment and Labor Flow*. New York: Cambridge University Press.

———. 1991. *The Global City*. Princeton: Princeton University Press.

Schwartz, Benjamin. 1995. "The Diversity Myth: America's Leading Export." *Atlantic Monthly*, May, 57–67.

Sengupta, Somini. 1996. "Immigrants in New York Pressing for Drive for Dual Nationality." *New York Times*, December 30.

Shumsky, Neil. 1992. "Let No Man Stop to Plunder": American Hostility to Return Migration, 1890–1924." *Journal of American Ethnic History* 11:56–75.

Smith, James. 1998. "Mexico's Dual Nationality Opens Doors." *Los Angeles Times*, March 20.

Smith, Robert. 1998a. "Notes for a Paper on Transnationalism in the Second Generation among Mexican Americans in Brooklyn." Paper presented at the conference Transnationalism and the Second Generation, Harvard University, April 3–4.

———. 1998b. "Reflections on the State, Migration, and the Durability and Newness of Transnational Life: Comparative Insights from the Mexican and Italian Cases." *Soziale Welt* 12:197–217.

———. 1998c. "Transnational Localities: Community, Technology, and the Politics of Membership Within the Context of Mexico–U.S. Migration." In *Transnationalism from Below*, edited by Michael Peter Smith and Luis Eduardo Guarnizo. New Brunswick, N.J.: Transaction Press.

Sontag, Deborah, and Celia Dugger. 1998. "The New Immigrant Tide: A Shuttle Between Worlds." *New York Times*, July 19.

Sontag, Deborah, and Larry Rohter. 1997. "Dominicans May Allow Voting Abroad." *New York Times*, November 15.

Soyer, Daniel. 1997. *Jewish Immigrant Associations and American Identity in New York, 1880–1939.* Cambridge: Harvard University Press.

Speranza, Gino C. [1906] 1974. "Political Representation of Italo-American Colonies in the Italian Parliament." In *The Italians: Social Backgrounds of an American Group,* edited by Francisco Cordasco and Eugene Bucchioni. Clifton, N.J.: Augustus M. Kelley.

Sutton, Constance. 1992. "Transnational Identities and Cultures: Caribbean Immigrants in the United States." In *Immigration and Ethnicity: American Society—"Melting Pot" or "Salad Bowl"?* edited by Michael D'Innocenzo and Josef Sirefman. Westport, Conn.: Greenwood Press.

Tomasi, Silvano. 1975. *Piety and Power.* New York: Center for Migration Studies.

Topp, Michael Miller. 1997. "The Transnationalism of the Italian American Left: The Lawrence Strike of 1912 and the Italian Chamber of Labor of New York City." *Journal of American Ethnic History* 17:39–63.

Waldinger, Roger. 1996. "Ethnicity and Opportunity in the Plural City." In *Ethnic Los Angeles,* edited by Roger Waldinger and Mehdi Bozorgmehr. New York: Russell Sage Foundation.

Waters, Mary, Philip Kasinitz, and John Mollenkopf. 1998. "Transnationalism and the Children of Immigrants in the United States: What are the Issues?" Paper presented at the conference Transnationalism and the Second Generation, Harvard University, April 3–4.

Wong, Bernard. 1998. *Ethnicity and Entrepreneurship: The New Chinese Immigrants in the San Francisco Bay Area.* Boston: Allyn and Bacon.

Wyman, Mark. 1993. *Round-Trip America: The Immigrants Return to Europe, 1880–1930.* Ithaca: Cornell University Press.

CHAPTER 3

The Generation of Identity: Redefining the Second Generation Within a Transnational Social Field

Georges E. Fouron and Nina Glick Schiller

Georges woke up laughing. He had been dreaming of Haiti, not the Haiti he had visited last summer, but the Haiti of his youth. But it wasn't actually the Haiti of his youth either, as he realized when he tried to explain to his wife, Rolande, the feeling of happiness with which he had awakened. He was walking down Grand-Rue, the main street of his hometown of Aux Cayes. The sun was shining, the streets were clean, and the port was bustling with ships. He and his friends were laughing, joking, and having a wonderful time. Once he was awake, Georges laughed again but this time not from joy. Georges had been dreaming of a Haiti that never was.

The Haiti of his Georges's youth had actually been more nightmare than joy. The Duvalier dictatorship was clamping down on all dissent. Wearing an Afro, speaking out at school, or joining any form of organization could lead to disappearance, beatings, imprisonment, torture, and murder. Besides being afraid, Georges was constantly anxious about how he would get an education and find some sort of a job. He couldn't even take his next meal for granted, although his father was the director of a technical school and his mother did sewing and fancy embroidery to supplement the family income.

Georges's joyful dream of his dear, sweet homeland would have been familiar to immigrants from around the world, whose days as well as nights are filled with memories of things past. In the pain of resettling in a new country, reminiscence is often replaced by nostalgia. The deprivations or repression that prompted migration often are put aside. This nostalgia persists even though for Georges and for millions of contemporary immigrants from all over the world, the longed-for homeland is a location of ongoing experience. These immigrants are transmigrants living simultaneously in two countries. They participate in personal and political events in both their home-land and their new land. They live their lives across borders in a social world that includes the often harsh realities of their homeland. Nonetheless, many immigrants continue, as does Georges, to dream of a homeland in which "the sun is shining and the streets are clean."

What of the next generation, who were born or grew up in the United States rather than in Haiti? How have they been affected by the fact that the pattern of their lives is shaped not only by their parents' nostalgia but also by their families' enduring transna-tional connections? And if, as we and a growing number of scholars have been docu-menting, immigrants' transnational social relations connect homeland and new land into a single social field, how do we delimit the boundaries of the generation born to immigrants, the second generation? After all, many young people living in Haiti are also children of immigrant families, living in Haiti while their parents or other rela-tives who maintain their households live incorporated into the United States.

In this chapter we employ a transnational perspective to examine the second genera-tion. We look at the effects of transnational migration on young people born in the United States of Haitian parentage and on young people living in Haiti within transna-tional social fields. We also examine the similarities and differences in identification with Haiti between children of Haitian parentage living in the United States and Haitian youth born in Haiti. Our conclusions are based on research we conducted on Haitian transnational migration and Haitian ethnic, racial, and national identities in New York and in Haiti. This research extended from 1969 to 1999. When we describe the experi-ence of one of the authors, we use the third person, referring to "Georges" or "Nina." To describe our joint analysis we speak in the first person plural. Between 1985 and 1997, in addition to participant observation, we conducted surveys, two in the United States and three in Haiti. In total we interviewed 229 poor and middle-class people and asked about the relationship between those who have left Haiti and those left behind.

To discuss the experience of a generation living within the daily realities of transna-tional migration, we will use quotations from interviews conducted in 1996 and 1997 with two samples of young people, one in New York and one in Haiti, and observa-tions of a conference called in New York in 1996 to build what became the Haitian American Community Action Network. While we draw on data from all the inter-views and discuss the identities of the second generation and how they vary over time and in location, degree of education, class position, and political involvement, we highlight the voices of youth who served as the unpaid staff of a radio program in Aux Cayes, Haiti, young people who participated in the 1996 conference in New York, and Haitian students at the State University of New York at Stony Brook. We present these particular voices because they contribute to the public debate within Haitian transnational social fields about the identity of the second generation and the rela-tionship between those in Haiti and the Haitian diaspora. However we wish to stress that there is not a single voice of Haitian youth, either in Haiti or in the diaspora. There are many experiences and imaginings of Haiti, of the United States, and of their rela-tionship.[1] We use our findings to argue for a new and expanded concept of the second generation and to examine long-distance nationalism as an ideology of belonging that extends across the territorial boundaries of states, as well as across generational divides (Anderson 1993, 1994; Glick Schiller and Fouron 2001).

Definition of Terms

A growing number of scholars are constructing a "transnational perspective for the study of migration" and documenting the connections that first-generation immigrants to the United States who are part of the "post-1965" immigration maintain with their native land (Glick Schiller, Basch, Szanton Blanc 1992; Glick Schiller and Fouron 1990; Goldring 1996; Guarnizo 1997; Kearney 1991; Mahler 1998; Margolis 1998; Portes, Guarnizo, and Landolt 1999; Rouse 1991, 1992; Smith 1995; Smith and Guarnizo 1998). Although there is now an emerging scholarship of transnationalism, there is no common understanding about what is meant by transnational migration. The effort to create a common set of definitions for the study of transnational migration is complicated by the fact that political leaders in many emigrant-sending countries are now working to engage their emigrant populations in economic or political projects. These leaders have developed a set of policies and laws that redefine membership in these emigrant-sending states, in some cases by constitutional changes that provide dual nationality to transnational migrants and their children (Basch, Glick Schiller, and Szanton Blanc 1994; Guarnizo 1998; Graham 1996; Sanchez 1997; Smith 1997, 1998b). Even those states that have not changed their legal definitions have formulated tax regulations or created public agencies that strive to incorporate emigrants and their descendants into the sending society.

To facilitate the study of the effects of transnational migration on the political identities of immigrants and their descendants, we propose the following definitions. Transnational migration is a process of movement and settlement across international borders in which individuals maintain or build multiple networks of connection to their country of origin while at the same time settling in a new country. Persons who live their lives across borders so that they are simultaneously incorporated in two or more states can be defined as "transmigrants" (Glick Schiller, Basch, and Szanton Blanc 1992, 1). That is to say, such migrants do more than stay in touch with family members left behind. They organize their daily economic, familial, religious, and social relations within networks that extend across the borders of two nation-states. Transnational connection takes many forms, all of which go beyond immigrant nostalgia in which a person who is removed from his or her ancestral land tries to recreate in the new land a sense of the old, through foods, music, and storytelling.

While transmigrants may emigrate and settle without returning home, they consistently engage in various social interactions that cross borders. Georges, for example, does much more than dream of Haiti. His transnational relations range from sending money and gifts to sporadic attendance at meetings, demonstrations, and forums called by various organizations that conduct activities in both the United States and Haiti.

Even in the periods when he did not visit Haiti, first because he was undocumented, and then because his burden of supporting family in the United States and Haiti left him no money to visit, he was embedded within transnational networks that intimately connected him to the place he continued to call home. We must point out that to speak about the transnational connections of persons who have emigrated from their homeland to settle abroad is to describe only one set of relationships that such persons establish. For example, many persons from Haiti have become well incorporated in their new country, developing relationships at work and in their neighborhood. Economic, religious, and social activities that link them to persons of varying nationalities with whom they may identify in various ways: co-worker, union member, neighbor, Catholic, Protestant, Mason, black, Caribbean, or woman. In this chapter we focus on the transnational domain of social relationships established by migrating populations not because it is their exclusive sphere of action but because the effects of this domain on the second generation have yet to be addressed.

The most useful way to conceptualize the domain created by the social relationships of persons who visit back and forth in their country of origin and persons who remain connected even if they themselves do not move is to speak of a "transnational social field" (Basch, Glick Schiller, and Szanton Blanc 1994; Glick Schiller 1999a; Glick Schiller, Basch, Szanton Blanc 1992, 1995; Glick Schiller and Fouron 1999). We build our understanding of social field on the network studies developed by the Manchester School of Social Anthropology (Barnes 1954, 1969; Mitchell 1969; Noble 1973; Turner 1967). A network is best understood as a chain of social relationships specific to each person. A social field can be defined as an unbounded terrain of interlocking ego-centric networks.[2]

The concept "transnational social field" provides a conceptual and methodological entry point into the investigation of broader social, economic, and political processes through which migrating populations are embedded in more than one society and to which they react. It facilitates an analysis of the processes by which immigrants as well as their descendants can continue to be part of the fabric of daily life in their home state, including its political processes, while they simultaneously engage in activities in their new country, at their jobs, in their neighborhoods, and as citizens participating in the political process. The study of transnational social fields focuses on human interaction and situations of personal social relationship.[3] Underlying the use of this concept is the hypothesis that ongoing transnational social relations foster different forms of social and political identification than connections made simply through transborder forms of communication.

To facilitate the analysis we differentiate between the maintenance of transnational networks and an ideology of belonging and call the ideology of belonging built within a transnational social field "long distance nationalism." Georges is not only a transmigrant but also a long distance nationalist. We define long distance nationalism as ideas about belonging that link people living in various geographic locations and motivate or justify their taking action in relationship to an ancestral territory and its government. Through such ideological linkages, a territory, its people, and its government become a transnational nation-state. Long distance nationalism binds immigrants, their descendants, and people who have remained in their homeland into a single transborder citizenry. It provides the transborder nationalist narratives that constitute and are constituted by everyday forms of state formation. As in other versions of nationalism, the concept of a territorial homeland governed by a state that represents the nation remains salient, but national borders are not thought to delimit membership in the nation. Citizens residing within the territorial homeland view emigrants and their descendants as part of the nation, whatever legal citizenship the émigrés may have.[4]

Long distance nationalism does not exist only in the domain of the imagination and sentiment. It leads to action. These actions link a dispersed population to a specific homeland and its political system. Long distance nationalists may vote, demonstrate, contribute money, create works of art, give birth, fight, kill, and die for a "homeland" in which they may never have lived. Meanwhile, those who live in this land will recognize these actions as patriotic contributions to the well-being of their common homeland.[5] Georges is a long distance nationalist not only because he dreams about Haiti but also because he takes action on behalf of Haiti while continuing to live in New York. He believes that when he assists family members in Haiti, speaks out about problems in Haiti, or counsels young people of Haitian descent born in the United States, he is working to reconstruct Haiti. People living in Haiti are also long distance nationalists if they continue to claim Georges as their own and maintain that he continues to be responsible for Haiti and that his actions abroad reflect on the reputation and future of Haiti.

Transnational migration and long distance nationalism are not new. In previous publications, Nina has explored the late nineteenth- and early twentieth-century nation-state building projects of U.S. immigrants in order to better understand the role of contemporary globalization in shaping long distance nationalism (Glick Schiller 1999a, b, c). As in the past, long distance nationalists today build their homelands and emigrant-sending states continue to claim the loyalty of their emigrants. However, current-day states no longer expect their emigrants to return home to rebuild the motherland; they are urged to do this work from afar. Recently, emigrant-sending states such as Mexico, Colombia, the Dominican Republic, Ecuador, Brazil, and Haiti have adopted policies that turned them into transnational nation-states. Many have changed their laws and created government agencies to ensure that transmigrants remain incorporated in their native land. Some governments have granted dual nationality so that emigrants can carry two passports; others have extended voting in the homeland to emigrants who have become U.S. citizens. Through these changes, as well as the establishment of special ministries responsible for the diasporic population, the political leaders of these countries signal that transmigrants, as well as their children, remain members of the nation of their birth. These countries urge their dual nationals to vote, lobby, and demonstrate on behalf of the land of their ancestors.[6] This alteration in the relationship between emigrant sending countries and their populations abroad has important consequences for a transnational second generation.

Concepts of the Second Generation

The emergence of a scholarship on transnational migration constitutes a challenge to the dominant model of the immigrant experience that has portrayed immigrants as "uprooted" and examines their incorporation into their new country without regard to their continuing relationship to their native land. Generated from the experience of European immigrants who arrived at the end of the nineteenth and the early twentieth century, the dominant model of immigrant incorporation projects a unilineal process of acculturation and assimilation that takes several generations (Gleason 1982; Gordon 1964; Simpson and Yinger 1958; Warner and Srole 1945). In this model U.S. society is defined as the sole domain of structural and cultural pressures that shape the identities and cultural repertoire of the second generation. Even the naming of immigrants' children as a "second generation" reflected and contributed to the notion of the incorporation of immigrants as a steplike irreversible process and one in which immigrant's children were socialized solely by forces within the land of their birth.

More recently, scholars concerned with a new second generation that is growing up in the wake of the recent immigration from Latin America, the Caribbean, and Asia have developed a more nuanced reading of immigrant incorporation. The emerging paradigm of immigrant incorporation foresees a range of trajectories for the second generation rather than a straightforward pattern of assimilation (Portes 1995; Portes and Zhou 1993; Rumbaut 1996; Stepick 1998; Waters 1996, 2000). Factors of race, class, region, and city of residence are seen as contributing to variations in the identities of the second generation whose parents were part of the post-1965 immigration.

For example, Alejandro Portes and Min Zhou (1993), working with data sets that included Haitian youth in Miami, theorized that race enters into the experience of second-generation youth in two contradictory processes, neither of which resembles the classic model of immigrant incorporation. Some second-generation youth who are racialized as black do assimilate rapidly but take on a black American identity. The adoption of this identity by a sector of second-generation young people constitutes a rejection of white mainstream culture and values that, through processes linked to race and class, marginalize black youth. In contrast, other sectors of the second-generation youth respond to racialization by joining with their parents in embracing the national identity of their country of origin. Mary Waters' research reveals a range of responses among Caribbean second generation youth in New York to the experience of racialization. These responses included "identifying as [black] Americans, identifying as ethnic Americans with some distance from black Americans, or identifying as immigrant in a way that does not reckon with American racial or ethnic categories" (1996, 178). (Alex Stepick [1998] has reported similar findings among Haitian youth in Miami). This significant rethinking of the Americanization process has not addressed, however, the transnational social and political processes that shape the lives and identities of a significant sector of both immigrants and their children.

In investigating the forces that contribute to these variations of identity, Portes and Zhou (1993), Stepick (1998), and Waters (1996) examine only the structure and processes within U.S. society. Furthermore, they tend to see racial and ethnic identifications as fixed in time and singular. That is to say, the model they develop suggests that a person develops only one racial, ethnic, or national identity and tends to keep it as he or she matures. But as young people mature they develop multiple, overlapping, and simultaneous identities and deploy them in relation to events they experience at home, at school, at work, in the country of their birth, and in the country of their ancestry.

At various conferences at which we have presented evidence of transnational migration, scholars who remain within the older assimilationist perspective have dismissed our work as only a "first-generation phenomenon" that will vanish with the coming of age of a second generation. Even if this were true, home ties would clearly be a phenomenon of note, since these ties affect the incorporative strategies of immigrants and the political rhetoric and practices of political leaders. Moreover, there has been little research about the degree to which children born in the United States embrace or reject transnational processes and relations.[7]

To establish the parameters in which members of the second generation develop their identities we need to employ both a concept of transnational social fields and an understanding that immigration is currently an ongoing process. Often discussions of the second generation implicitly assume that migration stops after the first generation. In this approach, whether in its classic or recent formulations, the old country is represented in the United States only by an aging population of immigrants; a second generation grows up as a cohort surrounded by people their age who were also U.S.–born and –bred. But this view of immigration was inspired by a migration stream that was abruptly cut by immigration restriction, depression, and world war. If attacks on immigration do not succeed in halting the flow of newcomers, and if the current pace of family reunions continues, young people born in the United States will continue to find in their households, and all around them, compatriots their age who recently have arrived from the home country.[8] These young people influence and socialize one another. In addition, immigrant households host a constant flow of relatives of various generations who engage in a circuit of visiting.

Once a migration is firmly established, child-rearing is a transnational process. This means that in research on the second generation, we cannot assume that adults who have immigrated and settled in the United States will have children born and reared in the United States. This is a question for empirical investigation. For example, many Haitian parents have children born in Haiti who are brought to the United States only when they are teens, children born in the United States after their parents have migrated but sent home to be raised in Haiti, and children born and reared in the United States. Consequently, households contain children with many different degrees of knowledge about Haiti.

Youthful Voices in New York

Her presence was not imposing. Her rhetoric was not fiery. She stood before the large lecture hall filled with people, mostly young, mostly Haitian, and spoke very quietly. But the audience hung on her words because she was Edwidge Dandicat, a successful author at the age of

twenty-seven. "I am not a politician," she told the audience. "I am just a Haitian and our com-
munity is in crisis." Her message was as much in her presence at this occasion as in her spe-
cific words. She seemed the perfect symbol to open this conference that had been called to
initiate the "Haitian American Community Action Network."

The Haitian American Community Action Network (HACAN) network was envisioned by the conference conveners as a means of "initiating a national network of community groups and individuals dedicated to promoting the well-being and the civil and political rights of Haitians in the United States" (HACAN 1996). But to many of the participants in the conference, the location of this Haitian community and the domain of community action were not stable. Dandicat stood as a symbol of "Haitian-American" success but on what ground did she stand? Dandicat ended her speech by quoting the slogan on the Haitian flag, "L'Union Fait la Force" (Through union comes strength). That flag along with the U.S. flag decorated the speaker's podium. Much of Dandicat's critically acclaimed fiction is set in both the United States and Haiti, carrying readers into the world of Haitian transmigrants who travel back and forth between Haiti and the United States (Dandicat 1996, 1998a, b).[9] Her life story, which was known to this audience, includes a childhood in Haiti, migration to the United States at the age of twelve, degrees from Barnard College and Brown University, and continuing ties to Haiti. Her English is flawless but she addressed the conference in Kreyòl.

The conference addressed political concerns in Haiti as well as in the United States. The first session, entitled "Building Haitian American Political Leadership," offered, "in an increasingly hostile environment, . . . a broad overview of the socio-political environment in which Haitian-Americans live." But the final session on the agenda, "Politics and Democratic Trials in Haiti," focused on Haiti and the responsibility of Haitian Americans to Haiti. "How can Haitian-American communities honestly contribute to Haiti's democratic well-being?"

Not all the organizers and participants at the conference were equally comfortable with the transnational scope of the agenda. There was a noticeable difference between the older generation and the youth, a second generation who had come of age within families structured by transnational migration and in the context of efforts of Haitian leaders to portray Haiti as a transnational nation-state. Those who spoke for an older generation of leadership saw the goal of the community action network in the terms of the traditional U.S. paradigm of immigrant settlement: the development of immigrants as an ethnic "community" that celebrates its roots but gets on with the business of carving a place for themselves within the U.S. political and economic structure. For example, Jocelyn McCalla (Americanized as "Johnnie"), in his forties and a spokesperson for the National Coalition for Haitian Rights (NCHR), the organization that attempted to launch HACAN, urged the audience to speak in "American" rather than "Haitian terms" "because we are here and we are here to stay." He made no mention of Haiti. He called on Haitian professionals to help improve life for Haitian immigrants. "We have more power than we think we have at the local, state, and federal levels. We should build strong lobbies. We should build alliances and we need to link up to other groups."

It should be noted that many in this older generation of leadership were engaged in politics in Haiti. However, they had learned in the United States to separate political organizations linked to Haiti from efforts to create ethnic constituencies. They had found that foundations and churches that helped fund Haitian community organizing efforts, such as the proposed network, expected to see ethnic activities focused on incorporating immigrants into the United States.

The majority of the participants in this conference and a significant section of its leadership came from a second generation that was born or has lived since childhood in the United States. This generation has a different vision of the meaning of community. Young, confident, well educated, they felt comfortable building an organization that connected them to Haiti as well as the United States. They simply did not acknowledge the boundaries. Their experience growing up in the United States convinced them that they needed to have a public identity. Public identity meant they had a label and a culture they could claim as their own. This identity became Haitian but for them Haitian was not confined to a concern for building a Haitian "community" in the United States. At one point, the assembled body was called on to chant, "A strong Haitian community equals a strong Haiti; a strong Haiti equals a strong Haitian community." Their ability to use the word *community*, sometimes for Haitians in Brooklyn, sometimes for Haitians in the New York metropolitan area, sometimes for Haitians in the United States, sometimes for the Haitian diaspora, and sometimes for all Haitians abroad and in Haiti, gave the slogan layers of meaning.

In three decades of research on Haitian incorporation in the United States, we have found an identification with Haiti to be common among persons of Haitian descent born in the United States. In certain ways our findings resemble those of Portes and Zhou (1993), and Waters (1996), who describe a sector of study of second-generation Caribbean youth who maintain an identification with the homeland of their parents. These findings take on new meaning, however, when placed within the transnational perspective on the second generation that we are proposing. To make this point we draw on quotations from eleven lengthy interviews Georges conducted in 1996 with seniors at the State University of New York at Stony Brook who were born in the United States but whose parents had emigrated from Haiti. All the students we interviewed spoke some Kreyòl but not all were fluent in Kreyòl and the interviews were conducted in English. Although education is highly valued by the Haitian immigrant population and a significant segment of Haitian young people in the United States have some form of post-secondary education,[10] these young people are more educated than many second-generation Haitian immigrants. The students we interviewed did not come from elite backgrounds, either in Haiti or in the United States; in the United States their parents worked as nurse's aides, office cleaners, and mechanics.

Although these students were U.S. citizens, none of them identified himself or herself as American.[11]

Georges: Do you classify yourself as Haitian-American, African-American, or Haitian?
Toufi: Haitian.
Georges: Haitian, no hyphen?
Toufi: No, no hyphen. I am a Haitian.

Sandra, age twenty-two, discounted the influence of birthplace on her identity:

> I know I say I'm Haitian because I have a Haitian background. My family is from Haiti and the only thing I have from here is that I was born here. I picked up the American culture, but at the same time, I think that about sixty percent of me, if not more, is Haitian. . . . I automatically say I'm Haitian.

Sandra maintains she has always thought of herself as Haitian, but several of these young people speak of their identity with Haiti as something that they consciously adopted as they grew up. Carline sees herself as growing up "more as an African American . . . but as of late incorporating more of the Haitian culture into my daily life." Toufi explains:

> When I went into high school, I started to realize a little bit more of who I was and started getting more in touch a little more with my Haitian side and that is the only side I have ever seen since then. And that is the side I want to help.

We have observed this maturing of a sense of Haitian identity among many young adults of Haitian parentage in the New York metropolitan area. It seems to be a direction taken more frequently by those who obtain higher education, but the acquisition of a sense of being Haitian also seems linked to participation in the work force in the New York metropolitan area. Whether they saw themselves as mostly or completely Haitian, all of the Stony Brook students expressed pride in being Haitian. As these young people matured they learned to turn to their Haitian origins as a wellspring of strength that allowed them to live their lives in the United States. Several directly said in almost the same words "Haiti is me, Haiti is my pride." To be Haitian is defined as being proud. When Claudia was asked, "What does it mean to you to be Haitian?" she responded, "A lot of pride, a lot of history, strength."

This pride in Haiti is linked to a catalogue of Haiti's historical accomplishments that were recited or referred to in each of the interviews. Among those accomplishments mentioned were that Haiti was "the first country to defeat slavery"; it is a country that maintained "an African religion," a country with its own language, a country that fought for its independence, and "the first black republic to defeat a white army." The statement that Haiti "defeated a white army" is highly significant. One of the forces that impel youngsters of Haitian descent toward an identification as Haitian is their racialization in the United States as blacks.

All of these young people held jobs while attending school, and all had their most direct experiences of discrimination in the work force. There, being viewed as black meant being defined as somehow not American. They said that they had learned that despite their citizenship and their fluency in English, the United States "is not your country."

These students were treated by the larger society as if they are African American and they experienced discrimination because of this identification. Yet, by the time they were teenagers they were not able to easily identify as African American. African Americans often treated them as different and sometimes inferior. Meanwhile, their parents continued to teach them to differentiate themselves from African Americans. As college seniors they chose to be Haitian, at least some of the time. However, we want to stress that they were not antagonistic to African Americans or to an overarching identity politics that united them with other blacks and placed them within an African diaspora. For them, being Haitian does not exclude them from other forms of identification.

Without a transnational perspective, these students' specification that they are Haitian can be interpreted as evidence of the persisting importance of ethnicity within American life. Pride in Haiti can be construed as a politics of cultural roots within a discourse about membership in a multicultural United States. Or continuing identification by a second generation with their ancestral homeland can be interpreted as solely a response to the racialization that the second generation experiences. And certainly several of the students told us that the discrimination they faced convinced them that they should "go back to some place where they expect something of you, where they appreciate you, where they don't discriminate against you." That place becomes your true home, no matter where you were born. For example, Toufi told us, "When I go home, there is no discrimination. I don't feel it."

An adequate interpretation of the experience of the second generation, however, must assess their transnational ties and experiences. All eleven of the students we interviewed were raised within transnational social fields. All but one had visited Haiti, and that one young woman's plans were abruptly disrupted in 1991 when the military coup against Jean-Bertrand Aristide made the prospective journey dangerous. However, direct experience in Haiti was only one aspect of their ongoing relationships to Haiti. Their childhoods were structured by the sending of remittances, packages, and news to and from Haiti and the visiting back and forth of various relatives. Sandra provided a description of the taken-for-granted interchange of visits: "My grandmother has come here. . . . I think only twice but that's because she was sick. My cousins have come from time to time, and I think all of them have come once or twice, but I think there are one or two . . . different cousins and aunts who haven't been here yet." All of these young people also grew up with and continue to confront their parents' relationships to Haiti. Of the eleven students, two had parents planning to return to Haiti to live, one to establish a business and the other to retire.

The transnational context of these students' lives makes it logical for them to see themselves not just identifying with Haiti but assuming some responsibility for Haiti. For example, Carline linked her ability to confront racism in the United States with her responsibilities to Haiti: "My strength derives from my Haitian nationality. I feel I have an obligation to Haiti." Sabrina had returned the previous year from her first trip to Haiti with a commitment to assume some of the burden of supporting kin in Haiti that had previously been carried by her mother: "What I do once a month is send money to my family, 'cause they are so much in need."

Haitian youth born in the United States and living within transnational social fields come to believe that identification with a homeland is a matter of action as well as words. Therefore when they speak about their Haitian identity they speak about future plans as well as their sense of self. All the students we interviewed had such plans that ranged from the personal to the political. But of course in this context the personal was political. To identify with another nation as part of a personal sense of self and to plan to take some action in relation to that nation provides a base for political leaders seeking to rally persons living in the United States on behalf of Haiti.

Some students planned to work in Haiti, others just to visit. Sabrina mentioned becoming a doctor and possibly opening a private practice in Haiti: "It would be good if I go back, and as far as helping my country and my people, that's something I would always do." In their discussions of education the students made a link between their Haitian identity and their education. They also told us that their obtaining an education reflected well on Haiti and provided them ways to help the country. We have found this elision between self and the Haitian nation among young people who grow up in Haiti, as well as among members of the second generation in the United States.

Two students envisioned for themselves a directly political role in relation to Haiti. Toufi told us: "I want to be involved in politics in Haiti. My father always tells me no because I may never be able to go back to Haiti, which would be a problem. True, but I just think I can go back and volunteer and do things."

In the 1960s young men who were born in Haiti but had emigrated to the United States often declared their intentions to become president of Haiti. Nina encountered this aspiration repeatedly when she worked with Haitian young people in Haitian summer youth programs in New York in 1969–70. By the 1990s, the situation had changed. The dream of leading Haiti had not disappeared but now Georges heard the same aspiration from a young woman born in the United States. Carline told Georges: "Well, one of my biggest ambitions is to get involved in politics in Haiti. And even one day run for president. . . . Even though I was born in America, . . . with or without a [Haitian] citizenship I still have patriotism for the country, so!"

It is important to note that Carline differed from the other students Georges interviewed. She had lived for significant periods of her life in both Haiti and the United States. Although born in the United States, she had been sent back to Haiti for part of her education. While Carline was the only young person in our sample to have had this experience, living for several years in Haiti is an important part of the socialization of many children born in the United States. In our assessment of the identities and loyalties of the second generation, we must consider the experiences of young people who grow up across borders. Youth, brought up this way, as well as young people born and reared in Haiti and then brought to the United States, often form a cohort within school populations in regions of the country with large numbers of Haitian immigrants, such as New York, New Jersey, and Miami. This cohort pressures other Haitian second-generation youngsters who know less about Haiti to identify themselves as Haitian and to become involved in activities linked to Haiti. All the students we spoke with described such pressures within the Haitian Student Organization at Stony Brook, in which all but one of them participated.

Many Haitian student clubs in New York, including the one at Stony Brook, have been active in articulating long distance nationalism and in building transnational activities that link them to Haiti. Students contributed to the movement against the

Duvalier regime and participated in Aristide's Lavalas movement.[12] By 1996 the political disarray in Haiti was accompanied by a lull in Haitian student activism in the United States. Those students who had not recently visited Haiti seemed removed from the country's political discourse. Nonetheless, we were told, "I have to defend Haiti. . . . I feel at times I am the voice of the country." It is also important to note that a core of the young people engaged in building HACAN who seemed more immersed in current transnational political discussion had come out of Haitian student clubs.

Claudia was among those of this second generation who envisioned themselves as a force to "rebuild Haiti." She told us:

> I have a lot of people who are just like me who are getting their education here who want to go back. . . . It can be, you know, a very fulfilling future as far as Haiti is concerned because a lot of us who are getting our education here we gonna plan to go back and to build the country. So I see, in a few years, Haiti will be a good country again to live in.

And Carline concluded: "I can see my future in Haiti. It could be here and helping over there or totally there. Definitely my eyes will be focused on Haiti."

These students take into their vision of the future not only their own experiences in the United States but also their parent's imagery of a beautiful Haiti that once was. Sabrina, for example, used the word "rebuild" in discussing her own plans for the future: "I hope for the best for my future, and as far as Haiti, it's my country and I will definitely be going back. . . . It can be rebuilt." Georges asked, "What do you mean rebuilt? Was there a time when it was beautiful?" And she replied: "That's all I heard, when I went to Haiti. All I heard was, 'You came at the wrong time. Haiti's at its worst. This was once a beautiful place.' "

Most of the students we interviewed were familiar with this projection of Haiti's past, the same imagery of Haiti that haunts Georges's dreams. Past becomes linked to the future. Politics and nostalgia meet in the concrete organizations, practices, and plans of the second generation to reconstruct and reclaim Haiti for their generation and for the future.

Youthful Voices in Haiti

In 1996 we visited Aux Cayes, Georges's hometown, as part of our research on long distance nationalism. On our first day in Aux Cayes, we turned on the radio and found ourselves in an air space that the young people in Aux Cayes were claiming as their own. A team of young women and men, most of them in their early twenties, were broadcasting a daily radio program, designed to speak to young people. The radio program was broadcast on Men Kontre (Hands together), a noncommercial station sponsored by the Catholic Diocese of Aux Cayes Church. Men Kontre originated under the Duvalier dictatorship as part of a broad-based social movement that led in 1986 to the toppling of the twenty-nine-year-old Duvalier regime. While many of the radio stations that had contributed to the struggle had been silenced by 1996, Men

Kontre continued to provide political information and serve as a political forum. The young people who participated in the station as either broadcasters or audience were linking themselves to a particular history of struggle against political repression and a particular discourse about the Haitian nation and state that had been shaped by a grassroots movement for social justice, more than a decade old, that demanded that the state take responsibility for the welfare of the nation.

At the time of our research the station's youthful broadcasters had successfully initiated a dialogue among the youth of Aux Cayes. The broadcasters called on their listeners to participate in the live broadcast by calling the station or, since most of their audience did not have access to a telephone, by writing to the station and receiving personalized answers. Hundreds of young people responded to this invitation to become "penpals" and wrote to the station.

We spoke with six members of the radio staff, one man and five women, ranging in age from eighteen to twenty-nine; their average age was twenty-three.[13] All six were born in the countryside. Four of the six had fathers who worked the land as "cultivators," selling crops to support the family; only one had a father with any formal training and profession.[14] Four had mothers who were *commerçante*, small-scale retailers selling agricultural products, cooked food, and a broad array of new or second-hand manufactured goods. Two of those interviewed had the same mother but because they had different fathers they had different family members living abroad.

These youth grew up in the crucible of political struggles that popularized a transnational project of rebuilding the Haitian nation-state. Before Aristide became president in 1991, Haitian political discourse sharply delineated between those living in Haiti and the Haitian diaspora. The diaspora were defined as outside of the nation or even traitors to it. In a sharp reversal, Aristide in 1991 began to define the Haitian diaspora as one of the territorial departments of Haiti (the Dixième or Tenth). The young people of the radio program staff responded enthusiastically to this redefinition as part of their embracing Haiti as a transnational nation-state. Though they were isolated from the rest of Haiti by poor roads and a grossly inefficient telephone service, they were connected to Haitians who lived in other nation-states. They understood that they inhabited a global terrain of settlement that included the United States (Miami, New York, Chicago, and Boston), Guadelupe, and France. This knowledge shaped their definition of the term *Haitian*. Marjorie, for example, who had an aunt and cousin abroad said:

> A Haitian is a person who is fighting for Haiti, who loves his brothers and sisters who live in Haiti, who loves the flag, who loves the culture. A person who is living abroad for a long time is a Haitian. Even if you are naturalized [as a U.S. citizen] you keep Haitian blood. The only way to keep them from being Haitian is if they cut their meat and took all your blood.

Her definition of Haitian extended into the second generation. She stated, "I believe if the parents are Haitian and always speak with him and say who he is and what nationality he is, that person is not totally [American]. He has Haitian blood in veins."

Carmelle took up this theme, differentiating between legal definitions of citizenship and questions of political loyalty by using the language of blood. She informed us, "According to the constitution of the foreign country, once you naturalize, you adhere to their nationality and reject your native one, but for me, regardless of what the other country says, you have Haitian blood in your veins."

By the using the concept of blood, Haitians in Haiti find a way to reclaim persons of Haitian descent as Haitians—even if those persons have changed their language, culture, and nationality. For this reason, all six members of the radio staff expressed opposition to the concept of dual nationality because they felt one could never stop being Haitian. They agreed that the ties of blood were not an abstract claim of identity—they came with an agenda. Those abroad were a key to changing Haiti, and the diaspora had obligations toward Haiti. They differed, however, about whether the diaspora has fulfilled these obligations. Anna explained:

> It is an obligation because they know the conditions the country is in and the sufferings that exist in Haiti. If the country was good, they would never have left. They know what they left behind. They know that they left these people in the same conditions that existed prior to their departure. How can they ignore them and not lend a helping hand?

The young people we interviewed in Haiti did not all have connections with family abroad and those who did have transnational family connections differed in whether these ties provided resources. The absence and degree of intensity of transnational family connections shape their life prospects, affecting both their daily standard of living and their sense of the future for themselves and for Haiti. While not all young people have transnational family connections, the fact that many do have such ties affects the outlook of the entire generation. Young people all over Haiti live within networks of people who do have family abroad and are aware of acquaintances who do receive money and benefits from such connections. Those who receive money and gifts from family abroad appeared more positive and self-confident. They expected either assistance in obtaining education in Haiti or sponsorship to go abroad and study. They prefer to study abroad.[15] Anna, whose parents are both in the United States, informed us: "Haiti doesn't offer any real university education. I have been calling my mother regularly, asking for my mother to send for me so that I can attend college in the United States."

In contrast, those without such prospects, although still in their twenties, were already bitter. Their sense of frustration was deepened by the widespread belief in Haiti that kin have an obligation to help their family. The transnational flow of money from families in the United States and Haiti while providing material evidence of interconnection, at the same time contributes to class divisions within Haiti and tremendous tensions within family networks that extend from Haiti to persons settled abroad. The transnational ties of Haiti's youth have been a basis for them to judge conditions in Haiti and envision themselves studying and working abroad.

As Carmelle, age twenty-three, stated:

> When I was young, I wanted to study medicine, but I never asked myself was it possible to get admitted to medical school. I thought that once I finished my studies, I could just go and register at the medical school, and get accepted. But, I used to hear people say that it is a comedy to be in *philo* [the terminal year of high school], but the tragedy begins when

you pass the exam. I am now realizing that it is true. I want to study, but the tragedy of the reality is that I can't.[16]

Carmelle abandoned her dream of becoming a doctor, and even though she obtained technical clerical training, she found herself without a job or a future. Her hopes lie in migration from Haiti. She told us, "If right now I could leave Haiti, it would be good for me." Emilia, looking at her older sister's fate, was even more despondent.

> Look at the others already living abroad. They are already working and making money. Even when I finish my studies I won't have anything to do in a country that doesn't offer you anything. Three of my mother's children grown and none of them is working and doing anything. What a sad story. Alas. Sometimes I sit and cry and cry because there is no future for me.

Given the worsening living conditions and the tenuous political situation, the staff of the radio program see their personal futures and the future of the country very much connected to the Haitian diaspora and especially to the United States. These youth were aware of the racial discrimination in the United States but nonetheless see it as a land of possibility rather than of restriction. Marjorie reported, "My aunt and boyfriend told me that they are mistreated a great deal because they are black. They reserve the harder, dirtier work for them." But she and the others wanted to go anyway. Without employment or educational opportunities in Haiti these young people saw no choice but to leave. They saw as a more insurmountable barrier to their aspirations the discrimination that they face in Haiti from the rich and powerful, who are still mainly mulatto. Only with a foreign education and money could they overcome the discrimination based on color and class background that they face in Haiti.

These Haitian young people saw themselves living in the United States and even obtaining U.S. nationality, but their goals were linked to their expectation that they would always remain Haitian and connected to Haiti. Their achievements would belong to Haiti and would contribute to a brighter future for Haiti and for their families remaining there.

Throughout the country Haitian youth have experienced the Haitian diaspora as a political force within Haiti. As Carmelle explained:

> [Those abroad] keep a keen eye on what is going on in Haiti. . . . The Dixième . . . did the same thing that we did in Haiti. We sent news bulletins and they used to organize demonstrations, voice their opinions, say what they liked and didn't like about what was going on in Haiti. As a result of those actions Aristide was able to return to Haiti.

Several of the program staff went on to say that while the diaspora met their political obligations to Haiti, they were failing to assist Haiti economically. For example, Anna told us:

> We have ample problems in Haiti. There are no roads, there are no industries. They could have invested in roads, in opening industries and creating jobs but they don't do that. The country is in poverty. They should have put their heads together. This is our country. This is their country too. They helped the country politically but socially the things we need, we don't see what they do for us.

Trained in activism, one of the young women, Marjorie, used the occasion of our interview to directly address the diaspora. Speaking into our microphone, she made a passionate appeal: "Those who are listening to my voice, I urge them to concentrate and remember what country they left behind. My brother, see the one on the ground, see the one who has nothing, who is on the ground, help him out."

She spoke of the need to "rebuild Haiti," evoking an image of a past Haiti that was better, stronger, more beautiful than the Haiti that was all around her. Another staff member told us: "You see, whatever used to be is falling in disrepair is being destroyed. . . . The country is going backward." In their nostalgia for the past these young people who have never left Haiti share the dream of Haiti that made Georges, living in Queens, New York, laugh in delight. That dream, filtered through the nostalgia that other second-generation Haitians living in New York learned from their parents, fuels their commitment to "rebuild Haiti."

In their nationalism and their view of the diaspora the young people at the radio station differed little from the thirty-six other young people we interviewed in Haiti in 1996, who were less politically active, and by and large had less education and fewer life opportunities. Of those thirty-six, eight were in Aux Cayes and twenty-eight were in Port-au-Prince. In wealth, they varied widely. One, the son of a prominent capitalist, held both a U.S. and a Haitian passport and who had houses in Miami and Port-au-Prince, and one was a homeless young man who supports himself by helping persons in an impoverished neighborhood to illegally tap into the electric lines. Twenty-one (60 percent) classified themselves as poor, thirteen (37 percent) as middle class, and one (3 percent) as a member of the bourgeoisie. Twenty-eight were students at the time of the interview, although among these some reported having received only a few years of schooling.

Despite the differences in their backgrounds and levels of education, the majority of the thirty-six young people (69 percent) expressed some degree of nationalist sentiment, although they were not as fierce in their nationalism as were the radio staff. Most (86 percent), like the members of the radio staff, believe that those who emigrate and change their nationality remain Haitian and therefore remain within the Haitian nation. And most (77 percent) also agree with the radio station staff in opposing a change in Haitian law to allow dual nationality for those abroad. They oppose this change not because they have a vision of a Haitian polity restricted to those who live in Haiti but because they believed the diaspora can contribute politically (53 percent) and in other ways (42 percent) to the future of Haiti. Most knew the word *diaspora* and of those who did only 16 percent saw it as a negative word.

Previous generations of Haitian youth had learned patriotic sentiments from nationalist rituals embedded in school curriculum and public ceremonies and national holidays. While many of these rituals had been abandoned by the 1980s, the young people in both Aux Cayes and Port-au-Prince grew up in a period of intense political mobilization and also repression. Beginning in the 1990s, the Lavalas slogans calling for rebuilding of the nation were all around them, as graffiti on the walls of houses, churches, and schools, in discussions on the radios that play incessantly in Haiti, and in the Roman

Catholic masses of liberation theology priests. They witnessed or participated in street demonstrations with similar slogans. Then between 1991 and 1995 they experienced the coup that sent Aristide into exile and the transnational resistance to the Haitian military dictatorship that followed.

The sense of awareness of this generation extended far beyond their neighborhood or city. They grew up in a media age dramatically different from what their parents had known. With the advent of cheap transistor radios and inexpensive tape recorders, even people in rural areas of Haiti can now listen to radio programs and exchange audio cassettes.[17] Because of the scarcity of electricity in rural areas, television is less prevalent there but some poor households in cities such as Aux Cayes black-and-white sets, and many households living on remittances have color television and video and compact disc players. Television and radio not only introduced images of U.S. and European music, life styles, and items of consumption; they also linked Haiti with the diaspora. By the end of the 1980s radio broadcast had become transnational. Interviews with Haitian scholars and political leaders in New York and Miami are broadcast in Haiti. News about life in Haiti broadcast in New York, Miami, and Boston features telephone conversations with correspondents in Haiti. Some talk shows include audiences calling in from Haiti and the United States at the same time (Glick Schiller and Fouron 1998). In the 1990s Georges's father-in-law in Aux Cayes regularly followed the radio station that periodically broadcasted interviews conducted with Georges in Queens.

However, despite their uniform socialization, not all youth held the same opinions. We found some evidence that young people's opinions are linked to their relationships within transnational social fields. Forty-two percent of those we interviewed lived in transnational households, that is, they had strong ties to family living abroad, defined by either regular remittance to their household or regular communications accompanied by assistance if needed. This group tended to be the fiercest nationalists and their nationalism was long distance. Because class status of a household in Haiti is often determined by whether the household receives regular remittances, differences in the degree of nationalist feelings also vary with self-ascribed class status.

Most of the youth, whether from a transnational household or not, displayed some degree of nationalist sentiment. However, except for the radio staff, those who were most strongly nationalist were those who received remittances. At the same time, most of those who displayed no nationalist sentiments had no contact with family living abroad. The radio staff were the exception: they had no transnational family ties but they displayed fierce nationalism. The source of their strong nationalism was their participation in a nationalist organization, the radio station whose Catholic leadership were part of significant transnational religious and political networks.

The link between Haitian nationalism and transnational ties among the youth is an important one to investigate further. Our exploratory research with small, snowball samples can only suggest a direction for further inquiry. However, our interviews reflect patterns we have been observing for many years. They are consistent with our analysis that there is no contradiction between living in a transnational social field and displaying Haitian nationalism. Those young people in Haiti and the United

States who live within transnational social fields learn to identify with Haiti, in part because they are positioned within this domain of interaction. At the same time, it is important to note that even young people who had no personal transnational connections often displayed some degree of long distance nationalism.

The Second Generation: A Redefinition

In this chapter we examine the identities of young people of Haitian descent in New York City and young people in Haiti and demonstrate that sectors of young people live within transnational social fields established by a networks that cross national borders. Our research on the establishment of transnational terrains that encompass several generations has implications for the concept of the second generation that extend far beyond the specifics of the Haitian case and unsettle the very notion of the "second generation." Far more is at stake here than academic definitions. Categories can illuminate or obscure political processes and the second generation is just such a category.

We suggest that it is time to redefine the second generation to include the entire generation in both homeland and new land who grow up within transnational social fields linked by familial, economic, religious, social, and political networks. In this approach, young people living in such fields would differ from those who may be exposed to various forms of transnational or global mediate but do not have direct contacts with persons abroad. However, much empirical research needs to be done to examine the degree to which network density, overlap, and the flow of various resources and personnel within these fields shapes the identity and actions of this second generation.

Our research on Haitians indicates that we must look transnationally to understand the dynamics that shape the identity of the children of immigrants living in the United States. This approach provides us with a more complex and dynamic explanation for the identity variability or "fluidity" (Vickerman 1999) encountered in contemporary second-generation researchers. We hypothesize that the children of immigrants living in the United States make their choices and move between different identities not only in relation to their experiences of racialization within the United States but also in relation to the degree to which their lives are encompassed within a transnational terrain. Two postulates emerge from this hypothesis. (1) Those young people who grow up within such a terrain develop a sense of self that has been shaped by personal, family, and organizational connections to people "back home." (2) At the same time, the production of self in terms of race, ethnicity, and nation is part of a political process that extends transnationally. Participation in transnational social fields can link U.S.–born young people to broader processes that define them as a political constituency that can act on behalf of this "home country."

If we define a second generation on the basis of transnational connections, then we must include children raised in the homeland. Some are children of U.S. immigrants sent "home" to be raised. Other children, while not directly the offspring of immigrants, are supported by relatives who have settled abroad. For example, many young people in Haiti, including eighteen in our sample of forty-two, were supported by transmigrants. They received remittances, regularly or when money was needed, from either one or both parents or a sibling of a parent. In most instances relatives abroad could be considered part of their household.

In the past decade increasing numbers of researchers on immigration have begun to acknowledge and study transnational households (Laguerre 1978, 1998; Lessinger 1995; Pessar 1995; Smith and Wallerstein 1992). Many children, living in emigrant-sending countries, depend for their sustenance, growth, and development on parents and other family members living abroad. These children are nurtured within a terrain of transnational connections, influenced by the economic, social, and cultural capital their parents obtain through emigration. If we can accept households as transnational, what about the generation produced within these households? We suggest that once we define households as transnational, the children living within them become part of a transnational second generation. Yet, once we take the step of including the children dependent on immigrants but still living in the homeland in our definition of a second generation, a further question follows. What of the other young people born within a field of social relations that links the home and host country of their parents through networks of economic activities, religious and social organizations, and transnational media? They too grow up within a transnational terrain that shapes the knowledge, consciousness, and identities of their generation. Young persons growing up in Haiti who are not part of transnational households also experience and are influenced by transnational connections. A transnational second generation can be defined as all persons born into the generation after emigrants had established transnational social fields who live within and are socialized by these fields, regardless of whether they were born or are currently living in the country of emigration or abroad.

It is important to distinguish between transnational connection and transnational identity. The national, racial, and ethnic identities of the transnational second generation must be the subject of research. Our Haitian research provides some preliminary indication, however, that among their multiple identities young people who live within transnational fields are most likely to become long distant nationalists. The young people we interviewed in New York as well as the HACAN activists were members of the transnational second generation. They were embedded in personal or organizational transnational networks. Our analysis of the forty-two interviews of Haitian youth we conducted in Haiti also indicates that those who were most fiercely long distance nationalists had either familial or organizational ties abroad.

To be sure, the Haitian elision of self, family, blood, race, and nation is the product of a two-hundred-year history of nation-state building, so that propensity of the second generation to embrace long distance nationalism is particularly strong (Glick Schiller and Fouron 2001). And even in the Haitian case, whether or not personal transnational connections are translated into political actions varies, depending on both the situation in Haiti and the conditions that Haitians face in the United States. However, the attraction for young people born in the United States to return and rebuild a homeland is a force that extends from beyond the particularities of Haitian history and deserves systematic cross-cultural exploration. Just as Georges is a long distance nationalist, so too are several of Nina's relatives who, as supporters of Israel, inculcate loyalty to Israel in their children through fundraising activities for Israel, including for youth programs there. The U.S. Zionist youth movement flourishes within a well-organized transnational institutional framework that builds long distant nationalism among people whose traceable ancestors never lived in Israel.

Developing this definition of a transnational second generation, which is bounded not by the territorial limits of a state but by the boundaries of social fields that stretch across national borders and link emigrant populations to an ancestral homeland, will greatly enhance migration studies. First, it will allow us to study transnational migration as a phenomenon that extends beyond a single generation. Second, it will allow us to ground and operationalize generational studies within transnational social fields. Moreover, such a definition approaches the entire topic of the second generation with new research questions. We can, for example, begin to explore the ways in which various types and densities of transnational connections shape the identities and political agendas of young people coming of age within transnational social fields, whether or not they themselves have migrated. As we indicate, among Haitian youth, involvement in organizations that have transnational linkages and residence in transnational households are two separate but significant paths to long distance nationalism.

Certainly this transnational definition of the second generation gave us insight into the generation that has come of age in both Haiti and the United States. Those who were born after the beginning of large-scale Haitian migration are affected by it, whether or not they are themselves children of immigrants. One of the outcomes of the establishment of transnational social fields has been the development of a sense of the continuity of Haitian identity after emigration and permanent resettlement. This means that many Haitian youth, regardless of whether they were born in the United States or Haiti and regardless of in which of those countries they grew up, are socialized into a Haitian identity that links persons in Haiti to the Haitian diaspora. Whatever their location, through the transnational media as well as from the adult transmigrants among whom they live, they are exposed to and respond to the same identity discourse. However, those who live in transnational fields are more prone to act as well as speak.

Haitian young people living in the different localities of the Haitian diaspora can be influenced by the same adults, as well as by the same political discourse. This is particularly true of those young people who participate in youth activities organized by the Catholic Church, whose clergy are members of transnational networks. For example, in 1998 the clergy from Aux Cayes who initiated the radio program there participated in a retreat for second-generation Haitian youth in New York. Within this transnational second generation, however, there are variations in the ways in which people participate in transnational social fields. A small but significant and vocal section of the transnational second generation move across borders, well incorporated into the United States yet actively participating in social and political processes in Haiti. A larger group is less likely to move but remains connected across borders in networks that can mobilize them politically in relation to Haiti, according to conditions and events in both in Haiti and the United States.

We found evidence of the effect of the dense transnational linkages in the response of Haitian youth to the false labeling of Haitians as carriers of the AIDS virus. Many of the Haitian young people who took to the streets of New York to protest against the stigma of the AIDS label began supporting transnational projects to rebuild Haiti. The second generation in Haiti meanwhile learned to look to the diaspora for the political power to change Haiti.

Although some members of Haiti's second generation living in the United States share with their peers in Haiti an understanding that they live in a transnational space, they have traveled to this place by a different path and they experience it in different ways. Youngsters living in Haiti in the wake of a massive out-migration were grappling with the disappointments of a bleak and unpromising future and looking to the Haitians of the diaspora for assistance in creating a brighter future. Those in Haiti, faced with the barriers of class, color, gender discrimination, political turmoil, and the lack of economic opportunity, see migration to the United States and the Haitian diaspora as the hope for both themselves and Haiti.

Meanwhile, some youngsters who are of Haitian descent living in the United States were reclaiming Haiti by reclaiming their ties with their ancestral land and reaffirming their Haitian identity. The members of the second generation in the United States see connection with Haiti as a way to escape racial barriers and the restriction of economic opportunities they increasingly are facing in the United States. Young Haitians in Haiti and in the United States hold different and disjunctive conceptualizations of both of these locations. By arguing that Haitians born and living in the United States and persons born in Haiti after the mass migration that began in the 1960s are part of a transnational second generation, we are not denying the very different experiences these two sets of people have or the very different adults they become. Young people brought up in the United States, whether they were born there or in Haiti, experience multiple assimilative pressures. They are very different culturally from people who never have lived in the United States. Nonetheless, the Haitian second generation, whether living in Haiti or in the United States, is coming of age in a different world from the one that shaped their parents, and the transnational linkages forged by their parents contribute to their shared membership in a single cohort. They are a single cohort because, although they are not pursuing the commitment to a transnational Haiti by following the same path, they believe they are traveling toward the same destination. Located in different daily realities, the members of this second generation share an "imagined community" in the past and in the future (Anderson 1991). They share a claim to a Haitian homeland and nostalgia for a Haiti that never was, binding them across national borders and across generations. Georges's nighttime dreams and the daydreams of the young people he interviewed in New York, Au Cayes, and Port-au-Prince become a single vision. Underlying their disjunctive images of Haiti and the United States is a common vision of a sweet Haiti of the past and a prosperous peaceful Haiti of the future.

The particularities of location within the transnational terrain matter greatly. The young people we spoke with in Haiti, despite all they share with those growing up in the United States, had a dramatically different set of educational, social, and political experiences. We wish to emphasize that when transnational second generations develop, they can contribute to political projects that join together personal self-identification with broader efforts to reconceptualize nation-states as polities that extend across territorial borders. For a transnational generation to be long distance nationalists in the sense that we have defined it, young people must not only grow up within a transnational field of social relations but also identify themselves with, and take action on behalf of, an ancestral homeland.

Our discussion of transnational migration, long distance nationalism, and the development of a transnational second generation should not be taken as either a celebration of or a denigration of these forms of interconnection across the borders of nation-states. The merits and problematics of the emergence of a phenomenon such as a transnational second generation can be judged only in terms of the goals and concrete achievements of a specific nationalist project. As we have argued elsewhere, the rhetoric and political practices of a transnational Haiti have so far had the effect of masking the Haitian state's lack of sovereignty (Fouron and Glick Schiller 1997; Glick Schiller and Fouron 1998). Debates about the relationship between states such as Haiti and the contemporary processes of globalization have been diverted into the efforts to rebuild Haiti by incorporating the Haitian diaspora. Yet the transnational experiences of the Haitians, including the development of a second generation, also contain possibilities to link struggles in Haiti for justice and equity with similar aspirations of people in other parts of the world. Many of these struggles come together when transmigrants in the United States unite in common cause with oppressed people, such as in the movement in the 1990s in New York to end police killings and brutality.

We also want to make clear that we do not believe that the continuation of transnational nation-state building across generations is an inevitable outcome of transnational migration. Even if politicians in emigrant-sending countries pass laws that extend forms of dual nationality into future generations as they have in the Dominican Republic, Mexico, and Colombia, they are not insuring the long distance nationalism of future generations. On the contrary, the situation we have observed in Haiti since 1996 shows us how nationalist fervor can rapidly turn to cynicism. The paralysis of the political leadership in Haiti, which included members recruited from the diaspora, created cynicism and a loss of nationalist fervor in members of the second generation in both the United States and Haiti. The interaction between transnational social fields and both the growth and diminution of a long distance nationalism that links populations across borders and generations must be systematically explored. Our purpose here is to take the first step by posing a transnational perspective on the second generation.

Notes

Acknowledgments: This chapter draws from research supported by grants or institutional support from the National Institute of Mental Health, the National Institute for Child Health and Human Development, the Wenner-Gren Foundation, the University of New Hampshire Graduate Dean's Research Fellowship and the University of New Hampshire Center for the Humanities, the Mellon Foundation's Global Migration Project at Yale University, the Rockefeller Foundation, and CEMI, UNICAMP, Brazil. We would like to acknowledge the encouragement and support of Patricia Pessar, Bela Feldman Bianco, Bert Feintuck, Marilyn Hoskin, Maurice and Solange Fouron, Max Bernard, Maud Fouron, and Stephen Reyna. Special thanks to members of the next generation, including Seendy and Valerie Fouron and Rachel and Naomi Schiller. Portions of this paper appear in Glick Schiller and Fouron 2001. The names of people interviewed in Haiti and some transmigrants have been changed.

1. Within the United States, the identities of the second generation are shaped by the particular Haitian settlement within which young people have grown up. Members of the second generation who live in the New York metropolitan area, the largest and oldest Haitian settlement, and a center of identity politics, may be more focused on their Haitian identity than those in South Florida, where the Haitian settlement is newer, has had a much smaller core of community activists, and faces a very different configuration of local ethnic politics. See Glick Schiller and Fouron 1998 for additional thoughts about the differences between the Haitian experience in South Florida and in the New York metropolitan area and Stepick 1999 for an ethnography based on the Haitian experience in South Florida. In our reference to Haitian immigrants of both the first and second generation we use the word *diaspora*, following a usage of the word that is now widespread both in Haiti and in Haitian settlements abroad. Until the fall of the Duvalier regime in 1986, the word *diaspora* was used by only a handful of Haitian leaders abroad to signal their continuing connection with the Haitian political process. Within a decade the growing visible participation of Haitians abroad in daily life in Haiti and in the Haitian political process popularized the word until it entered into the Kreyòl language. Most of the youth we interviewed in Haiti were familiar with the word and took it to mean Haitians living abroad. It is much less familiar to the second generation living in New York. As we show, they tend to use the word *community* in a way that extends the boundaries of community to include persons of Haitian descent in the many locations of immigrant settlement as well as in Haiti.

2. The term *social field* has also been used by Pierre Bourdieu to refer to "a network, or configuration of objective relations" (Jenkins 1992, 85).

3. We use the term *transnational social field* rather than "transnational community" (Goldring 1996) or "transnational locality" (Smith 1998b) because it is useful to be able to differentiate between various types of transnational connections. The terms *transnational community* and *transnational locality* are best employed for a very specific form of connection to a specific town or location of origin. Past generations of immigrants to the United States (Bodnar 1985; Chun 1990; Soyer 1997; Wyman 1993), as well as contemporary immigrants, have built hometown associations that closely link the locale of origin with members of that town that have settled abroad (Goldring 1996; Levitt 1998; Smith 1998b). Even in such cases the term *community* may be an ideological construction that obscures class differences. We prefer the concept of transnational locality for this set of transnational connections.

4. While many Haitians now use the term *diaspora* to describe those living abroad, we believe that it is important to distinguish between long distance nationalism and a diasporic consciousness such as that described by Paul Gilroy (1993). Diasporic consciousness does not focus on a particular nation-state building project. We also exclude the flexible use of citizenship found in Aiwa Ong's description (1999) of overseas Chinese who may have obtained citizenship in many states but identify with the nation-state of none of them.

5. In approaching long distance nationalism as both words and action so that nationalism con-

stitutes the state and is constituted by it we build on Craig Calhoun's statement (1997, 6), "There is nationalism as discourse: the production of cultural understandings and rhetoric which leads people around the world to think and frame their aspirations in terms of the idea of nation and national identity. . . . There is [also] nationalism as project: social movements and state policies by which people attempt to advance the interests of collectivities they understand as nations."

6. Increasing numbers of the leaders of these countries are transmigrants who were educated in the United States and maintain strong roots there. The president of the Dominican Republic elected in 1998 was a transmigrant with significant ties to Dominicans in New York (Guarnizo 1997).

7. Sunaina Maira's research (2000) among young people whose parents emigrated from India to New York City provides us with evidence of a second generation of Indians living within transnational social fields that connect them to India through both nostalgia and long distance nationalism.

8. Rob Smith (1998a) has made a similar critique of the research on the second generation.

9. Dandicat's third book, a novel that explores Haitian settlement in the Dominican Republic and the 1937 massacre of Haitians by the Trujillot government, has fanned Haitian nationalist sentiment among Haitian immigrants in the United States, including the second generation. The novel was published in English in 1998, and its Haitian readership is the highly educated sector of the Haitian second generation in the United States but its message was much more widely disseminated because the book has been discussed extensively on Haitian radio programs that are broadcast every day .

10. The 1990 U.S. Census (Bureau of the Census 1993) reports that 41 percent of Haitian immigrants have less than a high school education, 48 percent have at least a high school education, and 11 percent have college degrees or higher. Women are about as likely as men to obtain a high school or college education.

11. Three of these students saw themselves as both Haitian and American at the same time but more Haitian than American. They were generally not comfortable with seeing themselves as "hyphenated Americans," although one of the students explained that a high school teacher had instructed her that "Haitian-American" was her proper identity. The one young woman who identified herself as "Haitian-American" went on to explain "I think I'm Haitian before I'm American." The rest were adamant about the fact that they were only Haitian. Although in this chapter we are examining the Haitian long distance nationalism of these U.S.–born students, we are not claiming that this is their sole identity. We attribute some of their adamancy about their Haitian identity to their experiences on a college campus that demands an identity politics and to the fact that Georges, a faculty member on the campus who self-identifies as Haitian, did the interviewing.

12. Even when political repression in Haiti made it difficult for organizations in the United States to actually maintain ties to Haiti or develop ties, we found that Haitian organizations defined their activities in the United States as contributing to life in Haiti and as being part of Haitian life. In 1985 when we interviewed the leaders of Haitian clubs at various college campuses, the Caribbean Youth Association, composed of Haitians, and a soccer club. All but one of the persons interviewed saw the actions of their organization in the United States as contributing to Haiti, arguing that activities that took place in the United States ensured that "people from Haiti lived a better life."

13. All six closely resembled one another in their knowledge of and interest in questions of Haitian identity, their understanding of Haiti as a transnational nation-state, and their desire to migrate to the United States.

14. The use of the word *cultivator* rather than *peasant* reflects the class aspirations of these young people who have acquired a high school education. The word *peasant* when it is used in Haiti denotes the bottom of the society. In fact, those in the rural area have been defined as outside political society. Aristide, when he became president, discontinued the practice of issuing special birth certificates with the word *peasant* for those born in rural areas of Haiti. In contrast, the one professional parent was a land surveyor, a powerful position in the rural area because such persons must certify all land deeds and transactions.

15. Going abroad to study may not necessarily mean to the United States. Many young people are sent to Mexico, the Dominican Republic, or Europe to study fields such as medicine, agronomy, and engineering. With that diploma in hand, at a lesser cost than a U.S. education, young people may then be sponsored or find a way to migrate to the United States, where employment prospects and remuneration for professionals is higher. Even if they cannot enter the United States their foreign degrees will help them find positions in Haiti or set up their own practices. They re-enter Haitian society with the prestige of a foreign diploma as well was with the mystique of having lived abroad.

16. The young people at the radio station averaged 12.3 years of education. One was still attending school. The other five had completed their schooling, but two had only *rheto* degrees, and one had yet to pass the *philo* exam, meaning that half of those interviewed could not continue on to a university education in Haiti. In order to enter university in Haiti, a student must attend secondary school for six years and pass a competitive examination at the end of the fifth year (*rheto*) and the sixth year (philo). However, in the United States, a *rheto* diploma is considered equivalent to a high school diploma. For young people in Haiti who have not been able to obtain the resources, or have not been able to pass the *philo,* the only hope for further education lies abroad.

17. The Voice of American broadcasted a program in Kreyòl. Radio Tropicale is a radio station that broadcast simultaneously in Haiti and in the diaspora.

References

Anderson, Benedict. 1991. *Imagined Communities: Reflections on the Origins and Spread of Nationalism.* Revised edition. London: Verso.

———. 1993. "The New World Disorder." *New Left Review* 193:2–13.

———. 1994. "Exodus." *Critical Inquiry* 20 (winter): 314–27.

Barnes, J. A. 1954. "Class and Committees in the Norwegian Island Parish." *Human Relations* 7:39–58.

———. 1969. "Networks and Political Process." Pp. 51–76 in *Social Networks in Urban Situations,* edited by J. Clyde Mitchell. Manchester: Manchester University Press.

Basch, Linda, Nina Glick Schiller, and Cristina Szanton Blanc. 1994. *Nations Unbound: Transnational Projects, Postcolonial Predicaments, and Deterritorialized Nation-States.* Langhorne, Pa.: Gordon and Breach.

Bodnar, John. 1985. *The Transplanted: A History of Immigrants in Urban America.* Bloomington: Indiana University Press.

Calhoun, Craig. 1997. *Nationalism.* Minneapolis: University of Minnesota Press.

Chun, Sucheng. 1990. "European and Asian Immigration into the United States in Comparative Perspective, 1820s to 1920s." Pp. 79–95 in *Immigration Reconsidered: History, Sociology, and Politics,* edited by Virginia Yans-McLaughlin. New York: Oxford University Press.

Dandicat, Edwidge. 1996. *Krick? Krak!* New York: Vintage.

———. 1998a. *Breath, Eyes, Memory*. New York: Random House.

———. 1998b. *The Farming of the Bones*. New York: Soho.

Fouron, Georges, and Nina Glick Schiller. 1997. "Haitian Identities at the Juncture Between Diaspora and Homeland." Pp. 127–59 in *Caribbean Circuits,* edited by Patricia Pessar. Staten Island, N.Y.: Center for Migration Studies.

Gilroy, Paul. 1993. *The Black Atlantic: Modernity and Double Consciousness*. Cambridge: Harvard University Press.

Gleason, Philip. 1982. "American Identity and Americanization." Pp. 57–143 in *Harvard Encyclopedia of American Ethnic Groups,* edited by Stephan Thernstrom. Cambridge: Harvard University Press.

Glick Schiller, Nina. 1999a. "Transmigrants and Nation-States: Something Old and Something New in U.S. Immigrant Experience." Pp. 94–119 in *The Handbook of International Migration: The American Experience,* edited by Charles Hirschman, Philip Kasinitz, and Josh DeWind. New York: Russell Sage Foundation.

———. 1999b. " 'Who Are These Guys?': A Transnational Reading of the U.S. Immigrant Experience." Pp. 15–43 in *Identities on the Move: Transnational Processes in North America and the Caribbean Basin,* edited by Liliana Goldin. Austin: University of Texas Press.

———. 1999c. "Citizens in Transnational Nation-States: The Asian Experience." Pp. 202–18 in *Globalisation and the Asia-Pacific,* edited by Kris Olds, Peter Dickern, Philip Kelly, Lily Kong, and Henry Wai-chung Yeung. London: Routledge.

Glick Schiller, Nina, Linda Basch, and Cristina Szanton Blanc. 1992. "Transnationalism: A New Analytic Framework for Understanding Migration." Pp. 1–24 in *Towards a Transnational Perspective on Migration: Race, Class, Ethnicity, and Nationalism Reconsidered,* edited by Nina Glick Schiller, Linda Basch, and Cristina Blanc-Szanton. New York: New York Academy of Sciences.

———. 1995. "From Immigrant to Transmigrant: Theorizing Transnational Migration." *Anthropological Quarterly* 68 (1): 48–63.

Glick Schiller, Nina, and Georges Fouron. 1990. " 'Everywhere We Go We Are in Danger': Ti Manno and the Emergence of a Haitian Transnational Identity." *American Ethnologist* 17 (2): 329–47.

———. 1998. "Transnational Lives and National Identities: The Identity Politics of Haitian Immigrants. Pp. 130–61 in *Transnationalism from Below,* edited by Michael Peter Smith and Luis Guarnizo. New Brunswick, N.J.: Transaction Press.

———. 1999. "Terrains of Blood and Nation: Haitian Transnational Social Fields." *Ethnic and Racial Studies* 22 (2): 340–66.

———. 2001. *Georges Woke Up Laughing: Long Distance Nationalism and the Search for Home.* Durham, N.C.: Duke University Press.

Goldring, Luin. 1996. "Blurring Borders: Constructing Transnational Community in the Process of Mexico–US Migration." *Research in Community Sociology* 6:69–104.

Gordon, Milton M. 1964. *Assimilation in American Life: The Role of Race, Religion, and National Origins*. New York: Oxford University Press.

Graham, Pamela. 1996. "Nationality and Political Participation in the Transnational Context of Dominican Migration." Pp. 91–126 in *Caribbean Circuits: Transnational Approaches to Migration,* edited by Patricia Pessar. Staten Island, N.Y.: Center for Migration Studies.

Guarnizo, Luis Eduardo. 1997. "Social Transformation and the Mirage of Return Migration Among Dominican Transmigrants." Pp. 281–322 in *Transnational Processes and Situated Iden-*

tities. Special issue of *Identities: Global Studies in Culture and Power,* edited by Nina Glick Schiller, 4:281–322.

———. 1998. "The Rise of Transnational Social Formations: Mexican and Dominican State Responses to Transnational Migration." *Political Power and Social Theory* 12:45–94.

Haitian American Community Action Network (HACAN). 1996. Conference packet for Building a Haitian Community Action Network, New York, October.

Jenkins, Richard. 1992. *Pierre Bourdieu.* London: Routledge.

Kearney, Michael. 1991. "Borders and Boundaries of the State and Self at the End of Empire." *Journal of Historical Sociology* 4 (1): 52–74.

Laguerre, Michel. 1978. "Ticouloute and His Kinfolk: The Study of a Haitian Extended Family." Pp. 407–45 in *The Extended Family in Black Societies,* edited by Dmitri Shimkin, Edith Shimkin, and Dennis Frate. The Hague: Mouton.

———. 1998. *Diasporic Citizenship: Haitian Americans in Transnational America.* New York: St. Martin's.

Levitt, Peggy. 1998. "Forms of Transnational Community and Their Impact on the Second Generation: Preliminary Findings." Paper delivered at the conference Transnationalism and the Second Generation, Harvard University, April 3–4.

Lessinger, Johanna. 1995. *From the Ganges to the Hudson.* New York: Allyn and Bacon.

Mahler Sarah. 1998. "Theoretical and Empirical Contributions Toward a Research Agenda for Transnationalism." Pp. 64–100 in *Transnationalism from Below,* edited by Michael Peter Smith and Luis Eduardo Guarnizo. New Brunswick, N.J.: Transaction Press.

Maira, Sunaina. 2000. "Mixed Desires: Second-Generation Indian Americans and the Politics of Youth Culture." Paper delivered at the conference Diaspora and Displacement, Researching and Teaching the Asian Diasporas, Brown University, April 15.

Margolis, Maxine. 1998. *An Invisible Minority: Brazilians in New York City.* Boston: Allyn and Bacon.

Mitchell, J. Clyde, ed. 1969. *Social Networks in Urban Situations.* Manchester: University of Manchester Press.

Noble, Mary. 1973. "Social Network: Its Use as a Conceptual Framework in Family Analysis." Pp. 1–13 in *Network Analysis in Human Interaction,* edited by Jeremy Boissevain and J. Clyde Mitchell. The Hague: Mouton.

Ong, Aihwa. 1999. *Flexible Citizenship: The Cultural Logics of Transnationality.* Durham, N.C.: Duke University Press.

Pessar, Patricia. 1995. *A Visa for a Dream.* New York: Allyn and Bacon.

Portes, Alejandro. 1995. "Children of Immigrants: Segmented Assimilation and Its Determinants." Pp. 248–79 in *The Economic Sociology of Immigration: Essays on Networks, Ethnicity, and Entrepreneurship,* edited by Alejandro Portes. New York: Russell Sage Foundation.

Portes, Alejandro, Luis Guarnizo, and Patricia Landolt, eds. 1999. *Transnational Communities.* Special issue of *Ethnic and Racial Studies* 22:2.

Portes, Alejandro, and Min Zhou. 1993. "The Second Generation: Segmented Assimilation and Its Variants." *The Annals of the American Academy of Political and Social Science* 530:74–96.

———. 1996. *Immigrant America: A Portrait.* 2d ed. Berkeley: University of California Press.

Rouse, Roger. 1991. "Mexican Migration and the Social Space of Postmodernism." *Diaspora* 1:8–23.

Rumbaut, Rubén G. 1996. "The Crucible Within: Ethnic Identity, Self-Esteem, and Segmented Assimilation Among Children of Immigrants." Pp. 119–70 in *The New Second Generation,* edited by Alejandro Portes. New York: Russell Sage Foundation.

Sanchez, Arturo Ignacio. 1997. "Transnational Political Agency and Identity Formation Among Colombian Immigrants." Paper presented at the conference Transnational Communities and the Political Economy of New York, New School for Social Research, New York, February.

Simpson, George, and J. Milton Yinger. 1958. *Racial and Cultural Minorities.* New York: Harper.

Smith, Joan, and Immanuel Wallerstein, eds. 1992. *Creating and Transforming Households: The Constraints of the World Economy.* New York: Cambridge University Press.

Smith, Michael Peter, and Luis Guarnizo, eds. 1998. *Transnationalism from Below.* New Brunswick, N.J.: Transaction Press.

Smith, Robert. 1995. " *'Los Ausentes Siempre Presentes'*: The Imagining, Making, and Politics of Transnational Community Between Ticuani, Puebla, Mexico, and New York City." Ph.D. diss., Columbia University.

———. 1997. "Transnational Migration, Assimilation, and Political Community." Pp. 110–32 in *The City and the World,* edited by Margaret Crahan and Alberto Vourvoulias Bush. New York: Council on Foreign Relations.

———. 1998a. "Life Course, Cohort, and Gender as Variables Affecting Second Generation Transnational Life." Paper presented at the conference Transnationalism and the Second Generation, Harvard University, April 3–4.

———. 1998b. "Transnational Localities: Community, Technology, and the Politics of Membership Within the Context of Mexico–U.S. Migration." Pp. 196–240 in *Transnationalism from Below,* edited by Michael Peter Smith and Luis Guarnizo. New Brunswick, N.J.: Transaction Press.

Soyer, Daniel. 1997. *Jewish Immigrant Associations and American Identity in New York, 1880–1939.* Cambridge: Harvard University Press.

Stepick, Alex. 1998. *Pride Against Prejudice: Haitians in the United States.* Boston: Allyn and Bacon.

Turner, Victor. 1967. "Aspects of Sora Ritual and Shamanism: An Approach to the Data of Ritual." Pp.181–204 in *The Craft of Social Anthropology,* edited by A. E. Epstein. London: Tavistock.

U.S. Bureau of the Census. 1993. *1990 Census of Population. Foreign-Born Population in the United States.* Washington, D.C.: Government Printing Office.

Vickerman, Milton. 1999. *Cross Currents: West Indian Immigrants and Race.* New York: Oxford University Press.

Warner, W. Lloyd, and Leo Srole. 1945. *The Social Systems of American Ethnic Groups.* New Haven: Yale University Press.

Waters, Mary C. 1996. " Ethnic and Racial Identities of Second-Generation Black Immigrants in New York City." Pp. 171–96 in *The New Second Generation,* edited by Alejandro Portes. New York: Russell Sage Foundation.

Wyman, Mark. 2993. *Round-Trip to America: The Immigrants Return to Europe, 1880–1930.* Ithaca: Cornell University Press.

CHAPTER 4

Political Incorporation and Re-Incorporation: Simultaneity in the Dominican Migrant Experience

Pamela M. Graham

> If you, young mother, or you, elderly gentleman, or you, young student, feel the need to adopt the nationality of the United States in order to confront the vicissitudes of that society stemming from the end of the welfare era, do not feel tormented by this. Do it with a peaceful conscience, for you will continue being Dominicans, and we will welcome you as such when you set foot on the soil of our republic.
> —*Leonel Fernández, quoted in* New York Times, *October 12, 1996*

The president of the Dominican Republic, Leonel Fernández, made the above statement in 1996 in an address to Dominicans living in New York City, an important and supportive constituency. For migrants living abroad, "being Dominican" is a process with implications that go far beyond the symbolic. In 1994, the right to maintain dual nationality was formally approved by the Dominican Congress. Both Fernández and his closest competitor in the 1996 presidential elections, Jose Francisco Peña Gómez, supported expanded rights for Dominicans living abroad, including the establishment of representation of overseas Dominicans in the nation's major political bodies. By December 1997, the Dominican Congress passed an electoral reform law permitting voting from abroad, and de facto if not de jure representation of Dominicans living abroad has been created.[1]

The implications of voting rights from abroad are significant. The estimated five hundred thousand Dominicans living in the New York City area represent the third largest concentration of Dominican voters, following the cities of Santo Domingo and Santiago.[2] The last three presidential elections in the Dominican Republic had margins of victory far below the numbers of possible overseas voters.[3] With the establishment of institutional mechanisms for their participation and representation, migrants living abroad could have a significant influence on the outcome of national elections in their country of origin.

As these issues of involvement in the origin country have been debated and addressed, Dominicans have experienced a heightened visibility in New York state and local politics. Dominicans have been migrating to New York (and to other areas of the United States) in relatively large numbers since the 1960s, but for decades they existed as an "invisible" constituency within the New York City political arena. The redistricting of the New York City Council that took place in 1990–91 led to the creation of a new seat in northern Manhattan, an area with a concentrated population of Dominican residents. Since 1991 there has been a Dominican-born City Council member representing this district, and in 1996 a Dominican-born candidate won a recently redistricted New York State Assembly seat in northern Manhattan, defeating a non-Dominican incumbent who had held office for many years. Although rates of citizenship among Dominicans in New York and participation in formal political activity remain relatively low, there is an increased visibility of this community within the city, and a growing involvement of its members in local and statewide political institutions (Graham 1998).[4]

These events taking place in the Dominican Republic and in New York address many concerns and issues surrounding the political integration of migrants into the United States, and their roles within their country of origin. Proposals to curtail rights and access to U.S. government benefits only to those who possess citizenship has significantly altered the value of pursuing this status (Singer and Gilbertson 2000). Alongside this heightened pressure for legal residents to acquire citizenship is the lingering desire and outright need of many immigrants to retain political rights and citizenship of their country of origin. The desire to remain connected to the country of origin is fueled by the diverse economic roles that transnational migrants play in their "home" countries and is influenced by the perceived degree of openness (or lack thereof) of U.S. society to the integration of new immigrant groups into the political community. Sending states have sought the re-incorporation of overseas migrants, reflected in their willingness to change citizenship and electoral and economic policies to accommodate, court, or co-opt overseas nationals.

Conventional concepts of immigrant incorporation or assimilation, I argue, are limited in their ability to explain or even notice the rich political life that takes place across and over borders. Indeed, attachment to the home country has often been criticized as inhibiting the necessary development of loyalty and allegiance to the new nation. Instead of conceiving of a *choice* that must be made between loyalty to one or another political system, I argue that a process of simultaneous incorporation (or re-incorporation) into more than one national context can occur. Multiple political affiliations and identities can form, reflecting the realities of migrant engagement in more than one national economic or social arena. These political practices and their institutionalization through the alteration of nationally based political norms, laws, and structures culminates in the linkage of national or local political communities across borders. New reference points emerge, guiding the political options and choices that migrants and other political actors make.

The migration process occurring between the Dominican Republic and New York City illustrates this concept of simultaneous incorporation. In this chapter I examine the political development of Dominican migrant communities during the 1990s. Dominican migrants in New York have become increasingly important to their sending country and its government, *at the same time* as Dominicans migrants have achieved greater visibility and levels of formal participation in local New York City politics. Surveying these trends together highlights the ways in which economic and political resources cross borders, and the relationships that migrants have forged between acquiring more political power in the United States and receiving greater recognition in Dominican social and political arenas. Within these transnational political practices, Dominican national identity emerges as a strong resource deployed in both national contexts.

In the first section of this chapter, I discuss the concept of simultaneous political incorporation, considering possible determinants of its occurrence. Next, I turn to a discussion of Dominican migrant politics and review how and why a process of simultaneous incorporation has been unfolding. The research is based on fieldwork conducted in New York City and in the Dominican Republic throughout the 1990s, including in-depth interviews, attendance at a variety of meetings and events, and reviews of official documents, the Dominican and U.S. Latino press, and other published materials about this subject.

The Concept of Simultaneous Political Incorporation

Political incorporation involves entry into a nation-state's political system or its political community, in a process that is legally if not also socially sanctioned by that nation-state. As in the United States, the state may operate at different levels, with differing regulations governing who can participate in the formal political process. For example, some local elections for school boards do not require citizenship or even permanent resident status, whereas citizenship is required for participation at other levels. Incorporation may be reflected in engagement in both formal and informal political practices and is a much broader concept than naturalization to citizenship, which has often been used as a measure of migrant political assimilation.

Many different types of incorporation may exist, and they can be conceptualized along a continuum of alternatives. At one extreme migrants may become marginalized from the country of origin, maintaining few economic ties and withdrawing from social networks that include that country. As they construct new affiliations and identities, any participation that occurs will focus on the receiving country only. Such an outcome is reminiscent of theories of assimilation used in traditional literatures on immigrant incorporation that predict an increasing degree of "Americanization" as previous national identities fade or become symbolic or nostalgic (Abramson 1980; Alba and Nee 1999; Kazal 1995; Morawska 1990). At the other extreme, however, is

the opposite scenario; migrants may remain tightly connected to the country of origin, sending or investing money there and regularly communicating or traveling to
that country. Minimal contact or entry into the political arena of the nation of residence occurs. Re-incorporation into and membership in the nation of origin is much
more important than any assimilation into the nation where one resides. In fact, such
assimilation may be actively resisted and viewed as disloyalty toward the country of
origin. In between these extremes are a variety of possibilities, with differing combi-
nations of involvement or membership in the sending *and* receiving nations.

Sets of interests and opportunities will determine where migrants will fall on this continuum. The underlying economic and social organization of international migration is
one of the strongest generators of interest in being involved in both national political
systems. Migrants who operate businesses or labor alternatively on both sides of the
border will have concrete interests in state policies in both nations. For example, both
states retain the power to make policies and regulations that affect how easily migrants
can move themselves and their capital across borders and the legal status under which
they might labor. The organization of families and social groups across borders may
also give rise to interests in social and political policies in both national contexts.

These interests in the politics of both nations are mediated, however, by factors that
encourage or inhibit opportunities to participate in politics transnationally. The prevailing legal structures and norms of both nations can strongly influence whether
these interests are transformed into political action and thus affect the type of incorporation that may occur. For example, the lack of dual citizenship and prohibitions
on voting from abroad may prevent interested migrants from actively participating
in the country of origin. Conversely, a sending country that actively mobilizes and
promotes the maintenance of ties to the home country will enable the translation of
existing interests into actual participation across borders. The climate of reception in
the receiving society and laws governing naturalization and extension of political
rights to foreign-born residents can sharply define the options for political participation. Institutions such as political parties and interest groups (from either side of the
border) can be important agents in the construction of opportunities for transnational
political participation. Thus, the presence of transnational political interests, mediated by prevailing opportunities to participate in one or both systems, lead to a variety of possible degrees of incorporation into the sending and receiving nations.

Conventional concepts of immigrant incorporation focus on only a small part of this
picture, assuming most experiences will fall on either end of the continuum of incorporation. Recently emerging literatures on transnationalism focus more attention on the
middle spaces of the continuum of incorporation outcomes. The transnational perspective conceives of social fields and, by extension, political arenas that transcend political
boundaries (Basch, Glick Schiller, and Szanton Blanc 1994; Glick Schiller, Basch, and
Blanc-Szanton 1992). The dynamic nature of migration, often involving return or travel
to the origin country and the extensive relations carried on across borders broaden the
problematic of incorporation to take more than one national context into consideration.
While the concept of transnationalism has been used in many diverse ways, there have

been some common threads in research working with this perspective. This approach has questioned the role and strength of the state sovereignty in such contexts and explored the deterritorialization of the state and the resulting unboundedness of the nation. The in-between status of migrants, who exist "neither here nor there" as they maintain ties to both countries has also been a central concern.

The transnational perspective provides a useful tool for analyzing activities associated with recent international migrations. The concept needs to be refined, however, to be of greater use in explaining the practice of politics across borders.[5] First, many studies of transnational behavior have focused on documenting the existence and nature of relations between migrants and the home country but have not always consistently given enough attention to the place of such migrants within the receiving country. There is also need to distinguish between transnational behavior in the social, economic, and familial spheres and such behavior in the political arena. States retain high degrees of power in the organization of political space and activities but may not seek such degrees of control in economic, social, or private arenas. In addition to studies of migrant identity formation, there is the need to distinguish between transnational identities, transnational interests, and transnational practices and the relationships among them. Other concrete issues warranting more research are the timing and process of how nation-states have altered their laws and political norms to accommodate or mobilize nationals living abroad, with a recognition of how central such laws and norms are to delineating the opportunities for transnational political activity. Finally, the concept of the transnational social field may not be appropriate in describing political incorporation. Given the persistence of well-defined, nationally bound politics, we may be seeing interesting ways in which national political systems intersect at key moments, but not the creation of new systems free of national-territorial boundaries. Indeed, there may be a strengthening or reinforcement of national allegiances as laws on dual citizenship and participation in politics from abroad proliferate.

With such theoretical issues in mind, the remainder of this chapter looks to the case of Dominican political activity to explore the middle spaces on the continuum of incorporation, with an attentiveness to the factors that create or diminish opportunities to be involved simultaneously on both sides of the border.

The Political Incorporation of Dominican Migrants

Most Dominicans who have migrated to the United States arrived after the 1960s, joining the waves of "new" migrants entering the country after the major immigration policy reforms of 1965. The Dominican case rests within the context of multiple economic changes taking place at national and global levels since the 1960s, including alterations in the organization of manufacturing industries, the rapid growth of offshore assembly in export processing zones throughout the Caribbean, the similar growth of service economies in lesser and more developed countries, the effects of the Latin American debt crisis of the 1980s, and the shift to more open, export-oriented models of economic development (Georges 1990; Grasmuck and Pessar 1991). As in most other Caribbean nations, the migration industry evolved as an important means of alleviating unemployment and as a provider of foreign exchange earnings through investment and cash remittances sent by migrants living abroad. The use of migration has been by no means uniformly beneficial to the society or to individual participants; many Dominicans have lost their lives in attempts to make undocumented entries into the mainland United States or Puerto Rico, and others have met with little economic success once in the United States, incorporated into some of the most exploitative sectors of New York City's labor markets (Torres-Saillant and Hernández 1998).

The difficulties and challenges involved in migration have not dissuaded increasing numbers of persons from making the journey to the United States, however. New York City has been a prime destination, and by the late 1990s an estimated five hundred thousand Dominicans had settled in a geographically concentrated pattern within neighborhoods in Manhattan, Queens, and the Bronx (New York City Department of City Planning 1999, 18).

Throughout the past forty years, migrants have formed a variety of groups, organizations, and social clubs. Dominican nationality has operated as a cohesive bond, influencing the patterns of organizational development among migrants in New York, and has often superseded other bases of organization along class, racial, or gender lines. While such organizations serve cultural, social, or economic needs of Dominicans in New York, many migrant organizations have developed active roles in the sending country, engaging in fund-raising to assist communities of origin.[6] Instead of diminishing, linkages between the two sides of the migration process have increased and become more sophisticated.

The visible importance of Dominican national politics among migrants living in New York was the defining feature of earlier Dominican migrant political organization, leading many observers to assume that greater participation in local New York politics would not occur in the near future. However, during the 1980s and 1990s, Dominicans began to contest the characterization of their "invisibility" in New York politics, and many Dominican-origin persons stepped into positions of leadership through election or appointment to public office. At the same time, Dominicans also began to gain more formal legal recognition of the roles they have played in the economic and political life of their country of origin.

Dos Partes de una Misma Comunidad—Two Parts of the Same Community

In February 2000, a large conference called Dominicanos/Dominicans 2000 was held on the campus of the City College of New York, in northern Manhattan. Through a series of workshops on a variety of social, economic, cultural, and political themes, the young organizers sought to define and set an agenda for ongoing Dominican involvement in public affairs. Johnny Ventura, the mayor of the Dominican capital of Santo Domingo, addressed the large crowd at the closing session. He spoke of the achievements of Dominicans living abroad, and of their ongoing contributions to the development of their country of origin. He described Dominicans abroad as a bridge between cultures, an "indisputable part of us," and stated that those abroad and those in the Dominican Republic were "two parts of the same community."

As reflected in Ventura's comments, Dominican immigrants have achieved a degree of legal and symbolic recognition of the government of their country of origin. This recognition has not always been there, and Dominicans have worked actively over the decades to claim the right to exercise an ongoing role in the political process in the country of origin. Important developments in the 1990s have included the acquisition of dual nationality, the right to vote from abroad, and in less formal ways, increased levels of recognition and engagement with the Dominican government.

Several precedents existed for Dominican involvement in politics from abroad. Major political parties were established overseas early in the twentieth century and many important political leaders spent time actively pursuing their causes in exile.[7] The migration to the United States that began in the 1960s represented a new era in the Dominican Republic's migration history, but these movements had strong political elements as well (Martin 1966; Mitchell 1992). Many persons who opposed the election of Joaquín Balaguer to the presidency in 1966, and who had fought in the civil war in the Dominican Republic earlier in the 1960s, migrated to the United States and remained involved in Dominican politics. Even as motivations for migration to the United States shifted to more economic and familial reasons, the Dominican political parties formed strong networks among migrants. As the major parties set up offices overseas, they mobilized and directed political participation toward the country of origin.

Although the involvement of many migrants with political parties provided a means of ongoing participation in the home country, the legal and more formal recognition of migrants as a political constituency became an increasingly important issue in the 1990s. Without the ability to retain Dominican nationality, or participate in elections from abroad, the role and political power of migrants living abroad was limited.

The effort to acquire dual nationality was an initial step in creating a greater role for migrants in the country of origin. The Dominican constitution written in 1966 stated that the acquisition of another nationality would require the loss of Dominican nationality.[8] A constitutional amendment or revision was necessary to alter this provision, and carrying out such a reform was only within the power of the Dominican Congress.[9]

Several bills seeking to change nationality laws had been introduced during the 1980s but lacked sufficient support to be approved. Balaguer, president in 1966–78 and 1986–96, and members of the executive branch generally treated the nationality issue with neutrality, neither promoting nor strongly opposing it. By the early 1990s, members of the Congress, Dominican political groups in the United States, and Dominican political parties began to increase efforts to change the nationality laws.

In the early 1990s the Senate formed the Committee on the Affairs of Dominicans Living Abroad. Members of the multipartisan committee traveled to the United States in 1992 and 1993 to meet with individuals and groups within Dominican communities in the Northeast and in South Florida to discuss nationality and other political concerns (Informativo Dominicano 1992). The Dominican members of Congress used such occasions to express their support of the overseas communities.[10] While in New York in 1992, the Dominican Liberation Party (PLD) senator heading the committee stated that Dominicans abroad need representation given the reality of the large population of Dominicans living in the United States. He went on to say that, "in order to achieve respect, to achieve a share of power, they must have political power . . . and in order to have political power, it is necessary to have the right to vote . . . and to have the right to vote it is necessary to have double nationality" (*ListínUSA* 1992).

Members of Congress also participated in meetings and seminars held in the Dominican Republic, organized by both U.S. and Dominican-based groups, including political organizations, interest groups, and business organizations. Although many groups had members active in the United States and in the Dominican Republic, persons from New York were also invited to participate in the events held in Santo Domingo (*ListínUSA* 1993).[11] Many of the more active groups had members with strong ties to center and left political parties operating abroad, although some of the groups made efforts to promote their multipartisan nature.[12]

The Dominican parties were also important to this process of constructing dual nationality. Their ability to raise funds among Dominicans living abroad was predicated on the existence of a strong and ongoing interest in Dominican politics among such migrants. Their interest and participation would be strengthened if the legal right to continue being Dominican were available. It has been difficult to measure the exact influence of migrants on party fund-raising, but the extent of campaign activity abroad provides some indicator of their role. The New York–based Dominican press estimated in 1994 that the PRD raised several million dollars within a year, noting that the party's presidential candidate, Jose Francisco Peña Gómez, made seven visits to New York, New Jersey, and Massachusetts in the thirteen months preceding the 1994 elections (*ListínUSA* 1994).[13] In the 1996 presidential elections observers estimated that up to a third of the US$30 million raised by all three major parties came from overseas donations (González 1996, 19). The parties would have little reason to oppose any measure that would increase the power and visibility within domestic politics of Dominicans living abroad.

Proponents of dual nationality also used the more general economic role of Dominicans in the home country to justify the desire for continued access to the political system. Migration was often portrayed as an economically necessary and hopefully temporary process. The extensive remittances and capital earned abroad and directed back to the Dominican Republic out of familial and national allegiance formed the bases of arguments for maintaining rights and privileges of nationals to operate in the Dominican economy. One PRD senator supportive of changing nationality stated, "The Dominican community has made economic equilibrium possible through their support in foreign exchange earnings; without those economic resources and their honest work utilized to achieve domestic equilibrium, it would have been very difficult to surpass this period of crisis."[14] The text of one proposed reform stated, "Those Dominicans have triumphed in foreign lands maintaining in their hearts a love of the soil which gave birth to them— and they have contributed generously to alleviating the present problems of the country" (Rodríguez Pimentel 1992, 2). While campaigning in 1996 for the presidency, PRD candidate Peña Gómez, stated, "These people send back more than a billion dollars a year to our country. Their voices deserve to be heard" (*New York Times* 1996a).

Efforts to promote preservation of nationality also involved linking the position of Dominicans within the United States to their access to a dual national status. Discussions at group meetings and interviews with activists consistently revealed that naturalization was viewed as a practical, pragmatic step that simply enabled Dominicans to acquire a more secure status within North American society. Noting the relatively low naturalization rates among Dominican migrants, some argued that the fear of losing Dominican nationality stopped many from pursuing U.S. citizenship. Activists more involved in local politics in the United States frequently articulated the perception that naturalization and political power go hand in hand.[15] An interest group based within the Dominican Republic argued that "the possession of the nationality of the place of residence would give Dominicans more solidarity as a minority within the country in question, in order to claim and exercise their political rights" (Fundación Institucionalidad y Justicia 1993, 1). Being able to retain access to Dominican nationality would be important on a symbolic level as well. Naturalization would not necessarily reflect a renunciation or rejection of "Dominican-ness," especially if one could continue to hold Dominican nationality.

A political crisis following the 1994 presidential elections forced the process of constitutional reform to move forward. Balaguer claimed victory in the election, with a margin of the vote that was only 0.7 percent (*Notisur* 1994). Under national and international pressure and faced with documented allegations of fraud, Balaguer decided to negotiate with both opposition parties. In the days before his inauguration they signed a political pact mandating several constitutional reforms. The outgoing Congress, which had been involved in discussions of the nationality issue, was charged with approving the reforms. While provisions concerning presidential re-election and double-round balloting captured most of the attention, the nationality provision was also included in the reform package (Hartlyn 1998, 254; Oficina Nacional de Planificación 1994).

In the aftermath of the passage of this reform, efforts to reconceptualize and legally redefine nationality and citizenship continued with the ongoing attempt to achieve voting and representation rights within Dominican political institutions for nationals living abroad. Many of the groups active in nationality reform continued to press for voting rights from abroad. Organizations such as the Committee of Dominicans Abroad (CODEX) focused specifically on this issue and sought to lobby the Dominican executive and Congress in the effort to change access to the vote.

At the time of the nationality reform, in 1994, Dominicans living abroad had to return to the Dominican Republic to be allowed to vote. Unlike the nationality reform, the Congress had the power to change voting requirements through regular legislation. In 1996 the country's main electoral board, Junta Central Electoral (JCE), submitted a bill to reform the main electoral law to the Dominican Congress. Leaders of the two chambers of Congress agreed to form a bicameral committee to consider the reform (Bolívar Díaz 1997). After a year of review, the reform bill was passed in

November 1997, extending the right to vote in presidential and vice-presidential elections to Dominicans living abroad. Access to voting from abroad was to have been available by the 2000 elections, but the JCE reserved the right to determine exactly when voting from abroad can begin. Logistical problems have stalled implementation of the provision, and migrants were not yet able to vote from abroad as of the 2000 presidential elections.[16]

An important factor in the effort to change voting rights was the election in 1996 of a young lawyer in the PLD, Leonel Fernández, to the Dominican presidency. Fernández had been raised in New York City and had been a regular figure at PLD events in New York in the early 1990s. His program of government included recognition of Dominicans living overseas.

> The great population of Dominicans living abroad deserves a government that will take its problems into consideration. Our emigrants maintain a fond connection with their homeland and help in an extremely important manner with economic development. The PLD government will take into account the needs of Dominicans living abroad and will facilitate their return to the country, in such a way that they may be incorporated into social, political, and economic processes. (PLD 1996)

While the establishment of new legal rights has been an important marker of the increasing visibility of Dominicans living abroad, the relationship between the Dominican state and emigrants has been more visible than at any other time in recent history. Shortly after taking power, President Fernández appointed a long-time New York resident to the prized position of consul general for New York. Fellow PLD party member Bienvenido Pérez had also been active in an organization called Expresión Dominicana whose aim was to expand the rights of Dominicans with respect to the country of origin.[17]

Pérez sought to alter the traditional role of the consulate, from one of dealing with neutral bureaucratic procedures to one of pro-active advocacy for Dominicans living abroad (*New York Daily News* 1992). Upon assuming his new post, he stated in a press conference, "You can be sure that this consulate will defend [Dominicans] in a legal manner, and that we will make efforts to permanently defend Dominicans in New York" (*El Diario/La Prensa* 1996). In the wake of U.S. legislation in 1996 seeking to curb access to benefits by legal residents, he initiated awareness campaigns for Dominicans, sponsoring seminars throughout the city, and provided information in the consulate on U.S. naturalization and immigrant rights. At the same time, however, he stated in an interview, "I hope to make the consulate the fundamental link of our community overseas" (González 1996). His efforts were equally directed at promoting a closer relationship between the Dominican government and nationals living abroad.

The Dominican government has made efforts to include nationals living abroad in other, more formal initiatives during Fernández's presidency. In 1998, during a visit to New York, Fernández announced the opening of the Office of Foreign Investment, based at the Dominican Consulate. The office was designed to advise and facilitate investment by Dominicans living overseas. In addition, Fernández sought to implement more fairly existing import laws exonerating from duties personal effects and used cars brought into the Dominican Republic by returning migrants. The government also opened an office in 1996 devoted to providing information about customs and export issues. Dominicans living overseas were included in the general Diálogo Nacional (National dialogue) process that the Dominican president launched to encourage popular input into government and constitutional reform (*Boletín de Noticias* 1998). During a June 1996 visit by Fernández to New York, the Dominican Government sponsored an international exposition/conference at Riverbank State Park in northern Manhattan. The week-long conference featured forums on state reform, voting from abroad, and a variety of cultural events (*El Diario/La Prensa* 1998:23). More recently, the Central Electoral Board, the secretary of state for foreign relations, and the Presidential Commission on Reform and Modernization of the State sponsored a conference in the Dominican Republic in February 2000, focusing on the vote for Dominicans living abroad. Participants from the United States were involved in the forum (Junta Central Electoral 2000).

This level of activity and engagement between the Dominican government and overseas migrants is unprecedented. Prior to the establishment of dual nationality, Dominicans living overseas had few forums or legal rights within their country of origin. While Dominicans living abroad continue to operate at the margins of their origin country's political process, they have gained initial legal means for being more engaged in politics. The roles they continue to play in the Dominican economy creates a basis for retaining ongoing interests in the country's affairs, and the willingness of the Dominican state to extend rights and opportunities for participation has enabled the translation of interests into action.

Dominicans in New York Politics: We Came Here to Stay!

The same closing session of Dominicanos/Dominicans 2000 that featured Mayor Ventura's speech also provided aspiring U.S. Senate candidate Hillary Rodham Clinton a forum for addressing a new potential political constituency. Her attendance at the conference signaled the growing visibility of Dominicans as a political force within New York, with a host of pressing challenges and issues to confront. Identification with these realities was reflected in the words of a young Dominican organizer, who emphatically punctuated many of his speeches throughout the conference with the affirmation, "We came here to stay!"

This reality for many Dominicans has fueled their gradual emergence in local and state politics. While efforts were being directed at changing the Dominican Republic's legal and political institutions, activists in New York City faced the continuing challenge of gaining greater visibility and power within the city's political arena. Despite the existence of over 120,000 persons of Dominican origin within New York City by 1980 (New York City Department of City Planning 1992b) it was not uncommon to see Dominicans referred to as the "invisible" immigrants (Lescaille 1990). As Dominicans became more geographically concentrated in the Washington Heights/Inwood and Hamilton Heights neighborhoods, they formed a growing number of professional organizations, social and hometown clubs, and cultural groups (Georges 1984). Younger Dominican activists also formed community organizations focused on providing social services to residents of Washington Heights/Inwood. Dominicans became more directly involved in public affairs through the election of Dominicans to the Washington Heights school board and the mobilization of parents to take a more active role in school politics (Lescaille 1992; Linares 1989). Finally, several Dominicans were appointed to leadership positions within the Democratic Party and to posts on local community and city advisory boards. The much more visible political presence Dominicans in New York City achieved by the 1990s was the culmination of decades of growing organizational and political activity.

An important feature of the political development of the Dominican community in the 1990s was the creation of predominantly Dominican political districts and the election of Dominican-born candidates to city and state-wide offices. The creation of such districts for the New York City Council and for the New York State Assembly resulted from redistricting processes that sought to improve opportunities for fair and effective representation of previously underrepresented groups.

In 1989, the City Charter of New York was revised and the local legislative body, the City Council, was expanded from thirty-five to fifty-one seats (New York City Charter Revision Commission 1990). The creation of new districts was overseen by the specially appointed Districting Commission. The commission solicited proposals for districts from the public and held open forums throughout the city in 1989 and 1990, including one in Washington Heights that attracted many Dominicans. A group named the Northern Manhattan Committee for Fair Representation (NMCFR) submitted two proposals to the Districting Commission.[18] Consisting of mostly Dominican activists, many of whom had already served in public office, the committee sought "the creation of a Dominican-based Councilmanic District, that coinciding with a massive voter registration campaign would maximize Dominican political potential at the polls." The proposal also stated, "The Northern Manhattan Committee for Fair Representation believes that this is a viable district where the Dominican community can elect a candidate of their choice" (NMCFR 1991). Their proposed district was smaller in population than the required 139,000, but it would contain 44 percent Hispanic registered voters (compared with 32 percent in the old existing District 5) and a total Hispanic population of almost 78 percent. African Americans and whites would represent about 10 percent each of the total population. The proposal emphasized the economic role played by Dominicans in the area and confidence in their political position, stating, "The Dominican community in northern Manhattan has the population, voters, resources and potential leadership to elect the Dominican of their choice that would best represent the interests of Dominicans at the City Council" (NMCFR 1991).

The Districting Commission approved plans for a new District 10, covering much of Washington Heights in northern Manhattan. The new district contained a Latino voting age population of 75 percent (Berger and Reed 1991). The strong geographic concentration of Dominicans and the dominance of one common national origin in northern Manhattan greatly strengthened arguments in favor of adopting District 10. Unlike Latinos in Queens and East Harlem, Dominicans did not face the prospect of a district with sizable populations of other minority ethnic groups.

Four Dominican candidates ran for the new City Council seat in the 1991 elections. Educator Guillermo Linares narrowly defeated lawyer Adriano Espaillat, by a margin of only slightly more than three hundred votes in the Democratic primary (*ListínUSA* 1991b). The use of Dominican identity was a central part of the campaigns, even though the candidates differed in their length of stay in the United States and their connection to the Dominican political system. For example, Linares distributed campaign materials with Dominican flags printed on them. He also circulated an open letter from his mother, still in the Dominican Republic, asking voters to support her son and stating that she would be standing by the telephone waiting to hear of his victory. The flyer featured a picture of Linares and his mother, taken in a humble-looking house in the Dominican Republic. After the primary and only weeks before the general election, Linares traveled to the Dominican Republic to deliver an ambulance to his hometown of Cabrera. He also met with President Balaguer, leaders of the other two major parties, and the archbishops of Santo Domingo and San Francisco de Macorís (both major sending communities in the migration process) (*ListínUSA* 1991a). Upon returning to New York, Linares easily won the general election, against Dominican-born Apolinar Trinidad, who ran with the Conservative Party. Linares has twice won re-election to his City Council seat and has been faced with other Dominican-born rivals in each contest, including those backed by former opponent Espaillat (Jordan 1997).

Unlike the circumstances surrounding the City Council process, the 1992 redistricting for the New York State Assembly involved adjusting existing district lines to reflect population growth registered in the 1990 Census instead of the formation of a completely new district. Northern Manhattan's District 72 was one of the few redrawn districts that showed a significant increase in the percentage of Latino residents (78 percent after the redistricting as opposed to 68 percent before). As with the City Council District, new lines were drawn to maximize the chances of the election of Latino candidates, taking into account the patterns of settlement of Dominicans throughout the northern Manhattan area (Hanson and Falcón 1992). The long-time incumbent of District 72, John Brian Murtaugh, of Irish origin, was re-elected in his first post-redistricting race in 1994, defeating a Dominican challenger. But by 1996, Adriano Espaillat capitalized on the growing involvement of the district's Dominican population in politics and won the seat away from Murtaugh. Espaillat's victory was not a landslide, with a margin of only 196 votes out of a total of 6,400 cast in the primary. Although data on the ethnic composition of the vote is not available, the new district's high Latino population and the registration of 2,400 new voters in 1996, along with Espaillat's strong emphasis on his Dominican ethnicity (and Murtaugh's lack of the same) during the campaign, suggest that the issue of ethnic identity had become an important political factor (*New Orleans Times-Picayune* 1996).

While the creation of new political districts and electoral victories was a very visible sign of greater political involvement, less formal means of participation were also taking place. Dominicans have lived in areas of New York City challenged by higher than average poverty, unemployment, and crime rates, and along with other minorities have experienced tense relations with police. The killing of a young Dominican man in summer 1992 by a New York City police officer prompted several days of protests in northern Manhattan, attracting a significant amount of media attention.[19] This was probably one of the first times that Dominicans had captured the attention of the entire city (and country) while protesting serious problems in their communities. The issue of tense police-community relations continues to be important in Dominican neighborhoods and is underscored by well-publicized incidents of police brutality toward immigrants and minorities occurring in other parts of the city. Dominicans have joined with other New Yorkers in protesting the killing of the unarmed African immigrant Amadou Diallo and the abuse of Haitian immigrant Abner Louima by New York City police (*El Diario/La Prensa* 1999b).

This issue and many other challenges facing Dominicans in New York and elsewhere in the country have been driving ongoing efforts to organize, define political agendas, and pursue both formal and informal participation. While groups based within New York City's Dominican communities continue to play an important role in promoting greater involvement in politics, nationally based Dominican groups are also becoming more visible. The nonprofit organization Dominicanos/Dominicans 2000 was formed in 1997, drawing upon members of the Dominican Youth Union (Unión de Jovenes Dominicanos). This network of young Dominican-born and U.S.–born activists worked for three years to sponsor the national (and international) conference of the same name, which was directed at constructing "a national agenda for the advancement of the Dominican community in New York City and the United States" (Viñuales 1999, 1). The conference, held at the City College of New York in February 2000, attracted over fifteen hundred registered participants. The conference consisted primarily of workshops on health care, youth, law, interethnic relations, politics, economic empowerment, women and social change, the "diaspora and the island," the media, and the arts. Well-known Dominican leaders attended the event; a political workshop was led by Linares and Espaillat, who emphasized the importance of unity among Dominicans and the need to pursue naturalization and participation in U.S. elections. Other political leaders participated as well, including Manhattan Borough President C. Virginia Fields, Bronx Borough President Fernando Ferrer, U.S. Representative José Serrano (D), and Democratic Party leader Roberto Ramírez. But the emergence of new, young Dominican leadership was the most noticeable feature of what was probably the largest national organized political meeting of Dominicans and Dominican Americans to date.

The Dominican American National Roundtable (DANR) is another group that has emerged to follow similar goals—mobilization of resources and leadership to address policy issues of concern to Dominicans living throughout the United States (DANR 2000). Three national conferences had been held by early 2001.

The process of political incorporation among Dominicans has been the product of several factors. While many Dominicans travel and return to live in their country of origin, the realities of permanent settlement in the United States and the many economic and social challenges confronting Dominican neighborhoods in New York prompted efforts to obtain more political visibility and power. The organizational experience gained during the 1980s began the process of empowerment and was a basis for the new political opportunities appearing in the 1990s. The new wave of younger activists and the trend toward national level organization are products of the emergence of new generations of Dominicans and the growing dispersal of settlement of Dominicans throughout the country. Grass-roots movements have also been important to more informal political participation in the form of protests and demonstrations.

While grass-roots movements have been important, incorporation has also been influenced from above, in the form of norms, rules, and regulations surrounding the political process. For example, the creation of new political districts could not have been initiated at the grass-roots level. Federal and local efforts to address questions of minority participation provided the opportunity to pursue formation of predominantly Dominican districts. The response and involvement of activists was essential to the outcome of the redistricting processes, but local and federal states influenced how and when Dominicans organized. The increasing rates of naturalization among Dominicans in the late 1990s was prompted in large part by the wave of restrictive policies passed in the mid-1990s, limiting access to social benefits to citizens. While some of these measures have since been repealed, the experience highlighted the vulnerability of noncitizen residents and increased the value of naturalization. Many community organizations throughout Washington Heights carried out naturalization campaigns in the aftermath of the passage of the restrictive policies (Singer and Gilbertson 2000). While it is difficult to track the causality of current naturalization patterns, an increase augments the size of the Dominican electorate, and new Dominican-origin citizens can more easily sponsor ongoing migration of relatives.

Dominican national identity has been central to how immigrants have become more incorporated into the politics of New York City and New York State. National identity has been strongly present within efforts to gain political districts and in political races. In New York City's complex system of identity politics, "Dominican-ness" has been an acceptable and effective mobilizing tool. Within the city, the strong residential concentration of Dominicans has lessened the need to form coalitions with other groups in order to gain districts or win offices; Dominicans thus have been able to focus on a national, not a broader, ethnic identity. The fact that organizations in Washington Heights, including Dominican political parties, mobilize around national identity facilitates its continuing use in local and state politics.

Conclusion

Examining some of the most important political activity taking place among Dominican migrants in recent years reveals a complex picture, with the emergence of multiple identities and roles. A conventional assessment of incorporation that focused only on the activities of Dominicans with respect to participation and interests within the borders of the United States (or New York City) would omit important dimensions of the migrant political experience. Conversely, a study of the transnational involvement of Dominicans with the country of origin that failed to recognize their participation in politics in their "new" country would overlook this equally important dimension of the incorporation process. International migration is a complex political-economic event and it spawns equally complex interests that will not always "fit" neatly within existing political institutions and regulations, controlled and directed by nation-states.

The Dominican community in New York City has undergone a process of greater incorporation into local politics while pursuing an expanded role in the politics of the nation of origin. The community has not split into divisive segments, with some advocating greater activism in New York City and others promoting loyalty to the Dominican Republic. Some observers of the Dominican migration experience have expressed important concerns over the viability of this dual focus, and such concerns should form the basis for ongoing research (Torres-Saillant and Hernández 1998). At this time, however, patterns of convergence between involvement in these different national contexts appear to be more prevalent than sharp divisions in the focus of political activity.

The ability of Dominican migrants in New York to achieve representation and power within the city is linked to their social and economic position. In turn, the economic strength of the community affects its ability to contribute to development in the Dominican Republic. It thus becomes difficult to separate these arenas of political participation, even as more generations of Dominicans are born in the United States. The acquisition of dual nationality has been promoted with attention to its possible influence on encouraging greater rates of naturalization to U.S. citizenship. The economic importance of Dominicans to their country of origin, and the Dominican government's support of a sustained role for overseas migrants in Dominican politics has helped translate interest in home country affairs into active participation and engagement across borders. Those active in New York City politics have used Dominican identity as a basis for mobilization, thus encouraging a continued identification with the nation of origin. The emergence of new Dominican candidates running for state and national office signals the continuing importance of Dominican ethnicity in the context of even broader forums of representation. While it has been difficult to document the role of Dominican political parties in supporting candidates in New York City elections, these parties continue to be highly visible in the organizational landscape of the Dominican community.

It is important to emphasize that the concept of simultaneous incorporation is not being applied at the individual level, and unlike conventional notions of assimilation, sociocultural variables are not singled out as prime determinants of incorporation. Instead, this characterization of a community-level process of incorporation looks to structural economic and political factors to explain how and why involvement in more than one nation can occur among migrants. Individual level research will be useful to improving knowledge of who is likely to become involved in the transnational practice of politics, but there is a need to work at building knowledge of how broader, structural forces influence transnational politics.

Simultaneous incorporation should not be restricted to characterizing the experience of first-generation migrants. Participation in more than one national context is predicated upon ongoing economic relationships between the origin country and overseas migrant communities and upon the actions of the sending country government and actors in recognizing nationals living abroad as important constituencies. Furthermore, the political-institutional landscape in the receiving country plays an important role; the lack of easy or direct opportunities for incorporation and the encouragement of mobilization around ethnic and national identity will reinforce the retention of relationships with the origin country. The presence of these three sets of factors—transnational economic interest, sending-country policies, and the nature of reception in the receiving country—work together to create or to preclude the spaces and incentives for migrants to position themselves across national political arenas.

While the symbolic or psychological dimensions of retaining home-country identities and the imagined consciousness of a transnational community are important, these economic and political-institutional factors form the bases of the transnationally organized practice of politics among migrants. The initial experiences of the Dominican community in northern Manhattan illustrate this simultaneous incorporation process and encourage us to pursue new ways of thinking about transnational migration and its political consequences.

Notes

1. No formal mechanisms for representation of Dominican migrants within the Dominican Congress have been created. However, a member of the New York community was elected in 1998 as part of a slate of candidates from the country's second largest city. See Itzigsohn et al. 1999, 316–17.

2. It is difficult to obtain an accurate count of the number of Dominicans living in the United States or in New York City. Census Bureau data for 1997 estimates 632,000 Dominican-born persons in the United States. In New York City, there were 336,000 Dominican-born persons and 159,000 of Dominican parentage. The population of Santo Domingo in 1993 was 2.14 million, and the second largest city, Santiago, had 690,000 persons. See Hernández and Rivera-Batíz 1997, 11; Bureau of the Census 1997, 1.

3. For example, in the second round of the 1996 presidential elections Fernández won with about 72,000 more votes than Peña Gómez. In the controversial 1994 and 1990 elections, the margins of victory were about 22,000 and 25,000 votes, respectively. See data on the Dominican Republic posted in the Political Database of the Americas, <http://www.georgetown.edu/pdba/>

4. Of the almost nine thousand Dominicans admitted to the United States as immigrants in 1977, only 38 percent had naturalized by 1997, and of the almost thirteen thousand admitted in 1982, only 30 percent had naturalized by 1997 (Department of Justice 1999, 140–41).

5. For critical reviews of the concept of transnationalism see Glick Schiller 1999; Portes, Guarnizo, and Landolt 1999; and Smith and Guarnizo 1998. Studies of Dominican international migration employing this perspective include Graham 1996; Grasmuck and Pessar 1991; Guarnizo 1994; Itzigsohn et al. 1999; Levitt 1998. See also Smith 1995 and Goldring 1998 for studies of Mexican migration.

6. For example, in the aftermath of Hurricane Georges in September 1998, Dominicans in the United States sent large quantities of relief supplies and raised hundreds of thousands of dollars to assist victims. See *El Nuevo Herald* 1998.

7. The Dominican Revolutionary Party (PRD) was formed abroad in 1935 by exiled opponents of the Dominican dictator Rafael Trujillo. The frequent and long-time president of the country throughout most of the last quarter of the twentieth century, Joaquín Balaguer, also actively pursued his political career while in exile. During the 1950s, the small number of Dominicans living in the United States visibly protested the government of Trujillo, picketing the United Nations and various locations in Washington, D.C. Efforts to overthrow Trujillo were launched from abroad as well. See Graham 1996.

8. The primary rights associated with Dominican nationality and, by extension, citizenship include the right to vote and hold public office. Those born abroad of Dominican parents had until the age of eighteen to decide which nationality to adopt.

9. In order to change the constitution, both houses of the Dominican Congress (the Senate and Chamber of Deputies) must meet jointly, in which event they convene as the National Assembly. More than half the members of each house must be present to meet as the National Assembly. Constitutional matters must be considered in this forum, and decisions are adopted by an absolute majority of votes (Oficina Nacional de Planificación 1980, sec. A-1–4-1).

10. Notes from "A Forum on Dual-Citizenship for Dominicans in the United States," held at the City College of New York, New York, November 19, 1992.

11. The Federation of Dominican Associations in New Jersey (FADO), the Institutionality and Justice Foundation (FINJUS), Dominican Expression, the School of Legal and Political Sciences at the Autonomous University of Santo Domingo (UASD), the Federation of Dominican Businessmen in the United States, and the Foundation for the Defense of Dominicans Living Abroad were some of the groups involved in these efforts.

12. Interview notes, Santo Domingo, June 1995, and New York, June 1994.

13. Presidential elections continue to generate high levels of activity, with major parties holding large parades throughout northern Manhattan in the weeks preceding election day and political advertising appears on New York City television and radio stations with regularity.

14. Notes from file on dual nationality, U.S. Consulate, Santo Domingo, 1994.

15. A founder of one of the most prominent nationality-citizenship groups mentioned that he had just been appointed to a local community board within the New York City government. Interview notes, New York City, June 1994.

16. Immediately prior to the 2000 presidential elections, groups in New York criticized the Dominican Electoral Board for failing to making voting from abroad available. One major problem involved the *cédula* or identification card required of all Dominican voters. Dominican migrants had to return to the Dominican Republic to obtain these cards—a process that would significantly impede access to the vote even if it were available. See *El Diario/La Prensa* 1999a, 2000.

17. Interview and field notes, New York, 1992.

18. According to the records of the New York City Districting Commission, another proposal was submitted by the Dominican Research Center, apparently composed of a small group of Dominican activists. A written copy of this proposal was not on file at the Municipal Archives (Berger and Reed 1991, appendix 4, vol. 4).

19. The protests occurred just days before the start of the 1992 national convention of the Democratic Party, held in the mid-town area of the city. City officials feared that the protests might detract attention from the convention and portray a negative image of the city. See *El Diario/La Prensa* 1992; *New York Newsday* 1992; and *New York Times* 1992.

References

Abramson, Harold J. 1980. "Assimilation and Pluralism." Pp.150–60 in *The Harvard Encyclopedia of American Ethnic Groups*, edited by Stephan Thernstrom. Cambridge: Belknap Press of the Harvard University Press.

Alba, Richard, and Victor Nee. 1999. "Rethinking Assimilation Theory for a New Era of Immigration." Pp. 137–60 in *The Handbook of International Migration*, edited by Charles Hirschman, Philip Kasinitz, and Josh DeWind. New York: Russell Sage Foundation.

Basch, Linda, Nina Glick Schiller, and Cristina Szanton Blanc, 1994. *Nations Unbound.* Langhorne, Pa.: Gordon and Breach.

Berger, Joel, and Judith Reed. 1991. *Submission Under Section 5 of the Voting Rights Act for Preclearance of 1991 Redistricting Plan for New York City Council.* New York: New York City Districting Commission, June 17.

Boletín de Noticias. 1998. "Dominicanos de EE.UU. presentan propuestas para el Diálogo Nacional," February 20. <http://www.presidencia.gov.do/dialogo/20feb98.htm> (accessed May 10, 1998).

Bolivar Díaz, Juan. 1997 "Las modificaciones a la Ley Electoral y los comicios del '98." *Revista Rumbo* (March 24) Internet version <http://www.hispanet.com/resumen/juanbo.htm> (accessed April 1, 1997).

Dominican American National Roundtable (DANR). 2000. <http://danr.org/> (accessed February 2, 2000).

El Diario/La Prensa. 1992. "Reacciones de los líderes dominicanos." July 22, 4.

———. 1996. "Se posesiona nuevo consul dominicano." September 10, 6.

———. 1998. "Ha habido adecentamiento en la vida pública dominicana." October 6, 23.

———. 1999a. "Dominicanos que viajen a su pais podrán sacar su cédula de identidad." November 12, 13.

———. 1999b. "Ayer le toco el turno a líderes hispanos." March 23, 5.

———. 2000. "CODEX lamenta dominicanos en el exterior no tengan cédula." January 17, 12.

El Nuevo Herald (Miami, Fla.). 1998. "Desbordante apoyo a los dominicanos." October 3, 3A.

Fundación Institucionalidad y Justicia, Inc. 1993. "La Doble Nacionalidad en República Dominicana: Analisis de las Principales Propuestas Para su Adopción." Fundación Institucionalidad y Justicia, Inc., Santo Domingo. Photocopy.

Georges, Eugenia. 1984. "New Immigrants and the Political Process: Dominicans in New York." Paper presented at the conference Migrants in the City: Immigration Court, Labor Unions, and Ethnic Associations, New York University.

———. 1990. *The Making of a Transnational Community: Migration, Development, and Cultural Change in the Dominican Republic.* New York: Columbia University Press.

Glick Schiller, Nina. 1999. "Transmigrants and Nation-State: Something Old and Something New in the U.S. Immigrant Experience." Pp. 94–119 in *The Handbook of International Migration*, edited by Charles Hirschman, Philip Kasinitz, and Josh DeWind. New York: Russell Sage Foundation.

Glick Schiller, Nina, Linda Basch, and Cristina Blanc-Szanton, eds. 1992. *Towards a Transnational Perspective on Migration: Race, Class, Ethnicity, and Nationalism Reconsidered.* New York: New York Academy of Sciences.

Goldring, Luin. 1998. "The Power of Status in Transnational Social Fields." *Comparative Urban and Community Research* 6:165–95.

González, Juan. 1996. "They Cherish the Chance to Vote." *New York Daily News* May 17, 19.

Graham, Pamela M. 1996. "Re-Imagining the Nation and Defining the District: Dominican Migration and Transnational Politics." In *Caribbean Circuits: Transnational Approaches to Migration,* edited by Patricia Pessar. New York: Center for Migration Studies.

———. 1998. The Politics of Incorporation: Dominicans in New York City. *Latino Studies Journal* 9 (3): 39–64.

Grasmuck, Sherri, and Patricia R. Pessar. 1991. *Between Two Islands: Dominican International Migration.* Berkeley: University of California Press.

Guarnizo, Luis E. 1994. *"Los Dominicanyorks:* The Making of a Binational Society." *Annals of the American Academy of Political and Social Sciences* 553:70–86.

Hanson, Christopher, and Angelo Falcón. 1992. *Latinos and the Redistricting Process in New York City: An Assessment and Profiles of the New Latino Assembly, State Senate and Congressional Districts.* New York: Institute for Puerto Rican Policy.

Hartlyn, Jonathan. 1990. The Dominican Republic's Disputed Elections. *Journal of Democracy* 1 (4): 92–103.

———. 1998. *The Struggle for Democratic Politics in the Dominican Republic.* Chapel Hill: University of North Carolina Press.

Hernández, Ramona, and Francisco Rivera-Batíz. 1997. *Dominican New Yorkers: A Socioeconomic Profile, 1997.* New York: CUNY Dominican Studies Institute.

Informativo Dominicano. 1992. "Anteproyecto de ley sobre la doble ciudadania." Informativo Dominicano, Miami. Photocopy.

Itzigsohn, José, Carlos Dore Cabral, Esther Hernández Medina, and Obed Vázquez. 1999. "Mapping Dominican Transnationalism: Narrow and Broad Transnational Practices." *Ethnic and Racial Studies* 22 (2): 316–39.

Jordan, Howard. 1997. "Dominicans in New York: Getting a Slice of the Apple." *NACLA Report on the Americas* 30 (5): 37–42.

Junta Central Electoral. 2000. "Realizarán un Seminario sobre 'El Voto de los Dominicanos en el Exterior.' " Notas de Prensa, JCE <http://www.jce.do/notasdeprensa/npvotoext.htm> (accessed May 1, 2000).

Kazal, Russell A. 1995. "Revisiting Assimilation: The Rise, Fall, and Reappraisal of a Concept in American Ethnic History." *American Historical Review* 100 (April): 437–71.

Lescaille, Fernando. 1992. *Dominican Political Empowerment.* New York: Dominican Public Policy Project, Inc.

———. 1990. "The Invisible Dominicans." *New York Newsday,* September 21, 72, 74.

Levitt, Peggy. 1998. "Social Remittances: Migration Driven Local-Level Forms of Cultural Diffusion." *International Migration Review* 32 (4): 926–48.

Linares, Guillermo. 1989. "Dominicans in New York: The Struggle for Community Control in District 6." *Centro de Estudios Puertorriqueños Bulletin* 2 (spring): 77–84.

ListínUSA (New York). 1991a. "Joaquín Balaguer felicita Linares." September 25–October 1, 6.

———. 1991b. "Linares, un educador que se alzó con el triunfo." September 18–24, 3.

———. 1992. "Comisión del Congreso haré reunión sobre proyecto doble ciudadanía." November 18–24, 28.

———. 1993. "Seminario internacional en RD: Camino hacia la doble nacionalidad." December 1–7, 21–22.

———. 1994. "Nueva York: Importante plaza para partidos." March 2–8, 8.

Macchiarola, Frank J., and Joseph G. Diaz. 1993b. "Decision Making in the Redistricting Process: Approaching Fairness." *Journal of Legislation* 19:199–217.

Martin, John Bartlow. 1966. *Overtaken by Events: the Dominican Crisis from the Fall of Trujillo to the Civil War.* Garden City, N.Y.: Doubleday.

Mitchell, Christopher. 1992. *Western Hemisphere Immigration and United States Foreign Policy.* University Park: Pennsylvania State University Press.

Morawska, Ewa. 1990. "The Sociology and Historiography of Immigration." Pp. 187–238 in *Immigration Reconsidered: History, Sociology, and Politics,* edited by Virginia Yans-McLaughlin. New York: Oxford University Press.

New Orleans Times-Picayune. 1996. "Immigrant Voters Shaking Up Big-City Politics: Latinos Forming New Power Base." October 27, A12.

New York City Charter Revision Commission. 1990. "Final Report of the New York City Charter Revision Commission." Photocopy.

New York City Department of City Planning. 1992a. *Demographic Profiles: A Portrait of New York City's Community Districts from the 1980 and 1990 Censuses of Population and Housing.* New York: Department of City Planning.

———. 1992b. *The Newest New Yorkers: An Analysis of Immigration into New York City During the 1980s.* New York: Department of City Planning.

———. 1999. *The Newest New Yorkers: 1995–96.* New York: Department of City Planning.

New York Daily News. 1992. "Dominicans Get a Breath of Fresh Air: New Consul General a Big Hit." August 9, 11.

New York Newsday. 1992. "For Dominicans, This Is Not Over Yet." July 15, 39.

New York Times. 1992. "Angered by Police Killing, a Neighborhood Erupts." July 7, A1.

———. 1996a. "New York Dominicans Strongly Back Candidates on Island." June 29, 21.

———. 1996b. "U.S. Benefits Go: Allure to Dominicans Doesn't." October 12, A8.

Northern Manhattan Committee for Fair Representation (NMCFR). 1991. "A Proposal for a Dominican-Based District in Manhattan, Submitted to the New York City Districting Commission." Photocopy.

Notisur—Latin American Political Affairs. 1994. "Dominican Republic: Declaration of Balaguer Victory Does Little to Resolve Crisis." August 5.

Oficina Nacional de Planificación. 1980. *Manual de Organización del gobierno.* Santo Domingo, Dominican Republic: ONAP.

———. 1994. *Reforma del Estado: Constitución de la República.* Santo Domingo: ONAP.

PLD (Dominican Liberation Party). 1996. "Programa del Gobierno 1996–2000." <http://www.codetel.net.do/Leonel/extrajero.html> (accessed July 1, 1996).

Portes, Alejandro, Luis E. Guarnizo, and Patricia Landolt. 1999. "The Study of Transnationalism: Pitfalls and Promise of an Emergent Research Field." *Ethnic and Racial Studies* 22 (2): 217–37.

Rodríguez Pimentel, Hector. 1992. *Proyecto de Ley Tendente a Modificar La Ley #1683 de Fecha 16 de Abril de 1958, Sobre Naturalizacion.* Santo Domingo: Congreso Nacional, October 14.

Singer, Audrey, and Greta Gilbertson. 2000. "Naturalization in the Wake of Anti-Immigrant Legislation: Dominicans in New York City." Working Papers, No. 10, *International Migration Policy Program.* Washington, D.C.: Carnegie Endowment for International Peace.

Smith, Michael Peter, and Luis Eduardo Guarnizo, eds. 1998. *Transnationalism from Below.* New Brunswick, N.J.: Transaction Press.

Smith, Robert C. 1995. " 'Los Ausentes Siempre Presentes': The Imagining, Making, and Politics of a Transnational Migrant Community Between Ticuani, Puebla, Mexico and New York City." Ph.D. diss., Columbia University.

Torres-Saillant, Silvio, and Ramona Hernández. 1998. *The Dominican Americans*. Westport, Conn.: Greenwood Press.

U.S. Bureau of the Census. 1997. *March 1997 Current Population Survey*. <http://www.census.gov/population/socdemo/foreign/98/tab03–4.txt> (accessed January 15, 2000).

———. 1999. *Statistical Yearbook of the Immigration and Naturalization Service 1997*. Washington, D.C.: Government Printing Office.

Viñuales, David. 1999. "Llegamos para quedarnos." *Progreso: The Dominicans 2000 Quarterly Newsletter* 1 (fall): 1. <http://www.bls.census.gov/cps/pub/1997/for_born.htm> (accessed February 10, 2000).

CHAPTER 5

Suburban Transnational Migrants: Long Island's Salvadorans

Sarah J. Mahler

Though unbeknownst to the vast majority of New Yorkers and almost always unmentioned in popular depictions of New York's "glorious mosaic," there lives a teeming group of "immigrants"[1] from many nations—Salvadorans, Dominicans, Haitians, Koreans, Italians, West Indians—who number in the hundreds of thousands and who populate the extensive suburban tracts east of the city known as Long Island. Researchers and the public who readily acknowledge New York as the quintessential multicultural city as well as the gateway for generations of migrants to their new Promised Land are probably equally as likely to characterize Long Island as the antithesis of New York, as the bedrock of the white, middle-class mainstream. This portrait does not fit the contemporary reality; perhaps it never did. Though it is convenient and simple to divide the United States into diverse urban orbs and homogeneous suburban rings, certainly for metropolitan New York the picture is far more complex—and rich. Long Island's two counties, Nassau to the west and Suffolk to the east, exemplify a broadening national trend of ethnic and racial diversification within suburbia, particularly among those closest to the urban cores (e.g., Fong 1995). Long Island, total population some three million, is perhaps more unusual than other diversifying suburban regions because it has become a magnet for some migrants who do not follow the classic and stereotyped model of suburbanization. That is, they do not first spend years in the city and later, upon reaching some level of prosperity, resettle, according to the American dream, in suburbia. The reasons for this deviation from the model are complex and cannot be detailed in this chapter fully (see Mahler 1995 for a full discussion; Mahler 1996). What is important to underscore here is that Long Island, despite its stereotype, is at the forefront of twenty-first-century demographic and pluralistic trends. Fifty percent of the U.S.

population lives in suburbs and the numbers are growing. Suburban spaces where the so-called mainstream and the diverse newcomers must engage each other face-to-face are also growing; as they do they compel people to decide whether and how they will live together.

One important lesson established Long Islanders need to learn if they wish to have a harmonious future is that many "immigrants" are actually "transnational migrants." Conventional wisdom holds that people migrate to the United States seeking opportunities and relief from repression elsewhere, that they migrate permanently and return home only to visit, and that they and their descendants can be expected to assimilate to U.S. culture and laws over time. Many scholars take issue with these assumptions, arguing that generations of migrants, past and present, did and do not conform to this unilinear model (Foner 1999; Glick Schiller 1999; Guarnizo and Smith 1998; Wyman 1993). Nonetheless, this popular perspective is still applied to current migrants and lies at the center of debates over whether immigration to the United States should be curbed. In contrast to this unilinear model of migration—migration followed by resettlement and assimilation—scholars of transnational migration document how many migrants' lives span borders.

In this chapter I focus on one of the newest migrant groups to arrive on Long Island, Salvadorans, estimated at one hundred thousand. Most Salvadorans fled the civil war in their homeland during the 1980s and its aftermath and sought safe haven in the United States. I argue that Salvadorans live their lives transnationally; that is, they nurture a variety of ties to their communities of origin even as their day-to-day existence is largely focused on events and activities specific to Long Island. I also argue, however, that transnational migration does not develop merely through the desire of migrants to retain connections to their homelands. Transnational ties are promoted and impeded by a variety of factors, including demographic characteristics of the migrants themselves, such as education, the particular historical and structural conditions behind the migration and migrants' reception in the United States, and the level of activism displayed by the Salvadoran government. Feelings are important but they must be transformed into actions and these actions are conditioned by myriad factors endogamous and exogenous to the migrants themselves. The outcome of these actions—the development of transnational social fields—reflects these conditions as well. As in this case study, the complex interactions of these factors create serrated transnational terrains wherein the telltales of transnational connections are not evenly distributed throughout. For example as I show in this chapter, the lived reality of typical Salvadorans on Long Island is very focused on the local and is punctuated by transnational activities. In contrast, for the nonmigrant relatives and friends of these migrants in El Salvador, transnational ties are an inextricable feature of their daily life (see Guarnizo 1998 for development of quotidian life and transnational ties). This dissimilitude emerges vividly yet not contradictorily when migrants' lives are researched and documented transnationally— in their communities of origin and of resettlement.

Background to the Salvadoran Migrants on Long Island

Hundreds of thousands of Salvadorans fled their country for the United States during the years leading up to the civil war and for the decade that ensued (1979–92). During the civil war scorched earth policies, forced recruitment, terror and torture, and the appropriation of crops and livestock by both the military and the insurgents destroyed livelihoods and forced many to flee (Mahler 1995; Mahler 1996). Why did so many stream into the United States in particular? There was little historical precedent. Prior to the war, only a trickle of Salvadorans had migrated northward. The U.S. government supported the Salvadoran government and military in its war against left-wing insurgents, and so it denied Salvadorans fleeing the conflict status as refugees or asylees (Loescher and Scanlan 1986), leaving them more vulnerable to exploitation as undocumented immigrants. The answer to why so many fled to the United States is complex but reflects the geopolitical relationship between the United States and countries within its sphere of influence, particularly in the Americas. Scholars have noted that migrations are structured by colonial and neocolonial histories, bringing migrants from peripheral into core areas (e.g., Mitchell 1992; Sassen 1988). Moreover, Salvadorans were attracted to the United States by the greater economic opportunities that existed there than in El Salvador, a gap exacerbated by globalization. But the Salvadoran migration case, as in most instances of migration, is not a simple calculus of differences in economics between sending and receiving countries. Indeed, such disparities explain patterns of migration only in gross terms (e.g., Massey et al. 1998). Social networks of family and friends explain the particularities of migrations better. In the specific case of Salvadorans to Long Island, the earliest migrants relocated there for largely through chance; eventually, however, they played strategic roles in channeling the vast 1980s migration into certain nodes of opportunity on the island (Mahler 1995).

Salvadorans now comprise one of the largest immigrant populations in the United States, officially enumerated by the 1990 census at 565,000 but widely estimated by scholars at closer to 1 million (Funkhouser 1992; Mahler 1995; Montes Mozo and García Vásquez 1988). Half the population has relocated to the Los Angeles area, while 11 percent live in metropolitan New York, 9 percent in Washington, D.C., 8 percent in San Francisco, and 7 percent in Houston (Wisberg 1994). Perhaps counterintuitively, Salvadorans living in greater New York are concentrated on Long Island where they are estimated to number some 100,000.[2] The Long Islanders are predominantly people from the rural, eastern departments of the country, La Unión and Morazán in particular, whereas Salvadoran communities in other cities tend to be more representative of El Salvador's regions, social classes, and occupations (Chavez 1994; Chinchilla, Hamilton, and Loucky 1993; Funkhouser 1992; Hamilton and Chinchilla 1991; Lopez, Popkin, and Tellers 1996; Montes Mozo and García Vásquez 1988; Popkin 1995, 35–39; Rodriguez 1987). Additionally, the migration to Long Island was predominantly male until the late 1980s, reflecting the fact that men alone were forcibly recruited to serve in the civil war by both sides and often fled prior to or after serving.

Employment Niches

Salvadorans on Long Island typically labored in their homeland as poor peasants, day or permanent laborers on large farms, or seasonal laborers harvesting export commodities such as coffee, or they performed a combination of these subsistence and wage labor strategies. Even when landless, the majority owned their own modest homes located in *caseríos*—small hamlets constituting several dozen households of kin related through blood or marriage. According to oral histories of early migrants to Long Island, Salvadorans first arrived there in a trickle during the 1960s when factory and domestic work was abundant. Though these early migrants often hailed from El Salvador's middle classes, they initiated a pattern of employment in the island's poorest-paid sectors, a pattern still characterizing the migration today. To summarize an argument I develop elsewhere in greater depth (Mahler 1995, 1996), the Salvadoran migration to Long Island does not reflect classic, ecological theory where successful immigrant groups vacate inner cities for the suburbs. Rather, this case study illustrates how broader macroeconomic trends including the expansion of job opportunities to the suburbs and the shift from manufacturing to service sector employment expanded labor markets in suburbs attracting new immigrants directly to these areas (Bluestone and Harrison 1982; Sassen 1988).

Long Island's manufacturing industries flourished in the 1970s and 1980s, buttressed by military buildups during the cold war that favored major defense contractors on the island, even as manufacturing floundered in neighboring New York City. But the island's industries were bifurcated: native-born (and largely white) workers obtained higher wage and union jobs while Salvadorans, other Latin American migrants (including large numbers of Puerto Ricans), and African Americans were relegated to minimum-wage and dead-end jobs. Long Island's service industries expanded during these decades as well, raising demand for low-wage service workers in areas as diverse as child care, restaurants, and landscaping. Changing local demographics also opened employment opportunities. A drop in the birthrate in the 1970s and 1980s led to a decline in the availability of young native-born workers to take low-wage jobs at the same time that the number of elderly and two-parent working families had risen. This change escalated demand for low-cost service and factory labor, optimal niches for the newcomer Salvadorans.

Most Salvadorans on Long Island have few marketable skills because of their peasant backgrounds and tenuous legal status (described below), characteristics that proved well suited to many of the jobs created in the Long Island suburban setting. For example, they enjoy low levels of formal education, reflecting the fact that access to education in rural El Salvador has been historically limited (Reimers 1995). In a survey I conducted in 1989–90 of 202 adult Salvadoran English as a Second Language students, 32.2 percent had received less than five years of formal education and only 16.7 percent were high school graduates. Men work as landscapers, dishwashers, busboys, and assistant cooks and in factories and commercial cleaning; women work almost exclusively as domestics (child care and house cleaning) and in factories. According to the survey, men's median salary is $250 per week and women's is $200. Follow-up research I conducted during 1994–95, five years after the original fieldwork, documented little significant change in employment opportunities and practically no occupational mobility such as moving from the secondary to the primary labor force.

Legal Limbo

A principal reason behind Salvadorans' socioeconomic precariousness is their legal status. For political and historical reasons, permanent legal status has been difficult to obtain. Although nearly all Salvadorans migrated to the United States during El Salvador's civil war, they were systematically denied refugee or asylum status by the U.S. government throughout the 1980s. As a consequence, most entered and lived in the United States illegally. During 1987–88 close to 200,000 applied for permanent legal status ("green cards") through a legalization program (only 4,000 on Long Island, however) as legislated by the Immigration Reform and Control Act of 1986. During the 1980s and early 1990s, another 100,000 obtained green cards through other legal channels, but the vast majority continued to live precariously throughout the nation as undocumented immigrants (lacking authorization to work) until at least 1991. In that year and under considerable pressure from litigation, the U.S. government allowed Salvadorans to apply for Temporary Protected Status (TPS). TPS was enacted in 1990 after a decade of court cases filed against the Immigration and Naturalization Service by immigrant advocacy organizations. The organizations cited unfair denial of political asylum to Salvadorans (and Guatemalans), and their suits were resolved before trial with the offer of TPS to these national groups. Applicants received work authorizations, temporary status to stay in the United States, and the promise of being able to apply *de novo* for political asylum under a revised asylum process when TPS ended. TPS was extended several times before terminating in September 1995. At this point, those covered by TPS[3] were permitted several more months to file political asylum applications under a more equitable asylum system—but with a diminished chance of winning their petitions owing to the fact that the civil war had ceased years ago. In 1996, Salvadorans' chances were made even slimmer by the passage of the Illegal Immigrant Reform and Immigrant Responsibility Act. Among other things, the act gutted U.S. political asylum policies, precluded undocumented migrants from regularizing their status unless they returned to their homelands, and also implemented much more severe standards for the undocumented to win legal permanent residency through "suspension of deportation" (renamed "cancellation of removal"). Many Salvadorans in the late 1990s had been living continuously in the United States for over seven years and had U.S.–born children and other circumstances that could have been grounds for winning legal residency under "cancellation of removal." But the Illegal Immigrant Reform and Immigrant Responsibility Act closed this opportunity. The new legislation, as well as the anti-immigrant climate that inspired it, frightened Salvadorans on Long Island and across the country. The new legislation galvanized migrant and immigrant advocacy groups who helped usher in the passage of legislation offering limited relief, the Nicaraguan Adjustment and Central American Relief Act of 1997. This act principally affects Salvadorans by ostensibly lowering the standard for "cancellation of removal" to the pre-1996 regulations. I say ostensibly because lawyers who are filing cases on the island have found that the INS is not implementing the pre-1996 standards in many of the cases they are handling (CARECEN, personal communication). In sum, hundreds of thousands of Salvadorans still find themselves in legal peril in the United States.

Precariousness characterizes more than Salvadorans' legal status; day-to-day occurrences such as layoffs and illness, accidents, pregnancy, or the birth of a child can result in major loss of income, particularly for undocumented workers and those paid off-the-books, who are not entitled to unemployment compensation and other benefits. Moreover, during the winter many migrants on Long Island find themselves unemployed because their jobs are seasonal (e.g., landscapers and even house cleaners whose clients head south during these months). In short, Salvadorans on Long Island enjoy little security. They live in one of the country's wealthiest suburbs yet earn less than $1,000 a month according to my survey. Elsewhere I have written extensively about how disillusioned Salvadorans become with their lives on Long Island (Mahler 1995). Many regret their decision to migrate but relatively few entertain the notion of returning home permanently and few enjoy the luxury of returning temporarily. During the civil war, returning permanently was not an option for most and in the postwar era a crime wave has enveloped the country, discouraging people from returning even for visits.

Constraints on Mobility

Legal, economic and political constraints impede migrants' ability to travel back and forth between El Salvador and the United States. Perhaps the greatest obstacle is legal status. Lacking "green cards" (i.e. permanent residency), many cannot travel abroad freely and face the grim reality that if they return home, they will have to re-enter the United States illegally.[4] Such passage is expensive and dangerous. Prices for overland travel assisted by *coyotes* (smugglers) rose from $1,500 in the late 1980s to over $3,000 in the mid-1990s and now top $4,000. These are large sums of money that cannot be paid off easily with minimum wage jobs. Moreover, undocumented travel is so fraught with difficulty and danger that most informants told me they never want to go through the experience again. Mexico is notorious for its mistreatment of migrants headed for the United States, especially non-Mexican nationals (Castillo G. and Palma C. 1996; USCR 1991) and women, in particular.

Among the fortunate migrants who hold legal visas and therefore can travel with impunity, the high cost of airfare from New York ($500–$800 round trip) discourages frequent trips unless the cost is offset by converting travel into a business enterprise—such as operating as a courier. Salvadorans who fly pay a premium, because El Salvador is not a tourist nexus like the Caribbean or Mexico; it is not in a competitive market, so service is limited and expensive. Jacqueline Hagan (1994), in her study of

Mayan Guatemalans living in Houston, found that as migrants acquired legal status their involvement in transnational activities jumped dramatically. Her informants were aided as well, however, by their proximity to Guatemala. Salvadorans on Long Island are much more distant both geographically and legally. Under pressure from the United States, Mexico and Guatemala have strengthened their interdiction of undocumented migrants traveling through the isthmus and abuses are common (Castillo G. and Palma C. 1996).

Finally, Salvadorans are discouraged from returning to their homeland permanently or even temporarily by conditions of life there. During the decade of the civil war few even contemplated returning. After the peace accords were signed, I investigated their likelihood of returning and was told overwhelmingly that the aftermath of the war was perhaps worse than the war itself. Murder rates, for instance, have been comparable to those during the war (Johnson 1995). Fear still pervades people's attitudes, among Salvadorans both in the United States and in El Salvador. Many ex-combatants from both sides have turned to thievery, targeting returning migrants from the United States. Adding to the violence are thousands of gang members deported from the United States in recent years under provisions of the 1996 Illegal Immigrant Reform and Immigrant Responsibility Act. The country has been able to rebuild its infrastructure only very slowly after being severely damaged during the war, while job growth is stagnant—worst in the regions most Salvadorans on Long Island are from. Given all these inauspicious conditions in El Salvador, it is not surprising that returnees often reappear on Long Island within a year, claiming there were too few opportunities for them or that they simply could not adapt again to life in El Salvador.

The confluence of the aforementioned factors might logically suggest that the Salvadorans on Long Island achieve and nurture very few transnational links to their homeland. Indeed, in many writings on transnational migration to date, corporal mobility is depicted as an indispensable condition of migrant transnationalism (e.g., Basch, Glick Schiller, and Szanton Blanc 1994; Goldring 1996; Guarnizo 1994; Lessinger 1992; Ong 1993; Rouse 1990). Elsewhere (Mahler 1998) I have criticized this diacritic as too exclusionary of groups, such as the Salvadorans, whose own mobility is restricted. However, if they do live their lives transnationally, as I depict in the following section, then the fact that they surmount so many obstacles to do so is a testament to its importance.

The Salvadoran Transnational Social Field

Transnationalism is a highly contested area of inquiry where scholars are wrestling with its definition and objectives.[5] It does not help that the term *transnationalism* has been used in so many contexts that its definition cannot be assumed (see Guarnizo and Smith 1998; Mahler 1998). Here I employ a limited notion of transnationalism, one that relates to the activities of migrants that span borders—or transnational migration. This is the definition employed by several leaders of the field who organized a major conference to explore transnational migration in 1990.

> We have defined transnationalism as the processes by which immigrants build social fields that link together their country of origin and their country of settlement. Immigrants who build such social fields are designated "transmigrants." Transmigrants develop and maintain multiple relations—familial, economic, social, organizational, religious, and political that span borders. Transmigrants take actions, make decisions, and feel concerns, and develop identities within social networks that connect them to two or more societies simultaneously. (Glick Schiller, Basch, and Blanc-Szanton 1992, 1–2)

My approach to transnational description employs this definition broadly and then applies a research agenda that I have developed in depth elsewhere (Mahler 1998) and follow in abridged form here. Briefly, I advocate that researchers first explore holistically the transnational social fields constructed by groups of migrants; that is, they should identify and investigate as wide a variety of ties as are practiced. Then I argue for the creation of a typology beginning with a disaggregation of those ties that are practiced by large groups of transnational migrants from the case study (such as the majority) and those practiced by individuals only or by smaller groups. I further suggest that researchers analyze activities and ties by asking whether they are patterned along social characteristics, such as gender, class, age and generation, nationality, regionality, and mobility. Following this methodology reveals not only the breadth of the migrants' transnational social field but also its depth and overall topography.

Transnational Practices: The View from Long Island

By far the most widely practiced transnational activity among the Salvadorans on Long Island is the sending and receiving of letters, packages of goods (particularly clothes to El Salvador and medicines and Salvadoran cheeses from El Salvador), audio (and to a lesser extent video) cassettes, and, of course, dollars. That is, there are far more objects than people that flow through and around their transnational social field. People communicate with loved ones principally by letters; they telephone much less frequently for several reasons. Most communities of origin of the Long Island migrants have limited access to telephone services; telephone lines are scarce and cellular technology is incipient. Furthermore, telephone calls are very expensive, particularly collect calls from El Salvador, which often cost twenty dollars or more for three minutes. In contrast, letters are inexpensive and can be saved and savored; frequently I have witnessed stacks of old letters sitting prominently amid migrants' modest possessions.

How are these transnational objects delivered? Formal remittance agencies have long catered to urban residents; in the 1990s after the civil war ended they began to expand services into the countryside. But the first people to offer these services were personal couriers or *viajeros*, and they remain important in the communities of origin of the Salvadorans on Long Island. The early *viajeros* were the fortunate few to enjoy legal visas or green cards and who were willing to carry packages with them for friends and family when they traveled. The expense of travel, coupled with the risks they incurred by bringing goods for others into areas in the midst of civil warfare, inspired some to charge for their services and ultimately make a living this way. Currently, dozens of Salvadoran men and women on Long Island occupy this entrepreneurial niche, competing among themselves as well as with numerous formal remittance agencies (Mahler 1999). The *viajeros* travel between the two countries, following networks linking specific communities in one country with their corresponding communities in the other, bringing cash remittances down and letters, packages, cassettes, and fresh information back and forth. As such, they form a quintessential transnational corps. Their services range in their degree of personalism and in their sophistication, but they are used widely by migrants whose families live in the more remote areas of the country where formal remittance agencies provide limited service. Aside from the couriers there are other entrepreneurial travelers, such as petty merchants who buy goods in the United States for sale in El Salvador and long-distance haulers. Several small businesses on Long Island, for example, ship vehicles, machinery, and household belongings by tractor trailers driven overland and cargo containers loaded onto ocean vessels.

I have studied the *viajero* enterprise at length, even traveling with viajeros to El Salvador and observing their operations from both sides. The business, despite its seeming informality, is not truly small in scale. I have observed *viajeros* handle as much as $50,000 in one trip. Their efforts contribute to a staggering figure: total remittances to El Salvador from the United States are estimated to surpass $1.3 billion annually and signify the single largest source of hard currency to El Salvador (Torres A. 2000). In sum, remittances have become El Salvador's life blood and likewise for the communities of origin of the Long Island Salvadorans.

No other transnational activity practiced by the Salvadorans comes even near to being as widespread as sending letters and remittances. Aside from the abundance of remittance agencies, *viajeros*, and expensive telephone bills (calls from El Salvador are almost always made collect), other transnational linkages take some digging to find. Entertainers arrive quite regularly from El Salvador, dance bands and soccer teams in particular. Soccer is a major leisure activity among Long Island Salvadoran men, who have formed several leagues, each with a complement of locally sponsored teams. Probably the least developed aspect of this transnational social field is the media. For example, there are no radio stations that cater to the Salvadorans on the island, and Salvadorans can access only one program televised in El Salvador, an hour-long show on Salvadoran soccer that is broadcast on a local cable station one night a week. Quite in contrast, communities in El Salvador constantly hear about events in the United States by television, radio, and newspaper. Daily, these media pummel their audiences in El Salvador with information about the status of their compatriots in the United States. Newer communications technologies such as the Internet are being promoted by the Salvadoran government in its efforts to cultivate transnational ties and allegiances. For instance, millions of dollars are being invested to open technology centers in El Salvador so people can communicate by e-mail across borders. Though innovative, this state-sponsored transnational strategy is likely to fail with first-generation migrants at least on the island because most of them are marginally literate and economically too poor to afford home computers. I never saw a computer in a Salvadoran home on Long Island and saw only a couple in the Salvadorans' communities of origin. Indeed, in northeastern El Salvador people are very fortunate if they have electrical service and even rudimentary access to telephone services. In short, major infrastructural and human capital barriers—the legacy of regional underdevelopment—constrain growth of certain classes of transnational ties, technological in particular.

Another class of transnational ties frequently mentioned in the literature is hometown associations. Such associations connect communities in migrants' homelands with others in the United States and, at least ostensibly, collect monies to fund altruistic projects in the hometowns. They exemplify how transnational ties can transcend individual efforts to form more institutional linkages. I have heard of only four such associations in existence on Long Island and compared with other areas of Salvadoran settlement in the United States, such as Los Angeles, the Long Island associations are still in their infancy (e.g., Hamilton and Chinchilla 1999; Landolt, Autler, and Baires 1999; Torres A. 2000). Projects are organized and funded more ad hoc than through cultivated associations. For example, in one community on Long Island evangelical Christians from a specific sect known as the "Apostles and Prophets" funded the construction of a church in their rural village and an access road to it. Afterward, they also sponsored the installation of electrical service to the church, and church members whose homes are located along the road could pay individually for electrical service. In this case the organizers completely sidestepped local authorities to accomplish their tasks; usually hometown associations work more in tandem with the towns' mayors and other prominent figures (e.g., Goldring 1998; Hamilton and Chinchilla 1999; Landolt, Autler, and Baires 1999; Smith 1998). The blend of altruism and nepotism evident in this example highlights the need in studies of transnational activities to identify who gets involved and for what purposes. Recent comparative work on hometown associations, for example, has found that migrant entrepreneurs are much more likely to participate in these associations than are nonentrepreneurs (Luis Guarnizo, personal communication), but why they do is less well understood. Hometown associations are an interesting feature of transnational migration but one meriting careful evaluation. They do not attract participation representative of the greater migrant population and they serve interests that may not even reflect those of their constituency, especially by gender (Goldring 1996). They are relatively easy to research because they operate in public and this fact may help explain their abundant scholarly attention.

Another form of community-based assistance occurs in response to calamities such as Hurricane Mitch in 1998 and the series of devastating earthquakes in 2001. In both instances, Salvadorans on Long Island responded not only by sending remittances to their family members but also by taking up collections through churches and organizations such as the Central America Refugee Center to aid victims. Such humanitarian efforts are episodic but the fact that funds can be collected and sent reflects the greater transnational nature of the Long Island–northeast El Salvador migration.

Finally, no discussion of transnational ties linking El Salvador and the United States would be complete without addressing transnational gangs. In the 1980s, Salvadoran youth began forming gangs in large cities such as Los Angeles and Washington, D.C. These cities already had histories of gang activity and Salvadoran newcomers found it necessary to begin their own ethnic gangs in self-defense. So many members became involved in criminal activities that the United States now deports thousands of Salvadoran gang members back "home" each year after they serve their sentences in the United States. Upon deportation, some devote themselves to reconstituting their gangs on Salvadoran soil, others become conduits for transnational criminal activity linking Central America, Mexico, and the United States (Constable 1996; Johnson 1995; Jonas 1995, 6–10), and a few participate in "Homies Unidos" and other anti-gang organizations (Cruz and Portillo Peña 1998). Gangs also exist on Long Island but have arisen much more recently. A Salvadoran community organizer in Hempstead told me in 1997 that he knew of no true gangs on the island but that "posses" exist, small bands of youth, some of them transplanted gang members from other regions of the United States, who tag their turf with graffiti but are not generally involved in violent activities and crime. By 1998, police and community organizers on the island confirmed the presence of several Salvadoran gangs including one notorious gang whose local membership surpasses three hundred—La Mara Salvatrucha.

To summarize, the view of transnational migration examined solely from the vantage point of Long Island depicts a variety of practices, processes, and ties linking the Salvadoran population with individuals and communities in El Salvador. These linkages are dynamic; they are invented, re-invented, and transformed. However, I aspire to more than merely detailing a list of practices. I am interested in the degree to which people's lives are *lived transnationally*. To wit, I ask myself the research question, "What impact do transnational practices have on Salvadorans' everyday lives on Long Island?" Clearly, this question would yield a range of responses for unique individuals but my research leads me to a broad conclusion. Most Salvadorans on Long Island are consumed with their daily existence because of their precarious economic and legal situation. Consequently, transnational practices punctuate people's lives more than they dominate them. In other words, a typical person would communicate with family and friends in El Salvador through remittances, letters, and the like every few weeks or months though their thoughts surely migrate homeward far more often. Comparatively low levels of corporal mobility impede the development of stronger transnational linkages and hence of a transnational identity such as is found among Mexican, Dominican, and other transmigrant groups (e.g., Guarnizo 1994; Kearney 1995; Kyle 1995; Rouse 1992). Of course, corporal mobility is only one optic for understanding why Salvadorans, at least on Long Island, do not seem to generate deep transnational affinities and other reasons are developed further on in the chapter. What follows next, however, is a description of transnationalism visible from El Salvador, a view so divergent from the Long Island portrait that it begs its own description and analysis.

Transnational Practices: The View from the Communities of Origin

Given its rudimentary technological and transportation infrastructure and geopolitical marginalization, northeastern El Salvador would seem to be as remote from the world economy and transnational processes as any place could be. But as one's transnational gaze comes into focus, the area teems with ties to the outside, to the United States, and to Long Island in particular: Couriers arrive from and depart to the United States daily with remittances and letters; visiting migrants and returnees drive around in vehicles with U.S. license plates; and people sport tee-shirts given to them by migrant relatives with messages from the straightforward "New York: The Big Apple" to "I scored a goal at Jeremy's Bar Mitzvah party."[6] The few telephone company offices are constantly jammed with customers calling overseas; workers stated that 95 percent of all calls made are to the United States. And although in many areas television is just arriving along with electricity after years of limited service during the civil war, almost every-one has a radio and teenagers dance to a polyphonic mix of local *ranchera* (country), imported techno, and bilingual rap. Demographically, the region has staggering rates of emigration. For example, in 1997 I surveyed adolescent students and found that 95 percent of sixth to ninth graders had relatives living in the United States, averaging over six relatives per student. Moreover, 10 percent of their mothers lived in the United States, and 33 percent of their fathers. Nearly 70 percent of the students reported some family members living in New York State—by far the most traveled network. And students reported that remittances finance not only their living expenses but also their ability to study. Some 82 percent reported that remittances finance their schooling, allowing them to pursue an education instead of leaving school to work in agriculture, as was common in their parents' generation.

The most visually striking indicator of transnational ties is the construction of new and brightly painted houses made of concrete block and tiled floors. Such houses are telltale markers of migrant relatives and remittances, whereas houses made of wattle and daub or adobe with dirt floors, straw roofs, and no electricity reflect the continued poverty of non-migrant families. Detailed interviews with migrants as well as long-term residents of the Long Islanders' communities of origin document unequivocally that these transformations have been financed with migrants' remittances. Before the civil war, the population in these regions interfaced with the global economy only as marginal seasonal workers harvesting export crops such as coffee and cotton (Mahler 1995). Now to the untrained eye residents may still appear humble and Third World, but they are certainly hemispheric if not global in orientation.

Another marker of transnational ties are the scores of return migrants, overwhelmingly male, who are readily identifiable in El Salvador. They sport U.S.–style clothes and new pickups, often with license plates from the United States. They include a small number of U.S.–born children of migrants who are sent back to El Salvador to be raised by migrants' kin (usually during the labor-intensive preschool years and then returned to the United States to be educated there). More numerous are Salvadorans who enjoy legal immigrant status in the United States and who return for family and community events, such as marriages, baptisms, funerals, and village festivals. Increasingly visible are older returning migrants, generally men in their forties to sixties who fled El Salvador during the war, leaving behind their spouses and young children. With limited education and skills for advancing economically on Long Island, many of these men desired to return home—indeed their families begged them to return—but the families had also grown too dependent upon remittance income to forsake migration altogether. So, before returning, migrants first sponsor the migration of at least one child, grooming him or her in the basics of migrant life—housing and job. The children ensure that remittances will continue to flow homeward, cash that even highly self-sufficient farmers need to purchase fertilizers and pay for clothing, medical care, and so on.

The above examples point to the intergenerational reproduction of this transnational social field and in so doing they help illustrate transnational migration as a process more than the sum of events and practices. The illustration of everyday life in the communities of origin of the Long Island Salvadorans also documents the profound and pronounced effects of the migration. In contradistinction to migrants on the island whose lives are punctuated occasionally by transnational activities, their relatives and friends in El Salvador march to a transnational beat.

Contrasting Transnational Lives: Home and Abroad

Despite sharing a transnational social field, a transnational lifestyle, the lived realities of Salvadorans on Long Island contrast dramatically with those in El Salvador. On Long Island, migrants toil long hours at jobs and have little time for recreation let alone for participation in clubs, associations, and other institutional forms of outreach to their homeland. Their transnational ties consist primarily of objects that flow between themselves and their loved ones at home. A case in point is the life of Noemí Orellana.[7] Noemí earns her living on Long Island by splicing together income from selling Mary Kay cosmetics and from cooking meals for men who board in the same house she lives in. Between her work and caring for her daughter and two babies who later died from genetic disorders, Noemí has little time or resources to devote to her large family residing in El Salvador. She despairs most about her mother, who suffers from chronic health problems. Every few weeks Noemí drives to the home of a *viajero* to send a letter or two—occasionally with a modest sum inside—to her family or to pick up and pay for their letters to her.

In contrast, in the migrants' hometowns in El Salvador transnational ties bombard the senses and truly orchestrate the lifestyle of most people, such as mothers who wait desperately for that monthly remittance envelope and youth who refuse to harvest the land as they lust after the material trappings that older siblings and friends have purchased with dollars from El Norte. Typical of these residents is Flor Salvatierra. Flor's husband moved to the United States some five years ago, leaving her in charge of their six children. He found a job washing dishes on Long Island, where he works six days a week, ten or more hours a day. During a good month, Flor receives about $200 from her husband to supply her family's needs—never enough to feed, clothe, and school her brood. Flor frets constantly and calculates daily how much she believes her husband earns, how much he spends on his own needs, and why she receives so little. She monitors the arrival and departure of *viajeros* who might bring her next remittance, and she checks with neighbors and relatives for all news from the

United States. Flor's daily existence is transnationally wed to events in the United States, a world she has never seen but that she imagines constantly.

Whereas Noemí traces her origins to El Salvador but feels rooted to the exigencies of existence on Long Island, Flor is rooted to both simultaneously. Noemí may wish to return home, but she is impeded by factors largely beyond her control, factors that affect most Salvadorans on Long Island similarly. Ironically, these are also the same basic factors impeding Flor from realizing her dream of seeing the United States. First, both women are poor and have little formal education. For Flor this means that she cannot obtain a legal visa to enter the United States as a tourist because the embassy screens applications carefully to preclude entry to those most likely to stay and work illegally in the United States. Because she cannot obtain a legal visa, Flor would face paying up to ten times the cost of a plane ticket to hire a coyote and travel overland illegally (and dangerously). For Noemí, little education and low English proficiency signify poor job prospects, complicated, moreover, by her tenuous immigration status. These, in turn, limit her chances of escaping poverty, and poverty precludes her traveling home even if she could obtain legal permission to do so. Additionally, her circumstances do not permit her the luxury of getting involved in any hometown associations or other transnational civic actions.

In short, structural, legal, and socioeconomic factors constrain transnational practices for Salvadorans living throughout the social field. The constraints, in turn, produce interstices of opportunities for certain individuals, such as *viajeros*, who feel them less acutely than the majority population. *Viajeros* and other mobile individuals have played key roles in the performances of Salvadoran transnationalism, for they are a rich source of face-to-face communication. Yet it would be misleading to characterize them as the one essential ingredient of this transnational social field. In the Long Island–eastern El Salvador case study the most distinctive imprint left by transnational ties, I argue, is that left by letters, not bodies. Transnational projects such as constructing parks and refurbishing churches certainly leave an imprint as well, though one perhaps more symbolic than substantive at this point. Over the next years this relative emphasis on the flow of goods rather than people and of words more than projects is likely to change, particularly as more Salvadorans on Long Island obtain legal permanent residency and can return "home" freely and relatively inexpensively.

The Transnational Role of the Salvadoran State

Alongside the activities performed by individual migrants, small groups, and associations— transnational practices undertaken largely at the micro- and meso-levels— are efforts undertaken at the macro-level by the Salvadoran state to cultivate its expatriates overseas. These efforts are much like those of other governments in countries with high levels of emigration, both historically and contemporaneously (Basch, Glick Schiller, and Szanton Blanc 1994; Glick Schiller 1999; Guarnizo 1997), which have been termed "deterritorialized nation-state building" in some of the literature (e.g., Basch, Glick Schiller, and Szanton Blanc 1994). I prefer the terms *long-distance nationalism* (e.g., Anderson 1991; Glick Schiller 1999) or *transterritorial nation-state building,* which acknowledge the anchoring of these processes in real places even as they extend across them. Examples of such state efforts abound within the broader literature on transnational migration. In some cases, this governmental involvement reaches overseas to draw transmigrants back "home." The Philippines, for example, lures transmigrants and their wealth through a policy of tariff exoneration (Basch, Glick Schiller, and Szanton Blanc 1994, 257). The Mexican state, on the other extreme, has reached across its border into the United States for a decade through its Program for Mexican Communities Abroad. A division of the Ministry of Foreign Relations and coordinated through consulates and cultural institutes, the program intentionally foments ties among Mexican immigrants and their descendants to Mexico (Goldring 1998; Gonzalez Gutierrez 1997; Smith 1998). It works directly with hometown associations and encourages local, regional, and national Mexican politicians to court favor with their constituencies living in the United States.

Salvadoran officials and consular officers also have advocated on behalf of their citizenry resident in the United States, though their efforts can and should be examined with a careful eye to their objectives. To begin, it is important to reiterate that Salvadorans migrated to the United States and other countries in response to persecution perpetrated, largely but not solely, by their own government against them. Nonetheless, as El Salvador's dependency on remittances rose, the government implemented an activist policy with respect to the United States to keep Salvadorans from being deported and thereby insure a steady flow of remittances. Lobbying the U.S. government began in earnest in 1987, the year that the Immigration Reform and Control Act of 1986 (IRCA) became effective. IRCA offered legalization for some 200,000 Salvadorans resident in the United States, but its main purpose was to preclude undocumented migrants' access to the U.S. job market though the implementation of sanctions against employers hiring people without proper authorization. As sanctions were implemented in 1987 a great fear arose among Salvadorans that they would be massively deported. This fear reverberated across the transnational social field, stimulating a diplomatic visit by then-president of El Salvador Napoleon Duarte to Washington to make a direct appeal to President Ronald Reagan on the migrants' behalf. He argued that after nearly a decade of warfare, El Salvador was ill equipped to have hundreds of thousands of its citizens repatriated into a war-torn and economically devastated country.

The year 1987 marked the first real effort by the Salvadoran government to intervene on behalf of its transnational constituency, albeit more oriented toward protecting remittance flows that were and continue to be major factors in the country's economic health and hence its political stability (see Mahler 1999). Government officials have confided to me personally and repeatedly their concern about protecting remittance flows. In the years since Duarte's 1987 plea, each successive Salvadoran administration has made similar appeals aimed at permitting Salvadorans to remain in the United States as a measure to preserve remittances. In spring 1992 President Alfredo Cristiani met with President George Bush to discuss the impending termination of the TPS program for Salvadorans. Cristiani argued along the same lines as his predecessor that mass deportations of migrants would destabilize El Salvador, which in 1992 had finally signed peace accords but was in financial ruin. Cristiani knew his country could not absorb hundreds of thousands of returnees; moreover, the country desperately needed a steady supply of remittances to bring hard currency into the country, a necessity exacerbated by rapidly declining U.S. aid to El Salvador. Indeed, in the postwar years, U.S. aid to El Salvador fell precipitously from a high of nearly a half-billion dollars during the war to only $66 million in 1995. It is difficult to evaluate the impact of Cristiani's pleas on U.S. policy, but Salvadorans were granted extensions of TPS (later called DED or "Deferred Enforced Departure") by Presidents Bush and Clinton until the end of 1995. President Bill Clinton, succumbing to growing anti-immigrant pressures at home, then canceled the programs, arguing that Salvadorans could return without fear to their homeland. The news reverberated throughout the Long Island–eastern El Salvador transnational social field I was researching. In March 1995 as I visited the communities of origin of many of the migrants I knew from the island, I was peppered continuously with the same question: "Will the U.S. deport the Salvadorans when their work permits expire on September 30, 1995?" I knew that the answer was no, that the Immigration and Naturalization Service lacked a capacity for such large-scale round-ups, but also because the end of TPS/DED signaled the beginning of Salvadorans' rights to file new asylum applications.[8]

What neither I nor community groups who assisted the Salvadorans in filing the new applications anticipated was the next maneuver by the Salvadoran government. In 1995 under a mandate from the new president, Armando Calderón Sol, Salvadoran consulates began establishing assistance centers for asylum applicants. What ensued borders on the absurd. Salvadoran consular officials started helping migrants who had fled repression from the government to prepare testimonials documenting how they fled the repression and feared future repression if they returned home! When I called the Salvadoran embassy about the new program, I was told that the Salvadoran government was not trying to influence U.S. immigration policy. In an interview with the *New York Times*, however, the ambassador to the United States defended the practice by stating, "We're helping [the migrants] stay where they want" and added: "The problem is that there is not enough work to give these people in [El Salvador]. That's the main problem. If they go to El Salvador they will not be part of the economy" (Carvajal 1995). Her statements underscore how Salvadoran diplomatic policy with regard to the United States has become wed to and indeed is driven by migration. This orientation represents quite an inversion from the years of the war when cold war rhetoric and concerns dominated relations.

Another chapter in this strange diplomatic history began in summer 1997. With the passage in 1996 of the Illegal Immigration Reform and Immigrant Responsibility Act the U.S. Congress made it much more difficult to win asylum and apply for "cancellation of removal" (which would result in legal residency). As the changes in asylum and suspension policy began to be enforced in 1997, the Salvadoran diplomatic corps went into action anew. President Calderón Sol made a lengthy and pointed lobbying trip to Washington in June 1997. Salvadoran newspapers splashed his diplomatic maneuvers on the front page for a week; their president would return a hero or the country was doomed. This time the tactics employed were more involved. Calderón Sol retained a U.S. law firm to help him lobby and he did not limit his contacts to the U.S. president but lobbied key congressional figures as well. Additionally, the Salvadoran Embassy embarked on a public relations campaign to burnish the image of Salvadorans in the United States and to endear Salvadoran migrants themselves to their national heritage. Among other items, a colorful pamphlet was prepared called "Salvadorans in the US," which unabashedly presents Salvadoran migrants as a "very united and hard working people" and sings the praises of migrant good deeds at home (Embassy of El Salvador, n.d.). Embassy officials began cultivating relations with local hometown associations and immigrant centers, co-sponsoring beauty pageants and other fund-raisers. Calderón Sol visited several Salvadoran communities on his U.S. trip and his embassy personnel have attended meetings of the Salvadoran American National Network, a coalition of organizations serving Salvadorans in the United States. In September 1997, Calderón Sol and the network sponsored the first annual "Immigrant Week" to formally recognize the contributions of transmigrants to El Salvador's welfare. The week has become institutionalized since. Other notable efforts at transterritorial nation-state building include the inauguration of the "Casa de la Cultura" in Los Angeles and government sponsorship of a large convention in Los Angeles for community and business groups in June 1998. Another convention on Long Island took place in 1999 followed by more in Washington. Officials stated to me that their aims included improving relations between the government and its expatriate community and fomenting Salvadoran identity so that the second generation—those born in the United States—will not forsake their ancestors' homeland and thereby discontinue sending remittances.

The most recent phase of activism by the Salvadoran government is the October 1999 inauguration of an outreach program housed in the Ministry of Foreign Relations, much like the Program for Mexican Communities Abroad. The Office for Attention to the [Salvadoran] Community Abroad was formally established with the stated goal of "incorporating the Salvadoran community abroad into the process of national development by fortifying its links with El Salvador through national initiatives" (Government of El Salvador 1999). In an interview, the director further elaborated the office's mission as consisting of four areas of concern: (1) cultural exchanges and the integration of Salvadorans living abroad in the process of conceptualizing and promoting Salvadoran identity; (2) economic and commercial interchanges, as well as tourism linking Salvadoran communities abroad and in El Salvador; (3) efforts to work on collaborative projects to benefit social development in El Salvador, such as relations between the government and hometown associations; and (4) promotion of initiatives to strengthen the Salvadoran communities living abroad, such as distributing information about opportunities to legalize their status. A case in point is the publication by the Salvadoran government in 1999 of a brochure on the Nicaraguan Adjustment and Central American Relief Act of 1997 (NACARA) that was distributed to immigrants' rights centers by Salvadoran consulates. Entitled "La Ley NACARA Paso a Paso para los Salvadoreños," this document was designed to encourage Salvadorans to legalize their status and stay in the United States. Of course, the subtext is that those who stay will continue to remit homeward.

In sum, the development of transnational social fields is very much affected by the actions of states as well as those of individuals and groups. Activist governments, quite naturally, raise questions about their purposes. Salvadoran government policies, for example—most notably persecution—lie at the root of the Salvadoran migration itself. In an era when many nations depend on remittances for fiscal solvency (de la Garza, Orozco, and Baraona 1997; Orozco 1999; Torres A. 2000), defense of migrants can easily cloak more elite interests. Again, El Salvador is a case in point. In the postwar years El Salvador remains dependent on U.S. dollars but the source of the currency has shifted from U.S. economic and military aid to remittances to the shoulders of migrants—people who not too long ago were expendable for the state. Not surprisingly, the state has begun befriending the migrants, though many remain skeptical of these attentions. The peculiar history of the Salvadoran state and its expatriates abroad underscores the argument that transnational migration is best understood as an evolving process.

Conclusion

In this chapter I discuss a group of Salvadorans who migrated directly to the Long Island suburbs of New York and thus, for the most part, did not first settle in the city only to flee for the suburbs after acquiring a modicum of financial success. Suburbs have overtaken inner cities as the residential heart of the U.S. population and international migrants increasingly flock there too, but investigations of these new suburbanites have not kept pace. I show, however, that these Salvadoran migrants sustain ties to their communities of origin even as their day-to-day existence is largely focused on events and activities specific to Long Island. The lives of their relatives and friends in their homeland are also transnationalized, arguably more than for the migrants themselves.

These transnational ties do not develop in a vacuum but are promoted and impeded by a variety of factors, some endogamous and others exogenous to the migrants themselves, including migrants' human capital and access to travel home, the policies and actions of governments in the "host" and "sending" countries, and the economic and social conditions of the localities that this transnational migration is anchored in. These factors must be seen as a subset of a comprehensive list; there is not space here to address them all. The explication of all factors is not essential, however, to highlight the broader theoretical issue addressed here, that transnational processes are not "deterritorialized." Rather, in the words of Luis Guarnizo and Michael Smith (1998,11), "Transnational practices, while connecting collectivities located in more than one national territory, are embodied in specific social relations established between specific people, situated in unequivocal localities, at historically determined times." Transnational migration also does not develop merely through the desire of migrants to retain connections to their homelands or of states to make claims on them. Feelings, though important, must be transformed into actions. The outcome of these actions and the forces that affect them is the development of transnational social fields. As in this case study, the complex interactions of these factors create uneven and constantly changing transnational landscapes wherein the telltales of transnational connections are not uniformly distributed throughout.

Notes

Acknowledgments: I would like to thank Robert C. Smith for his helpful comments on the first draft of this chapter. Gratitude is also expressed to the University of Vermont and the University of Pittsburgh for funding much of the research cited in this chapter.

1. Following Roger Rouse (1995), I disdain the use of the word im-*migrant* for it implies that the migration is unidirectional and permanent. Studies that address transnational migration, such as this one, often question this assumption and, hence, this term. I substitute the more generic term *migrant* for instances where many scholars would inflect it as *immigrant* or *emigrant*. I employ these latter terms when appropriate to specific contexts.

2. This estimate is based on information received from local service organizations. The 1990 Census counted 19,152 Salvadorans. An alternate enumeration I conducted in a Salvadoran neighborhood on Long Island found an extremely high undercount on the order of 80 percent (see Mahler 1993) largely because of unusual housing arrangements. I believe that more than 20,000 Salvadorans are resident on Long Island but there is no way of obtaining an exact number, and so I have selected the estimate of those often cited by organizations on the island.

3. Not all Salvadorans who qualified for TPS applied—only 187,000 of the estimated 1 million Salvadorans in the United States applied for the program and even fewer renewed their status in later years.

4. The only option for legal travel available to many Salvadorans on Long Island occurred during the year TPS was granted. In 1991–92, the Immigration and Naturalization Service (INS) allowed Salvadorans with TPS to return home briefly to attend to emergencies. Now INS severely restricts extending such permission.

5. There are numerous metaphors in existence to signify transnational spaces. In another paper (Mahler 1998) I discuss each and argue for the adoption of "social field" as used in Basch, Glick Schiller, and Szanton Blanc 1994. I feel that this metaphor is most commodious and least confusing; however, it is not without its own drawbacks.

6. The information on this t-shirt has been slightly altered to protect the identity of the celebrants.

7. All personal names of informants used herein are pseudonyms.

8. Though TPS was designed to be temporary and controllable, by 1992 INS acknowledged that it was incapable of deporting large numbers of Salvadorans if and when TPS ended (*New York Times* 1992). Undertaking mass round-ups and deportation hearings and paying for migrants' passage home would be too costly. Ironically, the INS recognized that TPS/DED had permitted large numbers of undocumented migrants to obtain the very documents they would need to stay in the United States even if their legal status were suspended. That is, they acquired legal Social Security numbers and driver's licenses and other forms of identification that were sufficient under IRCA's provisions to "prove" their right to obtain employment. TPS/DED helped document the undocumented but it did not provide permanent legal status.

References

Anderson, Benedict. 1991. *Imagined Communities: Reflections on the Origins and Spread of Nationalism*. London: Verso.

Basch, Linda, Nina Glick Schiller, and Cristina Szanton Blanc. 1994. *Nations Unbound: Transnational Projects, Postcolonial Predicaments, and Deterritorialized Nation-States*. Langhorne, Pa.: Gordon and Breach.

Bluestone, Barry, and Bennett Harrison. 1982. *The Deindustrialization of America: Plant Closings, Community Abandonment, and the Dismantling of Basic Industry*. New York: Basic Books.

Carvajal, Doreen. 1995. "Salvador Helps Refugees Filing for Asylum in U.S." *New York Times*, October 27, A1.

Castillo G., Manuel Angel, and Silvia Irene Palma C. 1996. *La emigración internacional en Centroamérica*. Guatemala, Guatemala: FLACSO.

Chavez, Leo. 1994. "The Power of the Imagined Community: The Settlement of Undocumented Mexicans and Central Americans in the United States." *American Anthropologist* 96:52–73.

Chinchilla, Norma, Nora Hamilton, and James Loucky. 1993. "Central Americans in Los Angeles: An Immigrant Community in Transition." Pp. 51–78 in *In the Barrios: Latinos and the Underclass Debate*, edited by Joan Moore and Raquel Pinderhughtes. New York: Russell Sage Foundation.

Constable, Pamela. 1996. "'Peace Summit' Aims to Steer Young Latinos from GangØConstable, Pamela. 1996. "'Peace Summit' Aims to Steer Young Latinos from Gang

Violence." *Washington Post*, April 4, B5.

Cruz, José Miguel, and Nelson Portillo Peña. 1998. *Solidaridad y violencia en las pandillas del gran San Salvador: más allá de la vida loca*. San Salvador: UCA Editores.

de la Garza, Rodolfo, Manuel Orozco, and Miguel Baraona. 1997. *Binational Impact of Latino Remittances*. Claremont, Calif.: Tomás Rivera Policy Institute.

Embassy of El Salvador. n.d. *Salvadorans in the U.S.* Washington, D.C.: Embassy of El Salvador in the United States.

Foner, Nancy. 1999. "What's New About Transnationalism? New York Immigrants Today and at the Turn of the Century." *Diaspora* 6:355–75.

Fong, Timothy P.. 1995. *The New Suburban Chinatown: The Remaking of Monterrey Park, California*. Philadelphia: Temple University Press.

Funkhouser, Edward. 1992. "Mass Emigration, Remittances, and Economic Adjustment: The Case of El Salvador in the 1980s." In *Immigration and the Work Force*, edited by George J. Borjas and Richard B. Freeman. Chicago: University of Chicago Press.

Glick Schiller, Nina. 1999. "Transmigrants and Nation-States: Something Old and Something New in the U.S. Immigrant Experience." In *The Handbook of International Migration*, edited by Charles Hirschman, Philip Kasinitz, and Josh DeWind. New York: Russell Sage Foundation.

Glick Schiller, Nina, Linda Basch, and Cristina Blanc-Szanton. 1992. *Towards a Transnational Perspective on Migration: Race, Class, Ethnicity, and Nationalism Reconsidered*. New York: New York Academy of Sciences.

Goldring, Luin. 1996. "Gendered Memory: Reconstructions of the Village by Mexican Transnational Migrants." Pp. 303–29 in *Creating the Countryside: The Politics of Rural and Environmental Discourse*, edited by E. Melanie DuPuis and Peter Vandergeest. Philadelphia: Temple University Press.

———. 1998. "The Power of Status in Transnational Social Spaces." Pp. 165–95 in *Transnationalism from Below*, edited by Michael P. Smith and Luis E. Guarnizo. New Brunswick, N.J.: Transaction.

Gonzalez Gutierrez, Carlos. 1997. "Decentralized Diplomacy: The Role of Consular Offices in Mexico's Relations with Its Diaspora." Pp. 49–67 in *Bridging the Border: Transforming Mexico–US Relations,* edited by Rodolfo O. de la Garza and Jesús Velasco. Lanham, Md.: Rowman and Littlefield.

Government of El Salvador. 1999. "Dirección General de Atención a la Comunidad en el Exterior." <http://www.rree.gob.sv/sitio\sitio.nsf/pages/dgace>

Guarnizo, Luis E. 1994. "*Los Dominicanyorks:* The Making of a Binational Society." *Annals of the American Academy of Political and Social Sciences* 533:70–86.

———. 1997. "The Emergence of a Transnational Social Formation and the Mirage of Return Migration Among Dominican Transmigrants." *Identities* 4:281–322.

———. 1998. "The Rise of Transnational Social Formations: Mexican and Dominican State Responses to Transnational Migration." *Political Power and Social Theory* 12:45–94.

Guarnizo, Luis E., and Michael P. Smith. 1998. "The Locations of Transnationalism." Pp. 3–34 in *Transnationalism from Below,* edited by Michael P. Smith and Luis E Guarnizo. New Brunswick, N.J.: Transaction.

Hagan, Jacqueline Marie. 1994. *Deciding to Be Legal: A Maya Community in Houston.* Philadelphia: Temple University Press.

Hamilton, Nora, and Norma Stoltz Chinchilla. 1991. "Central American Migration: A Framework for Analysis." *Latin American Research Review* 26:75–110.

———. 1999. "New Organizing Strategies and Transnational Networks of Guatemalans and Salvadorans in Los Angeles." University of California, San Diego. Unpublished report.

Johnson, Tim. 1995. "Return of War Refugees Reshapes Rural Salvador." *Miami Herald,* May 30, A1.

Jonas, Susanne. 1995. "War and Peace in the Central American Diaspora in California." Center for Multiethnic and Transnational Studies, University of Southern California. Unpublished report.

Kearney, Michael. 1995. "The Effects of Transnational Culture, Economy, and Migration on Mixtec Identity in Oaxacalifornia." Pp. 226–43 in *The Bubbling Cauldron: Race, Ethnicity, and the Urban Crisis,* edited by Michael Peter Smith and Joseph R. Feagin. Minneapolis: University of Minnesota Press.

Kyle, David. 1995. "The Transnational Peasant: The Social Structures of Economic Migration from the Ecuadoran Andes." Ph.D. diss., Johns Hopkins University.

Landolt, Patricia, Lilian Autler, and Sonia Baires. 1999. "From Hermano Lejano to Hermano Mayor: The Dialectics of Salvadoran Transnationalism." *Ethnic and Racial Studies* 22:290–315.

Lessinger, Johanna. 1992. "Investing or Going Home? A Transnational Strategy Among Indian Immigrants in the United States." Pp. 53–80 in *Towards a Transnational Perspective on Migration: Race, Class, Ethnicity, and Nationalism Reconsidered,* edited by Nina Glick Schiller, Linda Basch, and Cristina Blanc-Szanton. New York: Annals of the New York Academy of Sciences.

Loescher, Gil, and John A. Scanlan. 1986. *Calculated Kindness: Refugees and America's Half-Open Door, 1945 to the Present.* New York: Free Press.

Lopez, David, Eric Popkin, and Edward Telles. 1996. "Central Americans at the Bottom, Struggling to Get Ahead." Pp. 279–304 in *Ethnic Los Angeles,* edited by Roger Waldinger and Medhi Bozorgmehr. New York: Russell Sage Foundation.

Mahler, Sarah J. 1993. *Alternative Enumeration of Undocumented Salvadorans on Long Island.* Upper Marlboro, Md.: U.S. Bureau of the Census.

———. 1995. *American Dreaming: Immigrant Life on the Margins.* Princeton: Princeton University Press.

———. 1996. *Salvadorans in Suburbia: Symbiosis and Conflict.* Boston: Allyn and Bacon.

———. 1998. "Theoretical and Empirical Contributions Toward a Research Agenda for Transnationalism." Pp. 64–100 in *Transnationalism from Below,* edited by Michael P. Smith and Luis E. Guarnizo. New Brunswick, N.J.: Transaction.

———. 1999. "The Salvadoran Remittance Business: The Role of Trust in a Transnational Enterprise." Paper presented at the American Sociology Association meetings, Chicago, August.

Massey, Douglas S., Joaquín Arango, Graeme Hugo, Ali Kouaouci, Adela Pellegrino, and J. Edward Taylor. 1998. *Worlds in Motion: Understanding International Migration at the End of the Millennium.* Oxford: Clarendon Press.

Mitchell, Christopher, ed. 1992. *Western Hemisphere Immigration and United States Foreign Policy.* University Park: Pennsylvania State University Press.

Montes Mozo, Segundo, and Juan García Vásquez. 1988. *Salvadoran Migration to the United States: An Exploratory Study.* Washington, D.C.: Georgetown University, Center for Immigration Policy and Refugee Assistance, Hemispheric Migration Project.

New York Times. 1992. "For Some in U.S., Peace in El Salvador Brings Fear." March 11, A14.

Ong, Aihwa. 1993. "On the Edge of Empires: Flexible Citizenship Among Chinese in Diaspora." *Positions* 1:745–78.

Orozco, Manuel. 1999. *Remittances and Development Activities in Four Countries.* Claremont, Calif.: Tomás Rivera Policy Institute and InterAmerican Dialogue.

Popkin, Eric. 1995. "Guatemalan Hometown Associations in Los Angeles." Center for Multiethnic and Transnational Studies, University of Southern California. Unpublished report.

Reimers, Fernando. 1995. *La Educación en El Salvador de Cara al SIglo XXI: Desafíos y Oportunidades.* San Salvador: UCA Editores.

Rodriguez, Nestor. 1987. "Undocumented Central Americans in Houston: Diverse Populations." *International Migration Review* 21:4–25.

Rouse, Roger. 1990. "Mexican Migration and the Social Space of Postmodernism." *Diaspora* 1:8–23.

———. 1992. "Making Sense of Settlement: Class Transformation, Cultural Struggle, and Transnationalism Among Mexican Migrants in the United States." Pp. 25–52 in *Towards a Transnational Perspective on Migration: Race, Class, Ethnicity, and Nationalism Reconsidered,* edited by Nina Glick Schiller, Linda Basch, and Cristina Szanton-Blanc. New York: New York Academy of Sciences.

———. 1995. "Questions of Identity: Personhood and Collectivity in Transnational Migration to the United States." *Critique of Anthropology* 14:351–80.

Sassen, Saskia. 1988. *The Mobility of Labor and Capital.* Cambridge: Cambridge University Press.

Smith, Robert C. 1998. "Transnational Localities: Community, Technology, and the Politics of Membership Within the Context of Mexico and U.S. Migration." Pp. 196–240 in *Transnationalism from Below,* edited by Michael P. Smith and Luis E Guarnizo. New Brunswick. N.J.: Transaction.

Torres A., Federico. 2000. "Uso Productivo de las Remesas Familiares y Comunitarias en Centroamérica." Mexico, DF: Comisión Económica para America Latina y el Caribe (CEPAL).

U.S. Committee for Refugees (USCR). 1991. *Running the Gauntlet: The Central American Journey Through Mexico.* Washington, D.C.: American Council for Nationalities Service.

Wisberg, Morton. 1994. "Specific Hispanics." *American Demographics,* February, 44–49.

Wyman, Mark. 1993. *Round-Trip to America: The Immigrants Return to Europe, 1880–1930.* Ithaca: Cornell University Press.

CHAPTER 6

Rules of the Game and Game of the Rules: The Politics of Recent Chinese Immigration to New York City

Zai Liang

On January 12, 2000, the *New York Times* reported that fifteen men from China were found in the giant freighter called the *Cape May* in Seattle, Washington. Three bodies of dead men were also found inside the cargo container (Verhovek 2000). These illegal Chinese migrants, the survivors and the dead, had just finished a fifteen-day journey inside the cargo container from Hong Kong to Seattle. A week earlier, thirty stowaways on cargo ships were found in Long Beach, California (Whitaker 2000). This series of episodes of stowaways in containers on cargo ships signals a new strategy of smuggling Chinese immigrants to the United States, often with the final destination of New York City. In June 1993, the tide of illegal Chinese immigration to the United States received national attention when the ill-fated *Golden Venture* ran aground off the coast of Queens in New York City, with 286 people aboard (Fritsch 1993). Since then, despite increased efforts by U.S. law enforcement agencies, the illegal Chinese immigrants continue to arrive in the United States by whatever means possible.

Neither an extremely large nor a new phenomenon, the recent flow of illegal Chinese immigrants nevertheless presents an interesting study. Most of the illegal migrants are from China's Fujian province in the southeast coast. It is notable that this area in particular has enjoyed economic advancement during China's transition to a market-oriented economy, with a rate of increase in per capita income that greatly exceeds the average rate for the rest of China (Liang and Ye 2001). Clearly, Fujianese are not fleeing poverty. Although most of these immigrants arrive in the United States without legal status, many of them end up staying and working, mostly in the New York metropolitan area. As a result, Fujianese are becoming the new blood in Manhattan's Chinatown and have had a major impact on the social, political, and economic life of the Chinese community. How was it possible for the Fujianese, who know nothing of the political and economic systems of the United States and who are without legal status, to manage to stay in the United States? In contrast to undocumented migrants from other countries, such as Mexico, these migrants are handled by smugglers (snake-heads) who are part of a very sophisticated and global network. They not only "take care" of undocumented migrants during the voyage but also coach them in what to say once they arrive in the United States in order to maximize their chances of staying. Often the smugglers suggest that Fujianese migrants seek asylum, because once individuals ask for asylum in the United States, it is very likely that they will not be deported immediately and will at least be given a hearing. Thus, asylum has become an important channel for undocumented Fujianese to stay in the United States. This chapter begins with some theoretical discussion of the role of the state and state immigration policies. Following the description of political asylum policies in the United States, it explores the extent to which recent Fujianese migrants to the United States take advantage of rules of the game, turning asylum policy in their favor. Finally, it discusses policy options for stemming the tide of illegal Fujianese immigration to the United States.

The Role of the State and State Immigration Policies

Partly because of an increase in international migration, the past two decades or so have witnessed significant advancement in international migration research, in both theoretical endeavors and empirical investigations. In a recent assessment of international migration, Douglas Massey (1999b) identifies four theoretical perspectives that can be fruitfully used to understand international migration: world system theory, social capital theory, neoclassic economic theory, and the theory of cumulative causation. These theories capture major forces that generate and sustain international migration: penetration of capital markets, motivations of individual actors, and social and economic structures that connect sending and receiving areas (Massey 1999b). However, there has been inadequate attention paid to the effect of the state and state policies on international migration (Massey 1999a; Portes 1999). U.S. immigration policy, from the early days of Chinese Exclusion Act of 1882 and Gentlemen's Agreement of 1907 to the recent enactment of the Illegal Immigration Reform and Immigrant Responsibility Act of 1996, has been a constant force in our decisions about whom we shall welcome to this country.[1] Given the large amount of immigration legislation passed since the late nineteenth century, it is surprising to see the lack of research in this area. Although there is still some question about how much immigration policies affect the trends of immigration during specific periods (e.g. Massey 1995; Zolberg 1999), research on the state and state systems has recently been identified as one of the promising areas of immigration research for the twenty-first century (Portes 1999).

Several scholars have theorized the role of the state and state immigration policy formation (Freeman 1992; Massey, 1999a; Zolberg, Suheke, and Aguayo 1986). Aristide Zolberg, Astri Suheke, and Sergio Aguayo (1986) show that international factors often play an important role in triggering refugee flows; thus a theoretical framework of refugees should reflect the transnational nature of the process. Gary Freeman (1992) addresses the politics of migration policies in developed countries. In dealing with the efficacy of state policies, Douglas Massey (1999a) identifies five factors that can be linked to the state capacity to implement restrictive immigration policies: strength of bureaucracy, demand for entry, strength of constitutional protections, independence of judiciary, and tradition of immigration. Although Massey's work provides crucial theoretical guidance in search of sources of state capacity on immigration policy, sorting out these issues through empirical realities is often a challenging exercise. Thus, Alejandro Portes (1999) remarks that one of the important questions at the center of the discussion regarding the role of the state should be, "How is it that, in the face of widespread public opposition to the continuation of large-scale immigration, governments in the receiving countries have proven unable or unwilling to prevent it?" (31). So far, theoretical work has focused on factors and forces that generate the rules that govern immigration policies. What is often ignored is how rules and regulatory policies are actually implemented. In particular, how immigration policies are perceived and used by immigrants to generate perhaps unintended consequences is another critical question. As the case of undocumented Fujianese migrants demonstrates, the rules of immigration are designed by the state to achieve certain objectives, such as rationalizing the immigration or asylum processes, but they can be used by potential immigrants to serve their own purposes, that is, entering and staying in the United States, that would not otherwise be possible.

Rules of the Game: U.S. Refugee and Asylum Policies

The idea of providing a safe heaven for people who suffer persecution (based on race, religion, or political ideology or for other reasons) has a long history in the United States. George Washington once stated, "The bosom of America is open to receive not only the opulent and respectable stranger but the oppressed and persecuted of all nations and religions: whom we shall welcome to a participation of all our rights and privileges, if by decency and propriety of conduct they appear to merit the enjoyment" (quoted in Tienda and Liang 1994, 331). Indeed, U.S. immigration history is full of groups that came to the United States for religious freedom: the British Quakers and the French Huguenots during the earlier period of immigration and Jews in the twentieth century. Gradually, however, the commitment to welcoming the persecuted has been superseded by a systematic policy governing the admission of refugees and asylees.[2] And now, the "bulk of contemporary refugees . . . are produced by war and by the systemic processes of authoritarian regimes or by a combination of both" (Zolberg 1987, 21). U.S. refugee policy has been particularly effective in bringing thousands of people from Vietnam and Cuba who otherwise could have suffered persecution because of changes in political regimes. U.S. refugee and asylum policy sometimes also targets specific domestic policies in the immigrant country of origin. In 1997, the U.S. Congress passed legalization that provides legal grounds for claiming asylum if Chinese can claim that they have been persecuted or have a well-founded fear of persecution because of their violation of China's one-child policy (Dugger 1997). The unintended consequence of this legalization, however, is that it actually provides a means for thousands of illegal Chinese immigrants to come to the United States.

Game of the Rules: Unintended Consequences of Political Asylum Policy

With the rise of undocumented migration from Fujian, China, a social science literature is quickly emerging (Chin 1999; Liang 2001; Liang and Ye 2001; Myers 1997; Smith 1997). Peter Kwong (1997), a long-time observer and activist in New York's Chinatown, sees the recent surge in illegal immigration from Fujian as driven by the search for cheap labor by U.S. employers. He further asserts that the large number of entering Fujianese has deteriorated the working conditions in Chinatown. Ko-lin Chin (1999) is the first to systematically collect information from undocumented immigrants. Because of the sensitive nature of the subject, Chin chose the snowball-sampling technique to draw his sample, mainly in Manhattan's Chinatown. Stressing the social organizational aspect of human smuggling, Chin's work sheds significant light into the smuggling process. Zai Liang and Wenzhen Ye (2001) identify several factors that are closely linked to the recent surge in Fujianese immigration to the United States: the historical legacy of Fujianese emigration, seafaring culture, penetration of market forces in recent years, and the involvement of smuggling organizations.

Previous efforts by social scientists suggest several factors that explain the process of coming to the United States. Clearly, the existence of a smuggling network is instrumental in solving many logistic problems. It is also well established that the large number of Fujianese immigrants already in the New York metropolitan area attracts more and more people into the migration process. With the expansion of a community of Fujianese immigrants and the emergence of service providers and Fujianese organizations, adaptation becomes easier with each influx. However, previous research on Fujianese immigration gave short shrift to the question of how undocumented Fujianese who were detected by Immigration and Naturalization Service (INS) officers managed to avoid deportation. The question is important because large numbers of Fujianese immigrants who arrived in the United States in recent years are undocumented. Although both Ko-lin Chin (1999) and Peter Kwong (1997) note that many Fujianese applied for political asylum, neither author treats it as an important instrument to facilitate Fujianese immigrants' permanent stay in the United States. According to Chin (1999), among the three hundred undocumented Fujianese migrants he interviewed, about 80 percent applied for political asylum. I argue that the current political asylum process in the United States has many loopholes that Fujianese immigrants are able to take advantage of so that they can stay in the United States regardless of whether their political asylum application is approved.

The Process of Applying for Asylum

When an individual arrives at the port of entry and asks for political asylum, he or she normally is sent to an INS detention center. Before 1997, asylum seekers were detained at the port of entry and scheduled for an exclusion hearing. The Illegal Immigration Reform and Immigrant Responsibility Act of 1996 modified the asylum procedures, effective April 1, 1997 (Department of Justice 1999). Under the new law, the process of asylum involves two steps. The first step is for asylum officers to conduct credible-fear interviews with asylum seekers: "The purpose of the interviews is to determine whether aliens might have credible fear of persecution and thus be eligible to apply for asylum before an immigration judge" (Department of Justice 1999, 75). Applicants tend to provide very emotional accounts of their lives, and INS officers, knowing the kinds of risk these applicants have taken to make it to the United States, are usually quite sympathetic. Therefore, with few exceptions, applicants are deemed to be reasonable candidates for asylum and are given the opportunity to present their case to an immigration judge in court, who will make a decision whether to grant asylum. Applicants who are turned down in the screening interview may request an appeal before an immigration judge. Once asylum officers decide an asylum applicant is a bona fide applicant, he or she can be released with a bond. Many Fujianese enjoy the benefit of having relatives already in the United States who can put up the money for bond. Before applicants can be released and given a hearing date, however, they must sign a legal paper agreeing to meet the following three conditions: (1) they will appear at the court on time; (2) they will notify the INS if their address or telephone number changes; and (3) should the location of their court hearing changes, they will appear at the newly designated court location. Most Fujianese are more than happy to sign this paper because they are so eager to be released. Applicants are given a work permit to make sure that they can support themselves during the waiting period before the court hearing (Chin 1999). Contrary to a common misperception, most undocumented Fujianese do appear in the court, because it is a win-win situation: it costs them almost nothing and once in court they have a chance of being granted political asylum and working legally.[3] Even if they are denied asylum, they still have a chance of appeal.

Major Causes for Asylum for Fujianese

The most frequently cited claim by Fujianese immigrants for asylum is China's one-child policy. The policy was implemented in the late 1970s as a nationwide campaign to reduce China's huge population. The policy has undergone some major changes in recent years. The most important change is the policy that allows peasants to have second baby if the first baby is a girl (Wang 1996).[4] Following is a typical story that was told by an asylum seeker from Fujian. Mr. Chen, a man in his mid-twenties was living with his girlfriend in China when a routine medical examination revealed that she was pregnant.[5] Both Chen and his girlfriend agreed that she should have an abortion because they felt that they were not ready to have a baby. However, the event took a ugly turn. Without their knowledge, a doctor inserted an intra-uterine device during the abortion operation. Later, on learning what had been done Chen went to complain to officials at the local family planning clinic. But his efforts were in vain. The local government threatened that if he and his girlfriend persisted in appealing this case they would be arrested to prevent further damage to the party and cadre elite. To avoid being persecuted by the local government, Chen got in touch with a local smuggler and came to the United States. His girlfriend came with him because she was afraid that the news of her pregnancy without marriage (*wei hun xian yun*) would spread in the local community and she would be condemned by fellow villagers.

Stories told by married people seeking asylum are similar to Chen's. Consider the case of Mr. Li, a peasant from rural Fujian. Li is in his forties. He and his wife have two daughters. The local family planning program officers, believing that the couple was planning to have another baby, asked Li to undergo sterilization surgery to make sure his wife would not become pregnant again. Li was very worried that he might not be able to work if he underwent such an operation and decided to come to the United States.

Lack of religious freedom is also frequently cited as the reason for seeking asylum. Fujian province is known as the "silk road on the sea" because its seaports have long been used for trade. Thanks to this openness to the outside world, Fujian attracted Christian missionaries in the nineteenth century. Nonetheless, although this religious legacy was revitalized during the era of China's economic reform, Christianity is not yet a mainstream religion and most people in Fujian are either atheists or Buddhists. One of the asylum applicants, Mr. Yang, told INS officers that he is a Christian and did not have religious freedom in Fujian. He reported the following incident to back up his claim. Visitors to Fujian are usually drawn to the many elegantly designed temples (mostly for Buddhists) in the province. From time to time, temples need to be renovated. Yang said that one day a local cadre asked him to donate money to help renovate a local temple. Being a Christian, Yang was very reluctant to contribute any money and his attitude angered local cadres and fellow villagers. As time passed by, his relationship with them deteriorated and eventually he decided to leave China to search for religious freedom in the United States.

Another cause for seeking asylum is the search for sexual freedom by those who are gay because China still treats homosexuality as a disease. Recently, Fujianese also claimed that they are persecuted by the Chinese government because they practice Falun Gong, a blend of traditional slow-motion exercises, ancient Eastern philosophies, and the beliefs of its founder, Li Hongzhi, who now lives in New York City (Rothenthal 2000). The Chinese government has declared the Falun Gong an "evil cult" (*World Journal* 1999f) and its members are prohibited from practicing together, although some still practice individually, mostly at home.

Political Asylum as a Channel of Immigration

The cases described in the previous section could all be genuine cases; the only problem is that some versions of them have been told many times by many applicants. I argue that most undocumented Fujianese political asylum applications are fraudulent and political asylum is simply an instrument to achieve the objective of staying in the United States.

Even before Fujianese arrive at the port of entry, they are couched by smugglers that if they are caught by U.S. law enforcement officers, the first thing they should say is that they want to apply for political asylum. In this sense, smugglers are transnational agents who make connections between immigrant-sending and immigrant-receiving communities. Their role in the process of migration is not only to persuade potential migrants to take the risks to migrate but also to maximize the chances of their staying in the United States. In fact the words *political asylum* are among the first English words migrants learn to speak. These words are so powerful that, once they are spoken, it is very difficult to repatriate Fujianese back to China. A twenty-three-year-old female migrant cited in Chin's book is a case in point. When detained at Kennedy International Airport and questioned about her fake documents, she reported to Chin: "I told him, as instructed by my snakehead, 'I am married. I already have a child, and I am now pregnant. The Chinese government was about to force me to have an abortion,' and so on and so forth. It was really a joke" (Chin 1999, 189).

Substantiating the argument that most Fujianese seek political asylum as a convenient means for gaining legal status in the United States are two patterns that emerge from an analysis of asylum application data prepared by the INS for the years 1984, 1995, and 1997. The first finding is that the rate of approval for asylum applicants from China has been very low. In 1984 the rate of approval for political asylum was only 5.3 percent (Department of Justice 1986).[6] The approval rate for asylum applicants from China increased to 12.0 percent in 1995 and declined to 5.8 percent in 1997 (Department of Justice 1997, 1999). This is clear evidence that, in the minds of immigration judges, the majority of the asylum applicants from China are not qualified to stay. The second pattern is that the rate of approval for asylum applicants from China is significantly lower than the rate of approval for asylum applicants from all countries. For example, in 1995, the approval rate for asylum from all countries was 20 percent, compared with the 12 percent for China. In 1997, the contrast is even more striking: the approval rate for asylum applicants from all countries was 19 percent, again compared with 5.8 percent for applicants from China.

This argument is further confirmed by findings in Chin's study (1999). In his interviews with three hundred undocumented Fujianese migrants located in New York City's Chinatown, Chin asked respondents for their reasons for immigrating to the United States. Sixty-one percent of the respondents answered making money. Only 9 percent answered avoiding China's one-child policy and 1 percent answered seeking religious freedom. Clearly making money was the biggest incentive for most Fujianese to come to the United States.

The case for political asylum has also been played into the ever-changing climate of

China's domestic politics and U.S.-China relations. The situation regarding Falun Gong illustrates the transnational character of asylum, as argued by Zolberg and colleagues (1986). On April 25, 1999, the practitioners of Falun Gong staged a ten-thousand-person sit-in in front of Beijing's Zhongnanhai compound, where many Chinese leaders reside. The Chinese government sees the Falung Gong as a source of potential trouble and a major threat to the regime's stability (*People's Daily* 2000) and since the demonstration has conducted aggressive campaigns against the group. Some leaders of the group have been arrested, raising concern in the U.S. government about violations of human rights. Some Fujianese, however, see the Chinese government's campaign against Falun Gong as new grounds for seeking political asylum. For many, these grounds are not legitimate. According to an article in the *World Journal* (1999e, f), in Fujian, a series of training schools for Falun Gong began to emerge in 1998. These underground training schools are designed to issue documents certifying that the bearer has completed training in Falun Gong. The document costs about four dollars. Undocumented Fujianese who are already in the United States can even receive "indirect training" and obtain a certificate that can be used in applying for political asylum. The *World Journal* gave as an example Mr. Lin, an undocumented immigrant living in New York City, who asked his wife to get a Falung Gong training certificate and used it to apply for political asylum. For those who are not able to get a certificate, other methods of fabricating an association with Falung Gong are available. During a protest in front of the United Nations organized by New York–based Falun Gong practitioners, many people with no connections to Falun Gong showed up eager to have their pictures taken with the demonstrators, hoping this evidence can be used someday for political asylum applications (*World Journal* 1999f). Recent evidence suggests smugglers also tap into this new issue of Falun Gong. One group has successfully smuggled well over four hundred Fujianese to Canada and the United States, and all the migrants were told to apply for political asylum because of Chinese government's persecution of Falun Gong members (*World Journal* 1999d). Some INS officials worry that the potential to seek asylum for membership in the Falun Gong may cause another big wave of human smuggling from China. On a recent visit to China's Fujian and Guangdong provinces, Jean M. Christiansen, regional director for INS, warned that only 13 percent of mainland applicants were granted political asylum and that Falun Gong members will be considered only "case-by-case" (*AMN* 2000).

Zealous Supporters of China

If, as many Fujianese claim, they are genuine applicants for asylum, one would expect that they will be very anti-China and the Chinese government once they are granted political asylum. Animosity toward the sending country is common among most other refugee communities. The most prominent example is the Cuban American community in Miami, whose anti-Castro sentiment was clearly manifested in the custody case of the Cuban boy Elián Gonzáles. But the Fujianese are anything but anti-China. In fact, the growing presence of Fujianese immigrants in Manhattan's Chinatown has changed the way China is perceived there. For a long time, Chinatown residents celebrated only the "double 10" holiday, October 10, the National Day of the Republic of China, established in 1911. Before China started opening up to the outside world in 1978, most people in Chinatown were anti–Communist China. With the entry of large numbers of Fujianese in Chinatown, however, in 1995 for the first time, Chinatown celebrated the China National Day of October 1. The celebration was due in no small measure to the backing of influential Chinatown Fujianese and Fujianese organizations (Kwong 1997). Fujianese organizations were also instrumental in organizing the celebration activities of Hong Kong's return to China in summer 1997. A casual survey of the groups most actively involved in the China Day parade in 1997 revealed that the Committee to Celebrate the Return of Hong Kong was chaired by Kai-shing Wong, of Fujianese descent and president of the United Fujianese Association and the Fukien-American Association. (Lii 1997). In addition, Steven Wong, spokesman for many Fujianese associations, walked in the first row of the celebration parade. Several major immigrant community organizations featured prominently in the parade, including Changle, Fuqing, Pingtan, and Lianjiang, all counties or cities in Fujian province, are the major communities that have been sending thousands of undocumented migrants to the New York metropolitan area. Furthermore, Fujianese in New York have strong connections not only with China in general but also with local government in Fujian. In November 1999, on a visit to New York's Chinese community, Pan Xincheng, deputy governor of Fujian province, was reported to have received a warm welcome at a banquet hosted by a local Fujianese community organization (*World Journal* 1999c).

Fujianese migrant organizations also frequently invite officials from the Chinese Consulate in New York City and Chinese representatives from the United Nations to join events sponsored by local community organizations. Once Fujianese migrants have a foothold in the New York region they tend to establish local organizations based on their community of origin in Fujian province. Most community organizations established in recent years are a result of the large flow of immigrants from Fujian. With few exceptions, whenever Fujianese establish a new community organization or celebrate the anniversary of a Fujianese community organization, Chinese officials are invited and often make some keynote speeches during the ceremony. In the month of April 2000 alone, Chinese officials in the New York area attended three community organization celebration events sponsored by local Fujianese immigrant groups.

Conclusion and Policy Options

This chapter focuses on the relationship between U.S. asylum policy and illegal migration and argues that the U.S. asylum policy is a magnet for attracting immigrants to the United States. The role of the state and state immigration policies are important topics that have not received sufficient attention from students of international migration (Massey 1999b; Portes 1999). In addition, how immigration policies are perceived and used by potential immigrants is even less understood. I tackle a small piece of the puzzle by examining U.S. asylum policy. Using the case of recent undocumented migrants from China's Fujian province, I suggest that U.S. asylum policy is closely linked to the rise of recent immigration from Fujian because, by claiming persecution from the Chinese government, most Fujianese end up staying in the United States. The "trick" has worked so well that many Fujianese now believe that once they land on the American soil, they are here to stay.

The successful stories of previous waves of Fujianese who claimed for asylum are very likely to be used continuously by smugglers as teaching materials when they prepare for smuggling the next waves of immigrants. This technique will spread out from earlier Fujianese immigrant cohorts to potential new immigrants from China. Thus, unless there is a major change in U.S. asylum policy and its implementation procedures, it is almost certain that we will see increasing immigration from Fujian province and perhaps other provinces as well, using asylum as a shelter for permanent settlement in the United States.

The "game of the rules" played by smugglers and Fujianese immigrants creates transnationalization of asylum policy in three ways. One is that smugglers are transnational agents who disseminate knowledge and tricks about asylum policy among potential migrants and thus facilitate settlement of Fujianese immigrants. Second, the "game of the rules" is also a transnational process as U.S.–China relations are constantly thrown into play. Thus, when the U.S. government expressed concern over potential human rights issues regarding Falun Gong practitioners, smugglers were quick to capitalize on the issue and make it a top priority for political asylum claims. Third, the entry of a large number of Fujianese immigrants in New York City began to change the dynamics of transnational policies. Initially political asylum seekers, the Fujianese immigrants have become active supporters of China and have helped transform transnational politics in Chinatown from anti-China to pro-China.

The issue of migrants' abusing the right to seek asylum in the United States also involves Canada. Recently, the United States stepped up Coast Guard patrol efforts to intercept ships carrying undocumented Chinese migrants. The idea is to intercept the ships and return them to China before they reach the United States and before anyone can claim asylum. Perhaps in response, smugglers increasingly use Canada as a transit country. Once these undocumented migrants arrive in Canada either by boat or by airplane they apply for refugee status and then disappear during the one-year review period required in Canada (Brooke 1999; *World Journal* 1999c). Most of them will be smuggled across the boarder to the United States, with the destination of New York City. The issue has ignited a big national debate about Canadian's immigration policy and the topic was even mentioned during Canadian government officials' diplomatic meeting with Chinese foreign minister Tang Jiaxuan in August 1999 (Brooke 1999; *World Journal* 1999b, d).

Similarly, the work of Rosemarie Rogers (1992) suggests that policy makers in Western Europe also show a growing concern with this problem, although Chinese are not the only abusers of asylum seekers in this region. Rogers stated: "The general assessment is that most applicants hope to use the system as a surrogate immigration channel. If their claim is rejected, they have nevertheless had the opportunity of living and perhaps working in the host country for several months or years, and, . . . after a negative decision most of those who wish to do so succeed in staying on illegally" (1992, 1122). Thus, this discussion of the "game of the rules" has much broader implications. In order to reduce the abuses of asylum policies, several European countries, including Britain, France, Austria, and the Netherlands, have recently tightened asylum policies (Freeman 1992; Lyall 2000).

In the wake of the *Golden Venture* episode in 1993, President Bill Clinton declared that illegal migration and human smuggling are threats to national security, and he ordered federal law enforcement agencies to combat the problem (Kwong 1997). Eight years have gone by, the human smuggling trade from China continues to thrive, and the newspapers continue to report incidents of the discovery of cargo stowaways. Clearly more needs to be done. A natural conclusion from this study is that with the Cold War over, the United States should rethink and redesign asylum policy so that abuse of the system can be minimized.

A realistic and comprehensive policy regarding undocumented immigration from China to the United States should begin with an effort to understand why international migration happens in the first place. As argued by Massey (1998), three fundamental forces are responsible for the rise in international migration throughout the world: market consolidation, human capital formation, and social capital formation. In the case of China the effect of market transition on international and social capital formation are particularly relevant. Since 1978, China has been moving toward opening its society and joining the world economy. The recent agreement with the United States on the terms for China's joining the World Trade Organization further signals China's determination. The integration of China into the world economy has had a tremendous impact on local communities in China, especially in communities where growth and development are most active, such as Fujian province. The penetration of market forces has generated opportunities, but also rising inequality, risks, uncertainties, and insecurity among traditional households. Under such conditions, households in China are eager to search for new ways to protect themselves against risk and uncertainty. Thus, sending a household member to the United States has become a common strategy in Fujian. At the same time, with the progressive expansion of interpersonal networks between migrants and nonmigrants, immigrant "success" stories are sent back and tips about how to get in and stay in the United States are exchanged with the sending communities, encouraging further emigration from Fujian (Liang 2001).

As China's market transition further deepens in both urban and rural areas, more risks and uncertainties will be created and more households are likely to decide to send someone abroad. The smuggling fee of forty thousand U.S. dollars may be high, but in the minds of many potential migrants, it can be paid off within a few years of hard work: then they can start saving and send money home. As Chin (1999) argues, some Chinese will attempt the illegal journey no matter what the cost. In the light of this fact, I suggest the following course of action.

First, U.S. law enforcement agencies need to coordinate antismuggling efforts with the Chinese and other transit countries' government with the objective of targeting smugglers. Human smuggling is a transnational operation and it must be dealt with as such. However, given the extremely lucrative nature of human smuggling, we must be realistic about how much we can expect to achieve in this regard as our experience of the war on drugs attests.

Second, major changes are needed in the U.S. asylum policy. Given the current prevalence of abuse of asylum policies, INS officials should carefully scrutinize asylum applicants and deport all fraudulent applicants. As the preceding discussion points out, the problem with the current asylum policy is that even if people are denied asylum, they are still able to stay. By implementing this "get tough" policy, however, we may encounter some difficult moral dilemmas. For example, in October 1999 the Chinese government announced more punitive policies against undocumented migrants. The new Chinese law calls for heavy fines and an increase in the term of imprisonment from two weeks to one year (*AMN* 2000).

Third, we need to create alternative channels for Fujianese to come to the United States. One possibility is to negotiate with China and create a temporary worker program, targeting major immigrant-sending communities in Fujian province.[7] Providing a legal channel for migrants to come to the United States will help them avoid illegal channels and reduce the human smuggling market. This temporary worker program would not be implemented in non–immigrant-sending communities because doing so may introduce more migrants in the future. Temporary worker visas could be valid for three years and renewable only once in a lifetime. These temporary migrants are likely to send back home enough remittances to stimulate economic development in the sending communities. Another possibility is to increase the immigration quota for China from the current twenty thousand to forty thousand. Twenty thousand is an absurdly low number given China's enormous population size and high demand from potential migrants to come to the United States. Massey (1998) makes a similar suggestion for a policy aimed at Mexico in order to reduce flow of undocumented Mexicans to the United States.

These policies, if implemented, are likely to reduce (though perhaps not eliminate entirely) the market for human smuggling from China to the United States. They will certainly minimize the abuses of the U.S. asylum policy for protecting human rights and justice. In the short run, these policies will introduce more Chinese migrants to the United States than what the current immigration law allows. But in the long run, the United States will certainly help to reduce the human suffering associated with smuggling, eliminate the incentives for illegal migration from China, and ease China's integration to the world economy.

Notes

Acknowledgments: This research was supported, in part, by the National Institute of Child Health and Human Development (1R29HD34878–01A2) and PSC-CUNY Research Award Program, whose support is gratefully acknowledged. I also thank Robert Smith and Dean Savage for helpful comments on an earlier version of this chapter.

1. It should be noted that, before the implementation of the First Quota Law of 1921, the restriction of immigration applied only to potential immigrants of Asian origin, not of European or other origins (Tienda and Liang 1994).

2. *Refugee* is defined as "any person who is outside his or her country of nationality who is unable or unwilling to return to that country because of persecution or a well-founded fear of persecution" (Department of Justice 1997, A.3–9). The difference between a refugee and an asylee is that the asylee is either already in the United States or at the port of entry.

3. There is an exception. For Fujianese who arrive in Canada, the percentage of asylum applicants appearing in court is rather small, around 47 percent in the first half of 1999 (Brooke 1999). Once released, most Fujianese will try to cross the border to the United States rather than wait for their court hearing.

4. Although this policy is clearly an institutional form of gender discrimination, the reality is that son preference is so strong among Chinese peasants, they will try to have a second baby regardless of the policy.

5. All names are fictional. Interviews with Fujianese migrants were conducted by the author and his assistant during 1998–99.

6. The approval rate for political asylum is calculated by dividing the total number of applicants granted during the fiscal year by the sum of following numbers: total number of applicants granted, total number of applicants denied, and total number of applicants otherwise closed.

7. I am aware of the long-term consequences of such a temporary migrant program (see Massey and Liang 1989). However, I believe that the overall benefits of such a program in the case of China outweigh the potential disadvantages.

References

Asian Migration News (AMN). 2000. "Intensified Campaign Against Illegal Migration." February.

Brooke, James. 1999. "Vancouver Is Astir over Chinese Abuse of Immigration Law." *New York Times*, August 29, L8.

Chin, Ko-lin. 1999. *Smuggled Chinese: Clandestine Immigration to the United States*. Philadelphia: Temple University Press.

Dugger, Celia W. 1997. "Dozens of Chinese from 1993 Voyage Still in Jail." *New York Times*, February 3, A1.

Freeman, Gary P. 1992. "Migration Policy and Politics in the Receiving States." *International Migration Review* 26:1144–67.

Fritsch, Jane. 1993. "One Failed Voyage Illustrates Flow of Chinese Immigration." *New York Times*, June 7, A1.

Kwong, Peter. 1997. *Forbidden Workers: Illegal Chinese Immigrants and American Labor*. New York: New Press.

Liang, Zai. 2001. "Demography of Illicit Emigration from China: A Sending Country's Perspective." *Sociological Forum*, December (forthcoming).

Liang, Zai, and Wenzhen Ye. 2001. "From Fujian to New York: Understanding the New Chinese Immigration." Forthcoming in *Human Smuggling: Comparative Perspective,* edited by David Kyle and Rey Kaslowski. Baltimore: Johns Hopkins University Press.

Lii, Jane H. 1997. "The New Blood in Chinatown." *New York Times,* "The City," June 22.

Lyall, Sarah. 2000. "Fortress Britain to Asylum Seekers." *New York Times,* April 27, A10.

Massey, Douglas S. 1995. "The New Immigration and Ethnicity in the United States." *Population and Development Review* 21 (3): 631–52.

———. 1998. "March of Folly: U.S. Immigration Policy after NAFTA." *The American Prospect,* no. 37 (March–April).

———. 1999a. "International Migration at the Dawn of the Twenty-first Century: The Role of the State." *Population and Development Review* 25 (2): 303–22.

———. 1999b."Why Does Immigration Occur?" Pp. 34–52 in *The Handbook of International Migration: The American Experience,* edited by Charles Hirschman, Philip Kasinitz, and Josh DeWind. New York: Russell Sage Foundation.

Massey, Douglas S., and Zai Liang. 1989. "The Long-Term Consequences of a Temporary Worker Program." *Population Research and Policy Review* 8:199–226.

Meyers, Eytan. 1995. "The Political Economy of International Migration Policy: A Comparative and Quantitative Study." Ph.D. diss., University of Chicago.

Myers, Willard H. III. 1997. "Of Qinging, Qinshu, Guanxi, and Shetou: The Dynamic Elements of Chinese Irregular Population Movement." Pp. 93–133 in *Human Smuggling: Chinese Migrant Trafficking and the Challenge to America's Immigration Tradition,* edited by Paul J. Smith. Washington, D.C.: Center for Strategic and International Studies.

People's Daily. 2000. "Officials from the State Council Answered Questions from Reporters of 'Wen Wei Pao' on Falun Gong." April 20.

Portes, Alejandro. 1999. "Immigration Theory for a New Century: Some Problems and Opportunities." Pp. 21–33 in *The Handbook of International Migration: The American Experience,* edited by Charles Hirschman, Philip Kasinitz, and Josh DeWind. New York: Russell Sage Foundation.

Rogers, Rosemarie. 1992. "The Future of Refugee Flows and Policies." *International Migration Review* 26 (4): 1112–43.

Rothenthal. 2000. "China Seizes 100 in Sect Trying to Celebrate Anniversary." *New York Times,* April 26, A8.

Smith, Paul J., ed. 1997. *Human Smuggling: Chinese Migrant Trafficking and the Challenge to America's Immigration Tradition.* Washington, D.C.: Center for Strategic and International Studies.

Tienda, Marta, and Zai Liang. 1994. "Poverty and Immigration in Policy Perspective." Pp. 331–64 in *Confronting Poverty: Prescriptions for Change,* edited by Sheldon H. Danzinger, Gary D. Sanderfur, and Daniel H. Weinberg. Cambridge: Harvard University Press.

U.S. Department of Justice. Immigration and Naturalization Service. 1986. *Statistical Yearbook of Immigration and Naturalization Service, 1984.* Washington, D.C.: Government Printing Office.

———. 1997. *Statistical Yearbook of Immigration and Naturalization Service, 1995.* Washington, D.C.: Government Printing Office.

———. 1999. *Statistical Yearbook of Immigration and Naturalization Service, 1997.* Washington, D.C.: Government Printing Office.

Verhovek, Sam Howe. 2000. "Deadly Choice of Stowaways: Ship Container." *New York Times,* January 12, A1 and A19.

Wang, Feng. 1996. "A Decade of the One-Child Policy: Achievements and Implications." Pp. 97–120 in *China: the Many Facets of Demographic Change,* edited by Alice Goldstein and Wang Feng. Boulder, Colo.: Westview Press.

Whitaker, Barbara. 2000. "Immigrant Smuggling Draws New Attention." *New York Times*, January 4, A14.

World Journal. 1999a. "Canadian Lax Immigration Policy Facing Challenge." September 12, A1.

————. 1999b. "Canada Uses Diplomatic Measures to Stop Human Smuggling." September 10, B1.

————. 1999c. "Fujianese Immigrants Have Banquet in Honor of Deputy Governor of Fujian Pan Xincheng." November 14, C3.

————. 1999d. "The Lesson from the Recent Wave of Smuggled Chinese in Canada." Editorial. August 15, A2.

————. 1999e. "Training Session for Falun Gong in China." November 21, A1.

————. 1999f. "Undocumented Migrants Use Falun Gong for Political Asylum." September 6, C1.

Zolberg, Aristide R. 1987. "Wanted But Not Welcome: Alien Labor in Western Development." Pp. 36–74 in *Population in an Interacting World*, edited by William Alonso. Cambridge: Harvard University Press.

————. 1999. "Matters of State: Theorizing Immigration Policy." Pp. 71–93 in *The Handbook of International Migration: The American Experience*, edited by Charles Hirschman, Philip Kasinitz, and Josh DeWind. New York: Russell Sage Foundation.

Zolberg, Aristide R., Astri Suheke, and Sergio Aguayo. 1986. "International Factors in the Formation of Refugee Movements." *International Migration Review* 20 (2): 151–69.

CHAPTER 7

Gendered and Racialized Circulation-Migration: Implications for the Poverty and Work Experience of New York's Puerto Rican Women

Dennis Conway, Adrian J. Bailey, and Mark Ellis

Puerto Rican women living in New York City represent a segment of a transnational community with some of the highest rates of poverty on the U.S. mainland. An important component of this poverty is employment experience. Latinas had labor force participation rates approximately 5 percent lower than non-Latinas in 1980 and 1990 (Perez and de la Rosa Salazar 1993, 193). Among Latinas, Puerto Rican women have especially low labor force participation rates, although these rates have not always been so low (Bean and Tienda 1987). In both 1950 and 1960, Puerto Rican women had higher participation rates than total U.S. females, but the decade of the 1960s saw a significant drop in the Puerto Rican labor force participation rate from 36.3 percent in 1960 to 29.8 percent in 1970 (Cooney and Warren 1979), a decline that continued through the 1980s (Bean and Tienda 1987).

The principal goal of this chapter is to theorize how the gendered and racialized circulation strategies of Puerto Rican women contribute to their poor economic standing in the United States. Human capital and underclass frameworks both suggest that migration selectivity partially accounts for the high rates of poverty in areas of traditional outmigration. The idea is that migration creates concentrated pockets of poor people, such as Puerto Rican women in New York, as other members of the group leave for greener pastures. In our view the principal flaw in this explanation is the absence of any consideration of the gendered and racialized context in which migration decisions are made. Migration is a process that originates in households with distinctive gender roles and unequal gender relations (Alicea 1997; Ellis, Conway, and Bailey 1996). As such, the poverty of Puerto Rican women in New York cannot be fully understood without reference to the way in which their ability to work, circulate, or engage in other strategies to improve their economic lot is gendered. In addition, there is little question that an understanding of Puerto Rican women's migration and poverty is incomplete without recognition of the additional disadvantage wrought by racialized labor and housing markets. Racist exclusion in New York may encourage circulation-migration by those who seek opportunity or escape from oppression elsewhere; it also increases the likelihood of poverty for those who do not move.

Thus, we believe a better understanding of the relationship between poverty relations and circulation-migration in New York City's Puerto Rican community will be gained from an account that builds on the racialized and gendered context in which they make migration decisions. Transnational scholarship has potential value for organizing such an alternative migration and poverty framework because it suggests ways in which material (and nonmaterial) conditions in immigrant transnational communities are linked to the social networks that connect individuals with opportunities (Smith 1997). Since our work seeks to describe the gendered and racialized nature of these network processes, we believe it can make a useful contribution to the corpus of scholarship that is attempting to explain the uneven distribution of poverty in immigrant communities and its relation to migration.

We think transnational theory is underdeveloped, however, with respect to understanding the importance and complexity of circulation migration in transnational communities (Conway 2000). International migrants use migration as a strategy to maximize individual or family social and economic well-being. They continuously assess their strategies in response to life-course events, structural economic change, and their own prior mobility experiences. Eventually, migration may become culturally embedded—an accepted, indeed expected, part of a transnational group's way of life—as movement to and from the original sending community becomes regularized. We argue in this chapter for a more detailed and thorough understanding of these mobility strategies in transnational communities and, in particular, for recognition of the role of gender and "race" in their construction. An examination of how these strategies are sensitive to gender and "race" will yield a more thorough account of poverty in transnational communities than that offered by alternative explanatory frameworks.

The remainder of the chapter falls into four sections. First, we critique the behavioral model of migration implicit in human capital and underclass accounts of migration consequences. Second, we argue that transnational scholarship needs to develop more nuanced accounts of the gendered nature of international migration strategies. Third, we propose a framework that combines behavioral insights into circulation migration strategies with gendered and racialized perspectives on the lives migrants lead within transnational communities. Fourth, we illustrate this alternative perspective with an empirical account of the complex relations between migration and employment experience for Puerto Rican women using a pooled sample of island-born and mainland-born

Puerto Rican women. We conclude with a summary and suggestions for future research on circulation-migration and economic well-being in transnational communities.

Migration and Its Connection to Puerto Rican Poverty

Demand-side explanations of poverty in the United States emphasize the importance of economic restructuring over the past three decades. These accounts explain the plight of Puerto Rican women in the labor market by reference to the precipitous decline of the manufacturing sector in New York City in general, and the downsizing of the textile industry in particular (Waldinger 1986, 1996; Wright and Ellis 1996). However, other immigrant groups have also arrived during periods of economic stagnation (for example, Cubans) and not suffered the same degree of impoverishment as Puerto Ricans. This inconsistency has led many researchers to link individual-level characteristics of Puerto Rican migrants to economic standing by using human capital frameworks (after Sjaastad 1962).

Thus, a popular explanation for the poor work record of Puerto Rican women on the mainland refers to their relatively unfavorable personal characteristics for employment. Grasmuck and Grosfoguel 1997 reports that Jamaican and Haitian women's incorporation into the New York economy is relatively successful when compared with Hispanic-Caribbean experiences of Dominicans and Puerto Ricans, alluding to the former group's common stocks of social capital, their initial higher educational attainments, higher occupational levels, and group heterogeneity as contributing factors of advantage.

Underclass scholarship has also implied that migration, and circulation migration in particular, may be directly associated with the low rates of labor force participation among Puerto Ricans. Indeed, several scholars have considered William Julius Wilson's underclass model for portraying Puerto Rican experiences in the United States (Wilson 1987; for Puerto Rican examples see Moore and Pinderhughes 1993; Tienda 1989; Tienda and Jensen 1986; for a more general discussion of the Latino case see Massey 1993; Moore 1989). Wilson argued that high rates of African American poverty in certain Chicago neighborhoods were linked to processes of economic restructuring and de-industrialization in the Rust Belt, selective out-migration, and an intensification of separation between the very poor and mainstream institutions and information. Falcón and Gurak 1994 argues that Puerto Rican migration has the effect of assembling in New York a negatively selected group of Puerto Rican women. The authors' explanation is that island-born women who are less educated and more likely to have experienced marital disruption are disproportionately attracted to and retained in New York. Also there is an out-migration from New York of Puerto Rican women who are positively selected on human capital characteristics.

However, there are misgivings about attempts to link migration and Puerto Rican poverty through underclass scholarship. First, empirical evidence from Galster and Santiago 1994 and Santiago and Galster 1995 questions the implicit link between central city location and Puerto Rican poverty. Second, Wilson's thesis is based on the historical and geographical experience of a limited number of African American communities, many in the Midwest. Chicago is not New York City. Indeed, New York's standing as a major immigrant gateway suggests that parallels with cities in the Midwest may be overdrawn (Enchautegui 1992; Melendez 1993). New York is the site of several transnational communities, including Puerto Rican settlements, that exhibit complex links between migration and economic outcomes (Smith 1997). In short, critics contend that underclass arguments oversimplify the composite of historical, cultural, and economic factors that contribute to Puerto Rican poverty (see Darder 1992; Hernandez 1990; Massey 1993; Moore and Pinderhughes 1993).

Third, culture of poverty arguments underestimate the pervasive effects of race and gender discrimination that are felt in labor and housing markets in the United States. Torres 1992 demonstrates that island-born Puerto Rican women suffer more wage discrimination than any other gender-nativity group of Puerto Ricans, holding constant human capital differences. Ortiz 1996 describes how Puerto Rican women have historically suffered ethnic discrimination in the garment industry in New York City. Borges-Mendez 1993 implies that employers may not retain (or hire) workers who expect to spend extended periods away from work because of personal and familial commitments in Puerto Rico. In this case, the act of circulation is negatively related to employment, because circulators are thought to lack the commitment to holding a steady job.

To these criticisms of underclass-led attempts to link migration and poverty we would add our own concerns about the behavioral model of migration that is implicit in both underclass and human capital formulations. Both theoretical frameworks suggest a simplified model of migration that sees migrants moving for overwhelmingly economic motives. As the historical and contemporary records suggest, however, migrants move for a complex suite of economic, social, cultural, and political reasons (Castles and Miller 1993; Wyman 1993). Furthermore, migrants often move in response to their own previous experiences of migration, that is, there is strong cumulative causation in migration networks (Massey 1990b).

We next consider an important recent drift in international migration scholarship that gives greater attention to these noneconomic and cumulative or recursive features of life in immigrant communities. Focusing on the construction of simultaneous daily lives in two or more places, transnational scholars probe the links between transmigration and the basis of community. Parts of this scholarship deploy economic sociology concepts to consider how material relations evolve in transnational communities. Because this chapter concerns itself with poverty relations we limit our discussion of the transnational literature to these accounts.

The Material Constitution of Transnational Communities

Much recent attention has been given to the central role of "transmigration" in fostering the basis of transnational communities in the United States (see Basch, Glick Schiller; and Szanton Blanc 1994; Glick Schiller, Basch, and Blanc-Szanton 1992; Kearney 1995; Levitt 1997; Rouse 1991). For Basch and colleagues (1994, 7–10), "transmigrants take actions, make decisions, and develop subjectivities that connect them simultaneously to two or more nation-states." Glick Schiller, Basch, and Szanton Blanc 1995 posits that three historically conjoining circumstances now encourage immigrants to live transnational lives. These are, first, general processes associated with the global restructuring of capital, second, the rise of racism directed at immigrants, and third, the demands of allegiance to a nation-state exacted from immigrants.

How, then, do transmigrants contribute to the material practices that constitute the basis of simultaneous daily lives? Descriptions of transmigrant material practices typically focus on flows of remittances from destination sites of economic production to origin areas. Many transnational communities remit large sums of capital to kin and community in origin regions (Durand, Parrado, and Massey 1996). This capital exchange creates opportunities for entrepreneurship, and the rise of courier services, financial intermediaries, and the like characterize transnational communities. Other niches—immigration lawyers, telephone offices, and travel agencies are prominent examples—also arise in connection with the construction of simultaneous lives (Jokisch 1997). Indeed, some authors view the operation of labor markets within transnational communities as examples of ethnic enclaves that permeate transnational, rather than metropolitan, spaces (Glick Schiller, Basch, and Szanton Blanc 1995).

Efforts to understand such material relations in transnational communities draws on scholarship in economic sociology that emphasizes the facilitatory and constrictive role of social networks (Grosfoguel and Cordero-Guzmán 1998). Social networks influence economic outcomes in ways specific to ethnic groups and local areas (Smith 1997). For example, on the basis of their work among two different Mexican transnational populations, Zabin (1994) and Mountz and Wright (1996) suggest that gender constructions restrict the access that potential women migrants have to economic spaces of production in the United States. However, Alicea (1997) highlights the complex articulation of gender relations between Puerto Rico and the United States and criticizes approaches that draw binary distinctions between island and mainland.

In addition to highlighting the role of gender, this emphasis upon how social networks influence the material circumstances of transmigrants also draws our attention to the racialized experiences of international migrants. The way that discriminatory and exclusionary practices connect racialized groups to specific economic positions and niches forms an important undercurrent in recent work on social networks (for example, Grasmuck and Pessar 1991; Smith 1997). Migrant people of color face a range of exclusionary practices in society that not only are coterminous with racism and ethnic discrimination but are embedded as structural forces in the class relations of capitalist society (Miles 1982, 1987, 1989). Everyday racism is one commentator's assessment of the day-to-day stresses and strains migrant people of color experience in "the other man's country" (Essed 1990).

Transnational scholarship thus provides us with a way of connecting transmigration processes to material relations by emphasizing gender and race constructions. However, just as we are critical of the model of migration assumed by human capital and underclass accounts, we harbor similar reservations about the way repetitive migration behaviors are theorized by transnational scholars. The transnational literature pays little attention to how individual and family migration strategies become culturally embedded. And, paradoxically, although much has been made of the gendered and racialized ways in which transnational community networks operate, little attention has been paid to the way the migration strategies of transmigrants are gendered and racialized. Indeed, Hondagneu-Sotelo and Avila (1997, 550) points to the assumption of genderless transnational migrants as a significant weakness in transnational scholarship. It is this particular concern we address below by extending our own work on gendered circulation strategies.

Gendered and Racialized Circulation Strategies

International migration involves the adoption, use, and modification of an extremely varied range of mobility and circulation strategies (Carnegie 1982). For example, in the Caribbean context, Conway (1988) describes conditional moves, decisions to return (impromptu and planned), decisions to postpone return, to return forever, or to never return, decisions to circulate, when to repeat a circuit, when to interrupt a circuit, when to choose an alternative intermediate destination, and so forth. These strategies are influenced by stage of the life course (Katz and Monk 1993), educational background (Bonilla and Campos 1985), previous experiences with migration (Gmelch 1987), macroeconomic conditions (Maldonado 1976), and cultural context (Conway 1988; Pessar 1997).

Migration strategies also emerge in response to a series of critical stimuli in the family and community (after Carnegie 1982). First, individual learning, directly and indirectly, occurs through group (spouse, family, community) behaviors. Second, mobility traditions are adopted as the social norm in a community, and the "reproduction" of mobility becomes a social-class norm for potential participants. Third, multi-local social networks and familial support strategies become established to accommodate the flexible movement patterns of participants. These behavioral effects can launch a relatively independent process whereby mobility strategies are prompted, relearned, and enacted through the interaction of a complex of circular and cumulative (causal) mechanisms (Massey 1988, 1990a, b). As migration begets migration, short-visit moves prompt longer visits, one family member's movement stimulates other family members' moves, and norms of regularized and repetitive international mobility may be established (Chapman and Prothero 1985; Jokisch 1997; Pessar 1997; Peterson 1958).

Our previous research indicates that it is crucial to understand how these migration norms are gendered (Bailey and Ellis 1993; Conway, Ellis, and Shiwdhan 1990; Ellis, Conway, and Bailey 1996). Men and women circulate with different goals in mind (see also Sutton 1992). Structural situations, household circumstances, and life course evolutionary changes combine to generate stress thresholds that initiate, constrain, and modify migration behavior for both men and women. These thresholds differ between men and women because of the gendered nature of work and household responsibilities. Our work on the migration strategies of Puerto Rican women shows that gender roles and relations have important effects on the decision to migrate, choice of destination, duration of stay, participation in social networks, and most generally the cumulative causation of migration and material conditions. This work also suggests that migration alters social and economic conditions in origins and destinations—in both families and communities—which in turn precipitates changes in gender relations in both sending and receiving communities. This recursivity is likely to have differential implications for the future migration decisions of Puerto Rican men and women.

How, then, do we begin to weave together our notions of gendered circulation migration with broader transnational scholarship? We start by assuming that the international circulation behaviors of women and men are prompted as critical thresholds of information and resources are reached, but that these decisions to move are made in households and other social contexts where gender relations are unequal. Patriarchal structures result in the initial circulation of many women as "tied-movers"— women who move because their husband or household moved in response to economic structures. But the experience of mobility may sooner or later translate to a volitional international move as women gain migration and employment experience. Thus Puerto Rican women's circulation shifts from structural initiation to behavioral continuation, modification, and perpetuation. Implicit in this view is the recognition that gendered roles and responsibilities are dynamic over the life course (and over geographic space). Women's decisions to remain outside the formal labor force, or to enter and exit the labor force frequently, are taken in the context of multiple levels of responsibility (for example, to self, family, kin, community) and may involve economic and noneconomic trade-offs. Earlier assessments of Puerto Rican women's motives for migration revealed the importance of noneconomic factors in return decision-making (Baerga and Thompson 1990; Conway, Ellis, and Shiwdhan 1990).

A full account of the migration of Puerto Rican women, including repetitive circulatory moves, must also recognize the effects of racist practices in U.S. society. Racist exclusion in U.S. labor markets prevents nonwhite immigrant groups, including Puerto Ricans, from gaining reasonable access to decent employment opportunities. Low wages and poor working conditions are usually the only employment option for many Puerto Rican women (Flores 1993). The poor remuneration from such jobs is unlikely to cover the cost of child care and other basic necessities. In these circumstances, both poverty and low rates of labor force participation are unsurprising among Puerto Rican women, whenever and wherever they live in the United States. Such conditions are likely to encourage Puerto Rican women to return to the island or circulate between island and mainland, because they either seek better employment opportunities or want to access superior and more welcoming family and community support structures. Gendered family obligations interact with mainland racialized experiences, further constraining or encouraging women's circulation migration depending on family circumstances and stage of life course.

In general, as transnational research ably demonstrates, nonwhite immigrants have developed a variety of strategies to minimize the impact of racist exclusion in labor and housing markets and to combat the psychological damage of racial oppression. For example, many immigrant groups have developed enclaves and employment niches as a means of overcoming the social, cultural, and economic disadvantages and alienation they experience in host societies. Another strategy is to minimize contact with the host society by maintaining economic and cultural links with origin communities rather than attempting to assimilate into host societies. This strategy may simply involve participation with other coethnic immigrants in activities that help to maintain the origin community financially, such as sending home remittances (Conway and Cohen 1998). Immigrants may also try to keep up involvement in origin community life by making use of electronic media such as video recordings of key cultural events. Circulation-migration and return migration are also important components of this strategy. Periodic return, plans for future return, and the idea of retirement (whether realized or not) in the origin community are all ways in which international migrants can sustain themselves while working in societies in which they suffer racial exclusion and oppression. Knowing that one can go back, or that one will go back after earning sufficient money to buy property and retire, may encourage nonwhite immigrants simultaneously to spend longer sojourns in racially hostile host societies and to maintain strong economic and cultural connections to sending communities.

In summary, circulation migration is a strategy used by members of transnational communities to negotiate shifting economic opportunities, life-course transitions, and cultural pressures in origin and destination communities. To understand the links between the circulation migration of Puerto Rican women and their poverty and work experience we must acknowledge the gendered and racialized context in which decisions to migrate and work are made. We must also pay attention to the ways in which these decisions recursively affect material conditions, social relations, and race and gender constructions in origin and destination communities. Alicea's work (1997) is suggestive of these recursive links by showing how the gendered subsistence activities of Puerto Rican women contributes decisively to the social construction of the Puerto Rican transnational community.

Thus the relationship between the incidence of international circulation, participation in the metropole's labor force, and "positive" (for example, education) and "negative" (for example, presence of children) traits associated with labor force participation are likely to be complex. In the remainder of the chapter we explore these relationships for a group of Puerto Rican women living in New York City. We use a unique pooled data set that differentiates the employment and circulation experiences of first- and second-generation Puerto Rican women. While the data do not allow us to flesh out all of the implications of the preceding statements they do make it possible to initiate an inquiry into three questions related to the themes of our discussion. First, how does international circulation affect labor force participation among Puerto Rican women in New York City? Second, do the work experiences of women who regularly circulate between the island and New York differ from the work experiences of women who do not regularly go back and forth? And third, does nativity affect labor force participation directly or indirectly through circulation migration strategies?

Labor Force Participation Among Puerto Rican Women in New York City

We emphasize the New York employment experiences of Puerto Ricans over the age of sixteen who were not in the armed services or institutionalized. Since we are interested in both current and past employment experiences our analysis must account for two groups of women: those currently living in New York, and those living in Puerto Rico who had prior work experience in New York. Lacking such a composite data-set we custom created a pooled sample of women that represents currently and previously employed women.

The New York Fertility, Employment and Migration survey (NYFEM) contains longitudinal information for 2,033 Puerto Rican women who were living in the New York Metropolitan region in 1985. These data are statistically representative of the proportion of Puerto Rican–born and U.S.–born Puerto Rican women. However, they do not include individuals who either were born in the United States and were living in Puerto Rico in 1985, or individuals who were born in Puerto Rico and had spent some time in New York before 1985 but had returned to Puerto Rico at the time of the survey. Both sets of individuals need to be incorporated into an analysis of the circulating population.

We are therefore obliged to supplement the NYFEM data with data taken from a second and comparable longitudinal survey conducted in Puerto Rico. Between September and December 1982, the Centers for Disease Control received completed surveys from 3,175 women living in Puerto Rico (the Puerto Rico Fertility and Family Planning Assessment, PRFFPA). These PRFFPA data are representative of first- and second-generation Puerto Ricans who were resident in Puerto Rico in the early 1980s. Pooling NYFEM and PRFFPA data thus provides information on all Puerto Rican circulators in New York.

In pooling the PRFFPA and NYFEM data we assume that both data-sets are representative of the Puerto Rican population at their respective sample locations. We use 1980 U.S. Census Bureau Public Use Microdata Sample data to correct for differences in sampling rates between New York and Puerto Rico. Our resulting composite data-set consists of 1,326 noninstitutionalized and non–armed services. Puerto Rican women over the age of sixteen. Of these 1,326 records 1,140 were randomly selected from the NYFEM data and supplemented with 186 Puerto Rican women with New York circulation experience taken from the PRFFPA data. We restrict our attention to women who had spent at least three months in New York after their sixteenth birthday, and this condition reduced the size of our pooled sample to 1,166 women.

The following information was collected for these 1,166 women: start and end date of each New York period of residence (sojourn); history of circulation; employment history; marital status and childbirth history; place of birth; education history. All dates are recorded to the nearest month. As with all retrospective data, we may expect some recall bias, but this can be minimized by focusing on the incidence of significant life course events such as childbirth, employment, and circulation rather than on the exact timing of these events.

Formally, we distinguish working women from nonworking women on the basis of employment in New York for at least one month. Similarly, women are classified as circulators if they spend at least three months in Puerto Rico following a New York spell of residence. Women are defined as married if they reported being in a formally recognized marriage union or if they reported being in a consensual union. We represent education experience with a surrogate measure of post–high school training or college experience.

Overall, our pooled sample indicates that island-born women (i.e., first-generation Puerto Ricans) comprise the majority segment of the community, rates of participation in the formal labor market are low, and the incidence of childbirth in the community is high (Table 7.1). This finding underscores the degree of interconnectedness between mainland and island milieus. For succeeding generations of Puerto Rican men and women, circulation migration has become a culturally sanctioned mobility response to the essentially neo-colonial web of interrelations between Puerto Rico and the United States (History Task Force 1979; Bonilla and Campos 1985).

Participation in New York's labor market may be influenced by mainland and island contexts in different ways. In the first part of the analysis we assess the overall relationship between international circulation and labor force participation. Approximately one-quarter of the sample had engaged in circulation behavior between New York and Puerto Rico. Circulating women are less likely to have worked in New York than noncirculating women (Table 7.2). An analysis of variance test confirms that being a circulator is associated with a lower mean incidence of employment in New York (p = .0328).

However, circulation propensity varies by nativity (Table 7.3). Whereas one-third of Puerto Rican–born women circulated, only one-eleventh of the mainland-born women circulated. Supporting other work in this area, we find that island-born women are much more likely to engage in circulation behavior than are second-generation women (those born in New York). International circulation—repetitive moves between island and mainland—is an important facet of daily life in many Puerto Rican communities in the United States (Santiago and Galster 1995).

Furthermore, the proportion of women who are ever employed is strongly associated with nativity (Table 7.3). Our data suggest that about 37 percent of Puerto Rican–born women who have lived in New York were also employed there. The majority, 63 percent, have not been in New York's labor force. Other studies have also

TABLE 7.1 Profile of Pooled Sample

Category	Number	Percentage of Sample	Category	Number	Percentage of Sample
All women	1,166	100	Mean year of life (age), Jan. 1982	28	
Puerto Rican–born	702	60.2			
U.S.–born	464	39.8	Circulators	307	26.3
Ever employed in NYC	502	43.1	Post–high school experience	216	18.5
Never employed in NYC	664	56.9	Have children (by Jan. 1982)	935	80.1

TABLE 7.2. Individuals by Circulation Status

Category	Circulators	Noncirculators
Number	207	859
Percentage of sample	26.3	73.7
Number ever employed	81	421
Percentage of circulation group	26.4	49.0
Number never employed	226	438
Percentage of circulation group	72.6	51.0
Number with post–high school experience	59	157
Percentage of circulation group	19.2	18.3
Number with childbirth	269	666
Percentage of circulation group	87.6	77.5
Mean year of life (age), Jan. 1982	33	26

found that approximately two-thirds of the island-born population are out of the labor force (Rodriguez 1989, 33, table 2.4, notes that 70 percent of Puerto Rican–born women were not working prior to the 1980 Census). By contrast, 53 percent of second-generation women worked in New York. A difference of means test shows that being born in Puerto Rico makes a women significantly less likely to be employed in New York, when compared with being born in the United States (p = 0.0001).

Any impact of circulation migration upon labor force participation appears to be mediated through nativity. In the second part of the analysis we examine in further detail how nativity is linked to labor force participation. Lower participation among island-

TABLE 7.3. Individuals by Nativity

Category	Puerto Rican–Born	U.S.–Born
Number	702	464
Percentage of sample	60.2	39.8
Number ever employed	257	245
Percentage of nativity group	36.6	52.8
Number never employed	445	219
Percentage of nativity group	63.3	47.2
Number who circulate	269	38
Percentage of nativity group	38.3	8.2
Number who did not circulate	433	426
Percentage of nativity group	61.7	91.8
Number with post–high school experience	108	108
Percentage of nativity group	15.4	23.3
Number with childbirth	625	310
Percentage of nativity group	89.0	66.8
Mean year of life (age), Jan. 1982	32	22

born women cannot be attributed solely to age variation between the nativity groups. The greater mean age of Puerto Rican–born women would suggest greater exposure to New York's labor market and thus an increased possibility of gaining employment: that there is no such increased possibility suggests that additional factors are responsible for lower employment participation among first generation women.

The finding that island-born women are less likely to have had post–high school education experience (Table 7.3) is consistent with other research findings that connect lower labor force participation to reduced stocks of education (less human capital). Furthermore, island-born women are much more likely to have had children (consistent with their age) than are second-generation women. Bean and Tienda (1987), in their comprehensive analysis of 1980 labor force participation rates for Puerto Rican women in the United States, concur that the connections between migration and the labor market standing of Puerto Rican women are mediated by life-course events, in particular the presence of young children (302). Similarly, the presence of young children, and the role of the woman as head of household, reduced the labor force participation of Puerto Rican women in 1960 and 1970 (Cooney and Warren 1979). Falcón, Gurak, and Powers 1990 reproduces these results for labor market participation of Puerto Rican women in New York and connects household arrangements with job interruptions, delayed entries to the labor force, and early abandonment of employment. Torreuellas, Benmayor, and Juarbe (1996) report a similar life-cycle relationship between reduced formal labor force participation and increased family responsibilities among first-generation Puerto Rican women in New York City. Zsembik and Peek 1994, a study of the return to work among mothers on Puerto Rico, finds that "women also blend work and family roles in response to their own opportunity structure and are not returning to work solely in response to economic need" (535). Overall, then, we may expect first-generation women to have lower labor force participation because they have more children and less education than second-generation women, and because of the cultural context that places value on child rearing.

In the final part of the analysis we examine the importance of education and family characteristics for explaining the labor force experiences of circulators compared to non-circulators. Is the effect of nativity on labor market outcomes reducible to the differences in educational and family characteristics between first- and second-generation women? In Tables 7.4a and 7.4b we consider the characteristics of working and nonworking circulators, by nativity. For island-born circulators, education does not appear to be a major characteristic associated with worked/never worked (that is, 16.2 percent of those employed had post–high school experience, while 18.0 percent of those not employed had post–high school experience). Similarly, childbirth does not differentiate the worked/never worked groups (in both cases proportions exceed 86 percent).

Findings for mainland-born women are even more striking in this regard. Here, post–high school education characterizes twice as many second-generation circulators who have never worked as have worked. Although some of this difference may be offset by the fact that women who have worked are five years older on average than those who have not worked, it seems to us quite plausible that some of the more educated

TABLE 7.4a. Individuals Who Circulate and Work, by Nativity

Category	Puerto Rican–Born	U.S.–Born
Number of women	68	13
Mean year of life (age), Jan. 1982	36	29
Number with post–high school experience	11	2
Percentage of group	16.2	15.4
Number with childbirth	61	12
Percentage of group	89.7	92.3

TABLE 7.4b. Individuals Who Circulate But Do Not Work, by Nativity

Category	Puerto Rican–Born	U.S.–Born
Number of women	201	25
Mean year of life (age), Jan. 1982	34	24
Number with post–high school experience	36	10
Percentage of group	18.0	40.0
Number with childbirth	173	23
Percentage of group	86.0	92.0

mainland women are circulating for non–labor market reasons. In previous work we demonstrated how the return migration decisions of women to Puerto Rico were heavily influenced by child-rearing and familial motivations (Bailey and Ellis 1993; Conway, Ellis, and Shiwdhan 1990). Seen in this light, it is more reasonable to suggest that the international circulation of Puerto Rican women has as much to do with communal and familial life as with labor market life and human capital markers.

To summarize, our findings demonstrate an apparent negative association between circulation migration and employment in New York City. Most circulators in our study were island-born women, and island-born women had lower participation rates than second-generation Puerto Rican women. Indeed, disaggregating the circulation–labor force participation relationship by nativity removes the statistical significance of the circulation-participation relationship for both island-born ($p = 0.4068$) and U.S.–born ($p = 0.9305$) women. Finally, we found that within the group of women who used circulation strategies, labor force outcomes did not match the kind of educational or life-cycle predictions suggested by human capital or underclass frameworks. We use the concluding section to place these results in the context of gendered and racialized circulation strategies and to discuss issues they generate.

Conclusions

This chapter provides further empirical support to the idea that circulation migration is a strategy widely used by Puerto Rican women. As transnational scholarship argues, circulation (or transmigration) is a defining characteristic of a transnational community. As such, circulation migration strategies will affect material outcomes, such as poverty relations, in the community both directly (for example, employer perceptions of circulators as lacking commitment to the labor force), and indirectly (for example, the renegotiation of island and mainland gender roles and associated networks of child-care activities). This leads to the first contribution of this chapter: Analyses of Puerto Rican poverty relations must simultaneously account for mainland and island contexts and the experiences of both circulators and noncirculators.

Methodologically, this conclusion obliges us to pool data to analyze the dynamics of the Puerto Rican community whose mainland and island experiences are so interwoven. Massey (1993, 463) has already noted: "A principal challenge for Latino researchers is to create national data sets that link comparable samples undertaken in sending and receiving areas. This design has been incorporated into several small scale studies . . . but it has not been implemented on a large scale using nationally representative data sets" (463). Later Landale combined NYFEM and PRFFPA data to investigate the union formation dynamics of Puerto Rican women (Landale and Hauan 1996), and Falcón and Gurak (1994) followed a similar aggregation to investigate migration/poverty linkages.

Theoretically, we argue that the established view of the recursive relations inherent in transnational communities should take greater account of the gendered nature of circulation migration strategies. As the second contribution of our chapter, our empirical analysis offers some support for this position. Neither education achievement nor family situation could, or should, be regarded as independent events that "trigger" particular labor market responses. Rather, these choices and contexts are best interpreted against the backdrop of ongoing identity construction in a transnational community, that draws upon both nonmaterial and material considerations.

Like others before us, we find that nativity differences in employment experiences persist. Island-born women were less likely to have higher education experience, and this fact partially explains their poorer labor market outcomes. However, among the group of circulating island-born women education is not a marker for employment. Other factors related to the gendered and racialized experiences of daily life in the United States for non-natives appear to be important. However, our quantitative data do not permit us to explore the complex ways gendered and racialized identity constructions impinge upon work experiences in the Puerto Rican community, and this will be an important area for further research.

Although we are satisfied that our findings apply to women who had lived in New York by the early 1980s, we do not claim they are replicated in other Puerto Rican communities on the U.S. mainland. Indeed, research suggests considerable geographic variation in migration, settlement, and socioeconomic practices and outcomes (Enchautegui 1992; Santiago 1992; Toro-Morn 1995). How geographic context ("place") affects the operation of gendered and racialized circulation strategies, and in turn influences transnational community life, employment structures, and networks, is one more fecund research avenue. How the evolving restructuring of New York City as a "World-place" and a gateway for other new immigrants also affects Puerto Rican women's life chances is another related question. There are few certain continuities, it would appear, though our theoretical framework is a useful and generalizable construct in which to situate further empirical explorations.

References

Alicea, M. 1992. *Dual Home Bases: A Reconceptualization of Puerto Rican Migration.* Chicago: Depaul University, School for New Learning.

———. 1997. "'Chambered Nautilis': The Contradictory Nature of Puerto Rican Women's Role in the Social Construction of a Transnational Community." *Gender and Society* 11 (5): 597–626.

Baerga, M. del C., and L. Thompson 1990. "Migration in a Small Semi-Periphery: The Movement of Puerto Ricans and Dominicans." *International Migration Review* 14 (4): 656–83.

Bailey, A. J., and M. Ellis. 1993. "Going Home: The Migration of Puerto Rican–born Women from the United States to Puerto Rico." *The Professional Geographer* 45 (2): 148–58.

Basch, L., N. Glick Schiller, and C. Szanton Blanc. 1994. *Nations Unbound: Transnational Projects, Postcolonial Predicaments, and Deteritorrialized Nation-States.* Langhorne, Pa.: Gordon and Breach.

Bean, F. D., and M. Tienda. 1987. *The Hispanic Population of the United States.* New York: Russell Sage.

Bonilla, F., and R. Campos. 1985. "Evolving Patterns of Puerto Rican Migration." Pp. 177–205 in *The Americas in the New International Division of Labor,* edited by S. E. Sanderson. New York: Holmes and Meier.

Borges-Mendez, R. 1993. "The Use of Latino Immigrant Labor in Massachusetts Manufacturing: Evidence from Lowell, Laurence, and Holyoke." Pp 104–24 in *Latino Poverty and Economic Development in Massachusetts,* edited by E. Melendez and M. Uriarte. Boston: Gaston Institute.

Carnegie, C. V. 1982. "Strategic Flexibility in the West Indies: A Social Psychology of Caribbean Migration." *Caribbean Review* 11:10–13, 54.

Castles, S., and M. J. Miller. 1993. *The Age of Migration: International Population Movements in the Modern World.* New York: Guilford Press.

Chapman, M., and R. M. Prothero. 1985. "Circulation Between 'Home' and Other Places: Some Propositions." Pp. 1–12 in *Circulation in Population Movement: Substance and Concepts from the Melanesian Case,* edited by M. Chapman and R. M. Prothero. New York: Routledge and Kegan Paul.

Comaroff, J., and J. L. Comaroff. 1991. *Of Revelation and Revolution: Christianity, Colonialism, and Consciousness in South Africa.* Chicago: University of Chicago Press.

Conway, D. 1988. "Conceptualising Contemporary Patterns of Caribbean International Mobility." *Caribbean Geography* 2 (3): 145–63.

———. 2000. "Notions Unbounded: A Critical (Re)read of Transnationalism Suggests that U.S.-Caribbean Circuits Tell the Story Better." Pp. 203–26 in *Theoretical and Methodological Issues in Migration Research: Interdisciplinary, Intergenerational, and International Perspectives,* edited by Biko Agozino. Aldershot, England: Ashgate.

Conway, D., and J. F. Cohen. 1998. "Consequences of Migration and Remittances for Mexican Transnational Communities." *Economic Geography* 74 (1): 26–44.

Conway, D., M. Ellis, and N. Shiwdhan. 1990. "Caribbean International Circulation: Are Puerto Rican Women Tied Circulators? *Geoforum* 21 (1): 51–66.

Cooney, R. S., and A.E.C. Warren. 1979. "Declining Female Participation Among Puerto Rican New Yorkers: A Comparison with White Non-Spanish New Yorkers." *Ethnicity* 6:281–97.

Darder, A. 1992. "Problematizing the Notion of Puerto Ricans as 'Underclass': A Step Toward a Decolonizing Study of Poverty." *Hispanic Journal of Behavioral Sciences* 14:144–56.

Durand, J., E. A. Parrado, and D. S. Massey. 1996. "Migradollars and Development: A Reconsideration of the Mexican Case." *International Migration Review* 30 (2): 423–44.

Ellis, M., D. Conway, and A. J. Bailey. 1996. "The Circular Migration of Puerto Rican Women: Towards a Gendered Explanation." *International Migration* (Geneva) 34 (1): 31–64.

Enchautegui, M. E. 1992. "Geographical Differentials in the Socioeconomic Status of Puerto Ricans: Human Capital Variations and Labor Market Characteristics." *International Migration Review*, 26:267–90.

Essed, P. 1990. *Everyday Racism.* Claremont, Calif.: Hunter House.

Falcón, L. M., and D. T. Gurak. 1994. "Poverty, Migration, and the Underclass." *Latino Studies Journal* 5 (2): 77–95.

Falcón, L. M., D. T. Gurak, and M. Powers. 1990. "Labor Force Participation of Puerto Rican Women in Greater New York City." *Sociology and Social Research* 74:110–17.

Flores, J. (1993). *Divided Borders: Essays on Puerto Rican Identity.* Houston: Arte Publico Press.

Galster, G., and A. M. Santiago. 1994. "Explaining the Growth of Puerto Rican Poverty, 1970–1980." *Urban Affairs Quarterly* 30 (2): 249–74.

Gardner, R. W. 1981. "Macrolevel Influences on the Migration Decision Process." Pp. 59–89 in *Migration Decision Making,* edited by G. DeJong and R. W. Gardner. New York: Pergamon Press.

Glick-Schiller, N., L. Basch, and C. Blanc-Szanton. 1992. *Towards a Transnational Perspective on Migration: Race, Class, Ethnicity, and Nationalism.* New York: New York Academy of Sciences.

Glick-Schiller, N., L. Basch, and C. Szanton Blanc. 1995. "From Immigrant to Transmigrant: Theorizing Transnational Migration." *Anthropological Quarterly* 68 (1): 48–63.

Gmelch, G. 1987. "Work, Innovation, and Investment: The Impact of Return Migrants in Barbados." *Human Organization* 46 (2): 131–40.

Grasmuck, S., and R. Grosfoguel. 1997. "Geopolitics, Economic Niches, and Gendered Social Capital Among Recent Caribbean Immigrants to New York City." *Sociological Perspectives* 40 (3): 339–63.

Grasmuck, S., and P. R. Pessar. 1991. *Between Two Islands: Dominican International Migration.* Berkeley: University of California Press.

Grosfoguel, Ramón, and Héctor Cordero-Guzmán. 1998. "Social Capital, Context of Reception, and Transnationalism: Recent Approaches to International Migration." *Diaspora* 7 (3): 351–69.

Hernandez, J. 1990. "Latino Alternatives to the Underclass Concept." *Latin Studies Journal* 1:95–105.

History Task Force. 1979. *Labor Migration Under Capitalism.* New York: CUNY.

Landale, N. S. 1994. "Migration and the Latino Family: The Union Formation Behavior of Puerto Rican Women." *Demography* 31 (1): 133–57.

Hondagneu-Sotelo, P., and E. Avila. 1997. " 'I'm Here but I'm There': The Meanings of Latina Transnational Motherhood." *Gender and Society* 11 (5): 548–71.

Jokisch, B. D. 1997. "From Labor Circulation to International Migration: The Case of South Central Ecuador." *1997 Yearbook, Conference of Latinamericanist Geographers* 23:63–75.

Katz, C., and J. Monk. 1993. *Full Circles.* London: Routledge.

Kearney, M. 1995. "The Effects of Transnational Culture, Economy, and Migration on Miztec Identity in Oaxacacalifornia." Pp. 226–43 in *The Bubbling Cauldron: Race, Ethnicity, and the Urban Crisis,* edited by M. P. Smith and J. R. Feagin. Minneapolis: University of Minnesota Press.

Landale, N. S., and S. M. Hauan. 1996. "Migration and Premarital Childbearing Among Puerto Rican Women." *Demography* 33 (4): 429–42.

Levitt, P. 1997. "Variations in Transnationalism: Lessons from Organizational Experiences in Boston and the Dominican Republic." Aspen Institute Working Paper, Aspen, Colorado.

Maldonado, R. M. 1976. "Why Puerto Ricans Migrated to the United States 1947–1973." *Monthly Labor Review* 99 (1): 7–18.

Massey, D. S. 1988. "Economic Development and International Migration in Comparative Perspective." *Population and Development Review* 14 (3): 383–413.

———. 1990a. "The Social and Economic Origins of Immigration, " *American Academy of Political and Social Sciences* 510:60–72.

———. 1990b. "Social Structure, Household Strategies, and the Cumulative Causation of Migration." *Population Index* 56 (1): 3–26.

———. 1993. "Latinos, Poverty, and the Underclass: A New Agenda for Research. *Hispanic Journal of Behavioral Sciences* 15 (4): 449–75.

Melendez, E. 1993. "Latino Poverty and Economic Development in Massachusetts." Pp. 15–37 in *Latino Poverty and Economic Development in Massachusetts,* edited by E. Melendez and M. Uriate. Boston: Gaston Institute.

Miles, R. 1982. *Racism and Migrant Labor.* London: Routledge and Kegan Paul.

———. 1987. *Capitalism and "Unfree Labour": Anomoly or Necessity?* New York: Tavistock.

———. 1989. *Racism.* New York: Routledge.

Moore, J. 1989. "Is There a Hispanic Underclass?" *Social Science Quarterly* 70:265–83.

Moore, J., and R. Pinderhughes, eds. 1993. *In the Barrios: Latinos and the Underclass Debate.* New York: Russell Sage.

Mountz, A., and R. A. Wright. 1996. "Daily Life in the Transnational Migrant Community of San Agustin, Oaxaca, and Poughkeepsie, New York." *Diaspora* 5 (3): 403–28.

Ortiz, A. 1996. "Introduction." Pp.1–32 in *Puerto Rican Women and Work,* edited by A. Ortiz. Philadelphia: Temple University Press.

Perez, S. M., and D. de la Rosa Salazar. 1993. "Economic, Labor Force, and Social Implications of Latino Educational and Population Trends." *Hispanic Journal of Behavioral Sciences* 15 (2): 188–229.

Pessar, P., ed. 1997. *Caribbean Circuits.* New York: Center for Migration Studies.

Peterson, W. 1958. "A General Typology of Migration." *American Sociological Review* 23:256–65.

Rodriguez, C. E. 1989. *Puerto Ricans: Born in the U.S.A.* Boston: Unwin Hyman.

Rouse, R. 1991. "Mexican Migration and the Social Space of Postmodernism." *Diaspora* 1 (1): 8–23.

Santiago, A. M. 1992. "Patterns of Puerto Rican Segregation and Mobility." *Hispanic Journal of Behavioral Sciences* 14:107–33.

Santiago, A. M., and G. Galster. 1995. "Puerto Rican Segregation in the United States: Cause or Consequence of Economic Status?" *Social Problems* 42 (3): 361–89.

Sjaastad, L. A. 1962. "The Costs and Returns of Human Migration." *Journal of Political Economy* 70:80–93.

Smith, R. C. 1997. "Transnational Migration, Assimilation, and Political Community." In *The City and the World,* edited by M. Crahan and A. Vourvoulais-Buch. New York: Council on Foreign Relations.

Sutton, C. R. 1992. "Some Thoughts on Gendering and Internationalizing Our Thinking About Transnational Migrations." Pp. 241–49 in *Towards a Transnational Perspective on Migration: Race,*

Class, Ethnicity, and Nationalism, edited by N. Glick Schiller, L. Basch, and C. Blanc-Szanton. New York: New York Academy of Sciences,.

Toro-Morn, M. I. 1995. "Gender, Class, Family, and Migration: Puerto Rican Women in Chicago." *Gender and Society* 9:712–26.

Torres, A. 1992. "Nativity, Gender, and Earnings Discrimination." *Hispanic Journal of Behavioral Sciences* 14 (1): 134–43.

Torruellas, R. M., R. Benmayor, and A. Juarbe. 1996. "Negotiating Gender, Work, and Welfare: Families as Productive Labor Among Puerto Rican Women in New York City. Pp. 184–208 in *Puerto Rican Women and Work,* edited by A. Ortiz. Philadelphia: Temple University Press.

Waldinger, R. 1986. *Through the Eye of a Needle: Immigrants and Enterprise in New York's Garment Trade.* New York: New York University Press.

———. 1996. *Still the Promised City? African-Americans and New Immigrants in Postindustrial New York,* Cambridge: Harvard University Press.

Wilson, T. D. 1994. "What Determines Where Transnational Labor Migrants Go? Modifications in Migration Theories." *Human Organization* 53 (3): 269–78.

Wilson, W. J. 1987. *The Truly Disadvantaged.* Chicago: University of Chicago Press.Wright, R., and M. Ellis. 1996. "Immigrants and the Changing Racial/Ethnic Division of Labor in New York City, 1970–1990." *Urban Geography* 17 (4): 317–53.

Wyman, M. 1993. *Round-Trip to America: The Immigrants Return to Europe, 1880–1930.* Ithaca: Cornell University Press.

Zabin, C. 1994. "The Effects of Economic Restructuring on Women: The Case of Binational Agriculture in Baja California and California." *Economic Development Quarterly* 8 (2): 186–96.

Zsembik, B. A., and C. W. Peek. 1994. "The Effect of Economic Restructuring on Puerto Rican Women's Labor Force Participation in the Formal Sector." *Gender and Society* 18 (4): 525–40.

Part II

Migration and
Socioeconomic
Incorporation

CHAPTER 8

Class, Race, and Success: Two Generations of Indian Americans Confront the American Dream

Johanna Lessinger

Asian Indian immigrants in New York City, like fellow Indians in the rest of the United States, have become noted for their unusually rapid and successful incorporation into the U.S. economy. As part of the large post-1965 migration from Asia, recent arrivals from India are often cited as an ethnic success story, as a group that has entered the professions or founded businesses and gone on to experience American-style suburban affluence within the first immigrant generation. (Helweg and Helweg 1990 and Saran 1985 take this viewpoint. Works by Indian American scholars, such as Prasad 2000 and Mazumdar 1989, are more realistic about class and racial cleavages affecting Indians.) Unlike many other groups of newcomers, Indians are perceived as having "made it" quickly and with relative ease, without waiting for the second or third generation's painful climb into the professional middle class that has characterized the incorporation of many other immigrant groups, past and present.

This image of rapid economic assimilation of Asian Indians within two decades of arrival is made possible by the backgrounds of most of the post-1965, first-generation Indian immigrants. By and large born into India's urban, professional middle classes, these migrants are well-educated, particularly in technical fields, fluent in English, sophisticated about the U.S. job market, and increasingly transnational. Many have prepared themselves for out-migration years in advance, by seeking out particular kinds of higher education, professional training, or investment opportunities that will maximize their access to student or immigrant visas and their chances for well-paid, permanent work in the United States. By this time, prospective arrivals can tap into well-established employment and educational networks both in India and in the United States.

Within a decade of arrival, a great many of these immigrants will be successfully placed in professional or entrepreneurial positions and will be strategizing to ensure that their children will be even better placed for professional careers, hastening, for instance, to get a two-year-old enrolled in a Montessori school "so we can be sure she goes to Harvard." Many of these children do indeed attend good universities and go into highly paid and prestigious professions. The pressure from their parents to take up science, medicine, law, or finance, to prosper professionally, to make money, and to succeed to their parents' class position is very great.

Recent immigrants, brown- to black-skinned, from one of the world's poorest countries, yet generally well-to-do and professionally established once here, Indian immigrants present an interesting problem in terms of the contradictions between the ethnic self-identity they have developed here and the ways in which they are incorporating into the larger society. In that incorporation, racial location, class status, and transnational Indian identity are still contentious and problematic to Indian immigrants in New York City and the tri-state area of New York, New Jersey, and Connecticut.

This chapter looks at some aspects of the process, particularly the issue of racial location and racial discrimination as experienced rather differently by two generations of Indian Americans. The first generation of Indian immigrants tends to see itself as white because of its pre- and postmigration class privilege and has been in some degree insulated by money, professional jobs, and suburban residence from some of the most direct expressions of U.S. racism and nativism. These experiences of class privilege and of racial location are somewhat different for their American-raised children, whose lives in school and college, as well as their entry into the work force, may have given them close encounters with U.S. racial realities. I argue that the second generation of Indian Americans is slowly developing a more sophisticated sense of self, less afraid to acknowledge a nonwhite identity in the context of New York City's ethnic politics. At the same time, I suggest that some of the first generation's transnationalism is fueled by either a rejection of or profound unease with U.S. racism and nativism.

After examining two instances of racial attack against Indians in the greater New York area, and tracing the Indian-American response, I conclude that in the twelve years between these attacks there has been a gradual evolution of racial/ethnic self-identification among Indian immigrants, spurred by the wider experience and more flexible understandings of younger people. That second generation, now entering the professions themselves, is finding a voice in adulthood and is willing to consider both a wider definition of identity and at least temporary ethnic political coalitions of a kind other New York ethnic groups have developed.

Ethnicity, Class, and Race

In the discourse of U.S. migration, Indians' economic success, their status as one of the country's several Asian "model minorities,"[1] has become a validation—both of the pay-off for hard work, optimism, and family values and of the conservative American myth that paints the United States as a land of boundless economic opportunity for all. The economic success of Asian Indians, like that of Korean and Chinese Americans, has also come to be read as a subtle reproach to those immigrant groups and native-born minorities, particularly African Americans and Hispanics, who have not been able to achieve the American dream as rapidly and effectively, who are seen as trapped in eternal poverty, social dysfunction, and inner-city misery.

Indian immigrants wholeheartedly embrace this view of themselves as an exceptionally well-educated, affluent, and well-integrated American ethnic group, moving at ease in the upper reaches of U.S. society. It is an identity that Indians celebrate repeatedly, in their media and through their community events. The ethnic leadership is drawn largely from elite individuals who approximate this ideal: doctors, engineers, university professors, bankers, large business owners. The same ideal of success is echoed in both press accounts and daily discourse in India, where the American migrant is simultaneously admired, envied, and despised—but always imagined as rich, powerful, and centrally located in his or her adopted society. The image of success is clearly central to Indian immigrants' sense of themselves, a cornerstone of both internal group structure and self-representation to the larger world of non-Indians, and an important aspect of their transnational standing in India.

At the same time, the first generation of Indian immigrants is still deeply imbued with strong feelings of attachment to India. Most still think of themselves as culturally Indian, devote time and effort to maintaining an Indian identity, and fret that their U.S.–born children are failing to achieve the same sense of attachment to an imagined homeland. Even those first-generation immigrants most determined to shed Indianness and to remake themselves as purely American often slip into a nostalgic yearning to "give something back" to India, if only to eradicate its embarrassing poverty and backwardness. The first generation is not, therefore, a population that is hastening to assimilate culturally. Many actively deny or resist cultural assimilation, feeling that they can enjoy the economic advantages of the United States and participate in its economic structure without major cultural concessions. Others feel that their partial Westernization, by virtue of elite Indian class background, is assimilation enough. In contrast, the second generation is more genuinely at ease with many aspects of American culture, from food to music to interpersonal relations. These younger people are more likely to stress the American in what many call their "hyphenated identity."

The widespread sense of passionate connection that Indian immigrants in the United States express toward India fuels the multitude of transnational structures that keep Indian immigrants here deeply involved with friends, relatives, business partners, political parties, religious institutions, and cultural movements "at home." Such transnational links are also exerting increasing pressure on Indian culture, accelerating a process of Westernization that has become increasingly American-inflected since the 1970s.

The images of success that Indian immigrants use to locate themselves socially within the United States contain implications about both class status and race—implications that are often confused and at odds with observed reality. In terms of class, first-generation immigrants take for granted the superiority of Indians. Many would like to think that the entire ethnic group is as well-off as the Silicon Valley millionaires who recently raised several million dollars for the Indian science and engineering colleges that educated them (see Dugger 2000). The Indian doctors who are building themselves Mogul-style trophy houses in the New Jersey suburbs (Gordon 2000) are admired and held up for emulation.

Yet the Indian immigrant population also contains large numbers of people holding far more modest jobs, particularly in New York City. For instance, 21 percent of the New York City Indian immigrant population held some form of blue-collar job in 1990, according to the Bureau of the Census. There are, in addition, large numbers of service workers and owners of small, almost marginal, businesses. The Indian proprietor of a grocery store or newspaper stand may own his own business and be able to support his family, but he clings to the margins of lower-middle-class respectability only by working seven days a week. The city's Indian taxi drivers, apartment house doormen, factory workers, deli countermen, and waiters are frankly working class. Moreover, their employment conditions and pay frequently parallel those of other new immigrants, both past and present, who have struggled to find and keep low-paid, insecure, and sometimes dangerous jobs. Looked at from this angle, Indian immigrant exceptionalism and privilege is far less visible. Nevertheless, the immigrant leadership continues to insist that the entire ethnic group must downplay such internal class cleavages, presenting the ethnic group "as a whole," with a "healthy image" (Abraham 1984, 1). There is, in fact, widespread insistence that the group, which the ethnic leadership refers to as "the community," is in fact a functioning moral community, despite widening geographical dispersal and clear class cleavages.

One of the effects of this stance is to hamper recognition of social problems experienced by Indian immigrants. Those Indian doctors, social workers, and progressive activists (see, for instance, Motwani and Barot-Motwani 1989, iv) who would like to mobilize community resources, as well as the resources of the larger society, to combat problems such as alcoholism, unemployment, wife battering, and AIDS among Indians, find their efforts snubbed, disparaged, and ignored. Organizations that try to build coalitions—whether with other Asian groups, with feminists, or with city social service agencies, find themselves sharply criticized as disloyal or as no longer Indian (Lessinger 1995, 129–54). These disputes, too, often take on a generational aspect, with younger people far less defensive than their elders about the possibility that Indians, like all other groups, suffer social problems. Indeed, younger people are far more likely to cite pride in being Indian American as a reason for the ethnic group to "take care of its own."

The other aspect of Indian immigrant self-identification, still more strongly marked by silence and denial, is that of race. The society of India experiences color consciousness and is deeply divided by class antagonism and caste prejudice, but it experiences nothing approaching the blunt dualism of hegemonic U.S. racial categories, which assign everyone to either "white" or "black" status, a categorization based on alleged skin color and geographical origins. This country's post-1965 influx of new immigrants has complicated but not displaced what Michael Omi and Howard Winant have called the United States' "racially bipolar vision" (1994, 154), so that the more newly arrived Hispanics and Asians form an awkward residual or intermediate category. For Asians, in particular, their place within this hierarchy is contradictory, since their "nonwhite" skins often inhabit "white" class or occupational locations.

In some sense the first generation of Indian immigrants in the United States is genuinely bewildered about where they might fit into this model, since so many Indians still identify themselves primarily on the basis of national origin, and their skin color varies widely. At another level, Indians, like other new immigrants, have been quick to absorb America's general prejudices against blacks, Hispanics, and the poor in general (Mazumdar 1989). The frankly racist views of ultra-conservative Indian American political commentator Dinesh D'Souza are simply an extreme variant of opinions circulating within sectors of the Indian immigrant population. At the same time, many first-generation Indian immigrants tacitly assume that they themselves are white, on the basis of class criteria. Since most have accepted the American folk model that tends to conflate race with class status and with social disabilities such as poverty, welfare dependency, and drug use, Indians assume that they—hardworking, family oriented, affluent, and upwardly mobile—must be white.[2] Their imagined group class status makes it so. The same kind of conservative denial that leads the Indian immigrant community as a whole to blot out distasteful realities such as drug abuse and homosexuality also renders it helpless to respond in the face of racism and nativism.

These "honorary whites," or what Nazli Kibria calls "ambivalent nonwhites" (1998, 71), are imbued with bourgeois ideals of individual achievement and self-reliance. They are stunned to find that the larger U.S. society considers them nonwhite and distinctly Other, often disregards their vaunted economic achievements, and makes them potential victims of racial/ethnic prejudice. Only a handful of Indian immigrant intellectuals and progressives have begun to confront the ambiguities involved in the group's claim to whiteness (see, for example, Mazumdar 1989; Prasad 2000; Radhakrishnan 1994; Sethi 1993; Singh 1996).

Additionally, it is worth considering briefly how the transnationalism of Indian immigrants is shaped by their racial and class location within U.S. society. The more affluent Indian immigrants are those best positioned to maintain transnational ties, to move comfortably in and out of both societies. Those with money and paid vacation time can travel to India yearly, whether to maintain personal ties or to invest money, taking their children with them. (Such trips are partly designed to enhance the Indian self-identification of the young.) Indian immigrant professionals and large-scale entrepreneurs, with large savings and technical expertise, are able to take advantage of Indian government investment schemes offering favored treatment to overseas Indians legally defined as nonresident Indians or NRIs (see Lessinger 1992a, b). In contrast, lower-middle-class or working-class Indians are less likely to visit India regularly, since both airfare and the concomitant exchange of gifts such travel entails are very expensive. If they do travel home, usually for purely familial reasons, they are certainly unable to start businesses there, fund their former colleges, or contribute to Indian political parties.

At the same time, the affluent are also far more likely to spend time and resources constructing a public Indian ethnic identity in the United States through membership in a network of Indian ethnic organizations, participation in ethnic public events, including planning and subsidizing them, and consumption in the form of tickets to expensive dinners and performances, travel to fancy restaurants in distant suburbs, or attendance at three-day conferences in resort hotels. And for all of the events, one must purchase the clothes to match. Inevitably, many of these events turn into celebrations of the economic achievement of the ethnic elite.

It is possible to argue that the kind of racial and cultural dislocation that many first-generation Indians feel in the United States, whether they fully understand it or not, may well fuel both their adherence to an Indian ethnic identity and their embrace of transnationalism. In particular, this sense of racial and cultural unease may explain the wide appeal within the Indian diaspora of the ultranationalist Hindu rightist groups that have established proselytizing and fund-raising units in the Indian immigrant communities of the United States, Canada, and Britain (see Kumar 1993, 10–12; Prashad 2000, 133–56; Rajagopal 1993, 13). The current anti-Muslim and anti-Christian rhetoric of the rightist groups in India parallels the discourses of racism and class prejudice found in North America and Britain and may validate social conservatism among immigrants. At the same time, the right's premise of a powerful and eternal (Hindu) Indian-ness is comforting to many whose sense of cultural security and identity has been battered by the process of immigration and partial acculturation.[3]

Indians in New York City

There were, according to the 1990 Census, 786,694 Asian Indians living in the United States, of whom approximately 75 percent were foreign-born (Bureau of the Census 1993b).[4] More recent estimates indicate that this population has grown to 1 million or more, and some 100,000 may live in New York City; throughout the 1990s New York City continued to attract almost 9 percent of the 34,000 new immigrants arriving annually in the United States from India. About two-thirds of these new arrivals to the city settle in the borough of Queens (Lobo, Salvo, and Virgin 1996, 12, 133), concentrated in particular neighborhoods that since the 1970s have developed a particular Indian identity through the distinctive ethnic shopping areas and the cultural and religious institutions they house (Khandelwal 1995; Lessinger 1995, 27–43). As these newcomers prosper and begin to think about homeownership, some will move to New York City's suburbs in Long Island, in Westchester County, or in adjacent parts of Connecticut and New Jersey. This outward dispersal of the affluent is visible in the higher per capita and household incomes of Indian immigrants immediately outside of New York City (see Appendix). The attraction of such suburbs is, as it is for much of the U.S. white population, better schools, better housing, more green space, and a general ideal of the good life.

Since the mid-1980s, a parallel trend has led a certain number of new immigrants,

Indians among them, to settle directly in the suburbs as soon as they arrive, with no intermediate sojourn in New York City (see Chen 1999; Edmondson 2000). Many Indians follow this pattern to join relatives already there; the relocation of service and high tech industries to suburban towns means New York City is no longer the sole source of good jobs in the area. The result is that an Indian immigrant population once centered largely on New York City now stretches into New Jersey and other suburban areas around the city. For instance, the New Jersey towns of Edison, Iselin, and Bridgeport now have Indian shopping areas that rival the Little India in Flushing, Queens. The demographic shift speaks strongly to Indian immigrants' aspirations for the trappings of U.S. middle-class affluence—a shiny new house, a lawn, one or more cars, well-funded schools, and suburban quiet. (Increasingly, these are also the aspirations of the once determinedly urban upper-middle class in India as well.)

Ironically, the movement of Indian and other Asian immigrants into formerly all-white U.S. suburbs seems to be creating new arenas for racial conflict and anti-Asian sentiment as disputes over new houses, new temples, or school curricula take on a nativist or racist tinge. Suburban life does not, therefore, wholly insulate Indian Americans from racial/ethnic confrontation, although the class nature of many suburbs mutes the overt violence of such clashes.

For all the drift to the suburbs, New York City retains its enduring attractiveness to huge numbers of new immigrants, among them large numbers of Indians. The primary lure of the city is not only the quantity but the sheer variety of work it offers. Indians, with high levels of labor force participation (73 percent, compared with 65 percent of the general U.S. population in 1990) and of college education (in 1990, 56.5 percent of the pre-1980 migrants and 48.3 percent of the 1980–89 migrants had bachelor's or postgraduate degrees, compared with 20.0 percent of the general U.S. population; see Appendix) have moved into professional jobs of all kinds: in the city's banking and insurance industries, in its universities and research centers, in its medical establishments, in its engineering and construction firms, and in its municipal bureaucracies. This kind of work has made it possible for almost 68 percent of pre-1980 immigrant households to earn $40,000 or above in 1990 (at a time when only 44 percent of all Americans earned over $35,000 a year), and 15 percent of Indian immigrants to earn $75,000 a year or more compared with almost 10 percent of all Americans earning at these levels.

At the same time, New York is an important center of international trade, offering scope for Indian importers and exporters, dealing in everything from cotton clothing to diamonds to leather goods and food products. Indians own a number of medium-sized hotels, own and sell commercial real estate, and run some of the remaining small manufacturing plants that remain in the city. Bright young Indian Americans, products of the city's many universities, are prominent in the small information technology firms that are springing up in downtown areas of New York, often displacing older small industries.

Because of its long immigrant history, New York has for generations been hospitable to the family-owned and family-run retail store, the underpinning of immigrant movement into the economic mainstream. Indians have also joined the ranks of small shopkeepers and retail-business owners. In the 1970s and 1980s many Indians created an ethnic specialty of running newsstands, particularly in the city's subways (Lessinger 1990). Today many newsstands are still Indian operated, but people have branched out to run small convenience stores and groceries, gas stations, and tire dealerships, Hallmark card and gift shops, or one of the city's hundreds of Indian restaurants. The sheer size of the Indian population in the area now makes it possible for many small entrepreneurs to concentrate on retailing to the ethnic market, selling specialized clothing, jewelry, food, tapes and videos, and electronic and household goods to fellow Indians.

The other half of this population, often overlooked, is made up of Indians who work in the service industry, and in the city's informal economy—some in its lower depths. The size and cultural vitality of the Indian immigrant population in New York is attributable not only to the presence of a suburbanizing elite but also to the class diversity within the immigrant population. This diversity—which so disturbs the Indian immigrant leadership—reflects New York's economy, with its wide spectrum of jobs and petty entrepreneurial niches. Amid the discourse of professional achievement, it is useful to remember that 21 percent of the Indian immigrant population holds some form of blue-collar job and that 41 percent of households in 1990 made less than $35,000 a year. Indian men, particularly the young and the elderly, are found as night clerks in stores, as deli countermen, as waiters, hotel clerks, doormen, and concierges. Indian men, alongside Pakistanis and Bangladeshis, are prominent as city taxi drivers (see Kolsky 1998); they spearheaded a recent taxi drivers' protest action.

For women who have only domestic skills to sell, there are many openings for housekeepers and babysitters to take over the traditionally female tasks of cooking, cleaning, and caring for children and the elderly in upwardly mobile households where wives as well as husbands now go out to work. A good deal of Indian immigrant prosperity depends on households' deploying all their adult members into the work force, including wives and co-resident extended family members. In this situation there is, inevitably, a strong demand for household help. Some of these domestic servants erupt into the news periodically with grim tales of abuse, withheld wages, and conditions of semi-slavery.

The second generation of young Indian Americans (as well as the group that calls itself the "1.5 generation," born in India but raised largely in the United States) has followed in parental footsteps. The children of professionals tend to go to elite colleges and enter highly paid professions, although some rebel against the success-money model to take up art, acting, writing, journalism, or social work. The children of the less affluent may, like other young Americans of their class and generation, go to community colleges or state colleges. Many major in business and accounting and go to work for small New York firms or open small businesses themselves. Unlike their parents, however, all of these young people avoid working in ethnic niches. They seem to be more widely distributed in all areas of the local economy.

Apart from its economic attractions, New York City also offers a social ambience that encourages both the public display of ethnic identity and covert ethnic competition. City officials and large numbers of New York residents genuinely conceptualize the city as multicultural, or, in the words of a former mayor, "a glorious mosaic." This does not mean that racism and nativism do not occur. It does mean that the official ideology discourages their overt expression, while fostering displays of ethnic diversity and pride. Indian immigrants have responded to this social climate by sponsoring parades, cultural festivals, and other civic events that help them construct their Indian-ness in public form. Both Vijay Prasad (2000, 102–25) and R. Radhakrishnan (1994, 219–33) note the synthetic quality in this search for cultural authenticity. However, for many Indians the official recognition of such events, which Indian organizations work hard each year to arrange and fund, is important as a token that Indians are officially recognized in the city's array of ethnic groups. Moreover, such recognition encourages the Indian elite in the illusion that the group is fully incorporated into U.S. society on the basis of their ethnicity.

The other aspect of New York's cultural life, which Indians have been slower to grasp, is the kind of ethnic competition that goes on in the city. Ethnic groups that are large, well organized, and vociferous get more and better resources: more police protection, more special school programs, more community centers, and more tolerance for activities that can be defined as part of ethnic culture. The reality of city politics is that smaller ethnic groups often have to forge ethnic coalitions if they want to make themselves heard. Thus, despite internal resentments, Dominicans, Colombians, and Puerto Ricans will in some circumstances present themselves as part of the larger category of Hispanics. Jamaicans and African Americans, in response to racial discrimination, acknowledge a common blackness. Immigrant and minority groups in New York have used the twin strategies, among others, of allying with other groups and invoking the rhetoric of civil rights and racial justice to make themselves heard.

This tactic has been almost impossible for the first generation of Indian immigrants to adopt, given their assumptions of ethnic superiority, uniqueness, and whiteness. During the late 1980s, when Koreans and African Americans in the city were involved in ongoing hostilities, a group of Koreans and Chinese tried to form a pan-Asian council to lobby for both public understanding and greater official protection. Invited to join the group, Indians sent no representatives and ignored the initiative. They evidently could not imagine themselves involved in the kinds of potentially violent racial frays, on streets and in shop fronts, that then troubled Koreans and Chinese. The Indians were deaf to the appeal of pan-Asian solidarity, of the kind that more politically sophisticated Asian American groups have been developing nationally for some time (see Lopez and Espiritu 1990; Omatsu 1994).

Not Yet at Ease

The stories that follow trace the economic and cultural incorporation of two successful Indian immigrant businessmen in New York City. Differing in cultural orientation (one is traditional by Indian standards, the other self-consciously modern), both men are part of the ethnic elite. Yet each, in his particular social context, has been forced to recognize that his foreignness and perhaps his color have been barriers preventing complete acceptance by American colleagues. What each story reveals is a resulting discomfort and unease with U.S. society, undercutting Indian immigrants' general insistence that successful incorporation into the U.S. economy implies smooth social acceptance and cultural integration. Each man has taken steps to insulate himself from the pinpricks of racism and nativism through self-employment and, in one case, by avoiding nonbusiness interaction with Americans.

Mr. T. is a member of a transnational trading caste that has operated businesses throughout Asia during the past two centuries. His unhappiness centers on U.S. business practices and a deep aversion to many aspects of American culture—a stance that puts him at odds with his children. Until recently, he confined himself to a largely Indian milieu in New York. Even now, embarked on business ventures that bring him into contact with non-Indians, he clearly fears mockery outside the Indian enclave.

T., a garment importer and real estate magnate in New York, comes from a former landowning family in Sind, now a province in Pakistan. He and his devoutly Hindu family fled to India in 1947 when the two countries were partitioned and Sindh went to Pakistan. Left impoverished by his father's death, T. dropped out of his New Delhi college and went to work for an Indian garment manufacturing firm in Hong Kong owned by fellow Sindhis. This job paid him very poorly but allowed him to learn the business. Convinced that his future lay in the United States, T. and a brother migrated to New York in 1970 and opened a tiny, one-man office to sell garments and cheap costume jewelry in New York. Much of the time T. supported himself by working for other Indians when his own business faltered, since he had no backing from the Hong Kong textile or clothing firms. For several years T. scraped by, living in a small, drafty room, subsisting on rice and lentils.[5]

Eventually the brothers accumulated enough money to open a larger office and to hire a few employees. "Having our own employees was a big thing for us," recalls T. Most of his workers are Indian; the only exceptions are a Chinese woman bookkeeper and a Jewish lawyer—employees who are unlikely to reveal his business secrets to other Indians. Like many other Indian entrepreneurs, T. still feels most comfortable managing Indian workers who are seen, in the words of another entrepreneur, as less "rough" and less lazy, than their (nonwhite) American counterparts. T.'s comments about blue-collar workers in New York show a good deal of casual prejudice against blacks and Hispanics.

In the 1970s the U.S. market for cheap, bright Indian clothing expanded and T.'s business boomed. Abandoning the costume jewelry part of their enterprise, the brothers put effort into buying and stocking a series of retail clothing shops in New York and in several other states. Within five years they had sold those shops, because, T. says, they found operating retail shops at a distance too risky and difficult. In fact, the brothers were never able to move beyond their kind of personalistic, hands-on management style, derived from India.

Instead the brothers turned their attention to Manhattan and Queens real estate. New York City was in the midst of a commercial real estate slump, and office and apartment buildings were being offered for sale relatively cheaply. By this time the brothers had sufficiently powerful networks in the United States, India, and Hong Kong, built up through their import business, to raise the needed capital. Real estate is now the major source of the family income. T.'s brother concentrates on investing in motels in southern states. T. focuses on New York real estate and is also involved in lending money to other businessmen who want to open retail shops.

Although his real estate business is now bringing T. into closer contact with white American colleagues, he only reluctantly attends business dinners or conventions, finding the style of social interaction, the food, and the drinking distasteful. He refuses all invitations to private lunches and dinners with these colleagues, citing his fear that out of politeness he might be forced to smoke, eat meat, or drink alcohol—all abhorrent to him.

T.'s social conservatism is visible in many areas. For instance, he forbade his son to attend a university out of state, insisting that an eighteen-year-old was too young to be so far from home. Instead, the boy is attending a less rigorous local four-year college and living at home. The boy and his sister mutter and roll their eyes, calling their father "totally clueless," but they obey him. T. continues to live in a heavily Indian area of Queens, where he has embellished the interior of a modest house to reflect his growing wealth. He devotes most of his nonworking time and energy to religious organizations and to the local Sindhi Association.

In the 1980s T. was toying with the notion of using his NRI status to start some kind of business, perhaps in scrap-metal reprocessing, in India. T. is clearly thinking about retiring to India, although he does not know whether he could stand the separation from his children. The economic appeal is the possibility of making still more money as an NRI investor. The emotional appeal is the possibility of returning to India to regain a true emotional homeland, after a youth and middle age of exile and dislocation from the area he still calls "my lost Sindh."

In contrast, Mr. H., the son of a sophisticated, Westernized, civil service family, is shaped by several generations of close contact with the British Raj. He is fluent in American culture and feels he has reached an admirable accommodation to it, "a blend of East and West." Yet H. is also unhappy in the United States because of loneliness and derailed career aspirations. He and several of his closest friends in New York have suffered discrimination in their careers, but it has been subtle enough that they have difficulty naming it. Their response to meeting the glass ceiling has been simply to step around the problem; they have the class resources to do so. As one of H.'s friends, an engineer, said, "When I realized I couldn't be chairman of the board in my company, I decided to start my own company." H. has done likewise.

H., from a highly educated professional family, attended one of Bombay's premier colleges. After a science degree there, he received an M.B.A. from a respected school of management that had strong ties to U.S. corporations. H. says he was already, at that stage in his life, considering a move to the United States and knew what he needed to do to get here. Understanding that engineers often encountered difficulty in finding work in the United States of the 1970s, he sought to supplement his degree with training in business and management. In pursuit of this goal he worked after graduation as a marketing executive in one of India's major conglomerates, beginning a self-conscious socialization into American corporate culture. He emigrated to the United States in 1970, sponsored by his wife's relatives. He remarked that, well before he actually left India, others within his social network had already made the voyage, "and we all discussed these things; we all knew what to expect."

H. already had friends working in banks in New York who helped him get a bank executive's job on arrival. With flawless English and polished manners, he rose from finance and corporate planning to become a vice president. During this period, H.'s highly educated wife also worked in a New York advertising firm and they lived in a prestigious Long Island town.

Despite his success, H. describes the eleven years following his emigration as a period of personal uncertainty and turmoil, in which he frequently wanted to return to India, in part because of homesickness and in part because of frustration at slow promotion within the bank. H. said he thought his situation was typical of that of many Indians in the United States: "We feel blocked. We rise rapidly but we then find we can't be one of the top ten [executives] in the company." H. refuses to attribute his experiences to racism or discrimination. He can only analyze the checks to his career as a closing of ranks against outsiders. As a friend of H.'s, who went through similar experiences, said, "They [white colleagues] all went to the same schools and the same colleges. They belong to the same clubs. Of course they favor each other."

After a brief, unhappy return to India to work as a vice president in a multinational company, H. came back to New York, to the relief of his wife. He had felt stifled in his prestigious office in Bombay, where he could not work as hard or as effectively as he thought he should. His wife, unable to find a job, felt suffocated under a daily diet of tea parties, tennis matches, and gossip.

Once back in New York, H. and two American partners established a firm that buys and resells real estate and manages corporate construction projects. Although still small, the firm is prospering. H.'s wide connections in New York banking circles and the active encouragement of former employers are of great help to him.

H. has already done some exporting to India and plans to branch out by establishing a factory there. He is actively researching the question of what products will sell and what kinds of Indian government assistance will be available to him as an NRI investor. His home state of Maharashtra is one of the most highly industrialized in India, so his elite family and friendship networks in Bombay should be useful to him if he decides to build a factory there. H. says he would not mind spending several months a year in India if he could do so as the owner of his own company and run it as he liked.

As a wealthy man, admired by other Indian immigrants, H. is a dutiful contributor and participant in the activities of the two major Indian organizations in the city, although he contrives to maintain an attitude of ironic detachment about the tone of some of their events. His own social life is spent among both Indian and American colleagues and neighbors. His fellow Indians consider him liberal, perhaps reckless, in his treatment of his daughters, one of whom was permitted to attend a disco with a mixed party of boys and girls on her sixteenth birthday. H. says that if the girl has internalized the right moral values he can trust her not drink or behave improperly with the boys. He is optimistically raising his children to "absorb the best of both worlds."

A common thread in these stories is each man's recognition that, for all his economic success, he is perceived as nonwhite by many American colleagues and subtly patronized or excluded on that account. Each has sought to deal with the issue by starting his own firm, shielding himself—as such a move has done for many other Indian immigrants—from direct encounters with prejudice. Each also was pursuing possible transnational business ventures in India. Ostensibly, such investments are simply a source of business profit in a situation where Indians may hold an economic advantage over foreign investors. In fact, there are also social and emotional implications; for both men India offers a potential refuge from strains of life in the United States. Furthermore, T. is the kind of person to whom the rhetoric of the Hindu right is most appealing. Pious, socially conservative, suspicious of Western culture, he may well be swayed by the Hindu right's promise of religious and cultural renewal combined with inclusion in a worldwide Hindu community. H., born and bred in an alternate Indian tradition of liberal secularism and scientific rationalism, is likely to be immune to such a movement.

Facing Harsh Realities

Indian immigrants in the United States do not, in general, suffer as much from overt racial discrimination or racial violence as do other nonwhite minority groups in this country (see U.S. Commission on Civil Rights 1992). In comparison with the large, urban, working-class South Asian population in Britain, battered by periodic explosions of racial prejudice (see Werbner and Anwar 1991; Robinson 1990), Indian Americans have a relatively peaceful existence, partially shielded by education, white-collar jobs, and well-to-do suburban neighborhoods. Nevertheless, despite a carefully constructed ethnic identity, Indians in the United States are not perceived as white.

For Indian immigrant children, the question arises early. Teachers in the New York City and suburban schools describe attempts to protect and comfort Indian American children who are subjected to merciless teasing from schoolmates because the Indians refuse to identify themselves as black (or Hispanic or Chinese—the recognized "other" categories in the area's dualistic racial model). Classmates accuse young Indians of being nonwhites who repudiated their color and tried to pass for white. "Who am I?" wept one Indian child to a teacher after a schoolyard fracas. "Am I black? Am I white? Am I Hispanic?"

Indian immigrant children who attend college, particularly at large universities, encounter for the first time a wider and more acceptable choice of identities: South Asians, people of color, Asian Americans. Through student activism, young Indian Americans may encounter their first forms of pan-ethnic identity construction by cooperating with Pakistani, Korean, or Chinese students. They may get to see ethnic or political coalitions in formation, as when a wide spectrum of student groups protests a campus outbreak of ethnic slurs. At family-oriented Indian immigrant conferences, young adults have confronted the parental generation over their prejudice toward Muslims and Pakistanis, or over their refusal to identify with other South Asians.

Older Indian immigrants have a far narrower range of experiences with racism, usually at work or in their neighborhoods, and they rarely have the chance to take action against it. They encounter a whole range of racist or anti-immigrant slights and slurs, some of which they do not at first recognize. People with strong Indian accents are told to "speak English—you're in America now," a comment that outrages those who pride themselves on their British-style education. Women frequently find their traditional clothing a source of unwelcome comment that ranges from well-meant but ignorant questions to muttered admonitions to "Go home and get dressed properly—why are you wearing your nightclothes on the street?" People who bring meals to work (for reasons of economy, ritual purity, and taste) are told their lunches are "weird" or "stinky." Well-intentioned suburban teachers, engaged in earnest efforts to validate their students' Indian identity against the racism of classmates, nevertheless fret that their Indian students "smell funny" and thus endanger the integrationist effort. African Americans know how wearing such petty insults can be, even if they do not threaten life and livelihood.

In suburban neighborhoods in which Indians are newcomers, prejudice may go beyond individual remarks to involve vandalized cars or mailboxes, insulting graffiti, shouted racial slurs from neighbors or passing carloads of youth. Indians' (and other new immigrants') efforts to transform their environment physically, and to build bigger houses, new businesses, temples, or community centers, often touch off litigation, accompanied by expressions of anti-Indian or anti-immigrant prejudice. Similar responses oppose the academic prowess of Asian children in local schools and parental demands for improved science teaching. The consensus among the white original inhabitants is that the newcomers should go back where they came from and stop trying to remake the community in their own (foreign) image.

What this material suggests, therefore, is that Indian Americans' experiences of race and racism are related to occupation, area of residence, and generation. The young, less able to insulate themselves from white Americans through self-employment, immersion in an all-Indian social milieu, or intense transnational involvement, have generally been obliged to see and experience their nonwhite status since childhood. Many succeed in confronting it openly. Because their American upbringing makes them more secure in this society, it is easier for younger people to acknowledge and live with the contradiction between nonwhite skin color and bourgeois class status.

The "Dotbusters" and the Generational Reaction

In 1986–87 there occurred a series of racial attacks against Indian immigrants in Jersey City, New Jersey, just across the river from New York. These "dotbuster attacks," as eventually they came to be known, were something of a watershed for the New York–area Indian community's sense of racial/ethnic identity. For the first time a group of Indians had become the focus of widespread resentment and hatred, expressed through physical attacks. As a local vein of racial/ethnic contempt for Indians boiled to the surface, the Indian immigrant leadership was exposed, left unable to analyze or respond to the situation. This failure was rooted in the ethnic leadership's narrow focus on preserving class distinctions within the population and on protecting the group's non-minority, honorary white image. Leaders could neither name the problem—racism and nativism directed against Indians as an ethnic group—nor draw on the repertoire of civil rights–style political protest that other minority groups in the greater New York area have often used successfully.

After a period of escalating harassment aimed at Indians in and around Jersey City (women insulted on the street, shopowners threatened, walls covered with graffiti, cars vandalized), a letter was printed in a local newspaper in the form of a manifesto announcing the formation of a group calling itself "The Dotbusters." (The "dot" referred to the cosmetic spot, or *bindi*, many traditional Indian women wear on their foreheads.) The group vowed to drive Indians out of the area by violence. Meeting no expressions of official outrage, the letter served both to publicize and to legitimate local anti-Indian prejudice, and its manifestations grew. Jersey City high school students were soon carrying "membership cards" identifying them as Dotbusters and joining enthusiastically in the harassment and vandalism.

The area in question was generally working-class, with a mixed African American, Hispanic, and white population and high unemployment levels. The Indians, recent arrivals to the United States and to Jersey City, were also not very prosperous and were highly visible as they tried to find work in factories, make a success of running small shops along once-blighted main streets, or live in large groups in rundown apartments. Rumors circulated that Indians had bought property with huge federal handouts from the Small Business Association. Many of the Indian women in the area did not work, since their English was poor. These housewives in their saris and bindis were particularly noticeable as they shopped on the local streets, and some of them were jeered at, pushed or shoved by young toughs who plucked at their clothing.

While the Jersey City police investigated these incidents in a lackadaisical fashion, the situation turned tragic. In separate attacks, two young Indian immigrant men were brutally beaten. Navroze Mody, a Citicorp executive returning from an evening out with a white friend, was beaten so fiercely by a group of Hispanic youth that he died of his injuries. The other young man, a scientist newly arrived in the United States and looking for work to support elderly parents, survived a similar attack but was left with permanent brain damage.

The reaction of Indians in the tri-state area was one of stunned horror—and immobility. People in New York City talked privately about their fears ("Am I next?"), now that they realized that there was a reservoir of anti-Indian hatred nearby, but they were also bewildered. What had they done to bring this reaction down on their heads? Hadn't they been model immigrants? Perhaps the Indians in Jersey City had failed to be good citizens, "too clannish" or too "pushy" in their efforts to start small businesses. Virtually nobody wanted to discuss these attacks in terms of racial bias. Rita Sethi, an activist at the time, notes in a 1993 article that even white liberals had difficulty in 1986–87 in seeing these as bias crimes, so accustomed were they to understanding racial violence solely in terms of blacks against whites.

The local chapters of the two major national Indian immigrant organizations, the Federation of Indian Associations and the Associations of Indians in American, declined to get involved. Some of the Indian ethnic elite, safe in New York–area suburbs, hastened to distance themselves from the Jersey City victims, noting that they had probably invited American hatred by "keeping to themselves too much" (that is, by living in large groups and speaking Gujarati) or suggesting that those in Jersey

City had asked for trouble by living in a racially mixed area of urban decay (that is, for being poor). In other circumstances, this entrepreneurial drive and this retention of Indian language, culture, and dress might have been applauded by fellow Indians. Meanwhile, New Jersey officials dragged their feet, refusing to treat the incidents as a pattern of bias crimes. At one point, since no outraged ethnic community was clamoring for justice, it seemed that Mody's murderers might never be caught and that the author of the menacing dotbuster letter might go unidentified.

To their lasting credit, a group of young, progressive students, based at Columbia University, rose to the occasion and took on the daunting task of organizing a response and pressuring New Jersey authorities to pursue the cases vigorously. The group, which called itself Indian Youth Against Racism (IYAR, later YAAR), spent several years in an effort that, members say today, permanently changed their lives. Some of the YAAR organizers said they themselves had first experienced racism as schoolchildren on Long Island. Initially YAAR offered emotional support to both injured men's families and helped them find legal advice. Activists spent hours in and around Jersey City talking to Indian immigrant residents to document the patterns of harassment. Once arrests were made, YAAR mobilized groups of students from neighboring colleges to attend court proceedings, keeping pressure on the county prosecutor to seek convictions. This effort lasted several years, as did an initiative to develop anti-bias curricula and teaching materials about India for local schools.

YAAR's work was lonely, as the students faced indifference or outright criticism from older Indians around them. As one young activist said, very poignantly, "I looked around for my community, and my community wasn't there." One other change was significant, however. YAAR organizers believe that the Indian American college students from New York, New Jersey, and Philadelphia, who faithfully attended the long-drawn-out trial of Mody's attackers, were part of an age cohort developing a sense of itself as South Asian or Asian American. Although just as upwardly mobile and bourgeois in outlook as their parents, they grew to see themselves not as white but as South Asian or Asian American, part of a minority ethnic group that could be victimized by racial prejudice but could also demand racial justice without loss of status.

Perhaps shamed by the activity of the young, an ad hoc group of older New Jersey Indians did finally manage to organize some meetings to respond to these events. This group soon split along class lines, with one faction led by a local doctor, the other by an elderly Gandhian who worked as a security guard. The doctor's group was nonplused to receive offers of support from established civil rights groups in New York City, to whom the situation was all too familiar. The Guardian Angels, a racially mixed group of New York City young people who had created their own uniformed safety patrols in troubled neighborhoods in the 1980s, spent some time roaming the streets of Jersey City and provided security at a rally. The Reverend Herbert Daughtry, a well-known African American civil rights activist from Brooklyn, offered his support and was reluctantly invited to speak at a protest rally. Nevertheless, real interethnic cooperation never got off the ground, since the Indians remained intensely embarrassed at the idea of launching protests or pressing demands on the state over an issue of racism.

When another clearly racist attack on a South Asian occurred in Queens, in fall 1998, it initially seemed as if a similar scenario of Indian community inaction was about to be replayed. After some hesitation, however, New York City Indians began getting tentatively involved, again prodded by the young. The beating victim this time was a Trinidadian man of Indian extraction. In New York City, Indians from India keep their distance from Indo-Caribbeans,[6] whom Indians disdain for their poverty, their lack of education, their ignorance of Indian culture, and their mannerisms, which are often more Afro-Caribbean than Indian. Nineteen-year-old Rishi Maharaj was set upon by Hispanic and Italian American youths shouting anti-Indian slogans and wielding baseball bats and was badly hurt. There were several witnesses to the attack on an Ozone Park street where Indo-Caribbeans are beginning to buy houses. The police quickly arrested the attackers, charged them with attempted murder, and listed the incident as a bias crime.

This time the Federation of Indian Associations did come forward to offer the victim and his family public support. Two articles written by a young Indian American reporter for the *New York Times* (see Sengupta 1998; Sengupta and Toy 1998), in addition to the determination of Maharaj's outspoken lawyer cousin, may have spurred some of this interest.[7] Three weeks after the attack, a sizeable demonstration was held outside the Queens County Court as supporters pressed for higher bail for the accused. Indo-Trinidadians, Indo-Guyanese, and Indians, holding signs and national flags, attended the protest in an unusual example of cooperation and solidarity. The protest demonstration was reported in unusual detail in the Indian immigrant media. In July 2000 a defendant was finally sentenced to eight years in jail after the Queens District Attorney argued that the attack was ethnically motivated.

This case, the first to push an immigrant leadership to action over an issue of racism, may indicate that Indian immigrants are taking their first tentative steps toward forming the kinds of alliance and political mobilizations that help give other ethnic groups leverage and visibility in New York City politics. It is still too early to tell whether these fragile understandings and coalitions will endure, but if they do, they will represent a further stage in Indian immigrants' political and social incorporation into local culture.

Conclusion

Indians, already well-integrated into the city's economy, are now taking the first steps toward political and cultural incorporation into local culture as well. To do so, however, they must first come to terms with the contradictions inherent in their own ethnic, racial, and class image of themselves.

Because of the unusually successful and speedy economic integration of Indians as a group, the first-generation Indian immigrant elite in and around New York has constructed itself as racially white, insisting that Indian immigrants have nothing in common with the low status new immigrants or with older racial/ethnic minorities in the area. Indian immigrants have steadfastly denied that they suffer discrimination or are victimized by prejudice, a position that parallels the leadership's denial of unemployment, underemployment, or other social problems experienced by Indians. The first generation's strong transnational identity as Indians has facilitated this position, by allowing people to lay claim to a national identity apart from, and superior to, the American understanding of race or ethnicity. I contend that some of the appeal of transnationalism for Indian immigrants is precisely their covert unease in American society—an unease partly cultural and partly a reaction to discrimination in schools, workplaces, and residential neighborhoods where Indians aspire to the cultural markers of whiteness. A claim of an overriding, transnational Indian-ness allows people to ignore, for much of the time, their racialized U.S. identity. Unfortunately, this self-image is occasionally brought up roughly against an alternative reality, as a few serious incidents of racial antagonism indicate. A transnational Indian identity means little to the average American, while Indian immigrants' claim to whiteness is rejected on the grounds of their skin color and general foreignness.

Both the French- and English-speaking Caribbean have proverbs that say, "Money whitens." India has comparable proverbs about Untouchables who grow rich and "ripen" into higher caste persons. The contemporary United States offers no such simple, unequivocal transformation of assigned racial identity through prosperity. Even wealthy and successful Indian immigrants, whose lives are in many ways "whitened" through money, may, like H., suffer checks to their careers on the basis of prejudice. Like many Indians in the Greater New York suburbs, they may encounter anti-immigrant feeling from neighbors. Lower-middle-class and working-class South Asians, of whom there are far more than the Indian immigrant leadership acknowledges, are more likely to suffer physical attack. The violent bias incidents described here both involved a classic scenario for racial violence: poor but striving members of a minority group move into neighborhoods inhabited by older, equally poor groups, either white or minority, which then launch attacks to defend "their" territory. There is, perhaps, a continuum of "whitening," but it is never a complete process, leaving even wealthy and well-established Indian immigrants vulnerable to racism and prejudice.

The interest in the cases of racial attack described here is how the "Indian community"—both an older, first-generation ethnic leadership and an increasing number of younger members—have responded. The younger people, whose own lived experiences do not conform to the "white" model their parents have constructed, are slowly rejecting aspects of that model. The growing influence of this second generation seems to have sparked the slow development of a more flexible, multilayered, and inclusive form of ethnic self-identification for Indians in New York, although the process is still in its infancy. Members of the second generation, less caught up in transnationalism, are far more likely to acknowledge themselves as Asians and as people of color, without feeling degraded by the classification. This generation is also keenly aware of the U.S. history of racism and racial categorization—indeed, many have experienced its effects for themselves. They do not argue that Indian immigrants stand outside this history. Nor does this generation frantically insist on its whiteness, preferring to stress its ethnicity as part of a multiethnic society. At the same time, in acknowledging minority status, this younger generation has been able to lay claim to the other half of the American racial history that keeps the ideals of the civil rights movement and the concern for social justice alive, particularly in a city like New York with its strong progressive tradition. As these lived experiences become part of the Indian American consciousness, the group moves closer to the American main-stream—multiethnic and contentious as it is.

Tables

TABLE 8.1. Socioeconomic Profile of Indian-born Migrants in New York City, 1990, as Percentage of Total

Households at or below poverty line	
Pre-1980 migrants	7.1%
1980–89 migrants	13.4
Households with income over $40,000	
Pre-1980 migrants only	67.8
Households containing 3 or more workers	
1980–89 migrants only	23.0
College graduates age 25 and older	
Pre-1980 migrants	56.5
1980–89 migrants	8.3

Source: Bureau of the Census 1993b.

TABLE 8.2. Median Individual Incomes of Men and Women Older than 25 in New York City and Surrounding Areas, 1990

	Men	*Women*
New York City	$23,936	$17,191
Mid-Hudson counties	$38,675	$25,214
Nassau-Suffolk counties	$42,530	$27,786
New Jersey	$34,489	$15,622
Connecticut	$53,203	$10,275

Source: Bureau of the Census 1993a.

TABLE 8.3. Household Income Levels of Indian-Born Immigrants in New York City, 1990, as Percentage of Total

Loss of income or no income	2%
Less than $15,000 a year	11
$15,000–$34,999 a year	29
$35,000–$74,999 a year	43
$75,000 and over a year	15

Source: Bureau of the Census 1993e.

TABLE 8.4. Median Incomes of Professionals by Ethnic Group, Entire United States, 1990

	Foreign-born	Native-born
All groups	$35,363	$31,008
Whites	$36,375	$31,574
Blacks	$30,345	$26,250
All Asians	$37,782	$34,634
Asian Indians	$40,625	$30,564

Source: Public Use Microdata Sample, U.S. Census 1990, cited in Bouvier and Simcox 1994, 43.

TABLE 8.5. Distribution of Asian Indian Professionals in Selected Occupational Categories, as Percentage of Entire U.S. Population, 1990

	Foreign-born	Native-born
Engineers	26.0%	21.9%
Math/computer experts	9.0	9.6
Doctors	19.6	12.0
College/university teachers	12.2	14.6
Health care and nursing	9.3	8.9

Source: Public Use Microdata Sample, U.S. Census 1990, cited in Bouvier and Simcox 1994: 27, 30.

TABLE 8.6. Occupational Distribution of Employed, Indian-Born Men and Women in New York City, 1990, as Percentage of Total

Labor force participation rate	73.5%
Managerial and professional	43.4
Sales and clerical	21.4
Services	14.1
Blue collar	21.0
Receiving public assistance[a]	3.4

Source: Bureau of the Census 1993a.
[a]Among Asian Indians, the bulk of those receiving public assistance are the elderly.

TABLE 8.7. Sector Distribution of Occupations Among Foreign-Born Asian Indian Men and Women over Age 16 in New York City, 1990, as Percentage of Total Sample

Construction	3.7%
Manufacturing	10.8
Transportation and communications	11.0
Wholesale	4.4
Retail	16.0
Finance, insurance, and real estate	11.8
Business services	4.5
Professional services	32.6
Public administration	4.4

Source: Bureau of the Census 1993c.

Notes

Acknowledgment: This research was begun in 1985–86 under a Rockefeller Foundation grant to study Indian immigrant businesses. It has continued, less intensively, since then, through observation, casual and structured interviews, attendance at community events, and a close reading of the immigrant media.

1. Chinese and Japanese Americans, but not Indian Americans, have bitterly criticized this "model minority" image for the damage it does to the ethnic groups involved. See Kwong 1987, 57–80; and Takaki 1989, 474–84.

2. Roediger 1991, 1994, and Singh 1996 (100) remind us that Indians are not the first group of recent immigrants to claim whiteness in an effort to advance their privileges in a new society.

3. It is important to restate that not all Indian immigrants support the program of the Hindu right in India. There are many progressive Indian immigrants in the United States, Canada, and Britain, particularly among students, intellectuals, and scientists, who have taken a stand against the Hindu right as it extends its ideological influence into the Indian diaspora. Many other people quietly regret the popularity of the Hindu right's "backward" ideas, looking nostalgically at the pluralistic ideals that India once espoused. Still others dismiss the controversy as "old-fashioned stuff, leftovers from India," irrelevant to immigrants in a new world.

Nevertheless, letters to the newspaper *India Abroad,* the programs of Indian associations, and the activities of religious groups all make clear that the Hindu right, particularly through the religious and cultural proselytizing of the Vishwa Hindu Parishad, has a wide and receptive audience among both Indian and Indo-Caribbean immigrants in the United States. Muslim and Christian Indians here are deeply distressed but find few avenues to protest since the rightist ideology has already declared them "not true Indians."

4. The Census category "Asian Indian" is, like all the other racial/ethnic categories on the Census, fraught with ambiguity. From the social scientist's point of view, the term *Asian Indian origin* is so open-ended that a wide range of people can choose this self-designation. In addition to migrants born in India and their American-born children, the category probably also counts large numbers of Indo-Caribbeans, along with migrants of Indian ancestry who have entered the United States from Africa, Britain, and Canada.

Sometime between 1990 and 1997, the Census Bureau downgraded its 1990 count of Asian Indians from 815,562 (cited in Gall and Gall 1993) to 786,694, of whom 593,423 were "foreign born"—not necessarily Indian born.

From 1990 figures, Doyle and Khandelwal 1994 identifies 94,590 Asian Indians as living in New York City itself. The 1990 Census (1993a) suggests that in New York City 42,674 of these people were born in India.

5. T.'s narrative, featuring his penniless arrival in the United States followed by early hardships involving cold, hunger, worry, loneliness, and cultural ignorance, contrasts poor new immigrants with present rich businessman and is in some ways stereotypical. These accounts, which highlight heroic individual effort and dauntless entrepreneurial spirit, downplay the support networks of relatives and friends that doubtless existed on both sides of the globe. The stories offer an insight into the way many Indian immigrants re-imagine their entry into a new society, and their vision of individual virtue that makes them both exceptional and worthy of present affluence.

6. Indo-Caribbeans, primarily from Guyana, Suriname, or Trinidad, are descendants of an earlier phase of the Indian diaspora. They were recruited between 1837 and the 1920s to work as indentured laborers in the Caribbean sugar economy. Subjected to extreme exploitation and political discrimination, first by the colonialists and then by Afro-Caribbeans, many have become "twice migrants" in Parminder Bachu's phrase (1993), moving on to the United States. In the past fifteen years their numbers in New York City have soared. Given the cultural differences and the recent separate histories, the two groups' social networks rarely intersect in New York, despite rhetoric about shared heritage and the enduring nature of Indian-ness across time and space.

7. Ironies of cultural misunderstanding remained, however. Reporters Somini Sengupta and Vivian Toy (1998) write that Federation of Indian Associations members visited Maharaj and his family and invited family members to attend an upcoming association function. Maharaj's lawyer cousin and others attended the event, all carefully dressed in Indian national dress. The women said they were virtually ignored once they arrived. The entire audience was focused on meeting visiting members of India's right-wing ruling party, for whom the event had been organized. The young women, who had hoped to rally support for Maharaj, left in disgust.

References

Abraham, Thomas. 1984. "Preface." P. 1 in *North American Directory and Reference Guide of Asian Indian Businesses and Independent Professional Practitioners*, edited by Thomas Abraham. New York: India Enterprises of the West.

Bachu, Parminder. 1993. "Identities Constructed and Reconstructed: Representations of Asian Women in Britain." Pp. 99–117 in *Migrant Women, Crossing Boundaries and Changing Identities*, edited by Gina Buijs. Providence: Berg.

Bouvier, Leon F., and David Simcox. 1994. *Foreign Born Professionals in the United States*. Washington, D.C.: Center for Immigration Studies.

Chen, David. 1999. "The Newcomers, Asian Middle Class Alters a Rural Enclave." *New York Times*, December 27, A-1 .

Doyle, Joe, and Madhulika Khandelwal. 1994. "Asians and Pacific Islanders Enumerated in the 1990 Census." Queens, N.Y.: Asian/American Center, Queens College, CUNY.

Dugger, Celia. 2000. "Return Passage to India: Emigres Pay Back," *New York Times*, February 29, A-1.

Edmondson, Brad. 2000. "The New Suburbanites, Immigration Nation." *Preservation*, January–February, 31–49.

Gall, Susan, and Timothy Gall. 1993. *Statistical Record of Asian Americans*. Detroit: Gale Research.

Gordon, Alastair. 2000. "Raj Style Takes the Silk Road to the Suburbs." *New York Times*, January 27, D-1.

Helweg, Arthur W., and Usha M. Helweg. 1990. *An Immigrant Success Story: East Indians in America*. Philadelphia: University of Pennsylvania Press.

Ignatiev, Noel. 1995. *How the Irish Became White*. New York: Routledge.

Khandelwal, Madhulika. 1995. "Indian Immigrants in Queens, New York City: Patterns of Spatial Concentration and Distribution 1965–90." Pp. 178–96 in *Nation and Migration: The Politics of Space in the South Asian Diaspora*, edited by Peter van der Veer. Philadelphia: University of Pennsylvania Press.

Kibria, Nazli. 1998. "The Racial Gap: South Asian American Racial Identity and the Asian American Movement." Pp. 69–78 in *A Part Yet Apart: South Asians in Asian America*, edited by Lavina Dhingra Shankar and Rajini Srikanth. Philadelphia: Temple University Press.

Kolsky, Elizabeth. 1998. Less Successful Than the Next: South Asian Taxi Drivers in New York City." *South Asian Graduate Research Journal* 5 (1): 1–13.

Kumar, Krishna. 1993. "Behind the VHP of America." *Frontline*, September 10, 10 12.

Kwong, Peter. 1987. *The New Chinatown*. New York: Hill and Wang.

Lessinger, Johanna. 1990. "Asian Indians in New York: Dreams and Despair in the Newsstand Business." *New Asia*, special issue of *The Portable Lower East Side* 7 (2): 73–87.

———. 1992a. "Investing or Going Home? A Transnational Strategy Among Indian Immigrants in the United States." Pp. 53–99 in *Towards a Transnational Perspective on Migration, Race, Class, Ethnicity, and Nationalism Reconsidered*, edited by Nina Schiller, Linda Basch, Cristina Blanc-Szanton. New York: New York Academy of Sciences.

———. 1992b. "Nonresident Indian Investment and India's Drive for Industrial Modernization." Pp. 62–82 in *Anthropology and the Global Factory*, edited by Frances A. Rothstein and Michael L. Blim. New York: Bergin and Garvey.

———. 1995. *From the Ganges to the Hudson: Indian Immigrants in New York City*. Boston: Allyn and Bacon.

Lobo, Arun Peter, Joseph Salvo, and Vicky Virgin. 1996. *The Newest New Yorkers, 1990–1994: An Analysis of Immigration to NYC in the Early 1990s*. New York: Department of City Planning.

Lopez, David, and Yen Le Espiritu. 1990. "Panethnicity in the United States: A Theoretical Framework." *Ethnic and Racial Studies* 13 (2): 198–223.

Mazumdar, Sucheta. 1989. "Race and Racism: South Asians in the United States." Pp. 25–38 in *Frontiers of Asian American Studies*, edited by Gail Nomura, Russell Endo, Stephen Sumida, and Russell Leong. Pullman: Washington State University Press.

Motwani, Jagat K., and Jyoti Barot-Motwani. 1989. "Introduction." Pp. i–iv in *Global Migration of Indian: Saga of Adventure, Enterprise, Identity, and Integration*, edited by Jagat Motwani and Jyoti Barot-Motwani. Commemorative volume. New York: First Global Convention of People of Indian Origin.

Omatsu, Glenn. 1994. "The 'Four Prisons' and the Movements of Liberation: Asian American Activism from the 1960s to the 1990s." Pp. 19–69 in *The State of Asian America*, edited by Karin Aguilar–San Juan. Boston: South End Press.

Omi, Michael, and Howard Winant. 1994. *Racial Formation in the United States from the 1960s to the 1990s.* New York: Routledge.

Prashad, Vijay. 2000. *The Karma of Brown Folk.* Minneapolis: University of Minnesota Press.

Radhakrishnan, R. 1994. "Is the Ethnic 'Authentic' in the Diaspora?" Pp. 219–33 in *The State of Asian America,* edited by Karin Aguilar–San Juan. Boston: South End Press.

Rajagopal, Arvind. 1993. "An Unholy Nexus: Expatriate Anxiety and Hindu Extremism." *Frontline,* September 10, 12–14.

Robinson, Vaughan. 1990. "Boom and Gloom: The Success and Failure of South Asians in Britain." Pp. 269–96 in *South Asians Overseas: Migration and Ethnicity,* edited by Colin Clarke, Ceri Peach, and Steven Vertovec. Cambridge: Cambridge University Press.

Roediger, David R. 1991. *The Wages of Whiteness: Race and the Making of the American Working Class.* London: Verso.

———. 1994. *Racial Formation in the United States from the 1960s to the 1990s.* New York: Routledge.

Saran, Parmatma. 1985. *The Asian Indian Experience in the United States.* Cambridge: Schenkman.

Sengupta, Somini. 1998. "Racial Motive Is Seen in Beating of Indian-American Man in Queens." *New York Times,* September 22, B-1.

Sengupta, Somini, and Vivian Toy. 1998. "Two Groups of East Indians Are Brought Closer, for Now." *New York Times,* October 7, B-1.

Sethi, Rita Chaudhry. 1993. "Smells Like Racism: A Plan for Mobilizing Against Anti-Asian Bias." Pp. 235–50 in *The State of Asian America,* edited by Karin Aguilar–San Juan. Boston: South End Press.

Singh, Amritjit. 1996. "African Americans and the New Immigrants." Pp. 93–110 in *Between the Lines: South Asians and Postcoloniality,* edited by Deepika Bahri and Mary Vasudeva. Philadelphia: Temple University Press.

Takaki, Ronald. 1989. *Strangers from a Different Shore: A History of Asian Americans.* Boston: Little, Brown.

United States Commission on Civil Rights 1992. *Civil Rights Issues Facing Asian Americans in the 1990s.* Washington, D.C.: Government Printing Office.

U.S. Bureau of the Census. 1993a. *1990* Census of Population. Public Use Microdata Samples. Washington, D.C.: Government Printing Office.

———. 1993b. *1990* Census of Population. "Selected Characteristics for Persons of Asian Indian Race: 1990." CPH-L-151. Washington, D.C.: Government Printing Office.

———. 1993c. *1990* Census of Population. "Income and Poverty Status in 1989–1990," CPH-L-80. Washington, D.C.: Government Printing Office.

Werbner, Pnina, and Muhammad Anwar. 1991. *Black and Ethnic Leaderships: The Cultural Dimensions of Political Action.* London: Routledge.

CHAPTER 9

Ethnic Niches and Racial Traps: Jamaicans in the New York Regional Economy

Philip Kasinitz and Milton Vickerman

International migration links distant places in direct, personal, and even intimate ways. Nowhere is this more apparent than in the longstanding relationship between the small island nation of Jamaica and the New York urban region. There are now at least 200,000 Jamaican-born persons in the region, a remarkable number of immigrants from a nation whose total population is only 2.6 million. Together with their U.S.–born children, Jamaican New Yorkers play a vital role in the regional economy, and the ups and downs of New York's economic fortunes are now clearly felt in Jamaica. Remittances from New York are one of the largest sources of foreign exchange for the Caribbean nation and make the difference between destitution and decent standards of living for tens of thousands of Jamaican families. Yet any sudden downturn in the Jamaican economy can send thousands of immigrants, legal and illegal, to the region.

In this chapter we examine the economic position of contemporary Jamaican immigrants in New York. On the whole this group has been relatively successful. Jamaican household incomes are higher than those of African Americans and their labor force participation is higher than for many comparable immigrant groups. The portion of Jamaican households living in poverty is lower than that of African Americans, Puerto Ricans, Dominicans, and Haitians and is only slightly higher than the U.S. average (for a more skeptical view on West Indian economic "success" see Model 1995). Like other contemporary immigrants, Jamaicans in New York have developed distinct niches within the regional economy (see Waldinger 1996), and these niches have aided the group's upward mobility.

Among Jamaicans, however, race seems to have shaped and sometimes truncated the development of these niches and limited the effectiveness of "social capital." Like African Americans (and unlike most non–West Indian immigrants), Jamaicans work disproportionately in the public and not-for-profit sectors, where opportunities for capital accumulation are limited and where dense networks of "connections" while not irrelevant for individual success probably "count" less than in the private sector. Like African Americans, Jamaicans suffer a marked discrimination in the housing market that effectively limits their access to employment opportunities in many of the outer parts of the region. Despite considerable mythology about West Indian entrepreneurialism, Jamaican self-employment rates are very low and Jamaican ethnic niches tend to be (to borrow Roger Waldinger's phrase [1996]) "non-hierarchical." Thus Jamaicans have not formed anything like the "ethnic enclaves" (see Portes and Manning 1986) seen among some other economically successful groups. They have little real control over the sectors in the economy in which they are concentrated.

In fact, we argue, the comparative ease with which English-speaking Jamaicans have been incorporated into the growing service sector has had both positive and negative consequences. It has opened access to employment in the mainstream economy. But it has prevented the formation of "Chinatown-like" autonomous economic structures (see Zhou 1992) and left Jamaicans, nearly all of whom are black (at least by North American standards),[1] vulnerable to racial discrimination. Further, Jamaican employment is far more niche-concentrated among women than among men. This fact points to the importance of gender, an issue rarely addressed in the "ethnic economy" literature. Jamaicans enter the U.S. economy with a long history of female labor force participation, and, we argue, much of the relative success of Jamaican households is due to the large number of Jamaican women working for wages, albeit often poor ones. Finally, it must be noted that while the Jamaican (and African American) public sector concentration (particularly in health care) may have been an advantage during the 1970s and 1980s, it turned into a disadvantage in the anti-government 1990s.

Enclaves, Niches, and Middle Men: Immigrants in the Changing Regional Economy

In recent years the economic roles played by immigrants has become a central theme in the study of international migration in the social sciences, and particularly in the burgeoning field of economic sociology (see, for example, Portes 1995). Many have argued that immigrant economic concentration, employment networks, and entrepreneurialism help to explain the relatively high rate of economic success among some immigrant groups, particularly when compared with native minorities. (Indeed, immigrant entrepreneurialism is now so frequently studied that it is important to remember that self-employment accounts for only a minority of the labor force in even the most entrepreneurial groups.) Further, it is argued that economic and cultural "ethnic enclaves" have forestalled some aspects of assimilation and may (ironically) maintain "immigrant advantages" in social and cultural capital into the second generation.

Alejandro Portes and Min Zhou (1992, 498) speak of the "peculiar American paradox of rising labor market marginalization of native born Blacks and Puerto Ricans, along with growing numbers and employment of third world immigrants." This "paradox" is found particularly in global cities, such as Los Angeles and New York, where in recent decades manufacturing jobs have been lost, poverty and unemployment among low-skilled native minorities have increased, and job opportunities for those with less formal education have dwindled, yet which nonetheless serve as magnets for immigration. Saskia Sassen (1988, 22) argues that in such cities the growth of professional employment creates demand for low-wage, low-skilled, service jobs, which are more attractive and accessible to immigrants than to native minorities. She also notes that immigrants are better able to take advantage of these opportunities because their survival strategies and their willingness to work at service jobs fit well with the organization of the urban service economy. Jamaicans' suitability for these jobs is further facilitated by the fact that the immigrants typically speak English and have at least moderately high levels of education, both characteristics more important in a service-oriented economy than in one dominated by manufacturing.

The literature points to several modes by which immigrants and minorities are typically incorporated into this sort of economy. The "ethnic enclave" model, epitomized by the Chinese in New York (see Zhou 1992) or the Cubans in Miami (see Portes and Stepick 1993) is characterized by a high degree of coethnicity among the owners and employees of firms, the spatial concentration of ethnic businesses (often corresponding to ethnic residential patterns) and sectoral specializations among immigrant businesses. In this model immigrants with a wide variety of skill and human capital levels can be absorbed into the enclave. Waldinger's (1994, 1996) discussion of ethnic "niches" probably comes closer to describing the situation of Jamaicans in the New York region—or at least situation of Jamaican women. For Waldinger, a "niche" is simply an overconcentration of members of an ethnic group in an area of specialization. Waldinger argues that immigrants' social networks, which connect them with job possibilities, combined with the racial prejudice and discrimination that leads employers to prefer to hire immigrants (including black immigrants) rather than native blacks, creates specialized ethnic niches in employment. Such "niches" come about in a variety of ways: Immigrants arrive with certain skills and abilities or disabilities. Jamaicans, for example, came with a tradition of female labor force participation and speaking English, a good match with the needs of the growing health care sector in the 1970s and 1980s. But more important than the initial reasons for going into a specific job is how a group comes to dominate an occupation and achieve "closure" over a niche by passing on vital information, formal and informal assistance and apprenticeships, references, and capital through kin and ethnic networks. Such networks, intentionally or not, make it harder then for non–group members to get "niche" jobs.

Another possible mode of incorporation, identified by Logan and his colleagues (Logan, Alba, and McNulty 1994, 695) is "ethnic assimilation," by which a group is

absorbed equally into all sectors of the economy, without forming distinct ethnic con-
centrations. In some ways this phrase describes the situation of Jamaican men—but
with one crucial caveat. If Jamaican men "assimilate" they do so into a "black" America, and their employment possibilities will be shaped by this fact. Thus, when they
are absorbed into the mainstream economy it will be into those parts of the mainstream economy open to black people, creating the strong possibility that the immigrants will be incorporated into the secondary labor market, where group members
are concentrated only as employees in disadvantaged economic sectors.

Other varieties of incorporation include the development of businesses based in
ethnic neighborhoods or on ethnically specific markets. In this case an entrepreneurial class arises primarily to serve the needs of the immigrant or ethnic community. By
contrast entrepreneurial "middleman minorities" serve constituencies other than
coethnics and often act as intermediaries between poor (frequently minority) consumers and the mainstream economy (see also Bonacich 1972; Light 1972; Light and
Gold 2000; Zenner 1980). All of these models stress the importance of immigrant
social networks that bring them more information about job opportunities and reas-
sure employers about their work habits (see Kasinitz and Rosenberg 1996).

Jamaicans in New York

Afro-Caribbean[2] immigrants, of whom Jamaicans are the largest single national group,
are relatively understudied, though Afro-Caribbeans have immigrated to the United
States in substantial numbers since the turn of the century and they rank among the
larger post-1965 immigrant groups. Indeed, they have been described as the "invisible
immigrants" (Bryce-Laporte 1972). Most scholarly and popular attention that the
group has received has focused on how West Indians construct their racial identity
(Foner 1987; Kasinitz 1992; Vickerman 1994; Waters 1993) or on what West Indian economic "success" (or lack of "success") implies about African Americans (Farley 1986;
Model 1991, 1995; Sowell 1981). Journalistic descriptions of the West Indian American
community frequently dwell on the "discipline," "family values," and "work ethic" of
a group that could produce a Colin Powell. That the same milieu also produced Louis
Farrakhan is less often noted.

While the literature tells us less about Caribbean immigrants in their own right, one
fact emerges clearly: Jamaicans, like other West Indians, travel. Faced with the limits
of the small, insular economies and perennially high rates of unemployment, they
have, for generations, left the island looking for a better life. Jamaica, like other Anglo-
phone Caribbean territories, has long sent its sons and daughters abroad—to Panama
to build the canal, to Cuba to cut sugarcane early in the century, to Costa Rica to work
on banana plantations, to Britain in the post–World War II period, and, throughout
most of this century, to New York.

The near simultaneous restriction of Caribbean immigration to Great Britain in 1962
and the opening up of immigration to the United States after the Hart-Cellar reforms in

1965, combined to make New York the destination of choice for Jamaican migrants. In the 1970s and 1980s skyrocketing inflation and the deteriorating Jamaican economy forced both the poor and the middle class to emigrate. During those decades the Jamaican unemployment rated stayed over 20 percent, hitting a high of 31.1 percent in 1979 (United Nations Statistical Office 1992).[3] Inflation averaged 18.5 percent a year during the 1970s and 16.0 percent during the 1980s (Deere 1990). The Jamaican dollar, which in 1970 could be exchanged for U.S. dollars at rates close to one to one, has repeatedly devalued; today is takes more than forty Jamaican dollars to buy one U.S. dollar. This loss of foreign exchange value is particularly devastating for a small country where many foodstuffs and other basic goods, as well as manufactured goods, have to be imported. One informant, a contractor and former cost surveyor with the Jamaican National Water Commission, describes his decision to emigrate in the early 1980s[4]:

> It was an economic thing. . . . I came to see if I can make life easier . . . although I was a civil servant I found that the cost of living was moving much faster than my salary. I owned two vehicles and when I looked around and saw the price of vehicles, how it was going up so fast, I saw there was no way I could replace them. And then my two children . . . come of age to go to college. . . . If I was wealthy, then I could send the children to school in this country [i.e., the United States] without coming [myself], but very few people can [afford to] stay in the West Indies and send a child to school in America.

The New York urban region is the largest single destination for Jamaicans in the United States, as it has been for most of the century. Of those who emigrated between 1972 and 1992, 53.4 percent settled in the region. Indeed, Jamaicans are one most regionally concentrated of major immigrant groups to the United States. The 1990 Census (Bureau of the Census 1993), which almost certainly undercounted the group, shows Jamaicans to be the second largest foreign-born population in the region. While this migration has slowed some since its height in the early 1980s—the number declaring their intention to settle in the region fell in the mid-1990s to about 10,000 a year, down from an all time high of 13,481 in 1989—it remains one of the principal sources of new immigrants to New York.

Further, with Jamaica's population now projected to reach 3.5 million by 2025 and economic development stagnating throughout the Caribbean region, there is every reason to believe that steady migration to the New York urban region will continue (*Miami Herald* 1997). Indeed, Jamaican officials point to the fact that the North American Free Trade Agreement (NAFTA), though Jamaica is not a party to it, may now reverse the modest employment gains Jamaica made in the 1980s in several sectors (most notably garment manufacturing) by encouraging the movement of jobs to Mexico (Patterson 1997).

Although economically motivated, Jamaican immigration is greatly facilitated by the family reunification provisions of U.S. immigration law. Between 1983 and 1991, of the over 90,000 Jamaican immigrants legally admitted to the United States, 90 percent entered the country[5] through family reunification provisions of the immigration law, and 64 percent through the "second preference"; that is, they were the spouses of permanent residents or the children of permanent residents and U.S. citizens . Of the 10 percent that came through occupational categories, the large majority came through the "6th preference," the nonprofessional occupational category frequently used by "live-in" domestic servants, which was severely cut back by the Immigration Reform and Control Act of 1996 (Department of Justice 1984–92).

Sixty-eight percent of Jamaicans in the region live in New York City. While this proportion is higher that for immigrants in general, it is lower than that of other pre-dominantly black immigrant groups (for example, 82.6 percent of Trinidad-Tobago immigrants and 82.9 percent of Barbarian immigrants in the region live in the city). In New York, Jamaicans generally share residential neighborhoods with other West Indians and, to a lesser extent, with Haitians. The largest single residential concen-tration is in central Brooklyn, most notably in the contiguous neighborhoods of Crown Heights (also home to a large number of African Americans and members of the Lubavitcher Hasidic Sect of Jews), East Flatbush, and Flatbush. More affluent members of the community have also settled in the suburb-like neighborhoods of South Eastern Queens along the Nassau County border, most notably in Laurelton and Cambria Heights. Others are now found in the working- and middle-class row house neighborhoods of the North Western Bronx, especially Williamsbridge and Wakefield. Significant numbers of poorer Jamaicans, particularly recent immigrants, can also be found in East New York, Bushwick, and Bedford Stuyvesant, all areas they share with African Americans and other recent immigrants (Kasinitz 1992; New York Department of City Planning 1992; Nossiter 1995).

The largest suburban concentration of Jamaicans is in southern Westchester, most visibly in Mount Vernon, where from 1985 to 1995 the mayor, Ronald Blackwood, was a Jamaican American. There is also a growing Jamaican community in Rockland Country (Spring Valley's mayor, Allan Thompson, is also Jamaican American) and in northern New Jersey, notably in Montclair and Englewood, and small Jamaican com-munities in Hartford and New Haven, Connecticut—partially the result of recent sub-urban expansion from New York and partially as a result of older immigration, some of it descended from Jamaican migrant farm workers in the Connecticut Valley. Jamaicans in the suburbs usually share neighborhoods with African Americans. Not surprisingly, suburban Jamaicans are more affluent than those in the city, who are more likely to be recent arrivals. The 1990 Census (Bureau of the Census 1993) found that while only 30.7 percent of Jamaican households in the region live in the suburbs, 46.9 percent of those with incomes over $75,000 do. Still, the majority of Jamaicans at all income levels live within the city limits. Given the Jamaican propensity for home-ownership and the concentration of middle-class Jamaicans in those parts of the city closest to and most physically resembling the suburbs, it seems reasonable to con-clude that the urban concentration of Jamaicans is largely the result of racial discrim-ination in suburban housing markets.

Concern has been raised by George Borjas (1990) and others that the human capi-tal stock of recent immigrants has declined relative to what it was two decades ago. Interestingly, Jamaicans in New York make this observation about their own community, frequently maintaining that many more of the recent immigrants are coming from the poorest and least educated sectors of Jamaican society. They sometimes talk about the emergence an immigrant "underclass." This notion, although reinforced by the rising visibility of Jamaican organized crime in the late 1980s (see Gunst 1995), is only weakly supported by Immigration and Naturalization Service data. In the late 1970s professionals and managers and administrators constituted 12 percent of Jamaican immigrants annually. In the mid-1990s they generally accounted for about 6 percent. Education levels among immigrants, however, did not fall dramatically. In the New York urban region labor force participation was only slightly higher for high school graduates than for dropouts (Department of Justice 1973–96).

Niches and Networks: Jamaican New Yorkers in the Regional Economy

Like most other immigrants, Jamaican workers in the New York metropolitan region tend to be concentrated in certain occupations and sectors. These occupational niches have grown up gradually and reflect the skills, cultural preferences, and human capital within the group, as well as the structures of opportunities available to them within the regional economy and actions taken by the group to create "ethnic networks" through which employment information and referrals may flow.[6] The specific circumstances of Jamaican immigrants, however, have shaped their experience in several unusual ways.

As English-speaking immigrants, Jamaicans may have easier access to some jobs than do other immigrants. Whereas linguistic isolation limits members of other groups to ethnic enclaves, or to fields that require few language skills, such as manufacturing, Jamaicans were able to take advantage of the growing number of retail, clerical, and personal service jobs in the New York urban region during the late 1970s and 1980s. Thus, Jamaicans were not heavily represented in the declining manufacturing sector during this period, a fact that allowed them to avoid the most negative impacts of economic restructuring. In 1990 Jamaicans, especially women, who outnumber men among Jamaicans in the labor force, were overrepresented in retailing, personal and household services, and particularly health care, all areas where language skills are required (see Table 9.1).

Jamaican women are also heavily represented in the finance, insurance, and real estate sector, which had grown markedly in the decade preceding the 1990 Census. Many of these jobs appear to have been clerical, and here again the immigrants' English-language abilities allowed them access to growing sectors. Even in the least well paying jobs English-language skills helped Jamaican women. For example, among the 13 percent of Jamaican women listed as working in personal services, many were working in domestic child care. Jobs in this area, while poorly paid, grew in number during the 1970s and 1980s as more and more middle-class women with young children entered the labor force (indeed, the 13 percent figure is almost certainly an

TABLE 9.1 Jamaican Immigrants Ages 16–65 by Industry, New York Urban Region, 1990

	Male (N = 39,237)	Female (N = 54,905)
Agriculture and mining	0.6%	—
Construction	11.0%	0.6%
Manufacturing	8.4%	4.4%
Transportation and utilities	13.5%	3.3%
Wholesale trade	3.1%	1.3%
Retail trade	11.9%	7.9%
FIRE[a]	9.9%	10.9%
Business services	1.1%	2.2%
Personal services	11.5%	13.0%
Health care	7.5%	30.6%
Education	2.6%	5.1%
Social service	1.8%	5.4%
Public administration	3.4%	2.2%
Armed forces	0.3%	0.1%
None reported	13.4%	13.0%

Source: 1990 Census, Public Use Micro Sample. New York urban region: The Thirty County Regional Plan Association definition of the region.

[a]*Fire, insurance, and real estate.*

undercount, as this is an area in which undocumented immigrants are often employed, and thus one where census data is particularly suspect). English facility clearly gave Jamaican and other West Indian immigrants an advantage over non–English-speaking immigrants in competing for these jobs (see Colen 1987, 1990).

At the same time, as black immigrants, Jamaicans may find their opportunities limited by racial discrimination in hiring and credit availability and, in some parts of the region, by job location because of segregation in the housing market. Jamaicans may be aided, however, by affirmative action programs and policies, which are far more effective in the public sector than the for-profit sectors of the economy. Thus, their fate is in many ways tied to that of African Americans and, like African Americans, they have become increasingly concentrated in the public sector (see Waldinger 1996). Over 28 percent of Jamaicans in the region worked in the public or not-for-profit sectors in 1990 (Table 9.2), a remarkable figure given the fact that many civil service jobs require U.S. citizenship. In New York City, the percentage is even higher.

Yet Caribbean hiring networks, while functioning within a racially defined opportunity structure, have led to outcomes in the labor market quite different from those of African Americans. Jamaican-born immigrants in the region have notably high rates of labor force participation, and the rate of female labor force participation for ages sixteen through sixty-five is particularly high (79.5 percent in New York City, 78.6 percent in the region as a whole). Remarkably, these figures vary little by education. Labor force participation is only slightly lower (and public assistance use only slightly

TABLE 9.2 Sector of Employment for Jamaican Immigrants Ages 16–65, New York Urban Region, 1990

Class of Worker	New York City	Suburbs	Total Region
Profit	65.2%	69.0%	66.5%
Not-for-profit	10.8%	10.7%	10.7%
Government	18.5%	14.8%	17.2%
Self-employed	5.6%	5.4%	5.5%
Total number reporting occupation	65,158	34,090	96,248

Source: Bureau of the Census 1993.

higher) for high school dropouts than for high school graduates. And the household poverty rate among Jamaicans is lower than for most comparable immigrant groups in the city, and 46.9 percent of Jamaicans had income over $40,000 (Table 9.3).

These low rates of household poverty, however, are in part the result of larger numbers of people in the low-wage service sector labor force. In addition to the high rates of female participation, it is worth noting that 25.5 percent of Jamaican households (26.6 percent of those who arrived since 1980) include three or more wage earners. Compared with other immigrant groups this is not particularly high, which is in itself fairly amazing.

The economic importance of public and not-for-profit sector jobs in the West Indian community may also explain the disproportionate amount of political activity on the part of Afro-Caribbean immigrants (particularly Jamaicans) compared with other recent immigrants. Of the three post-1965 immigrants in New York's City Council, two are West Indians: Jamaica-born Una Clarke and Lloyd Henry, who hails from Belize (the other immigrant is Guillermo Llinares from the Dominican Republic).

TABLE 9.3 New York City Immigrants, 1990

Country of Origin	Percentage of Household in Poverty	Percentage of Household Income	Percentage of Household with 3 or More in Labor Force
Jamaica	13.9	46.9	23
Dominican Republic	34.1	23.4	32.6
China	20.5	34.4	20.2
Italy	10.4	43.2	6.4
USSR	32.8	28.1	33.1
Guyana	13.9	46.3	24.4
Haiti	18.4	40.0	24.2
Columbia	17.1	36.1	8.4
Poland	13.4	28.8	8.4
Ecuador	18.4	38.1	23.1
Trinidad	17.2	42.1	23.1
Korea	17.6	38.9	20.2
India	11.5	54.7	22.4

Source: 1990 Census, Public Use Micro Sample.

Another Jamaican immigrant, Nick Perry, represents East Flatbush in the State Assembly, and numerous children of earlier West Immigrants hold public office in New York. By contrast despite their "model minority" image, there are no Chinese-, Korean-, or Indian- born elected officials in New York today, nor are there any South Americans except on local school boards. Ironically, while political participation is often seen as an indicator of "assimilation," Jamaican elected officials have also been aided by their high degree of residential concentration (in part a result of racial segregation), which has created predominantly Caribbean districts.

The Jamaican female labor force is particularly concentrated, with 30.6 percent in the health care industry (Table 9.1). According to the U.S. Census Bureau's three-digit occupation codes (Table 9.4), of those Jamaican women aged sixteen through sixty-five who reported an occupation, 30.5 percent of those living in the city and 29.5 percent of those living in the suburbs were nurse's aides, orderlies, attendants, or registered or licensed practical nurses (for an in-depth study of nurse's aides, see Foner 1994). Clerical workers (often in health care bureaucracies) and domestic workers account for a large number. The top ten reported occupations account for 50.7 percent of all Jamaican female occupations in the city and 50.8 percent in the suburbs.

This concentration—which cannot be explained by pre-migration occupations—differs from the patterns of other highly occupationally concentrated immigrant groups in that it is not the result of coethnic employment. Indeed, very few Jamaicans work for other Jamaicans. Less than 6 percent of Jamaicans reported any self-employment income in 1990, and many of these were in very small enterprises (Table 9.2). In contrast, high levels of Jamaican female concentration reflect patterns of network hiring and referrals.

In the case of the domestic employment parallel, networks of largely female employees and employers sometimes develop, as the following account illustrates. It should be noted that none of the women in this example had done domestic or health care work in Jamaica (all names are pseudonymous).

Mrs. Bradford, who lives in Crown Heights and is in her sixties, came to the United States when she was nearly forty. Like many of her friends she was sponsored by an American family to work as a domestic. In Jamaica she had been a quality control inspector in a West Kingston garment factory. Employment with the original family soon "fell through" because of visa problems. Faced with the daunting prospect of finding a new job in a strange country, she turned to Mrs. Poole, a co-worker from the garment factory who had emigrated some years before. Mrs. Poole, who now worked as a domestic, helped her find a "sleep-in" job with a family in Westchester, which Mrs. Bradford held for seven years, eventually leaving this job for one on the Upper East Side, which she obtained by placing an ad in the newspaper. Two years later, in search of work once again, she turned to another former Kingston co-worker, Mrs. Damon, who had formerly worked as a domestic but who had recently become a Licensed Practical Nurse in a nursing home. Mrs. Damon was the most upwardly mobile member of Mrs. Bradford's circle of former Kingston co-workers, and along with her husband and the help of a "pardner" (rotating credit association) she had recently purchased a home in Queens. With her help, Mrs. Bradford obtained another position.

TABLE 9.4 Occupations of Jamaican Immigrants in New York City and the New York Urban Region, 1990

Jamaican-Born Females, New York City		*Jamaican-Born Males, New York City*	
Occupation	Total Reporting Occupation N = 38,910 (%)	Occupation	Total Reporting Occupation N = 21,875 (%)
Nurses's aides, orderlies, and attendants	21.4	Guards and police, exc. public service	4.2
Registered nurses	7.5	Truck drivers	4.2
Secretaries	6.0	Construction laborers	3.5
Cashiers	3.5	Janitors and cleaners	3.3
Teachers, elementary schools	2.5	Carpenters	3.0
Maids and household workers	2.4	Registered nurses	3.0
Administrative support occupations, including clerical	2.1	Managers and administrators	2.7
Bookkeepers, accounting and auditing clerks	1.9	Supervisors and proprietors, sales occupations	2.7
Managers and administrators	1.9	Accountants and auditors	1.8
Data-entry keyers	1.7	Cooks	1.7
Top ten occupations as a percentage of all occupations	45.5	Top ten occupations as a percentage of all occupations	24.7

Jamaican-Born Females, Suburbs *(New York Urban Region, excluding New York City)*		*Jamaican-Born Males, Suburbs* *(New York Urban Region, excluding New York City)*	
Occupation	Total Reporting Occupation N = 24,552 (%)	Occupation	Total Reporting Occupation N = 19,076 (%)
Nurse's aides, orderlies, and attendants	20.5	Janitors and cleaners	7.5
Registered nurses	7.7	Truck drivers	3.5
Secretaries	4.7	Carpenters	3.3
Private household cleaners and servants	3.4	Assemblers	3.2
Cashiers	3.2	Automobile mechanics	2.9
Maids and household workers	3.1	Accountants and auditors	2.7
General office clerks	2.9	Supervisors and proprieters, sales occupations	2.6
Bookkeepers, accounting and auditing clerks	2.1	Managers and administrators	2.5
Typists	1.6	Miscellaneous food preparation occupations	1.9
Data-entry keyers	1.6	Cashiers	1.8
Top ten occupations as a percentage of all occupations	49.2	Top ten occupations as a percentage of all occupations	31.9

Source: 1990 U.S. Census Public-Use Micro Sample.

About this time Mrs. Bradford took in a roommate, Mrs. Clarke, a younger Jamaican woman who also worked as a domestic. Mrs. Clarke contributed to the rent and Mrs. Bradford helped look after Mrs. Clarke's children. Mrs. Clarke worked for a Jewish family who needed additional help on the weekends. She referred them to Mrs. Bradford, who was then in need of an extra part-time job. Over the next decade Mrs. Bradford in turn referred several other former Kingston neighbors and co-workers to this family, who often employed several part-time domestic workers during the Jewish holidays. The wife in the employing family, in turn, referred several of these women to her friends, who were looking for domestic help. Mrs. Clarke eventually became a Licensed Pactical Nurse and bought a home in East Flatbush. (From field notes, 1995)

Thus, as this case illustrates, in addition to direct referrals, social networks pass along valuable information on how to find jobs (for instance, Caribbean domestic workers sometimes report finding jobs though "ads" in the *Irish Echo*) and contacts with agencies. Through passing on referrals and knowledge, the social networks of Jamaican domestic workers, health care workers, and clerical workers facilitate access to certain jobs. Yet this control over knowledge is a far cry from the sort of ethnic control and autonomy that the classic "ethnic enclave" provides. Further, while Jamaican women may be seen as having an "ethnic niche" in Waldinger's sense (1996), it is a low-paying niche. And their concentration in it is less attributable to any particular predisposition toward domestic and health care work than it is to the fact that both areas expanded rapidly in New York in the 1970s and 1980s. By 1992 health care accounted for 12.6 percent of all employment in the region (Lowenstein 1995). Although there is no question that domestic employment is under counted in official statistics, the huge increase in the number of middle-class women in the labor force clearly opened numerous, if poorly compensated opportunities for immigrants, as the problems of Zoe Baird, Kimba Wood, and Linda Chavez have all demonstrated.

Compared with self-employment, however, these niches provide few opportunities for upward mobility and capital accumulation. Even though some West Indians have made inroads into hospital administration and several have become prominent in the unions that represent health care workers, high skill levels and successful networking among nurses do not open for them the kinds of opportunity that come with self-employment and entrepreneurship. If Jamaican concentration in the service sector provided access to some growing sectors of the economy, it provided few of the entrepreneurial opportunities usually associated with ethnic economies.

Further, Jamaican men display a far lower level of occupational concentration than do women. According to Census Bureau statistics for 1990, the top ten occupations account for only 30.1 percent and 31.9 percent of Jamaican male employment in the city and suburbs, respectively (Table 9.4). The most common jobs are listed as security guards, truck drivers, construction, janitors, and carpenters—but none of these accounts for more than 4.2 percent in the city. A slightly higher number of men than women are self-employed (8.4 percent in the city, 8.5 percent of men ages sixteen to sixty-five in the region). This difference is mainly an outgrowth of skilled labor in construction and contracting, and marginal self-employment in jitney van, taxi, and car service driving.

These "dollar vans" (so called because the standard fare is one dollar), offering a form of privatized mass transit, provide a clear case study of the limits of often-celebrated immigrant entrepreneurialism. Jitney vans cruise the Caribbean neighborhoods and directly (and illegally) compete with city buses by offering lower prices and more frequent service. This practice is to some extent a continuation of a Caribbean tradition: in Jamaica and other parts of the Caribbean jitney vans ("tap taps") have proved such a vital complement to underfunded mass transportation systems that they eventually had to be legalized. In New York, Caribbean elected officials are now also fighting to legalize this service. Yet, while the one journalistic study of dollar van drivers praises their "enterprising" zeal, it also makes clear that many of the men in this niche took up this illegal mode of self-employment only after finding themselves unable to secure adequate employment in traditional blue-collar jobs, and often despite considerable experience and skills (see Husock 1996). Thus the question is whether this mode of self-employment is a first step toward an entrepreneurial career or whether such shoe-string entrepreneurialism is simply a disguised form of unemployment. There are also some concentration, small but growing, of Caribbean men in skilled labor—a fact attested to by the increasing number of backyard machine shops and tool rental facilities appearing in East Flatbush, another direct importation of the Caribbean tradition into New York. Yet many Jamaican men report strong barriers to joining white-dominated skilled trades and construction unions and racial discrimination in finding jobs as contractors. Several informants report leaving skilled trades for low-level clerical work for this reason, and in two cases from the Vickerman sample (see Vickerman 1994) men who had worked as supervisory construction workers for a major British firm in Jamaica reported being unable to break into this industry in New York even at the lowest levels. One eventually went back to Jamaica, while the other, following what we suspect is the more typical pattern, switched occupations, becoming a chauffeur. Blue-collar Jamaican men find more open opportunities in emerging fields not yet dominated by existing white ethnic networks. For example, anecdotal evidence suggests that a Jamaican "micro-niche" may be emerging in cable television installation. This niche, like the dollar vans, is partially a continuation of a Caribbean tradition—satellite dishes have been common in Jamaica for over a decade—and partially an adaptation to the structure of the New York labor market. It is a job that calls for a variety of blue-collar skills, albeit at fairly rudimentary level; installers need a basic knowledge of carpentry, electrical work, and construction. Yet, because the technology itself is new (New York being one of the last places in the country for cable television to become widespread), the niche is not already monopolized by a craft union or networks. Private security work was another a growing if poorly paid field in New York during the 1970s and 1980s.

Thus, Jamaicans men, benefited by a knowledge of English but excluded by racial discrimination and existing networks from many traditional blue-collar jobs, are more likely to see education and professional credentials as the route to upward mobility. And while the professions and positions in bureaucratic organizations (particularly public sector bureaucracies) may provide opportunities for both individual advancement and network building, they do not, by and large, provide anything like the opportunity for employment of coethnics that small business ownership does. In fact, the nepotistic employment practices often celebrated as ethnic self-help and enclave building in the private sector would be considered corruption in the public sector.

Why the Lack of Jamaican Entrepreneurs?

Relatively few Jamaicans work for other Jamaicans or are employed in businesses serving a largely Jamaican clientele. There is plenty of theoretical enthusiasm for the entrepreneurial route of upward mobility within the Jamaican community, and there is a long tradition of business formation and marketplace activity by the black Jamaican peasantry, particularly among women (see Mintz 1974). In Jamaica the small size of the economy has forced many poor people into self-employment, and small-scale entrepreneurialism is celebrated as a form of autonomy and self-determination in Garveyite and Rastafarian ideologies. Yet among black Jamaicans self-employment is generally associated with marginal activities among the lower class: peddling—a traditionally female-dominated sector ("higglering" in Jamaican parlance)—and craft making for the tourist market and subsistence farming in rural areas; jitney cab ("robot") driving and backyard auto-repair shops in urban ones. Rarely has self-employment been seen as a route of upward mobility for black and mixed-race Jamaicans aspiring to middle-class status. Instead, traditionally they have looked to higher education for access to prestigious occupations and professions (Foner 1973; King 1987; Smith 1965). Large-scale entrepreneurial activities, by contrast, have long been dominated by Jamaica's white, Middle Eastern, and Asian minorities. Only since the 1970s, thanks to a combination of government policies and the flight of much of that traditional elite during the Democratic-Socialist Michael Manley administration, have blacks had significant access to the entrepreneurial sector (Stone 1988, 1991).

In Caribbean communities in New York numerous businesses that serve Caribbean clienteles have sprung up. Many of these—restaurants, bakeries, record stores, catering halls, and shipping, insurance, and accounting firms in particular—are owned by Jamaican immigrants. Others, most notably groceries and fruit-and-vegetable markets, are dominated by members of other immigrant groups (as the 1990 Church Avenue boycott made clear).[7]

In New York today several organizations exist to promote the creation of Caribbean businesses. Una Clarke, the Jamaican City Council woman who represents East Flatbush, lists among her proudest accomplishments the formation of a collective of West Indian small-garment manufacturers through which women who had been sewing for local consumers out of their homes are able to professionalize their operations. Even here, however, it should be noted that the state sector—public officials and state-supported chambers of commerce—often leads the way.

Many Jamaican men work in construction, a field in which it is common for skilled employees to become independent contractors. Yet here too, as Waldinger (1995) observes, Caribbean contractors have been largely excluded from the white-dominated networks that control access to larger jobs. Like African American contractors, they have thus had to rely on political contacts and affirmative action set asides to gain access to public sector contracts. This reliance, Waldinger notes, can be a marked disadvantage since governmental contracts are accompanied by state "requirements and dependence on union labor [which] expose black builders to risks from which their . . . counterparts are sheltered (Waldinger 1995, 578).

There is also considerable attention to entrepreneurialism by those who celebrate the Jamaicans as an immigrant success story (relative to African Americans). Early waves of West Indian immigrants were often depicted as striving small-businessmen in both sociological and journalistic accounts that continue to be repeated over the years (see Reid 1939; Glazer and Moynihan 1963). For a discussion of this literature and its ideological implications see Kasinitz 1988). Anecdotal accounts of the business-creating role of Jamaican rotating credit associations have made their way into the sociological literature through the influential work of Ivan Light (1972) and continue to be repeated (see Granovetter 1995) despite the fact that studies of Caribbean rotating credit associations consistently show that they are generally used to save for consumer goods and housing, and only very rarely used for business capital accumulation (see Bonnett 1982).

The fact remains that Jamaican self-employment remains low (5.5 percent in the region, 3.9 percent in the city), far lower than in many immigrant groups with comparable labor force participation. There are several reasons. First, Jamaicans harbor a cultural predisposition for seeing education and the professions as routes to upward mobility (see Austin 1984; Foner 1973). Despite the much-honored tradition of market women (or "hagglers), black Jamaicans actually are underrepresented in the most easily accessed entrepreneurial niches (such as small retailing) in Jamaica. Among Jamaican New Yorkers today, homeownership remains a far more culturally resonant sign of achievement than business ownership. In addition, many Jamaicans report difficulty in obtaining credit, which they perceive as the result of racial discrimination. Finally, racial segregation has concentrated most Jamaicans in the inner city residential areas, with weak local markets and strong competition from other immigrants.

Black Immigrants and the Perils of Concentration

Traditional assimilation models generally assumed that "American" culture and identity was higher status than the immigrant culture. Thus, it is preferable in the wider society's eyes to be an American than an immigrant. Warner and Srole (1945) note in their classic statement of what "assimilation" meant in the 1940s: "In any judgements of rank, the American social system, being the most vigorous and having also the dominance of host status, is affirmed the higher. Since the child identifies himself with it, his position in the present reciprocal is higher" (145).

This preference may still be basically true for "white" immigrants assimilating into a "white America." If, however, immigrants lose their ethnic distinctiveness only to become indistinguishable from native blacks or Latinos, the "host" country status may not be "affirmed the higher." Today, when for some groups assimilation means joining the street culture of the urban ghetto, "becoming American" can be every immigrant parent's worst fear for their children (see Foner 1987; Kasinitz 1992; Vickerman 1994; Waters 1993; Woldemikael 1989).

In many ways the circumstances of Jamaicans are shaped by their racial identity. Like African Americans, a high proportion of Jamaicans workers—surprisingly high for a group with only moderate rates of naturalization—are in the public and not-for-profit sectors. Yet their rates of labor participation are higher and numbers receiving public assistance are significantly lower than for African Americans, and lower than for several other immigrant groups as well. In short, during the 1970s and 1980s Jamaicans were generally successful at getting a foothold in the low-wage end of the growing service sector. Yet the positions they tend to occupy offer less opportunity for enclave formation and thus for "segmental assimilation" (Portes and Zhou 1993) than those of other immigrant groups with similarly high labor force participation.

Despite some suburbanization in the past decade, Jamaicans, as black immigrants, are also affected by residential racial segregation within the region, which may limit their opportunities in industries concentrated at the outer edge of region (although there is some evidence of very long-distance commutation). Further, racial segregation makes it difficult for middle-class Jamaicans to establish middle-class neighborhoods of their own or to move into predominantly white middle-class neighborhoods. This may have a significant impact on the second generation, because many Jamaican American children grow up in high-crime ghetto areas despite their parents' high rate of employment (Massey and Denton 1993).

Indeed, because of their concentration in racially segregated ghettos, Jamaicans often find themselves zoned into some of the most troubled public schools in the region. Yet their position in the labor market means they are even more in need of educational credentials than other immigrant groups. While English-speaking West Indians generally have higher household incomes than the Latino immigrant groups (and native blacks), the very success that West Indians have had in inserting themselves in the growing and often bureaucratized mainstream service sector has left them in positions where the use of ethnic connections and networks is highly contingent on educational credentials. Knowing many people who are nurses, physical therapists, or mid-level white-collar workers in the finance industry will be of little use to second-generation youth if they do not have the college degrees that such positions require, and if racial segregation keeps these young people living in dangerous neighborhoods and attending inferior high schools, few such college degrees will be forthcoming.

It is also probable that second-generation West Indian youth will be reluctant to take many of the jobs the less well off of their parents hold: homes attendants, domestic workers, drivers, and security guards, all jobs that require a great deal of face-to-face contact, sometimes quite intimate, with typically white employers. (Ironically it is the major West Indian "advantage"—English fluency—that opened these jobs to the immigrants in the first place.) Further, as they come to resemble African American youth culturally, it is likely that whites may be reluctant to employ second-generation West Indian youth in such jobs.

Jamaicans (particularly Jamaican women) did relatively well in the 1980s in part because they went into expanding, if low-wage, sectors. Often it was race that directed them to niches— particularly to the public sector with its relatively nonracial employment policies. At the same time, ethnic (as opposed to racial) networks developed and created niches distinct from those of native African Americans. Several of these sectors, however, look extremely vulnerable in the near future. Health care employment, government employment, and clerical employment have all fallen since the 1990 Census and can be expected to fall further. Jamaicans are overrepresented in all of these sectors. The anticipated funding cuts in Medicare and Medicaid, as well as the declining support for public hospital in the New York metropolitan, area are particularly ominous for Jamaican workers.

There are niches and there are niches. Jamaicans have built "niches," but not "enclaves." Their low rate of self-employment means that their success or failure is more tied to the overall economic health of the region—particularly to the public sector— than are many other groups. The facts bear out the popular stereotype about Jamaican capacity for "hard work." The Jamaican propensity for small business, however, is largely a myth, despite ideological and political support both from within the community and from outside.

In the end, the lack of a Jamaican "ethnic enclave" may promote "assimilation" in the traditional cultural sense of the term. This means, however, assimilation into "black America." Second-generation Jamaican Americans, living in largely African American communities without the protection of an ethnic enclave, are likely to share much of the fate of those communities.

Notes

Acknowledgments: An earlier version of this chapter was presented to the annual meeting of the Social Science History Association, Chicago, November 16, 1995. Many thanks are due to Mary Waters and John Mollenkopf for their comments and advice.

1. While most Jamaicans are considered "black" in Jamaica, a sizable minority is considered "brown" or "colored," as distinct from "black." In the United States this distinction becomes meaningless. As these immigrants are phenotypically indistinguishable from lighter-skinned African Americans they are generally considered black by North American standards. There are also a small number of Jamaican immigrants of partially Chinese and Indian descent. Yet while they might be considered Asian in Jamaica, their partially African ancestry means they too will generally by seen as "black" in the United States.

2. The term *Afro-Caribbean* is used here (as it commonly is in New York) to denote *non-Hispanic* immigrants from Caribbean nations—including the mainland Caricom member nations of Guyana and Belize. The term *West Indian* is used more narrowly to indicate English-speaking

Caribbean immigrants. These immigrants tend more or less to form a single ethnic community in the United States. They live in the same neighborhoods and have similar employment patterns and think of themselves as a common group ("one nation divided by water"), and indeed they were part a common political unit until the verge of independence in the late 1950s. Thus, much of what is said in this chapter about Jamaicans might also be said about Trinidadians, Guyanese, Barbadians, and others. If all fourteen tiny Commonwealth Caribbean "nationalities" are thought of as one group, they become the largest immigrant group in the New York City. Jamaicans alone were, as of 1990, the second largest foreign-born group in New York and the fifteenth largest in the nation. They rank tenth among immigrants admitted to the United States between 1989 and 1993.

3. This despite various efforts by the Jamaican government to expand the definition of *employed* by redefining informal economic activity, such as occasional street vending ("higg-lering" in Jamaican parlance), as employment.

4. The male informants quoted in this chapter were interviewed as part of Milton Vicker-man's study of 119 Jamaican men in the greater New York metropolitan area. The men were located through a cluster sample and each was interviewed by Vickerman in an unstructured format for one to three hours during 1989 or 1990. For a more complete description of the sample, see Vickerman 1998. The female informants were located, also through a cluster sample, by Vickerman and Kasinitz in 1994 and 1995.

5. That is to say, *officially* entered. Many of course were here illegally for years before offi-cially "entering" the country under this status.

6. For more on Afro-Caribbean hiring networks see Waters 2000. For an overview and case study of the role of networks in inner city job placement in contemporary New York, see Kasinitz and Rosenberg 1993, 1996.

7. Even in the Caribbean-dominated business niches with Caribbean customer bases, anec-dotal evidence suggests a preponderance of minority owners *within* the community, that is, Asians and other "middle-man minorities" from the Caribbean.

References

Austin, Diane. 1984. *Urban Life in Kingston Jamaica: The Culture and Class Ideology of Two Neigh-borhoods*. New York: Gordon and Breach.

Bonacich, Edna. 1972. "A Theory of Middleman Minorities." *American Sociological Review* 38:583–94.

Bonnett, Aubrey, W. 1982. *Institutional Adaptations of West Indian Immigrants to America: An Analysis of Rotating Credit Associations*. Washinton, D.C.: University Press of America.

Bryce-Laporte, R. S. 1972. "Black Immigrants: The Experience of Invisibility and Inequality." *Journal of Black Studies* 3:29–56.

Colen, Shellee. 1987. "Like a Mother to Them: Meanings of Child Care and Motherhood for West Indian Child Care Workers in New York." Paper presented at the annual meeting of the American Anthropological Association, Chicago, November 22.

———. 1990. "Housekeeping for the Green Card: West Indian Household Workers, the State, and Stratified Reproduction in New York." Pp. 89–118 in *At Work in Homes: Domestic Work-ers in World Perspective,* edited by Roger Sanjek and Shelle Colen. Washington, D.C.: Ameri-can Anthropological Society.

Deere, Carmen D. 1990. *In the Shadow of the Sun.* Boulder, Colo.: Westview Press.

Farley, Reynolds. 1986. "The Myth of West Indian Success." National Academy of Social Sciences Report no. 6. Commission on Behavioral and Social Sciences and Education, National Research Council, Washington, D.C.

Foner, Nancy. 1973. *Status and Power in Rural Jamaica: A Study of Educational and Political Change.* New York: Teachers College Press.

———. 1987. "The Jamaicans: Race and Ethnicity Among Migrants in New York City." Pp. 131–58 in *New Immigrants in New York,* edited by Nancy Foner. New York: Columbia University Press.

———. 1994. *The Caregiving Dilemma: Work in an American Nursing Home.* Berkeley: University of California Press.

Glazer, Nathan, and Daniel P. Moynihan. 1963. *Beyond the Melting Pot.* Cambridge: MIT Press and Harvard University Press.

Granovetter, Mark. 1995. "The Economic Sociology of Firms and Entrepreneurs." Pp. 128–64 in *The Economic Sociology of Immigration: Essays on Networks, Ethnicity, and Entrepreneurship,* edited by Alejandro Portes. New York: Russell Sage Foundation.

Gunst, Laurie. 1995. *Born fi' Dead: A Journey Through the Jamaican Posse Underworld.* New York: Henry Holt.

Husock, Howard. 1996. "Enterprising Van Drivers Collide with Regulation." *City Journal* 6 (1): 60–68.

Kasinitz, Philip. 1988. "From Ghetto Elite to Service Sector." *Ethnic Groups* 7:173–204.

———. 1992. *Caribbean New York: Black Immigrants and the Politics of Race.* Ithaca: Cornell University Press.

Kasinitz, Philip, and Jan Rosenberg. 1993. "Why Enterprise Zones Won't Work." *City Journal* 3 (4): 63–71.

Kasinitz, Philip, and Jan Rosenberg. 1993. "Why Enterprise Zones Don't Work." *City Journal* 3 (4): 63–71.

———. 1996. "Missing the Connection: Poverty, Social Isolation, and Employment on the Brooklyn Waterfront." *Social Problems* 42 (2): 180–96.

King, Ruby Hope. 1987. *Education in the Caribbean: Historical Perspectives.* Kingston, Jamaica: University of the West Indies.

Light, Ivan. 1972. *Ethnic Enterprise in America: Business and Welfare Among Chinese, Japanese, and Blacks.* Berkeley: University of California Press.

Light, Ivan, and Steven J. Gold. 2000. *Ethnic Economies.* San Diego: Academic Press.

Logan, John R., Richard Alba, and Thomas McNulty. 1994. "Ethnic Economies in Metropolitan Regions: Miami and Beyond." *Social Forces* 72 (3): 691–724.

Massey, Douglas, and Nancy Denton. 1993. *American Apartheid.* Cambridge: Harvard University Press.

Miami Herald. 1997. "Sharp Rise Forecast in Region Population." June 5.

Mintz, Sidney. 1974. *Caribbean Transformations.* Baltimore: Johns Hopkins University Press.

Model, Suzanne. 1991. "Caribbean Immigrants: A Black Success Story?" *International Migration Review* 25 (2): 248–76.

———. 1995. "West Indian Prosperity: Fact or Fiction?" *Social Problems* 42 (4): 535–52.

New York City Department of City Planning. 1992. *Demographic Profiles: A Portrait of New York City's Community Districts from the 1980 and 1990 Censuses of Population and Housing.* New York: Department of City Planning.

Nossiter, Adam. 1995. "A Jamaican Way-Station in the Bronx." *New York Times,* October 25.

Patterson. P. J. 1997. "The Weakening of U.S.– Caribbean Economic Relations." *New York Carib News*, September 9.

Portes, Alejandro, ed. 1995. *The Economic Sociology of Immigration: Essays on Networks, Ethnicity, and Entrepreneurship.* New York: Russell Sage Foundation.

Portes, Alejandro, and Robert D. Manning. 1986. "The Immigrant Enclave: Theory and Empirical Examples." Pp. 47–68 in *Competitive Ethnic Relations*, edited by Joane Nagel and Susan Olzak. Orlando: Academic Press.

Portes, Alejandro, and Alex Stepick. 1993. *City on the Edge: The Transformation of Miami.* Berkeley: University of California Press.

Portes, Alejandro, and Min Zhou. 1992. "Gaining the Upper Hand: Economic Mobility Among Immigrant and Domestic Minorities." *Ethnic and Racial Studies* 15(4): 491–521.

———. 1993. "The New Second Generation: Segmented Assimilation and Its Variants." *Annals of the American Academy of Political and Social Science* 530:74–97.

Reid, Ira De A. 1939. *The Negro Immigrant: His Background, Characteristics, and Social Adjustment, 1899–1937.* New York: AMS Press.

Sassen, Saskia. 1988. *The Mobility of Labor and Capital: A Study in International Investment and Labor Flow.* Cambridge: Cambridge University Press.

———. 1991. *The Global City.* Princeton: Princeton University Press.

Smith, M. G. 1965. *The Plural Society in the British West Indies.* Berkeley: University of California Press.

Sowell, Thomas. 1981. *Ethnic America.* New York: Basic Books.

Stone, Carl. 1988. "Race and Economic Power in Jamica." *Caribbean Review* 16 (spring): 10–34.

———. 1991. "Race and Economic Power in Jamaica." In *Garvey: His Work and Impact*, edited by Rupert Lewis and Patrick Bryan. Trenton: African World Press.

United Nations Statistical Office. 1992. *Monthly Review of Statistics.* New York: United Nations.

U.S. Bureau of the Census. 1993. *1990* Census of Population. Washington, D.C.: Government Printing Office.

U.S. Department of Justice. Immigration and Naturalization Service. 1984–92. *Immigration and Naturalization Service Yearbook* for 1983–91. Washington, D.C.: Government Printing Office, 1984.

———. 1973–96. *Immigration and Naturalization Service Statistical Yearbook* for 1972–95. Washington, D.C.: Government Printing Office.

Vickerman, Milton. 1988. *Crosscurrents: West Indian Immigrants and Race.* New York: Oxford University Press.

———. 1994. "The Responses of West Indians to African-Americans: Distancing and Identification." *Research in Race and Ethnic Relations* 7:83–128.

Waldinger, Roger. 1987. "Changing Ladders and Musical Chairs: Ethnicity and Opportunity in Post-Industrial New York." *Politics and Society* 15 (4): 369–401.

———. 1996. *Still the Promised City: African Americans and New Immigrants in Post Industrial New York.* Cambridge: Harvard University Press.

Warner, W. Lloyd, and Leo Srole. 1945. *The Social Systems of American Ethnic Groups.* New Haven: Yale University Press.

Waters, Mary C. 1990. *Ethnic Options: Choosing Identities in America.* Berkeley: University of California Press.

———. 1994. "Ethnic and Racial Identities of Second-Generation Black Immigrants in New York City." *International Migration Review* 28 (4): 795–820.

————. 1995. "The Intersection of Gender, Race, and Ethnicity in Identity Development of Caribbean American Teens." In *Urban Adolescent Girls: Resisting Stereotypes,* edited by Bonnie Leadbeater and Niobe Way. New York: New York University Press.

————. 2000. *Black Identities: West Indian Immigrant Dreams and American Realities.* Cambridge: Harvard University Press.

Waters, Mary C., and Karl Eschbach. 1995. "Immigration and Ethnic and Racial Inequality in the United States. *Annual Review of Sociology* 21:419–46.

Woldemikael, T. M. 1989. *Becoming Black American: Haitians and American Institutions in Evanston, Illinois.* New York: AMS Press.

Zenner, Walter P. 1980. "Economics and Ethnicity: The Case of Middleman Minorities." *Ethnic Groups* 22:185–87.

Zhou, Min, and John Logan. 1989. "Returns on Human Capital in Ethnic Enclaves: New York City's Chinatown." *American Sociological Review* 54:809–20.

CHAPTER 10

Neither Ignorance nor Bliss: Race, Racism, and the West Indian Immigrant Experience

Vilna Bashi Bobb

West Indians arrive with conceptions of race and racism different from those found in the United States. However, among the immigrants who are linked in the social network, time and experience in the United States seem to lead to common understandings about the U.S. race system.[1] Among them are three ideas: "American society is racist"; "We do not have such racism back home"; and "We can ignore the racism that exists in America." Some hold this third belief despite having been directly affected by racist behavior themselves. The published literature on race and black immigrants offers some explanations for these sentiments. My data suggest that it is incorrect to assume, as some do (Sowell 1978), that the "successful" black immigrant need not contend with racism in U.S. society. Rather, I show that many "successful" West Indian immigrants express knowledge of racial problems in U.S. society and that some describe themselves as direct targets of racist behavior. I argue that the migration experience itself (i.e., having a society of foreign origin as a social referent) and the immigrant's participation in a social network mediate the effects of racism and racial stratification on these immigrants.

In this chapter, I describe the ways that West Indians understand and adapt to race and racism in the United States. I show how these processes are influenced by the immigrants' experience in their country of origin and their membership in the immigrant social network in the destination country. That is, I examine how the demography and sociology of immigration shape the ways black immigrants come to understand race and racism in the United States, and the responses immigrants may have to racist experiences. The analysis developed here is based on ethnographic research of two West

Indian immigrant social networks, where respondents were interviewed about their immigration and resettlement experience in New York City.

I use the ethnographic method to research the West Indian immigrants' experiences of race and racism in the United States. That is, in the interviews I conducted for this study, I did not directly ask respondents what they thought about the U.S. system of racial stratification; nor did I ask how they adapted to it. I defined neither race nor racism for those I interviewed. Instead I let the respondents and data speak for themselves. These data suggest that demography (specifically, the influence of population composition, and the movement between international borders) has important effects on one's outlook on racism. There are sociological effects as well, of which participation in an immigrant social network seems to be most important, since the immigrant network is an important entity through which immigrant social acculturation and economic integration generally occurs (Bashi 1997, 1998a; Boyd 1989; Hagan 1994; Massey et al. 1987). The first part of this chapter discusses the various responses that West Indian immigrants exhibit during their ideal-typical adaptation to race and racism in the United States. The second part explains the role of demography and the influence of membership in an immigrant social network on immigrant adaptation to life in a racialized social system. Finally, I suggest that the immigrant social network has a role in helping the immigrant define and adjust to what he or she perceives as the U.S. racial system. By implication, then, those who do not benefit from immigrant network membership (i.e., native-born African Americans, and the native-born second-generation offspring of West Indian immigrants) will not be similarly insulated from the racism that accompanies social life in the United States.

Methods

Using a snowball sample technique (Goodman 1961), I interviewed sixty-four persons in two networks (which I call A and B here) comprised of families of West Indian immigrants now living in the New York Metropolitan Area (including Newark, New Jersey, and Long Island, New York) and their relatives "back home." Network A originates in St. Vincent and the Grenadines, Network B in Trinidad and Tobago. Although there were a small number of immigrants from elsewhere in the West Indies,[2] about 90 percent of the sample came from these islands. Together, forty-four immigrants were interviewed in New York, twenty-five in Network A and nineteen in Network B. I also went to the West Indies to interview family and friends of these New Yorkers—people who were connected to the network but not themselves émigrés. In total, twenty people were interviewed in the West Indies, eight in Network A and twelve in Network B.

The interviews were modeled after the open-question/open-response method developed by Robert Weiss (1994). This method does not use an instrument or follow a strict list of questions but suggests the interviewer follow a "substantive frame" through which he or she may be sure all the topics of interest are covered. The purpose of the larger project was to determine how these West Indian immigrant social networks formed and operated (see Bashi 1997, 1998a). Race and racism were topics that emerged during our discussions about their expectations before immigration and the reality of life after moving to the United States. Thus, the data for this chapter come from work on a larger study of West Indian network immigration.

The interviews were begun with two unrelated, unacquainted persons who were asked to identify people whom they had helped, or tried to help, come to the United States. Respondents were also asked to identify people who had helped them come to the United States. The snowball developed, then, as I followed these leads. If the person being interviewed allowed it, the interview was tape-recorded. Whether or not tape recording was allowed, I took extensive notes. Most interviews were transcribed, and both interview notes and transcribed interviews were printed and coded for use in Ethnograph, a popular software program used for qualitative analysis. I let the sampling method dictate the period of immigration that would be studied and the list of islands from which the connected individuals would come. The oldest immigrant interviewed came to the United States in 1930; the youngest came in the 1980s. It should be noted that the respondents in the sample come from several different islands in the West Indies, settled in different parts of the New York area at different times, and are related to each other in very different ways. I limited the network sample neither by time nor by the geographic origin or destination of the immigrants who would be considered for interviewing.

Comparing Racial Structures

For analytical purposes, I define *racial stratification* as a social system that classifies people according to a hierarchy of specific phenotypic categories, or *races*. (The American racial system is one that is largely dichotomous, where whites occupy the top rungs of the racial hierarchy, and blacks the bottom rungs.) I define *racism* as the process that maintains this hierarchy. Some key mechanisms of this process include racial stereotyping and discrimination in housing, labor, and other markets.

Racial categories, the racial hierarchy that comprises them, and the political, social, and economic systems that support racial stratification, together, make up what I call a *racial structure*. Racial structures vary across historical time and over geographic space. People who are born and raised in a given racial structure become socialized into that structure. Immigrants, however, must adapt to the new racial structures to which they are exposed when they relocate to the destination country.

The responses that West Indian immigrants have to the U.S. racial structure are in part shaped by the pre-migration experiences they had in their countries of origin. Immigrants characterize the racial systems of the West Indies as different from those in Western cities (mainly London and New York) to which Caribbean people move (Bryce-Laporte 1972; Gopaul-McNicol 1993, Sutton and Makiesky 1975). Here I briefly recount the perceptions West Indians hold about race and racism in the West Indies,[3] describe the ways they came to understand U.S. racism and its corresponding racial hierarchy, and discuss how they cope with these realities.

The West Indians in my sample explained that they were shocked or surprised by racism in the United States, saying, "We don't have that back home." As one respondent relates:

> Racism is not really a priority there [in the West Indies], you know. You don't look at a black and white situation. You more look at an economic situation, you know. It doesn't matter really whether you're black or white or whatever it is. If you don't have the money you don't have the position in society that I'm talking about. If you have the money you have the position. But when I came here I realized that not only is there economics you have to deal with, you have to deal with the color of your skin, so that was kind of a shock to me.

Another respondent, living in Tobago, questions whether it is race that one is seeing, or if it is just the economic inequality that accompanies class differences.

> Racism? In Tobago? I don't know. What is racism? They talk about it, talk about it, talk about it. We have it, but is it really classism? Let's say you have two men, one black and one white, and they both went to school. But what if one have more money?

According to these respondents, although the racial hierarchy in the West Indies is as a system coincident with the distribution of access to resources, it does not, in itself, hinder access to socioeconomic opportunities. These immigrants described race in the West Indies as more like a class system; other researchers have published similar findings (Dominguez 1975; Foner 1985; Gopaul-McNicol 1993). But we know that class, race, and color are also intertwined in the United States (Keith and Herring 1991). The way these immigrants speak about their race-class stratification system is different from how they speak about that in the United States. Ira Reid (1939) and Christine Ho (1991) describe how class and race are interconnected in the Caribbean. According to Ho (1991, 151), the West Indian system is "a three-tiered, color-class hierarchy in which social class distinctions often dwarfed racial considerations." Though the sources on which Virginia Young (1993) relies in this excerpt focus on Jamaica, what she writes about race does seem to apply to other West Indian islands.

> The reason racism is so often difficult for many West Indians to articulate is that "color and class interweave to such an extent that it is nearly impossible and in any case impractical, to separate each from the other" (Phillips, 1976, p. 27). This claim can be further empirically supported if one looks at the social structure. Kerr (1952), Hendriques (1953), Miller (1967) and De Albuquerque (1989) all contend that the lighter-skinned people, including the Chinese, tend to belong to the upper social class, while people of darker skin color tend to belong to the lower class. There is a very small middle class, made up of mulattos or blacks, while the large lower class is predominantly black with a few mulattos (Phillips, 1976). The fact that whites, who number less than 5% of the population, completely dominate the upper class, while the blacks dominate the lower and middle classes seems to confirm that ethnic differences are reinforced by socioeconomic differences. (35)[4]

There are many ways in which social lives are organized to illuminate to its members how racial structures operate. Although I discuss only two here (population composition and social networks), political and economic systems are much more powerful influences. For example, apartheid-like systems will more strongly influence outlooks on a society's racial hierarchies, regardless of the population composition and the presence and effectiveness of networks. However, I argue that race plays itself out not just on a macro stage but also on micro- and mid-range levels of society, and these other levels are also important in shaping the everyday lives of people in all categories of the racial hierarchy. The point I am making here is that what is often misread as cultural differences among racial subgroups may indeed be evidence of differences in adaptations to racial structures, which in turn may be caused by positioning in socioeconomic structures. It is too simplistic to read the West Indian responses to racism as resulting from their having a different "culture." Instead, I argue that their worldview emerges from a particular socioeconomic positioning that occurs as part of the migration process itself (see also Bashi Bobb and Clarke 2001). This positioning, as population subgroups of various kinds ("minority" groups and social networks), is described nearer the conclusion of this chapter. I digressed here to explain that micro-level socio-structural contexts that are associated with membership in particular population subgroups influence one's understanding of racial systems, even if they are arguably not the only or even most important influences. To begin, I describe the responses West Indians have to the U.S. racial structure upon their arrival and demonstrate how these responses may change over time.

West Indian Immigrant Responses to the U.S. Racial System

Racial systems vary by country and historical time, that is, racial categories and the hierarchies that comprise them are neither constant nor transferable across sites and settings (Bashi 1998b). Thus, it is no surprise that when West Indians arrive in the United States, and are exposed to racism here, they soon begin to understand that this is not the same hierarchical system to which they are accustomed in their countries of origin.

Realization

Many respondents did not expect to encounter the U.S.–style racism that faced them upon arrival and thus were surprised by their first encounters with it. Others had some prior knowledge about racism in the United States before they migrated. And that knowledge made some, like Natalie,[5] afraid.

> Oh, [New York] was different. You know, a big city. It was kind of scary coming at that age [fourteen]. You heard so much good and a lot of negative things about New York. The negative was the one that I was scared about. Like the racial problems here, that sort of scared me. I learned about them back home, by watching TV, reading the newspaper. At that age, my impression was that you wouldn't know how to speak to people of other races. You were kind of afraid to approach them cause you didn't know what they thought about you and stuff like that. I was afraid, not that something would happen, but that I would be rejected. It wasn't until my twenties that I experienced blatant racism, though.

Joan Anne and her husband also arrived with knowledge of racial strife in the United States and were angered by it. For some time after their arrival, they refused to travel outside New York, believing that their anger at the extent of racism they found in U.S. society would draw them into activism in the Civil Rights movement. Joan Anne explained, "We did not grow up in an atmosphere where you were subjected to that kind of behavior. So putting us in up here, my husband was afraid that we would react under pressure. You know how folks were reacting in the West Indies . . . because we are not going to stand for it." Anita, who returned to Union Island (St. Vincent and the Grenadines) after living in New York for a few years, expresses a similar view.

> Racism? We never knew what the word was. White people were here on the island. They see us and we see them. They hire us, but here you just do business. In New York, you see differently. You say to yourself, "Why are these people behaving like that? We did them nothing." We are shocked that they don't accept us. They are our destruction. West Indians are shocked because they are fool-hearted.

Although some respondents reported that they knew about racial problems in the United States before migrating, almost all were shocked and surprised to experience racism once they arrived. Many newcomers did not know racist behavior when they first saw it.

> Oh man, you know, you may realize my personality is a jovial one, so maybe they used to give me a racist remark and maybe I used to just overlook it and say it's stupid. But when you just come to the United States and because you're not accustomed to racism you, you're not sensitive to it. Yet after [some time] you become sensitive to racism. I mean I start knowing what is a racist remark, but when I just came, I didn't know. I thought they were just making a joke or something.

These sentiments are not unusual among those that I interviewed for this study. Other researchers (see Foner 1985, chap. 2, esp. p. 45; Gopaul-McNicol 1993, chap. 5; Young 1993, 107) have uncovered similar sentiments from West Indians in the United States and England.

It is doubtful their surprise comes from not knowing what racism is. Although many were aware of the existence of racism and racial animosity in the United States, it is more likely that these immigrants simply failed to see themselves as potential targets of racism. That is, they may have thought that racism was something that happened only to American blacks, and as foreigners they would be exempt from such treatment. Or, perhaps, they were aware of U.S. racism but thought it was something one might encounter rarely, as was the case when they lived in the West Indies. Perhaps they did not understand racism to be as pervasive influence in the daily lives of African Americans until they became aware that they themselves experienced it daily. Initially, many West Indians do not realize that certain negative acts may be racist. Rather, they only gradually recognize and label them as such. Indeed, some realized only in retrospect that some of their negative experiences were the result of racism.

America was what I expected it to be, because I read a lot about America before I came. I would say, though, that I didn't encounter . . . I mean I'm talking about the negative aspect of the race relations. But now when I look back, especially when you are looking for jobs you realized that there was a lot of subtle type of discrimination. It wasn't that flagrant because you go in an agency and they have all these signs telling you they don't discriminate against race, color, but as far as getting the job is concerned.

This quotation suggests that the respondent is not sure whether it is one's race or one's color against which employers might be discriminating. Two other respondents, one living in Brooklyn and the other in Trinidad, expressed concern that the likelihood of this kind of confusion may induce black people to make accusations of racism for which they have no proof. Other interviewees downplayed racism's impact, describing it as just another one of the components of a more generalized culture shock (that, among other things, included surprise at the ability to speak informally to bosses and for younger people not to "respect their elders"). Some discussed being victims of discrimination from whites as well as from African Americans—the former a group who demonstrated racial prejudice while the latter seemed to dislike West Indians because they were foreigners. As this respondent suggests, all such forms of discrimination are to be ignored.

In Union Island, there's no great population of white people, but the tourists came there and we treated them like people. I lived in St. Vincent, where there is a good enclave of so-called white people and we worked together but we didn't see black and white, we saw people. We worked together, socialized together . . . . So when coming to America, and they were calling you "black," [saying] "West Indians come from a tree," "You're a monkey," "Why don't you go back where you came from?" . . . And you're trying to serve them! You work in the hospital and they would spit on you and tell you don't touch them and tell you to take your black so and so away from them . . . . That was dramatic to me because I never had experience of people spit on me. I mean, my first [response] was to hit back. Someone spit on me and call me black! And then my cousin say, "If you want a job you can't do it." You got to swallow your teeth and take it. Even after graduating from school with a B.S. degree and you go in a white place . . . . Even black Americans discriminated against us, saying to us on the job that those of us from the Caribbean think we're superior. They resented us. So it was strife not only against the white people but also the black people from America calling us black monkeys coming by the banana boat. But after a while you learn to rise above it, like water off the duck's back.

Most, however, talked only of white racism, maltreatment that clearly came in response to what they perceived as one's blackness. Ellie, a young immigrant now fourteen years old, was quite sure she knew that being black was the problem.

When I came up here I had to start learning what racism was. Because when you go to the stores and stuff like that, people follow you around, you go on the bus and people hold their pocketbooks. So, I want to know why, you know, why when I come to America people do this? What is so different? They don't discriminate because you're West Indian. They are discriminating against you because you're black. Period.

NEITHER IGNORANCE NOR BLISS   219

Immigrants begin to see that they are targets of racist behavior after experiencing racist episodes repeatedly. These can be personal encounters, which often happen at school or at work.

> I took anything racial, especially then [when I first arrived], at face value. The older woman I was tutoring in math was pleasant. But my friend was telling me, "Oh, you're so stupid. She's racist! What in the hell make you think these white people are your friends? She's just using you!" Well, that was my first time [experiencing racism], and I just couldn't understand. I said, "You don't even know her. How could you just look at a person and hate them?" She said, "Oh, I don't hate them, they hate me." Ha, ha, ha. . . . And now, in retrospect, I see exactly what she was saying.

A young black man reported:

> I worked on commission, but [my boss] would always hold on to the money 'til the very last. He would get paid, but he wouldn't pay me. And we had many arguments about getting paid. So that's one of the first things I began to realize, you know, how whites treat blacks.

And in another account, a man reports that it was his mistake to respond to racism directed at him—even as he paradoxically explains that such racism did not really bother him.

> I had several [racist] experiences in Arkansas when I was working as a night manager. I had people call me nigger and boy, [saying,] "You can't even count, what took you so long to give me my change?" you know, and they'll hold up two bills, U.S. currency bills, and say, "Do you know this is a $20 and do you know this is a $5, eh boy?" and stuff like that. . . . I made a mistake and lost my cool once. This man told me, "You people don't know how to count. Why do they have people like you behind the counter anyway?" and I told him, "So that I can take [steal] your money! Do you want your change or not?" Ha, ha, ha. Even more so when I went into people's homes, and I wouldn't be allowed to go in certain areas in the house, you know, when I used to work with this construction guy. They wouldn't allow me in, or if they are going to give me water, they will give it to me in some disposable cup or something. But it never bothered me, because I knew what I came here [to this country] for.

Many finally simply conceded the inevitability of racism. It was not uncommon for immigrants to conclude that racism was just a part of life in the United States, and one must just accept it.

> It's a hurt you learn to deal with. Eventually you just go on and do the best you can knowing that racism—you know it was here before I came, it's going to be here probably after I'm gone. But I did my best to take a stand on it, you know, for a very long time. Even now, you know, I'm still aware that it exists . . . there's no way, you know, you can deny it once you go out into the business world. Even working in the school system.

Thus, among the immigrants in these networks, there are mainly two ways of rationalizing the reality of racism in the United States.[6] On one hand, most of those I interviewed cope with racism by deciding to "overlook" or "ignore it." On the other hand, although many feel that they can safely ignore racist acts, some devise strategies of avoidance. In the extreme case of avoidance, the immigrant decides to leave the United States and return home.

Ignoring It

One widespread response to white racism by West Indian immigrants was simply to overlook or ignore it. Some respondents even stated that racist acts do not bother them. One man recounts his experience at a party in Arkansas:

> The highlight of the music was playing "Dixie" on the piano. "I wish I was in the Land of Dixie." Can you imagine this? And I joined them singing, yes I did. [*His wife argues with him that he didn't know what this meant.*] Of course I knew what it was. [*His wife says, laughing,* "Those white people thought you were crazy."] No, if you're the only black person in the crowd, and they're singing . . . . What do you want me to do, do you want me to show them I'm offended by it? I wasn't. It doesn't make any difference to me whether they're singing "I wish I was in the Land of Dixie," or whatever, because I don't really care as long as you don't hurt me physically.

Immigrants may believe that they can ignore racist acts, especially in the period immediately following their arrival. As stated, they often report that they did not see race as a unique social system (i.e., separate from class) back home. This perception might lead them to fail to expect race in the United States to be a separate system. Even as they begin to "see" racism in the United States and identify it as such, they understandably may not attribute it to a racial system. Instead, they may see racist behavior as an individual attribute, emanating from the racist's own ignorance about black West Indians. Thus, a nurse relates:

> I did private-duty nursing for the rich Jewish people, and one woman said, "Oh, you speak such good English. Where did you learn to speak such good English?" I was mean and I said, "Oh, while I was swinging from tree to tree, the missionaries left books and I would read." And she thought I was serious. She told people on her job that her mother's nurse was whatever. . . . So the doctor came the next day and said, "Miss, did you tell Miss WhateverHerNameWas that you were swinging from tree to tree?" I said yes. [He said,] "She is not very bright and she has been telling people you said this. Well, will you please correct her and tell her that it's not so?" I eventually spoke with her and told her that we had schools and vacations and shops and everything we do here, but on a smaller scale. That was one of the things that . . . and pulling your hair to see if it was real. But now everybody goes to Jamaica and St. Thomas and travels around, so I guess they're more educated. They had a lot of money, but they weren't intelligent people at all.

Some respondents say that racism does not bother them. "After all," they conclude, "I am here to accomplish something"—that is, do better socioeconomically than they did back home, get an education, get enough money to send remittances, or to send for someone less fortunate. They refuse to let racism stand in their way, particularly because they see their position in New York as superior to the one they had back home.

I didn't know about racism back home. Here, I was the only black guy in fourteen white guys on the [water tunnel construction] gang. I had goals I'm trying to achieve and I never let it bother me. There's a saying: "As long as your paycheck is right."

Others rationalized the inevitability of racism further, saying that, yes, there is racism, but life is too good in New York to think of leaving. One respondent, Natalie, described her feelings of anger at being called "nigger" as she walked on a street near her home. I asked her if she felt differently about New York following this experience.

No, because I guess New York was a place where everybody wanted to come to, so stuff like that you tend to overlook it, internalize it, you try to avoid situations where this happens.

James recounts his experiences with racism, then:

I knew I came to get an education but I knew in my mind that if I have an opportunity to live here, I'll live here. And, yeah, I was better living here irregardless of whether I have legal status or not. You will have to come and pick me up and put me in a plane because I ain't moving. I'm not going anywhere. Life is sweet. [*Laughs*] Especially in New York City.

Two of my New York informants—one who lived in England for quite some time—did talk about differences between British- and American-style racism. Both agreed that British-style racism was more overt, but one preferred the more direct racism of the British over the subtle racism of Americans, since British racism is so obvious that "you know where you stand."[7]

Avoidance

Usually, when people spoke of the inevitability of U.S. racism their words implied that they cannot simply ignore racism but instead must avoid situations where they might be exposed to it.

Everyone here experiences prejudice, especially [where I work,] in the hospital, where you see all kinds of people. I used to do private-duty nursing, where patients abuse you. It hasn't happened to me, but I've seen them spit in your face. Prejudice is overt in the South, but more covert in the North. Here [in New York], it's more hypocritical. They won't tell you to your face. It doesn't bother me, because I don't invite them to my house. And, I know who I am.

The man who found himself singing "Dixie" with his hosts says:

And another time I was invited to a wedding but I didn't go to this one. Everything was going to be Southern style with the Confederate flag draped along the aisle and the groom was going to be dressed in Confederate uniform and everything was going to be Southern style where they have this racist attitude. I didn't tell anyone, but I was invited though. "I had to work"—that was my excuse.

Medford, who returned to Trinidad after living in New York, said:

> As an individual you could develop your own protective systems. My personal thing is, I can make the world better for *me*, by changing my attitudes and what I do. It will not change the system, but I could get an area in the system where I could operate. For instance, you go to Bank A, and get that sort of behavior. Then try Banks B, C, D, E, until you get a bank that treats you how you want to be treated. Now it has not changed the fact that Bank A is racist. But I would no longer be dealing with that racist bank. And that is basically how I see most things. I cannot offer a wholesale idea for the entire system, but individuals, I feel, because we have a choice, can choose to be in a place where we are comfortable.

Some immigrants were more resolute about avoiding their exposure to white people. One woman explained that she did not want whites for neighbors because she did not like their behavior and felt that they did not control their children. Another woman speaks of avoiding doing business with whites.

> I knew all these things [about racism in the United States] before I came here. I would hardly spend my money in a neighborhood that is white. Why do that when I can spend my money down on 13th Avenue? They don't come up in Flatbush or on Church Avenue where I live to come and spend their money. I can't separate myself from them totally, but there are some things I don't do at all. And that's because I came here well informed.

Another man took avoidance of U.S. racism to its extreme, being so vigilant about "remaining completely divorced from the American psyche and system" that he chooses never to live in the United States.

> I go to North America once a year. It's the land of many opportunities. [But] the value of life doesn't seem to be focused in the right direction. First you have to deal with the problem of race. It's difficult to understand and accept. You can have immigration from all over the world: China, the Caribbean, Mexico. . . . These people arrive in North America. And you have Native Indians. Yet, when you visit you get the distinct feeling from the majority of white folks that it's the inalienable right of one particular race to have first choice. The Native American as well as all nonwhites are treated or regarded as not altogether equal. I think that's what's basically wrong with America. Arising out of that you have discriminating practices and racism in all levels of government and in society. This necessarily leads to strife. Unless America deals with this it will self-destruct. America is the land of many great opportunities. But unless you can enjoy a certain quality of life, I consider that life in the Caribbean, for a professional person is much better. When I compare North America to St. Vincent, that's the reason I didn't want to go.

To summarize, these data suggest that when West Indians first arrive, many are not immediately aware of the extent of U.S. racism and its applicability to them. Even those immigrants with prior knowledge of racial problems in the United States may be shocked and surprised when they first encounter racist attitudes and behaviors directed toward them. Immigrants from the West Indies do not enter the United States "thinking like a minority"—that is, necessarily expecting racist behavior from whites—but some come to accept the inevitability of racism as a fundamental fact of life in New York for those with black skin. As a result, some attempt to ignore racism,[8] or say it does not bother them. They try to detach themselves from racist acts that directly target them or in which they are indirectly involved, through either rationalization or avoidance. Immigrants in New York are there because they seek a better material existence. Many stay in New York and try to avoid either contact with whites or situations where racist acts are likely. Some even decide that this struggle is not worth it and instead choose to leave New York altogether. No matter what the response, they all come to realize that racism is a central feature deeply rooted in the very fabric of American life and social structure.

Demographic Influences on Conceptions of Race and Racism

Population composition may be one factor important in shaping our understanding of how this race-class connection is manifested in everyday practices of racial discrimination. All else being equal, in societies where there are more whites than blacks, the influence of racial discrimination may be easier to see than the influence of class, whereas in black-majority societies, the influence of class may seem greater than that of race. Of course, not all things are held constant across populations of like racial compositions—certain political and economic configurations (such as systems of apartheid or Jim Crow) will have a marked influence on the psychological impact of racism on the population's subgroups. However, population composition may indeed have some effect, independent of politics and economics. If so, then being socialized in the black-majority islands of the Lesser Antilles may shape one's thinking about oneself. As an example, note how a Vincentian woman decribes her inability to think like a "minority."

> [Our] whole orientation is that [education] is the key [to social mobility]. We come from a society where there is some racial difference but . . . the concept of being a minority is foreign to me. I realize, yes, black people are minorities [here] but I don't see myself as a minority because I didn't grow up being a minority . . . . You realize that [because] you are a black immigrant you never had a minority attitude. To think like a minority you have to be trained to think that you are a minority . . . . Regardless of what other black people in this country tell you, you weren't socialized that way, so it really never impact you. [It's only later,] when you realize that your color is an issue, and compounded with your color is your accent, . . . and all of a sudden you start realizing not only have I made enormous sacrifices and have achieved despite those odds, but I'm even lower now than I ever was because not only am I out of money, I'm out of money in a foreign country, educated now to know differently and expect more, and only to experience so much less. . . . It becomes very demoralizing and demotivating, then you really start to empathize with the black experience in this country.

A population's racial composition has both historical and contemporary influence on the social relations. This same woman speaks about the historical significance of a black majority population.

> I mean slavery is slavery. I'm not minimizing the mental impact and the physical debilitation on a racial population, but I'm saying when you have slave masters who are the mi-

nority—even though we came from a level of servitude—there was a level of respect, and that respect was based on fear. It's a different level of fear when you're a majority and there's one white man, than [there is] when you're a minority and there are many white people. I'm not saying there weren't beatings and all that kind of things, but not to that extent in the Caribbean. All you had to have was one beating, beat that slave, and they would poison three or four of your animals. And that white man would get up that morning and see three or four of his animals dead and he knew that he try that shit one more time and he was going to be dead. Because those people cooked for him. They fed his children and believe you me, the message was loud and clear that you can't beat and kill everybody. You did certain things that instill a certain level of fear, but everybody knew their boundaries. Well, this didn't happen in this country because you had a minority, and what we know as slavery is not your experience of slavery, so the black experience here is not the black experience there.

The effect of the racial composition in these islands is not just a historical artifact. If one has fewer encounters with whites, and sees blacks in all levels of socioeconomic strata, it is plausible that one may perceive an absence of racism. A man living in the West Indies explains:

> From the top of your head it's easy to say we don't have racism in the West Indies. Here, the majority of people are colored. Everyone you meet in the street is black. Whites own businesses. But they know that they depend on blacks to buy from them. Once in a while you may come up against a brick wall. But generally you may not see yourself with a problem. I would agree—we really don't have a race problem.

That the West Indies has a white minority and black majority has several effects. There are at least four reasons why the minority/majority population composition of the West Indies may encourage a vocabulary of class to predominate in the descriptions of social stratification in the West Indies.

First, in the West Indies racial stratification is not highly visible. There, where there are black people who hold some powerful political and economic positions, successful blacks are visible in everyday life. That is, most whites will be "rich," but not all blacks will be poor, because, absent a system of apartheid, there are too few whites to occupy all seats of power. Blacks, by their sheer number, occupy many different levels in the class system.

Second, the vocabulary of racial enmity has necessarily been muffled by the social limits deemed pragmatic by whites who are the minority population. The limited number of whites constrains the way they can behave toward blacks, even if they hold racist beliefs. Vehement racial ideologies, such as the ones that have historically occupied prominent social space in the United States and South Africa, would not be as pragmatic for white minority populations such as those in the West Indies. There, instead, a colonial ideology predominates (de-emphasizing race and emphasizing a hierarchy of culture—with the values of the "motherland" on top and the "natives" on the bottom).

Third, the classifications by color in West Indian racial systems differ from the black/white dichotomy of the European and U.S. systems, where the former is mostly described as having a third, or middle category, "mulatto" or "colored." Few whom I interviewed elaborated on color classification schemes in the West Indies. A respondent in Barbados reports:

> It used to be that you had to be white to work in banks and on Broad Street years ago. Then it was [that you had to be light skinned]. But now it doesn't matter. In all honesty we can't say there isn't any problem at all. Whites still do their best to keep down blacks, but they can't do much.

This "colored" or "mulatto" class had access to better schooling, jobs, and housing than the white elite structure made available to the colored class. Mulattos were deliberately treated differently from the darker-skinned blacks, making them a buffer "race" and reducing the ability of coloreds to achieve levels of mobility equal to that of neither mulattos nor whites.

Fourth, the socioeconomic structure of opportunities in Third World former colonies ensures limited access to upward mobility, regardless of race or color. For example, under the British-style educational system of some West Indian islands, entrance into secondary schooling is by examination and the number of slots are limited. Thus, only a few of the most talented will have a chance for higher educational opportunities. In another example, one can also note that Third World economies such as these can hardly employ all those who need jobs, one important reason that out-migration has been an important safety valve for the West Indies throughout its history.

In a less-developed economy that works in the favor of only a very few, nearly everyone is in the same poor socioeconomic boat—this, and the fact that blacks are in the majority, helps to obscure the ways race constrains social mobility and maintains socioeconomic stratification. In the West Indies, both the small number of whites and the countries' Third World status ensure that there is little room at the top for a black person to readily see himself as socially isolated because of his race. (This, however, does not mean that racism does not exist there—a point to which I return below.)

A racialized society's population composition greatly defines the separate social spaces racial groups occupy. The situation is quite different for native-born blacks in the United States, who must break into a white-occupied social space in labor and housing markets in order to achieve social mobility.[9] For them, social structures are racially segmented, recreating racial differentiation in social and economic arenas that keep white-occupied social space intact (Cose 1995; Massey and Denton 1993; Sullivan 1989; Waldinger 1995). West Indians in U.S.–based networks, however, may not need to penetrate white social space to achieve their first steps toward social mobility, because the social network brings immigrants into new and established economic niches. When one is an immigrant to a country where one's assimilation is made to a minority social space, being part of a social network can have an important mitigating influence on social mobility and one's cognizance of the debilitating effects of racial stratification.

The Influence of Network Membership on Conceptions of Race and Racism

Immigrant social networks are made up of international movers who are linked to other migrants from the same points of origin and also to friends and family members who remain in the country of origin (Bashi 1997; Massey et al. 1987). As a group, network members assist others in the network with information, financial and physical resources, and other kinds of resources that assist in international migration and resettlement (Bashi 1997, 1998b; Hagan 1994). In so doing, immigrant networks foster subsequent migration, since the information veteran immigrants provide through their networks can be used to lower the risks to migration for individuals and families still residing in the country of origin. Some also see the importance of networks in defining a space for political and socioeconomic action (transnationalism), exercising political and economic power in a social space that remains separate from both the sending and the receiving societies involved (Basch, Glick Schiller, and Szanton Blanc 1994). Networks, then, link sending and receiving countries, contributing to the self-sustaining nature of international movement. Thus, the "social network" has emerged as the concept that can best explain both the context in which the decision to migrate occurs and how international movement is operationalized through the immigration and resettlement processes.

Migration research to date tends to support the commonly held idea that immigrants send for one another in migration "chains." It is assumed that as new immigrants integrate themselves into the new society they send for others, until the process of subsequent migration forms a chain of immigrants who arrive at different times, all from the same place of origin. These chains link veteran immigrants (former newcomers themselves) already in the destination country to newcomers who will soon arrive with help from the veteran immigrant.

This process is not generally seen as one that distinguishes among potential newcomers—all who remain "back home" are seen as potential migrants, as long as they have connections to immigrants in the destination. I have shown in other research, however (Bashi 1997, 1998a), that immigrant networks are formed in highly structured ways—not in indiscriminate chain-migration patterns as is popularly assumed, and in ways somewhat beyond the control of the potential migrant. My research suggests, in fact, that veteran immigrants have the power to decide who may join the network, when, and under what circumstances—serving as hubs in a network comprised of hubs (who send for others) and spokes (who are sent for) in a hub and spoke network (Bashi 1997, 1998a). Thus, these veterans, or hubs, both create and control the expansion of the immigrant social network. By so doing, they also create and control the economic and housing niches to which they integrate those newcomers they send for. By implication, then, these hubs also create and control, perhaps to a lesser extent, the larger immigrant community to which they bring the newcomers they choose to assist.

The existence of immigrant networks among groups of foreign origin has been well documented (Hagan 1994; Massey et al. 1987; Thomas and Znanecki 1996). Research exists to support the idea that networks separate and isolate immigrant and native groups in the labor and housing markets (Kasinitz and Rosenberg 1996; Massey and Denton 1984; Waldinger 1995). It is well known, too, that native-born blacks used networks of friends and family to learn of job and housing opportunities that encouraged migration to the northern United States in the first half of the twentieth century (Marks 1983). Furthermore, contemporary networks among African American communities have also been documented to provide social support, but mainly among people who share both the same race and same class positions (Cross 1990; Stack 1974). Native-born people of all colors have social networks, as do all immigrant groups—including foreign-born blacks. The individual that functions outside of a social network is the rare exception. Network membership shapes the worldview of its members, and one's racial worldview is no exception. Then, the case I make here is twofold. West Indian immigrants, as well as other racial-ethnic groupings, have social networks that isolate network members from the larger society because they create pockets of within-group support that also separate and isolate groups from the larger society. Moreover, this social isolation shields (as an individual and as a group) the West Indian immigrant as a black newcomer from immediate exposure to and consciousness of the ways race and racism function in the United States.

Newcomers to the United States who arrive with the help of a network are not pushed into the larger society but instead have, waiting for their arrival, a ready-made community of immigrants. These networked immigrants work together and live near one another, most often in primarily West Indian neighborhoods, and in workplaces where West Indians predominate because networks foster the creation and maintenance of economic niches in the labor market and the housing market. The immigrant network is the primary means by which newcomers find jobs and housing. The network also connects people to consanguine and fictive kin back home. An insular community consisting of immigrants from the same point of origin, the network gives its members material and emotional support and separates them from the larger society in many different ways. Because this support and separation coexists with network membership and participation, being in an immigrant social network (at least initially) emotionally and psychologically insulates black immigrants from U.S. racism.

Being an Insider

Even as socially isolated as West Indians are who live and work within immigrant social networks, it is not true that racism does not affect them. In fact, my respondents report having had several racist encounters, and some report episodes that are far from innocuous. These West Indian immigrants are able, however, to detach themselves from U.S.–style racism by overlooking racist acts, ignoring racist behavior, or avoiding situations where racist episodes might be likely. I contend that their membership and participation in the social network largely enables this detachment.

The implications of membership in an immigrant network on racial attitudes and responses to racism are at least three. The first effect is psychological; the immigrant experience in general, and membership in the social network in particular, allows black immigrants to insulate themselves, emotionally and psychologically, from U.S.–style racism. The second effect is influenced by economics; network membership helps one to achieve what is perceived as "success," compared with American-born blacks, in housing and labor markets. The third effect is psychosocial and results from an interaction between the psychological insulation offered by the network (the first effect) and the advantages realized in housing and labor markets (the second effect).

Until a black immigrant realizes the pervasiveness of race in the life of a black person in the United States, he or she is largely unaware of the effect that being black in the United States has on one's life chances. This ignorance is a shield against the discouragement one might feel knowing that having black skin means something negative to those who may be able to affect his or her social mobility. There are many ways it can be easy for a new immigrant who arrives with the aid from a social network to be "protected" from this realization, because network membership can be a kind of prism through which the effects of racism can be distorted.

Immigration is selective. Only those with the means and motivation to migrate do so. The most capable arrive and participate in the housing and labor markets here in the United States. They usually come to urban areas, and specifically to jobs and industries that center and depend on immigrant labor (Sassen 1988). They are not randomly distributed throughout the labor and housing markets (Kasinitz and Rosenberg 1996; Massey and Denton 1993; Piore 1979; Waldinger 1995). If one arrives with the help of a network one will automatically be connected to other immigrants. So, generally, they do not face open-market competition. Concurrently, immigrants who are network members will be somewhat isolated from society at large and more immersed in an immigrant socioeconomic subsystem. This is true for all who migrate with the help of a network, regardless of race.

Whether immigrants find work through a labor recruiter or through their connections with a social network, they are likely ultimately to work in a place where there are other immigrants like them. There, they will encounter West Indians during most of their workday. Even if problems with racism exist, and even if these encounters become intolerable enough for the worker to seek out a job change, immigrants who are members of networks that have marked off labor market niches can (because of their access to network knowledge of jobs) more easily change to a new job in the same industry, leaving behind that particular racist whom they may believe has a personal problem working with blacks. The idea of systematic racial discrimination would evolve to a new immigrant only slowly, after prolonged job searches outside the niche, or after repeated exposure to racist behavior within the job niche.

Housing is the other socioeconomic area in which West Indian immigrants are isolated. Newcomers voluntarily find and may desire housing where other immigrants live. Black immigrants in search of housing, then, do not harshly or even consciously confront the involuntary nature of racial segregation in housing markets. In addition, racially segregated housing means that black people (immigrants included) are less likely to live around whites, so even if they face racist behavior at work, they may leave it behind them when they go home.

Immigrants follow one another in a chain or hub and spoke system, finding jobs and housing through the immigrant social network of which they are members (Bashi 1997, 1998a; Bryce-Laporte 1972; Massey et al. 1987; Sassen 1988). The very nature of network membership allows immigrants to avoid much contact with people outside the network, and they need not be aware of the effects of race in the United States in order to get their first job and a place to live. They may even change jobs and homes a few times before they have had much exposure to the larger society in New York. Thus, it is not just the emotional support from network members, or an inherent group culture, that allows West Indian immigrants to feel they can ignore racism. Black immigrant social networking gives members social support, as well as access to housing and job niches that allow them to cope with and slowly adapt to the racial stratification they face when they arrive.

Networks create two social processes that may enable West Indian immigrants to ignore racism for some time, feel it does not apply to them, or otherwise detach from U.S. racism. One process is social isolation—West Indians live and work among other immigrants and may not be as exposed to racism (at least in the initial period after arrival) as is the average person in New York City with a "black" phenotype. Another process is that of social mobility, which provides first a labor market "floor," through which even undocumented immigrants may use the network to find jobs, and, second, a measure of upward mobility at least to the outer boundaries of the network's labor market niche. Problems arise for immigrants when they seek mobility beyond the purview of the network. Racism is certainly a factor in immigrants' lives well before they reach this point, as the testimonies of the interviewees suggest. However, once they desire mobility outside of the network's grasp, they will lose the "protection" and insulation that same network offered in earlier stages of the settlement process.

Increased Exposure to Racism When Reaching Beyond the Network

Newcomers who arrive with assistance from social networks are somewhat "protected" from fully conscious knowledge about or exposure to racism but probably not for very long. Eventually, they realize that racism is systematic and that they are not exempt. This realization may occur, as noted above, through unavoidable and repeated exposure to racism within network niches. It also occurs when the immigrant steps outside the purview of network influence and is most obvious when an immigrant is ready to attempt even greater upward mobility in larger housing and labor markets.

One immigrant, who earned her Ph.D. here and built an extremely successful professional career, reports:

> So you come [and get an education] and you make that sacrifice and you work and you do well and you expect that the next thing that is going to happen is that you're going to show

up and you're going to get a job, a good job, and you realize, hey, there is no job, and that is the shocker. Then you realize. Now you start dealing with social problems. . . . I think that's the time when you really realize that there is something beyond education, it's something beyond effort. . . . And no matter how much experience you have and how much you show that you've been able to defy all the odds, you know, and still succeed, there is still not parity. And then I think that is the turning point for the immigrant, to where you become aware now of the other societal problems that exist in your new country that will impact your ability to succeed. And all of a sudden you say, "What was that effort for?" You know? Because I made all of this effort, and all of a sudden I'm not going to succeed because I don't have an opportunity. I'm not going to be given the opportunity.

West Indians who reach the limits of the network's ability to assist their upward rise in the labor market will find themselves facing racial discrimination that pervades the U.S. labor market as a whole. That West Indians face labor-market discrimination contrasts with the idea that one's cultural values cause one to strive and succeed where others fail (Glazer and Moynihan [1963] 1970; Sowell 1978). Culturalists suggest that race does not affect social mobility. However, immigrant status is reason enough to strive for economic success, fully independent of one's "culture." Most newcomers are unknowing of the ways black skin will affect socioeconomic outcomes in the United States. It is that very attempt at upward mobility that forces the black immigrant to confront the barriers that the U.S. racial system brings to him and native-born blacks and not to the immigrant or native-born person who has white skin.

Employer willingness to recruit and preferentially hire immigrants (Waldinger 1995) and differential immigrant network access to job niches (Hagan 1994) suggest that for West Indians job searches—especially within niches—are easier than they are for African Americans. According to Bonacich ([1972] 1994), this special treatment is enough to create antagonism between the two groups of "blacks"—which may be one explanation why West Indians feel the pressure of job competition from African Americans they encounter.

> The central hypothesis [of the theory of ethnic antagonism] is that ethnic antagonism first germinates in a labor market split along ethnic lines. To be split, a labor market must contain at least two groups of workers whose price of labor differs for the same work. The concept "price of labor" refers to labor's total cost to the employer, including not only wages, but the cost of recruitment, transportation, room and board, education, health care (if the employer must bear these), and the costs of labor unrest. (475)

Whether or not one endorses the split labor market hypothesis, it is true that both immigrant status and network regulation of immigrant job performance lowers the price of West Indian labor to the employer, relative to U.S.–born blacks. First, the network lowers the cost of recruitment to employers, through which immigrant hubs and others find jobs for newcomers. Second, the network incorporates the means for selecting potential immigrants on their willingness and commitment to work hard, and it can also sanction poor workers. This labor control further lowers the costs of labor for employers. Thus, network members may get a "leg up" from their association with other immigrants and the niches to which they are attached, and the labor market "floor" for African Americans may be lower than as the floor on which West Indian immigrants stand (Waldinger 1996).

Ira Reid (1939), in his classic and seminal study of black immigrants, suggests that West Indians are "relieved" to live among other blacks, but he gives no evidence to support this statement. Perhaps at first they do not mind living among other black homeowners, or in a predominantly West Indian neighborhood. Nevertheless, it does not follow that these immigrants will long be pleased with that outcome once they begin to realize that racism is systematic. They come from predominantly black populations—perhaps living among other blacks is not something they think of in negative terms. But more likely, they are less bothered by living among other West Indians who share similar cultural traits.

Black immigrants may or may not prefer integrated communities as African Americans do (Massey and Denton 1993). At least initially, segregated housing may be a shield from racism. It is to be expected that when a family is successful enough, they will desire larger, better housing in better school districts. These moves will likely encourage black immigrants to move outside of the neighborhoods where they began their climb up the U.S. social ladder. And when they begin to search for better housing, particularly those amenities (larger and better housing, in better school districts) that correlate with neighborhoods with larger numbers of more affluent whites, they are certain to confront the racism that pervades U.S. housing markets (Massey and Denton 1984, 1993).

Being an Outsider

If one is not a member of the immigrant social network, then, of course, none of the benefits of network membership accrues. Two groups considered briefly in this section are not members of the West Indian immigrant social network and have different experiences with the U.S. racial system as a result. They are the second-generation children of immigrants, and African Americans.

Disadvantaged American blacks, by lacking membership in these immigrant networks—with well-established labor market and housing market niches—lack the opportunity to advance by using these network to bring them better housing and jobs. They also are unable to avail themselves of the psychological insulation that comes with the ability to think, for example, that one is a black immigrant—and different from native-born blacks (African Americans), who are grouped at the bottom of the racial hierarchy. Thus, for African Americans, the combined effect of lack of socioeconomic access and lack of a foreign referent may be that one may feel little sense of one's agency to change one's own socioeconomic situation (Cose 1993; Massey and Denton 1993). Successful immigrant networks enable easy access to jobs (e.g., in some niches, new immigrants need only have the recommendation of one who already works there to secure employment, and assistance in renting or buying homes. African Americans do not have open access to these networks, even if they have an interest in securing the jobs these immigrants might hold (Kasinitz and Rosenberg

1996; Waldinger 1995). While their own African American networks may provide psychological and economic support (Stack 1974), which may counteract anti-black stereotypes (blacks are bad; blacks are lazy; etc.), the networks available to the average African American may have fewer of the relevant "success stories" that are available to the average immigrant network member.

Too, members of the second generation lack their parents' vision of an alternative society, which allows the first generation to deny the messages that the racial hierarchy sends about the characteristics of people with a "black" phenotype. The second generation—being a subgroup of the native-born black population—grows up in the U.S. racial system, under the psychological influence of what it means to be black in America. Thus, the source of their parents' psychological insulation (the foreign referent that involves an alternate racial system, where class is seen as the more important factor) is no referent for the native-born child. And the parents' alternative vision, or expressions of the ability to ignore racism, can be experienced as a denial of the second generation's reality. Certainly, the second generation's potential employers do not see them as different. They do not have accents, the one cultural marker that employers and others can readily use to recognize the difference between West Indians and African Americans. Thus, the children of immigrants have neither the psychological shelter nor the vision of the network as an opening for career advancement that the network was for their parents. The experience of the second generation is very different from that of the immigrant.

> Oh yes, if you were born here, you're born with . . . you're socialized to be a minority. My children are minorities; I will never be a minority. Because again, they look at things based on the society they live in. When I came to this country I have already been socialized. . . . I came with what were the realities for me in my country . . . so it takes me time to understand and figure that out, [and then] it's too late. I've already invested too much to even convince myself that they are met. . . . Once you have made an investment, you buy into a strategy, and it's a helluva thing to convince yourself that you're wrong. So I have to ditch this strategy, and that's not easy to do. So for us as immigrants who came with that socialization and that strategy, we've invested too much when you came not knowing the social structure, and you went full speed ahead on one track . . . and you're too far down the pipeline now to abandon it. And it may be easier in the world of investment to ditch [a strategy] because it's other people's money, ha ha ha, so let them belly up to the loss and write it off for taxes. But when it's your life you don't ditch it. You ride it out and you hope by riding out you get some type of satisfaction, or you could maneuver the process, and somehow it may not be utopia but something will evolve. [But for your kids, it's different.] I mean, you tell them what you know to be your reality and they look at you and say you are a lunatic and they go on and do whatever the hell they want to do. You're either beating the hell out of them or you get so frustrated and say maybe they're right and just leave them be. This is their country. What do I know?

Second-generation blacks, even as children, will see very different kinds of social barriers than do their parents, who have as a reference point the remembrance of a different life "back home." Immigrant parents also have an immigrant ethic (which encourages them to strive for their targeted goals, despite whatever obstacles they might face), other network members (who buoy them with financial and emotional resources in times of trouble), and the many models of success that veteran immigrants in the network represent. Since the second generation has a different reference group, these things are not necessarily resources for the immigrants' native-born children.

Even if second-generation immigrants are still able to get housing and some jobs through the network, two forces play against the likelihood that the network will work for them as it did for their parents. First is a sense of mobility that suggests that the children of immigrants should take jobs outside the purview of the network. For the most part, only those children in these networks who are willing to work in the areas of the labor market where the network strengths lie can benefit from network job contacts (in the networks I studied, these were water and subway tunnel construction, domestic work, nursing, and civil service). Thus, the information about immigrant niches in the primary labor market may not be as useful to the upwardly mobile second generation who attempt to move upward or away from where their parents stand. Although a network's information about available jobs may be more useful to the second generation in an ethnic enclave economy than to the second generation looking to rise in the primary labor market, West Indians are not in enclave economies. Second, parents may not want their children following in their footsteps. For example, a mother who bought her house and sent for her children through her career as a domestic may not see it as a positive thing if her daughter, too, works as a domestic.

Finally, children are not similarly protected from racism because they have to traverse social space their parents (at least immediately) do not. The children of immigrants—and immigrant children, for that matter—come into contact with the white world daily (with white teachers, school officials, store owners, police officers, etc.) and do not in their waking hours spend most of their time with coethnics. Also, they may not get support for their alternative worldview from their immigrant parents. For even if these parents become cognizant of their child's different reality, to admit that difference is possibly to concede that racism might defeat them. That is, to recognize the effect of racism on one's life chances—as the immigrant adult will not do—is to agree that the adult immigrant's worldview may represent a losing strategy.

Even though young immigrants benefit from network membership more than the second generation does, they may also experience the network differently than do their older network counterparts. For example, the youngest immigrants move directly into school, and not work, and therefore their social experience is very much like that of the second generation. Ellie, who is quoted above describing her experience being followed in stores, here explains why she and her immigrant grandmother (who said that racism does not bother her) have very different responses to racism.

> I'm fourteen and I came in 1990. With my grandmother's case it's different, because when she came she went straight to work. So, she don't have to go to school, she don't really have to go to the stores and stuff like that, like the younger folks have to.

The experience of the immigrant who relocates as an adult is different from that of the young immigrant. Children of West Indian immigrants do not so much choose between membership in an ethnic group (West Indian) and a race (black) as they try to navigate a system that recognizes blackness on sight and recognizes ethnicity for black native-born people rarely, if at all. Thus, when Mary Waters (1996) tallies the numbers of young West Indians who call themselves black and those who call themselves West Indian, she misunderstands that, for young black immigrants, and especially for the native-born black children of immigrants, no choice exists between ethnicity and race (Bashi 1998b). Ethnic recognition would come only for those children who choose to claim an ethnicity by choosing to struggle against being defined as black by those who equate black race with black phenotype, that is, a racial system that includes white adults such as teachers, school officials, store managers, and other whites with authority, as well as the young white peers they encounter in school.

Conclusion and Implications

Despite achieving what is perceived as "success" relative to U.S.–born blacks, West Indians who emigrate to the United States believe that the United States is a racist society. Thus, racism affects them, certainly at least to the extent that they are able to identify and name it when they see it, and more important, to the extent to which it affects them directly. Some immigrants sooner or later realize that one's difficulty in the United States comes not just from the struggle one should expect in moving to a new country and beginning at the bottom of the job ladder but also from being black. Even if West Indians do "succeed" socioeconomically, their social mobility does not exempt them from racist animosity, any more so than it does for native-born middle-class blacks (Cose 1995).

In sum, West Indian immigrants to the United States do not immediately understand the U.S. racial structure and the ways that racist behavior by North Americans will apply to them, but neither are they ignorant of the existence of racist ideology in the United States. I present here an ideal type of immigrant adaptation to racism as if it progresses along a timeline coincident with the length of stay in the United States and exposure to racist behaviors by whites. Initially, West Indians may not be aware that racist behavior by whites is intentionally directed toward them, but for many there is a period of realization. Some choose to respond to this realization by ignoring the racist behaviors of others or by avoiding contact with whites altogether. But the West Indians I interviewed all developed a consciousness about the U.S. racial structure and racism by whites toward blacks (including those who are foreign-born), even if in the end they believed they could ignore racism.

I contend that the experience of growing up in a black-majority society in their countries of origin and enjoying membership in an immigrant social network in the United States allows black immigrants emotionally and psychologically to insulate themselves from U.S.–style racism for some time. After moving to the United States, an immigrant has the opportunity to see the stratification system at work, as his or her daily interaction with whites brings the understanding that racism is part of the daily experience when one is of "black" phenotype and encounters whites who demonstrate discriminatory practices. Even while this awareness emerges, however, immigrants, by their participation in the immigrant social network, are to some degree insulated from the full effects of racism in the United States. The network acts as a shield in three ways. One, it may limit interaction with whites who may behave in a racist manner. That is, although they are in the primary and secondary labor markets and not in ethnic enclaves, black West Indian immigrants work and live alongside other immigrants like them, because their social space is mainly limited to job and housing niches. Two, these niches bring to the West Indian immigrant population a degree of socioeconomic success relative to their native-born black counterparts, and thus socioeconomic separation from them. Three, the labor market success that members receive along with access to these labor- and housing-market niches belies the racist stereotypes about the inability of black people to succeed in the United States. On three levels, then, this separation allows an insulation (which has both psychological and physical counterparts) from racist enmity.

There is an important corollary here: people who are not similarly full members of these social networks will not be able to take complete advantage of this insulation. I maintain that, generally speaking, the second generation is in this category, as are native-born African Americans. Neither group has the markers of difference—accents—which may make whites treat them better. Nor do they have an idyllic vision of life "back home" to sustain them, or the escape hatch of becoming a returnee when they become fed up.

Being an immigrant striving to find work and earn a better living than one could back home gives the newcomer one outlook and set of experiences, while having black skin in the United States gives another. All immigrants go through the first struggle. For West Indians, movement to the United States brings the unique problem of being rendered invisible (Bryce-Laporte 1972), because to most Americans they are indistinguishable from the African American population. The foreign referent (an orientation in a society socially and politically structured to inhibit "thinking like a minority"), however, coupled with the socioeconomic isolation that network membership in the destination country brings allows West Indians to discount the effect of racism on their lives—at least in the time nearer to arrival and integration in the immigrant network. To the degree that West Indians may separate themselves ethnically (a project with which an accent helps greatly) or socioeconomically (a project that is aided by the immigrant social network, particularly in the help it offers in finding work and housing) they may be able to articulate the ability to disregard racist animosity.

> You know, you have blacks on one side and whites on one side and unless you're a foreign black they look at you like you're diseased or something, you know. Where black folks are afraid to walk on the same side of the streets as the white folks. It was just gross. A country so advanced to be so stupid, you know. I could never see the reason for it and I really never accepted it.

Notes

1. Although racial systems differ between the United States and the Caribbean, they also differ among the islands themselves (see note 4). This variation among racial systems in the West Indies is not discussed here but will be addressed by the author in future research and writings.

2. Two respondents were from the Virgin Islands, two were from Grenada, and three were from Barbados.

3. There are similarities and differences in the conception of race in the West Indies. Racial composition in the Caribbean varies by island, and these differences have some impact on the responses to race both in the country of origin and in the United States. But I focus only on the similarities of racial systems in the West Indies, saving a discussion of inter-island differences for another publication.

4. In this passage Young (1993) cites the following: K. De Albuquerque (1979), "The Future of the Rastafarian Movement," *Caribbean Review* 9 (4): 22; F. Hendriques (1953), *Family and Color in Jamaica* {London: Eyre & Spottiswoode}; M. Kerr (1952), *Personality and Conflict in Jamaica* (Liverpool, England: University Press); E. L. Miller (1967), "A Study of Body Image, Its Relationship to Self-Concept, Anxiety, and Certain Social and Physical Variables in a Selected Group of Jamaican Adolescents," master's thesis, University of the West Indies, Kingston, Jamaica; A. S. Phillips (1976), *Adolescence in Jamaica* (Kingston, Jamaica: Jamaica Publishing House).

5. All names given in the text are pseudonyms.

6. These responses are not mutually exclusive. That is, some immigrants may ignore direct racist verbal or other types of attack when they experience them and try to avoid them otherwise.

7. This perception contradicts Foner's suggestion (1985) that West Indian immigrants can more easily tolerate racism in New York than in London, since in New York the native-born African American population acts as a social buffer between the West Indian immigrant and the white population. By contrast, in Britain, where West Indian immigrants are the first resident-black population, immigrants are directly targeted for racist acts and their presence is seen as the root of many social ills.

8. Respondents did express sentiments that can be read as sympathetic with African Americans. Statements along these lines indicate they believed that living under racism like this from birth would cause one to become discouraged. Other comments suggest that they understood the African American experience was different, and worse, than their own. Their feelings about African Americans, and what they see as the African American experience, however, are not directly addressed here.

9. Douglas Massey and Nancy Denton (1993) suggest that white-occupied social space is becoming less and less visible to those who live in predominately black and poor urban ghettos, while the social space occupied by blacks is harder for whites to see and understand. Residential segregation ensures that blacks and whites live very different lives of affluence and poverty, affecting both the culture and socioeconomic factors that impact the quality of life for both groups.

References

Basch, Linda, Nina Glick Schiller, and Cristina Szanton Blanc. 1994. *Nations Unbound: Transnational Projects, Postcolonial Predicaments, and Deterritorialized Nation-States*. Langhorne, Pa.: Gordon and Breach.

Bashi, Vilna. 1997. "Survival of the Knitted: The Social Networks of West Indian Immigrants." Ph.D. diss., University of Wisconsin, Madison.

———. 1998a. "Hubs, Spokes, and a Culture of Reciprocity: Elements of an Immigrant Social Network." Paper presented at the annual meetings of the American Sociological Association, San Francisco.

———. 1998b. "Racial Categories Matter Because Racial Hierarchies Matter: A Commentary." *Ethnic and Racial Studies* 21 (5): 959–68.

Bashi Bobb, Vilna, and Averil Clarke. 2001. "Experiencing Success: Structuring the Perception of Opportunities for West Indians." In *West Indian Migration to New York: Historical, Comparative, and Transnational Perspectives,* edited by Nancy Foner. Berkeley: University of California Press.

Bonacich, Edna. [1972] 1994. "A Theory of Ethnic Antagonism: The Split Labor Market." In *Social Stratification: Class, Race, and Gender in Sociological Perspective,* edited by David B. Grusky. Boulder, Colo.: Westview. Reprinted from *American Sociological Review* 37:547–59.

Boyd, Monica. 1989. "Family and Personal Networks in International Migration." *International Migration Review* 23 (3): 638–70.

Bryce-Laporte, Roy Simon. 1972. "Black Immigrants: The Experience of Invisibility and Inequality." *Journal of Black Studies* 3:29–56.

Cose, Ellis. 1995. *The Rage of a Privileged Class.* New York: HarperCollins.

Cross, William E. Jr. 1990. "Race and Ethnicity: Effects on Social Networks." Pp. 67–85 in *Extending Families: The Social Networks of Parents and Their Children,* edited by Moncrieff Cochran, Mary Larner, David Riley, Lars Gunnarsson, and Charles R. Henderson, Jr. Cambridge: Cambridge University Press.

Dominguez, Virginia R. 1975. "From Neighbor to Stranger: The Dilemma of Caribbean Peoples in the United States." Antilles Research Program, Occasional Papers #5, Yale University.

Foner, Nancy. 1985. "Race and Color: Jamaican Migrants in London and New York City." *International Migration Review* 19 (4): 708–27.

Glazer, Nathan, and Daniel Patrick Moynihan. [1963] 1970. *Beyond the Melting Pot: The Negroes, Puerto Ricans, Jews, Italians, and Irish of New York City.* 2d ed. Cambridge: MIT Press.

Goodman, Leo A. 1961. "Snowball Sampling." *Annals of Mathematical Statistics* 32:148–70.

Gopaul-McNicol, Sharon-Ann. 1993. *Working with West Indian Families.* New York: Guilford.

Hagan, Jacqueline María. 1994. *Deciding to Be Legal: A Maya Community in Houston.* Philadelphia: Temple University Press.

Ho, Christine. 1991. *Salt-Water Trinnies: Afro-Trinidadian Immigrant Networks and Non-Assimilation in Los Angeles.* New York: AMS Press.

Kasinitz, Philip, and Jan Rosenberg. 1996. "Missing the Connection: Social Isolation and Employment on the Brooklyn Waterfront." *Social Problems* 43 (2): 180.

Keith, Verna M., and Cedric Herring. 1991. "Skin Tone and Stratification in the Black Community." *American Journal of Sociology* 97 (3): 760–79.

Mahler, Sarah J. 1995. *American Dreaming: Immigrant Life on the Margins.* Princeton: Princeton University Press.

Marks, Carole. 1983. "Lines of Communication, Recruitment Mechanisms, and the Great Migration of 1916–1918." *Social Problems* 31 (1): 73–83.

Massey, Douglas S., and Nancy A. Denton. 1984. "Racial Identity Among Caribbean Hispanics: The Effect of Double Minority Status on Residential Segregation." *American Sociological Review* 54:790–808.

———. 1993. *American Apartheid: Segregation and the Making of the Underclass.* Cambridge: Harvard University Press.

Massey, Douglas S., Rafael Alarcón, Jorge Durand, Humberto González. 1987. *Return to Aztlán: The Social Process of International Migration from Western Mexico.* Berkeley: University of California Press.

Piore, Michael J. 1979. *Birds of Passage: Migrant Labor and Industrial Society.* Cambridge: Cambridge University Press.

Reid, Ira DeAugustine. 1939. *The Negro Immigrant: His Background, Characteristics, and Social Adjustment, 1899–1937.* New York: Columbia University Press.

Sassen, Saskia. 1988. *The Mobility of Labor and Capital: A Study in International Investment and Labor Flow.* New York: Cambridge University Press.

Sowell, Thomas. 1978. "Three Black Histories." In *American Ethnic Groups,* edited by Thomas Sowell with Lynn D. Collins. Washington: Urban Institute.

Stack, Carol B. 1974. *All Our Kin: Strategies for Survival in a Black Community.* New York: Harper Torchbooks.

Sullivan, Mercer L. 1989. *"Getting Paid": Youth Crime and Work in the Inner City.* Ithaca: Cornell University Press.

Sutton, Constance R., and Susan R. Makiesky. 1975. "Migration and West Indian Racial and Ethnic Consciousness." In *Migration and Development: Implications for Ethnic Identity and Political Conflict,* edited by Helen I. Safa and Brian M. DuToit. Paris: Mouton.

Thomas, William I., and Florian Znaniecki. 1996. *The Polish Peasant in Europe and America: A Classic Work in Immigration History.* Edited by Eli Zaretsky. Urbana: University of Illinois Press.

Waldinger, Roger. 1995. "The 'Other Side' of Embeddedness: a Case-study of the Interplay of Economy and Ethnicity." *Ethnic and Racial Studies* 18 (3): 555–80.

———. 1996. *Still the Promised City? African Americans and New Immigrants in Postindustrial New York.* Cambridge: Harvard University Press.

Waters, Mary C. 1996. "Ethnic and Racial Identities of Second-Generation Black Immigrants in New York City." In *The New Second Generation,* edited by Alejandro Portes. New York: Russell Sage Foundation.

Weiss, Robert. 1994. *Learning from Strangers: The Art and Method of Qualitative Interview Studies.* New York: Free Press.

Young, Virginia Heyer. 1993. *Becoming West Indian: Culture, Self, and Nation in St. Vincent.* Washington, D.C.: Smithsonian Institution Press.

CHAPTER 11

Peruvian Networks for Migration in New York City's Labor Market, 1970–1996

Alex Julca

How do immigrant networks evolve and unleash large-scale immigration? Do networks of help and reciprocity help immigrants to cope with market instability? This chapter analyzes the case of Peruvian immigration to New York City through participant[1] observation over four years, using census data and data from interviews with sixty-five people living in Queens[2] and Brooklyn (all names of interviewees are pseudonyms), to shed light on the dynamic processes of kin and *paisano* networks in contemporary labor markets. While industrialization in Lima opened up possibilities for upward mobility to primarily Andean parents between the 1930s and the 1960s (first-generation migrants), increasing urban stratification caused their endeavors to fall short. First- and second-generation Andean immigrants have carried the baton since the late 1960s by developing long-distance international networks. In 1996 there were about 80,000 Peruvians in New York City, of whom about 64,000 were legal residents.[3]

This chapter has three parts. The first introduces the Peruvian community in New York City through three periods of historical development and then explores the corresponding structural composition of the New York City labor market. Discussion of the structure of the labor market emphasizes the level of job security (degree of unsteadiness), immigrant skills, state intervention, and degree of immigrant access to this market. The second part begins by defining Peruvian networks and the culture of social relations involved, continuing on to the analysis of the role of networks among Peruvian kin and *paisanos* for immigration purposes, and concluding with a discussion of the kinds of socioeconomic responsibilities assumed by members. The third part highlights the dynamic interaction of these two elements, labor market and networks: while the networks struggle to decrease the negative effects of unsteadiness in the labor market, many Peruvian immigrants continue to face challenges to their living conditions from the volatile political economy of New York City, and the relationships among network members are constantly transformed in the process of reacting to the unsteady market.

Although this chapter concentrates on the micro-level dynamics of network formation among Peruvians, the context is the increasing globalization of the economy and Peru's accelerated crises as key stimulating factors, which propels migration from Lima to the United States. Hence, the globalization process is at work in two ways. It helps cause the initial flow of migrants from Peru, whose weak position in the global economy creates macro-economic pressures for migration. It then shows up locally as New York City's labor markets are transformed over the course of the past thirty or more years into a global city, one possessing an hourglass economy: many jobs for the high skilled at the top and the low skilled at the bottom, but fewer ways to start with low skills and move into the middle class (Harrison 1997; Sassen 1991). One result of globalization's effects in Peru and in New York is the emergence of the transnational networks analyzed here.

Historical Evolution of Peruvian Networks in New York City

The migration process itself (first from the Andes to Lima starting in the 1940s, then from Lima to New York City after the late 1960s) has transformed kin structure and created new relationships. Long-range networks of support for the nuclear family have often weakened links with other relatives as well as *paisanos,* although relatives sometimes reencounter each other in New York City after a period of little communication in Lima. For example, during the first generation's migration from Quechua villages to towns and cities (1940s to 1960s), some kinship group members developed a separate integration into Lima's society. Even when they maintained contact with members of the extended family, urban life in Lima encouraged them to develop new network branches on the job and in the neighborhood. As a result, migrants' children developed even weaker ties with their extended families. However, the migration of the second generation to New York City (parents, sons, and daughters) added a new tone to kinship ties. Immigrants have sometimes relinked with extended family here, or relied on strong ties with former co-workers, friends, or neighbors from Lima. Reliance on strong ties with friends was especially common in the initial period of the late 1960s and early 1970s when the presence of kin members, and especially nuclear family, was not likely in New York City.

The Peruvian community in New York City has evolved through the following phases. From the late 1960s to the late 1970s, Peruvians arrived with documents (i.e., as "tourist visitors"). From the early to late 1980s, Peruvians arrived increasingly as undocumented immigrants, many later becoming legal U.S. residents through the 1986 "Amnesty Law." Since 1990, a Peruvian community has emerged, made up of a complex set of transnational immigrants, who are a combination of U.S. citizens, legal residents, and the undocumented.

Peruvian Networks from the Late 1960s to the Late 1970s

Although the Peruvian presence in the United States can be traced to the immigration of experienced Peruvian miners and Andean women to California in 1848 for the gold rush (Monaghan 1973), contemporary Peruvian migration networks in New York City were formed through a different process of social transformation. In the late 1960s in Lima, the growth in frequency and means of international communication was accompanied by an explosion in the urban population, which was predominantly young and literate. At the same time in the United States, the demand for manual labor for factories, in New Jersey and New York City in particular, intersected with the U.S. immigration law of 1965, which favored "family reunion" immigration.

In the 1970s, tourist visas to the United States were relatively easy to get in Peru. Travel agencies in Lima organized "tours" to the United States, whose real purpose was to facilitate immigration. These firms were in charge of requesting tourist visas for the travelers. The one-way airfare of $250 was funded from personal savings and loans from family members or close friends. Given the long-term scope of the migration enterprise, U.S. immigration meant a future source of social and economic capital for all people involved. Expected earnings in the United States were from eight to ten times higher than in Peru, and immigration would improve access to social services (such as running water and education); both were basic factors for stimulating immigration. However, immigrants were not fully aware that some expenditures in the United States were also higher than in Peru (e.g., rent), and that work, although available, would be physically straining, often involving a ten-to-twelve-hour workday, and a six-to-seven-day workweek. The responsibilities of sending remittances or of funding other relatives' immigration encouraged immigrants to work even harder.

Friends and *paisanos* were crucial for securing a foothold in New York City during this early Peruvian flow of immigration. Families slowly followed "pioneers" who established a beachhead upon which further immigrants disembarked. Full family immigration was not the most distinctive feature of these first years, partly because new immigrants were mostly young people (twenty to twenty-five years old). They took this opportunity with its aura of risk and adventure. Once in New York City they had to confront crucial challenges, such as gaining status as legal residents, learning basic English, and finding a permanent job. To solve these issues and to save enough to bring more family members to the United States often took several years—in some instance ten years or more. Not until the early 1980s did the "family reunion" type of immigration gain momentum and maturity.

Peruvian Networks in the 1980s

At the macro level, the 1980s brought additional reasons for Peruvians to consider international migration. On one hand, the state of extreme violence resulting from the conflict between the Peruvian military and the forces of Shining Path had made the political scene very unstable and oppressive. On the other hand, the Peruvian economic situation deepened into crisis, with hyperinflation reaching 2,350 percent in 1989. This environment of economic and civil insecurity prompted would-be political refugees and economic migrants to flee Peru in increasing numbers, which is reflected, for instance, in the 100 percent growth of the Peruvian immigrant flow to New York City between 1980 and 1990 (Rodríguez 1995). This rapid growth of the immigration flow was made possible by the workings of the international kin and kith networks already established in the 1970s.

In contrast, however, to the easy absorption of immigrant labor in the 1970s, by the 1980s the New York City labor market had acquired a quite gloomy outlook. But also by the late 1970s obtaining a tourist visa had become more difficult because one had to produce documentation before the U.S. Consulate in Lima that one had enough financial resources—with bank certification—for a trip to the United States. This procedure often included showing proof of enough funds for hotel and discretionary consumption. Moreover, the U.S. Consulate increasingly required documentation of regular cash deposits and withdrawals from bank accounts, a secure job, and justification of the possession of wealth in fixed assets (house and car) for traveling abroad as a tourist. As a consequence, Peruvians increasingly came across the Mexican border, using underground multinational networks for immigration to the United States. The average cost of $4,500 for each new immigrant was again funded, as in the 1970s, by close family members or friends.

The critical situation of increasing numbers of undocumented immigrants, Peruvians included, was eased during the 1980s. The Immigration Reform and Control Act of 1986 granted amnesty to undocumented workers, and several hundred thousand people "came forward by the cut-off date of May 4, 1988" (Castles and Miller 1993). Presumably the fear of an amnesty hoax prevented even more undocumented immigrants from coming forward. Pepe, who was living in Brighton Beach (Brooklyn) in June 1989, told me about Peruvians who applied for legal residence under this edict from the Immigration and Naturalization Service (INS): "Under this amnesty program many in this neighborhood applied for residence. However, there was also fear in the community that this might be just a hoax of *la migra* [the INS] to catch illegals. . . . And yet, some recent Peruvian arrivals, in collaboration with their lawyers and some INS officials, have applied for this amnesty as if they had arrived well before 1986 and they have gotten their green cards."

The legal amnesty for undocumented immigrants helped Peruvian immigrants to put down more secure roots in New York City and sponsor more family immigration (documented and undocumented). Moreover, some businesses founded by Peruvians who had come to the United States in the late 1960s and early 1970s were more firmly established, including restaurants and travel agencies in the Bronx and Queens. Command of English, acquired on the job and by personal commitment outside of work, played a key role in helping these entrepreneurs develop business plans by facilitating the legal, logistic, and marketing relations involved in running a business. The new ventures included retail stores, restaurants, and travel agencies. Increasingly, Peruvians with a secure job that paid social benefits were also able to pay the mortgage for a house either in Miami or in upstate New York. In general, institutional and transnational ties with Peru were further fostered. Owners of these businesses promoted additional legal immigration to the United States by sponsoring kin or *paisanos* who wanted to come to New York City. And yet, the general character of most Peruvian kin and kith networks had primarily a working-class face (Bureau of the Census 1993a, b, c).

Peruvian Networks in the 1990s

There are some signs that Peruvian immigration continues at a similar pace as in the 1980s. The first reason is that the Peruvian economy has become increasingly even more fragile. Less than 15 percent of the working population in Peru have secure jobs, with wide unemployment among the ranks of young people. However, the labor market and the political environment in New York City have also limited immigrants' upward mobility. The unsteadiness of the U.S. labor market has intensified, following deregulation and restructuring from an industrial to a service economy. The competition among Hispanics and with other immigrant groups for finding jobs has substantially increased (Waldinger 1995). And yet the balance leans toward more Peruvian immigration, which also raises awareness of a high presence of undocumented immigrants.

The unstable labor markets in Lima and in New York City have increasingly prompted legal Peruvian residents to live in both cities almost simultaneously, traveling back and forth. They work for a short time in New York City, save, then buy clothing and electronic paraphernalia, which they sell in Lima. These Peruvians become couriers for New York City residents, transmitting remittances in kind and money to families in Peru.

Unsteadiness and Structure of New York City's Labor Market

The employment picture for Peruvians in New York City (from the late 1960s to the mid-1990s) appears strikingly similar to what they left behind in Lima. The demand for commodities and the massive social mobility brought about by Peruvian modernization in the early 1940s was not accompanied by a boost in the demand for steady labor like the demand that inspired the late nineteenth-century immigration to the United States (Golte and Adams 1986). Peruvian immigrants in New York City are currently facing a similar period of economic change unaccompanied by the creation of enough steady jobs. As has been widely discussed in the migration literature, there have been two general shifts in the U.S. labor market over the past thirty years: the evolution from an industrial to a service-based economy and the decline in job security (unsteady labor market) associated with deregulation (Harrison 1997; Massey et al. 1996; Sassen 1988, 1991). Accordingly, the tendency for new immigrant communities to fill menial jobs has persisted.

Job security is defined by the market characteristics of the activity itself (seasonality and growth), underlying inequalities, the degree of deregulation, the strength of the relationship of the worker with management inside the workplace, and the market "niche" that the employing firm has. Recent statistics indicate that a large proportion of Peruvians are working in occupations that are likely to offer insecure employment and low wages. This trend has persuaded Peruvian immigrants in New York City to have 1.5 or 2 jobs to comply with their personal and social responsibilities. A comparison of the kinds of job in which Peruvians have found regular employment in New York and the kinds of job held by their Hispanic counterparts and by all workers in New York reveals some inequalities (Table 11.1). The rate at which Peruvian immigrant women are employed in the service sector (home care for the elderly, cooking, cleaning, babysitting), 13.3 percent, is much higher than the 10.0 percent average for all Hispanic working women and nearly double the 7.4 percent average for the total New York female working population. In contrast, in the basic office work category ("technical, sales, and administrative support"), where the work is a little cleaner and less physically stressful, the proportion of Peruvian women employed, also 13.3 percent, is much lower than both the 17.1 percent for Hispanic women, and the 20.5 percent for all women. Peruvian men[4] are more significantly employed in physically demanding blue-collar jobs, represented by the categories "precision production, craft and repair" (skilled manual labor such as in car mechanics) and "operators, fabricators and laborers" (heavy physical labor such as in construction work). Interestingly, this characteristic is shared by the entire New York working population, as is the more general trend of just over 40 percent of women participating in the New York labor market.

The overwhelming majority of Peruvian immigrants are not unionized, and manual work is often seasonal. Interviews indicate that the work load in garment factories also tends to vary with the fashion seasons, and contrary to stereotypes, both men and women are employed in these establishments. Furthermore, Peruvians are underrepresented in the occupational group most strongly correlated with job security, "managerial and professional" jobs: 13.8 percent of all Peruvians hold such jobs compared

TABLE 11.1 Percentage of Employed Peruvians, Hispanics, and Total New Yorkers, by Occupational Group, 1990

	Peruvians[a]		Hispanics		Total New Yorkers	
	Total	Female	Total	Female	Total	Female
Managerial and professional	13.8	5.9	15.8	8.0	30.0	10.0
Technical sales, and administrative support services	23.6	13.3	29.3	17.1	33.1	20.5
	28.4	13.3	23.1	10.0	14.4	7.4
Precision prod. and craft	13.1	1.1	10.1	1.3	9.4	0.8
Operators and laborers	20.5	6.4	20.9	6.9	12.0	3.0
Farming and fishing	0.6	0.1	0.8	0.1	1.1	0.2
Total	100	40.1	100	43.4	100	41.9

Source: Based on the Bureau of the Census 1993c, Employed persons 16 years and over.

[a]Includes U.S.-born Peruvians. Peruvians number about 5 percent of all Hispanics.

with 15.8 percent of all Hispanics and the almost double 30.0 percent of the total population. The tendency toward insecure employment is also captured in the unemployment figures for Peruvian immigrants in New York City: 8.7 percent for Peruvians over sixteen years old, 11.3 percent for Peruvian women (Bureau of the Census 1993c, 313).

As for the characteristics that Peruvian immigrants bring to the labor market, these include a skills "mismatch" and lack of command of English. Peruvian immigrants in New York are on average thirty years old, and most of them are sons and daughters of previous migrants from the provinces of Peru to Lima. One reason their parents made the move to Lima was to guarantee their children a high school education, and in fact Peruvians in New York State are highly likely to have a high school diploma: 82.4 percent of Peruvian men and 83.2 percent of Peruvian women in New York State between the ages of twenty-five and thirty-four are at least high school graduates, and 13.0 percent of legal Peruvian immigrants over twenty-five have completed college studies (Bureau of the Census 1993c, 309). Thus, most Peruvians in New York City have higher qualifications than what the market demands.

Growing up in Lima also provided most Peruvian immigrants with urban job skills such as construction, mechanics, driving, electronics, and sewing, and, among professionals, accounting, engineering, teaching, and administration. However, even in those cases where Peruvians bring with them skills that are in demand in New York City, differences such as the traffic flow, urban structure, tools, work space, and administrative organization mean that immigrants have to learn new features on the job, passing through a "get used to" process. As Perico in Astoria says, "It is not difficult to learn how to install parts and fix these windows [which are different from those found in Lima], but I also have to learn where to buy them and their proper English names. Or when installing tiles on the floor [a better paid skill], the technique, basic materials, and tools are different from the ones used in Lima, so I would like to learn that."

Lack of command of English does not prevent an immigrant from finding a job, but it greatly reduces promotion potential and the possibilities of switching from temporary to permanent employment. Furthermore, English skills qualify an immigrant for cleaner and less physically stressful jobs, such as secretarial and sales positions. In New York City only 42 percent of Peruvians have strong English proficiency, which is lower than the Hispanic average of 56 percent (Bureau of the Census 1993c, 244, 309), which in turn is lower than the non-Hispanic white average of 90 percent (Rodríguez 1995). Peruvians quickly learn that language limitations reduce the scale of informational resources to Spanish newspapers, Spanish television channels, and communication with other Latinos. Command of English links the immigrant to wider job networks and increases his or her desirability to an employer because the employing firm also wants to access wider networks. For instance, Pepe, who lives in Brighton Beach (Brooklyn), in 1989 was not promoted to foreman in a private construction firm in Manhattan because his English was poor. He knew that learning English would have improved his ability to deal with Manhattan residents and his prospects for mobility in the construction sector in general.

Frequently Peruvians learn English on the job, beginning with basic words and phrases used colloquially. They then increase their vocabulary as they are exposed to circles of other English speakers, such as bilingual Puerto Ricans and non-Latino bosses and co-workers, and people they meet and must deal with outside of work, including other apartment tenants, landlords, telephone operators for public utilities, and grocery store owners. English proficiency is crucial at jobs with high potential for promotion, such as building maintenance and administration, in addition to construction. "My husband decided to learn ten new English words a day [twenty years ago], and that is how he improved," Luisa, Víctor's wife, commented. Víctor's English proficiency was enhanced also by his work as a doorman in a building in midtown Manhattan, where most of the residents did not speak Spanish. Víctor and Luisa live in Jackson Heights (Queens). Whenever time constraints work against the desire to overcome lack of English proficiency, Peruvian parents register their children at English or bilingual schools. "When we look for an apartment or need to call AT&T, Luisito reads the newspaper or talks on the phone," said Sophia, who lives in Flushing, praising her ten-year-old son. Sophia intends to raise a child who will offset her own educational shortcomings.

State intervention in the labor market leaves clear marks on immigrant mobility options, to which immigrants respond by gathering substantial economic and informational resources from the network. Because there is no more powerful barrier to immigrant settlement and social mobility than the condition of being undocumented, Peruvian community networks are structured around the distinction between "legals" and "illegals." "How did you come [undocumented through Mexico or with legal visa]?" would be the first question—right after exchanging names—that an "old" Peruvian resident would ask of a recent immigrant to New York City. According to the answer, many "old" Peruvians (documented and undocumented) will use the answer to evaluate the degree of risk and trust for entering into social and economic commitments with their fellows.

The need to legalize immigration status to better access the labor market makes obtaining residency the highest priority for undocumented Peruvian immigrants. Legal immigrants can more easily use formal channels for their job search, such as newspaper want ads, employment agencies, and New York City government offices, and can therefore have fuller access to the spectrum of labor demand at shops, factories, and subcontractor and service establishments than their illegal counterparts, to whom these avenues are generally closed. In construction work, legalization increases the possibility of finding employment with a firm that can sponsor union membership, and thus the possibility of more steady work and social benefits. Obtaining a "green card" plus a job with social benefits means an immigrant will have deeper roots of incorporation into U.S. society, including active citizenship, since now the immigrant has "something to thank this country for." But legalization in itself is not enough. Access to better-paying or less physically stressful jobs that do not involve manual labor require further language and professional qualifications and the right contacts. Nonetheless, a legalized immigrant experiences less psychological pressure than does the undocumented immigrant, who leads a fugitive life and for whom every day is a series of risk-filled events.

For the legalization process, Peruvian immigrants use illegal as well as legal strategies. For example, sometimes INS employees can be bribed to facilitate status, and some U.S. residents can be paid off to enter into fake marriages. According to a sotto voce motto among members of the Peruvian community: "To marry a legal resident [or get the green card] is like winning the Lotto or even better. Puerto Ricans and other legal residents know this, that's why they charge from $2,500 to $3,500 to arrange marriages. They need the money anyway—many of them live on welfare." Although some immigrants obtain false green cards and false Social Security numbers to access certain jobs, they are never certain that these false documents will be accepted at another job. Furthermore, lack of permission to work can also prevent immigrants from obtaining other documents, such as driver's licenses or bank cards, which in turn close the avenue to other jobs and credit opportunities.

Kin and Kith Structure of Peruvian Networks

The use of kin and *paisano* networks by Peruvian immigrants to find jobs is rooted in the social fabric of negotiated help and reciprocity, inculcated since childhood. There are three basic circles of relatives tying Peruvian immigrants together: nuclear family, extended family, and *paisanos*. Of all the kin to whom an immigrant is related, the closest ties are to the nuclear family. Families in Peru have on average four or five children, and siblings are particularly important in the migration endeavor because they have been brought up to support one another as well as their parents. Moreover, older children have the responsibility to help raise their younger brothers and sisters and give advice and support even in adulthood. In New York City, brothers and sisters are the first to be called upon to mobilize the community to find a job for the newly immigrating younger sibling. The reciprocal sense of obligation between siblings is so strong that monetary advances may be returned in the form of nonmonetary favors (such as house construction, chores, babysitting, job search, and information sharing), making the means for meeting obligations more flexible. However, for the same reason and because of the density of reciprocal ties, conflicts between siblings might have a disturbing effect on network dynamics by breaking or transforming the tie.

Members of the extended family provide the same type of information or financial assistance as the nuclear family but are less obligated to do so. Nonetheless, if an immigrant is the first person in his or her nuclear family to immigrate to New York City, he or she will try to find out if any extended family live in the area, though the less flexible relationship of rights and obligations may persuade immigrants to concentrate their energies on developing stronger ties with *paisanos* and friends.

Whereas in Peru *paisanos* are related by descent from the same geographic space (often from the Andes), in New York City *paisanos* include all Peruvians, and the term might even be extended to other Latino immigrants. Dario says, "I am more *paisano* with somebody from Cuzco in the Andes, but I am also *paisano* with any Peruvian. Maybe the Dominican lady from the video store is like a *paisana*, too, because she speaks Spanish." If a person is the first in the family to immigrate, he or she might build a *paisano* network by asking neighbors, colleagues, or schoolmates in Lima for contacts in New York City, and once in New York City by seeking out other Peruvians.

Most Peruvian immigrants after arrival try to reach out beyond their kin to *paisanos* by participating in church, soccer, school, and party activities. The contacts made here will be vehicles for information and better jobs, second, part-time jobs, and immigrant legalization endeavors. However, the predominantly reciprocal relationship in the nuclear family has as its counterpart a more negotiated relationship among *paisanos*. Conflicts may occur because its values and relationships and the money involved are not homogeneous (Zelizer 1994). If ties between *paisanos* are weak or semi-weak they will not loan money without charging "loan shark" rates of interest, because for some Peruvian families money made by lending is fundamental for their economic living. The practice of charging a high rate of interest is also due to the high possibility that the borrower will default on the loan, where there is neither a formal enforcing mechanism nor as strong a sense of moral obligation as exists between family members.

Although the nuclear family is the basic resource for help and reciprocity, there is no neat division of Peruvian networks in New York City into the two categories kin and *paisanos*. Each migrant's particular history creates the actual possibility for using the potential link between two points—nuclear family, extended family, or *paisanos*—in the network. Perhaps during his or her lifetime, the migrant will not develop even 50 percent or his or her networking possibilities. Migrants, however, keep in mind each feasible useful tie, new or old, developing some while abandoning others. "I meet people in the subway, at my job, anywhere. . . . I especially cultivate relationships with my aunts, uncles, and cousins. . . . One has to *sembrar* [sow] here and there," Perico confessed.

Strategic and Bounded Economic Roles of Peruvian Networks

An important issue for Peruvian immigrants is how to contact the labor market. Peruvians' knowledge of the wide New York City labor market is limited to what their contacts tell them. For a new immigrant, particularly if undocumented, the network of information for jobs consists, basically, of kin, close family friends, and telephone numbers of contacts given by friends in Lima. Luis, who arrived in New York City six months ago, said, "I am going to visit a Peruvian friend in New Jersey. I asked him on the phone about a job and he wanted me to come to his house to talk about it." Luis lives in Flushing (Queens) and works in a carpentry shop around this area. His friend has lived in New Jersey for about twenty years and currently works as a doorman at a three-star hotel. Before leaving Peru, Luis compiled a list of addresses of people whom he could contact in the New York area, some of them collected when these people returned to Peru to visit. Luis brought this list even though his mother and sisters, already living in Queens for about three years, offered to host him and put him in contact with his new employer. His faith in the contacts he can make through the network is matched by employers' support for the strategy, because "network hiring, in which current employees bring their friends and relatives to fill vacant jobs, eliminates many costs of recruitment and training while providing high quality employees, since co-workers are only likely to bring into the workplace new workers who will be dependable" (*Migration News* 1995).

For Peruvians, as for some other immigrant communities, the purpose of immigration is to improve the social and economic welfare of the family, not just that of the individual immigrant. To make this goal feasible, Peruvian immigrants share what might be called a culture of social and negotiated reciprocity, in striking contrast to the predominant culture of individual self-sufficiency prevalent in the United States.[5] Although investment in social relations is strongly stimulated by long-term benefits, in the short term there is an expectation of concrete rights and obligations. If in the short term there are no signs of reciprocity, the tie has a strong possibility of breaking or of developing only weakly (particularly if lack of reciprocity is a trend).

Peruvian migrants on the move know that there is more risk than certainty in what lies ahead, so their strategies tend to be to tie to one another, to exchange resources, and to assign different roles, as well as to punish those who "misbehave." For example, help in pursuing studies might be compensated with household work and a place to stay with a "voluntary" contribution from the weekly wage; an uncle praises a nephew's accomplishments in exchange for the nephew's advice to the uncle's child; a reduced rent is granted in exchange for "voluntary" babysitting a few hours a week. Networks, ultimately, become a special and crucial kind of asset, with expected short- and long-term social and economic returns. Thus, their power is greater than that of a purely economic investment.

Socio-Economic Commitments, Tensions and Dynamics of Reciprocity

The opportunity for economic and social improvement opened to the family by immigration cannot occur without draining the resources available to the network (in both the Lima and New York City branches). The immigrant, therefore, assumes the responsibility to reciprocate by complying with commitments to family and *paisanos*. Social commitments might include repaying debts, sending remittances, and helping other members of the family to immigrate. The ability for the new immigrant to comply with these social responsibilities, however, will depend on the job or jobs he or she finds in New York City and on his or her actual ability to save.

Pressure to repay debts affects the job in three ways: first, the immigrant must perform well on the job, or even overperform, in order to keep it; second, the immigrant attempts to become skilled as soon as possible; and third, he or she is likely to take a second job or additional shifts. New immigrants are likely to arrive in New York City with debts or social commitments, whether they arrive legally or illegally and whether or not they have family in New York City, partly because the average income in Peru is about $120 a month, while the cost of airfare to New York City is $1,200. If the immigrant is undocumented, the costs may rise to around $5,000. These costs demand the participation of kin, *paisanos*, and friends, who sometimes will be lending their life savings. The immigrant turns to close family first, but if they do not have the resources, the immigrant will then turn to extended family, or to close friends and *paisanos*. The best results are achieved by those who have well-cultivated relationships with some of these network contacts. Of course, if the immigrant has contacts already earning dollars in New York City, it may be easier to raise funds for immigrating (Massey and García 1987). And the probability that the New York City contact may advance money for the immigration expenditures is higher the closer the family relationship.

Would-be immigrants do not only call upon the network for financial resources. The immigrant leaving Lima may ask for assistance with taking care of children while he or she is away, or with cooking if the mother is immigrating. More to the point, it is understood that brothers and sisters of a woman whose husband is immigrating will look out for her while he is away, and vice versa. Outside the family, would-be immigrants ask friends and *paisanos* in Peru to put them in contact with any relatives they may have in New York City. Once the immigrant settles in New York City, he or she then reciprocates, again sometimes using informational or labor resources rather than money, for example, by passing on to Peru information about job opportunities in New York City or by sending gifts or by sending back goods requested from the United States for family or *paisano* businesses based in Peru.

Nonfinancial assistance is particularly important for women with young children in New York City, since even if a job is available, they cannot work until they find a babysitter. If parents or other kin are not available at home, child care will involve stringent time coordination and probably require assistance from close friends (or neighbors) outside the home. When child care cannot be arranged, jobs or promotions are simply not taken. Elsa is a dramatic case, since she works the nightshift as a data-entry operator at the U.S. Post Office, and her cousin Perico takes care of her child at night. Even with this assistance, Elsa expresses the extreme stress to which she is subject, in her comment, "Sometimes I only get two hours of sleep."

If the immigrant was able to borrow from family, the repayment obligation may be tempered by social processes. For example, maybe the immigrant can find a job someday for the son of the sister who lent him the money. However, the extended family tends to be less flexible than the nuclear family when lending money because something the immigrant does for the nuclear family will not necessarily help the extended family financially: if married, the extended-family member is supporting a separate nuclear household. The extended family usually expects repayment as soon as they learn that the immigrant has obtained a steady job in New York City.

Remittances are a second social responsibility that immigrants using the family network assume. When a person immigrates, social improvement for the family is only potential. The immediate effect is to cut physical contact, particularly difficult for other members of the nuclear family (spouse or children). The immigrant needs to send remittances to Peru as soon as possible as a sign that the immigration process is worth the effort and will improve the family's well-being. Among the different kinds of remittance obligations, those to spouse and children back in Peru are strongest. They should be large and especially stable. The spouse and children need funds for housing, food, and school. Even if the spouse works in Lima or has already immigrated to New York, the he or she is obligated to send remittances to children. Although varying in degree, this commitment is permanent and nearly unbreakable.

Immigrants also tend to help parents who are still in Peru by sending them remittances. Although pensions for senior Peruvians are often not sufficient to cover basic living expenses, the ones who have siblings overseas probably do not depend for their entire income on the immigrant's remittance because their other children also help support them, each according to his or her means. Remittances to parents may take the form of goods or currency for living, for health care, or for birthday and Christmas gifts. "Today I will send the remittance in kind to my mother, poor woman, she will be needing it," "La Cholita" would say, on one of the occasions on which she sent *encomiendas* to her family. Even grandparents, who often had helped parents to raise the kids, are subject to attention from Peruvian immigrants, who send them remittances when not sponsoring them to come to *"los Estados Unidos."*

Sometimes remittances flow the other way and parents use their skills to help their grown children. For example, when parents who are construction workers might help to build or improve their children's homes, either in Lima or in New York City. María invited her father to New York City on a tourist visa so that he could visit her and his grandchildren but also assist in the construction of the sewage system for her new house. "Here it's different," her father told me. "The parts are generally plastic, not like in Peru, where they are usually metal. But some of the parts might be interchangeable, so I am taking a few back to Peru to use with my clients."

Immigrants with some years of settlement in New York City also send remittances to the family for buying land (in the countryside or the city), for buying material to construct a house, or for opening or improving a small store. The house might be for the parents or it might be for the immigrant's dream house, to be occupied on his or her return to Peru at some future date. In either case, the siblings might live in the house temporarily in return for taking care of parents or preparing for the immigrant's return.

Whereas with parents the immigrant has an obligation to give without expecting to receive anything in return, with siblings there is an ongoing back-and-forth relationship of benefit and obligation. The immigrant might, for example, fund an entrepreneurial venture in Peru, such as a store or a restaurant, so that a brother or sister could earn a living. But along with the funding would go the expectation that the sibling would use part of the income to support the parents. Supporting parents or helping younger siblings could be the reciprocal obligation in lieu of repaying the total loan in currency.

The best way for an immigrant to help his or her family, however, is to bring a family member to New York City. But first the immigrant must spend two or three years establishing himself or herself and in that time presumably become a legal resident, find a stable job, and perhaps accumulate some buffer savings.

Peruvian networks facilitate accumulation of the savings necessary to meet social obligations such as debt repayment, remittances, or funding new immigrants is through the organization of *juntas*. This financial mechanism is the Peruvian immigrant version of the "rotating credit association" studied by Geertz and Granovetter (cited in Portes 1995a, 137–42). A *junta* is a savings and credit system organized by a group of six to ten immigrants, documented and undocumented. Mutual trust among the members of the *junta* is the key to its success. Group members are often related by kinship, *paisano*, and job-ties and are not necessarily Peruvian. They may be Colombian, Puerto Rican, Dominican, or Ecuadorian. Each member deposits a certain amount of money weekly, and one member has the right to use the total money gathered. "We deposit $100 each week; for example, next week it's my turn, so I will receive $1,000 because we are ten members. This money I will use to buy a video camera and to send money for Christmas to my relatives in Peru," Jenny explained to me. She added, "In this way one can 'see' the money, because if we don't do this, money disappears like magic. Do you want to take part in this *junta*." The person who organizes and administers the junta benefits by receiving the first week's "pot" but in return for this right assumes the obligation to cover any member's default or delay in the weekly quota.

The enforcement of the social commitment is based partly on the immigrant's own shared belief in family care and reciprocity, and partly on the immigrant's thirst for prestige and power (control) over resources. However, the immigrant may not be able to pay back the debt as quickly as the creditor desires, or the immigrant may find a conflict between debt repayment and remittance obligations. The network has social enforcement mechanisms to promote repayment, despite such conflicts, through the flow of information between its New York and Lima branches. For example, the people the immigrant is staying with in New York City are often related to the creditor in Lima. Through them, it is not difficult for the creditor in Lima to learn the level of the immigrant's success in New York City. Furthermore, the immigrant still has family in Lima who want to maintain good relationships with the benefactor who granted the loan.

Cash constraints may lessen the amount of but do not excuse regular debt repayments or remittances. Perico, for example, working an average of three or four days a week in his first year in New York City, earned about $13,000, of which $2,200 went to repay debts and $3,500 was remitted to his wife and children. However, he has not finished repaying his debts, and remittances to his family sometimes fluctuate. "If it were not for my debts, I would be saving to legalize my immigration status, so I could visit my family in Peru and eventually bring them here," Perico added.

A humble way to gain prestige is to meet one's social obligations. Thus, the immigrant who pays his or her debts on time, sends remittances to Peru, or makes it possible to bring a new immigrant to New York City also forges prestige in his or her family and close friends in both Lima and New York City. To be able to fulfill all these commitments often means that the immigrant has a regular stream of income of one or several jobs and so could likely serve as a liaison with other Peruvians or family members for job recommendations and various kinds of contacts. The person who administers successful *juntas* also gains a reputation as trustworthy and reliable, making it easier for him or her to organize new ventures.

Those who do not comply with the network's moral code, however, are punished. For example, Duly, a New York City resident for two years, would inform her friends about her "ungrateful" brother: "Esteban is a bad son because he never sends his mother a penny." To repeat, conflicts based on perceived breakdowns in reciprocity between brothers and sisters can generate transformations in the network itself, possibly manifested in less dense or tight ties between them. Another example of the network's disapproval concerns Camilo, who worked as a stevedore in Lima before immigrating to New York City. He could not repay on time the expenses incurred by the Peruvian woman, owner of a garment factory, who funded his immigration through Mexico. He had to tolerate the teasing of his friends and harassment in the street by his creditor. According to his friends he might not have put enough effort into complying with his debt, and as a result he does not enjoy the trust of the Peruvian neighborhood in Brighton Beach (Brooklyn). Thus, even though he has been in New York City for several years, his job and housing situation remain fragile.

The ultimate punishment that the network can impose on a defaulting member is de facto, often temporary, ostracism. Fausto provides an example. He is a legal resident in the United States, speaks English, and has regular employment. He invested $60,000 in a fourteen-wheel tractor-trailer for a business in Peru hauling freight across the Andes. He financed the purchase through a combination of personal savings, banks loans, and a personal loan from his aunt in Lima. The collateral for the bank loan was his aunt's house. After several months of operation, the tractor-trailer suffered a serious breakdown that Fausto could not afford to repair. His aunt demanded that Fausto return to Peru or pay the overdue debt, but he could do neither, leaving the aunt in the position of repaying the debt herself or losing her house. In attempting to control the situation, Fausto wound up accumulating additional debts in New York. Finally, he fled to a Peruvian friend in Ohio to escape the moral censure of his family network.

Dynamic Links Between Peruvian Networks and New York City Labor Market

Unsteadiness in the labor market has four visible effects on the workings of Peruvian networks: it increases the new immigrant's dependence on the host network; it requires flexibility in the length and location of the workday, which affects the role of members of the household; it increases reliance on network contacts beyond kin; and it increases the importance of bringing additional family members to New York City. Increased dependence on the host network occurs during the first period of adaptation. Since obligations are more elastic between nuclear family members, an unreliable job situation makes it more important for the new immigrant to be hosted by nuclear family. The advantage of relying on nuclear family rather than extended family or *paisano,* in terms of favors or loans, is that the time frame and form for meeting the respective obligation tend to be longer and more flexible, respectively. In terms of jobs, nuclear family is likely to be more diligent about locating one for the new immigrant. In terms of housing, the nuclear family is more likely to endure overcrowding and delayed payment of the rent. The absence of family members in New York City, for example, made Dario's situation more precarious. When hosted by his *paisano,* Pepe, he had to make rent and utility payments immediately. Close kin would probably have been more flexible in the first months while Dario looked for work.

Because of unsteadiness in the labor market immigrants might take on a second job, or they might work overtime at their first job or take home piece work that could be for their own employment or for that of other household members. For example, sewing and jewelry making are activities subject to household (often kin) involvement. Although this strategy brings work stress home, it does not necessarily decrease time shared with family. Rather, it changes the activities and roles that family members play while at home. The net benefit is the higher likelihood of accumulating savings to comply with social commitments, in addition to coping with basic economic needs. The likelihood that two or more household members become involved in wage-earning activities is probably the reason Peruvian annual household income in New York City averages $25,000, among the highest in the Latino community (Rodríguez 1995).

The unsteady labor market also increases reliance on contacts with *paisanos* and friends, pushing immigrants to make contacts beyond kin networks among *paisanos* and relatives of friends, friends of relatives, friends of friends, old friends and former neighbors from Peru, and new neighbors and co-workers in New York City. Among undocumented Peruvians, this drive to build ties beyond kin is also stimulated by the need to make contact with people who can assist in getting the legal ID necessary to get a job (a Social Security card, or a sponsor for a work permit). Strong ties among *paisanos* are fostered, for example, at the soccer gatherings that take place almost every day in various public parks in Brooklyn and Queens, among men on weekdays and with family participation on weekends. These are propitious occasions for exchanging information about jobs, wages, and legalization—as well as for getting updates on various social issues in the Peruvian community, such as parties, gossip, Spanish television soap operas, boyfriends, girlfriends, and news from Peru. Frequent informal gatherings at the household level and beyond, including different kinds of weekend family parties (for welcoming new arrivals or celebrating baptisms, birthdays, and holidays), and informal conversations at the workplace all help to keep the networks lubricated. In general, other Latino friends and intermarried couples are invited to Peruvian parties. Sometimes as many as 50 percent of the guests are other Latino non-family members who, together with Peruvians, dance Dominican *merengue* for most of the party.

The fourth effect of the unsteady labor market is to increase the importance of bringing additional family members to New York City. An unreliable job means unreliable income, so the probability that any one person can send remittances to Peru regularly is lower. However, if the family sends additional members of the same nuclear household to New York City, there will be two positive effects: the presence of more than one household member in New York decreases the probability of fluctuating remittance flows, even if the paychecks for each person continue to be unsteady, and there will be fewer dependents in Peru relying on the remittances.

Conclusion

Peruvian kin and *paisano* ties have enabled and constrained the attainment of upward mobility in the unsteady New York City labor market over the past thirty-five years. Peruvian immigrants face different degrees and kinds of risk according to their positioning and the strength of ties to their nuclear network. The alternatively harsh, thoughtful, strategic, and risky decision-making of Peruvian immigrants reflects the uncertain political economy in which they have been operating. It also reflects their determined defiance of this uncertainty and their attempts to exploit the opportunities it sometimes presents. Whereas the New York City labor market puts downward pressure on the improvement of Peruvians' economic livelihood, kin and *paisano* transnational networks of help and reciprocity create the actual space for contending formal limits to upward mobility. These social networks represent a transnational response by migrants to a structural situation of global inequality at two sites. Just as their networks aided them in responding to the global inequality that yielded the macro-level causal factors for migration in Peru, so too they have helped them in adapting to the unsteady labor markets that confront them in the global city of New York.

Relations between and among kin and *paisanos* have structured Peruvian networks, determining the nature and limits of mutual aid and conflict negotiation. Furthermore, the unstable nature of immigrant links to labor markets has led to greater reliance on interpersonal networks, as well as on different network structures. Network membership is in itself an asset with short-term costs balanced against short- and long-term insurance for a wide variety of risks, some of them quite unknown at the time of investment. What is particularly important to note is the changing nature of the social bonds of trust and solidarity in the context of Peruvian immigration, with immigrants striving in the unsteady conditions of the New York City labor market.

More specifically, controlling for job insecurity and wage levels, Peruvians have found ways to increase their potentials for economic and social growth: first, through multiple incomes earned within a household, and, second, through social arrangements to share undertakings and nonmonetary resources. Given diminishing job security and a downward trend in real wages, this process has not occurred without tight economic constraints and risks of defaulting on commitments. And yet, without disregarding the conflicts among kin and *paisanos* carried along the way, social undertakings such as remittances, loans for airfare, helping kin construct a home, *juntas* and job search assistance have reinforced community-based support, even as they have transformed the customary ways that Peruvians build and reinforce ties to one another. As a Peruvian immigrant told me on the subway at six o'clock one weekday morning on the way to his construction job, "We have to help each other, that is the only way."

Notes

Acknowledgments: The author thanks the MacArthur Program on Globalization and Liberalism at the New School for Social Research for supporting this research.

1. I myself immigrated to New York City from Lima in the 1990s, a step that was made possible by my parents' migration from the Andes to Lima in the 1960s.

2. About 40 percent of the Peruvians in New York City reside in the Borough of Queens, in neighborhoods such as Astoria, Elmhurst, Jackson Heights, Woodside, Corona, Flushing, Richmond Hill, and Jamaica-Hillcrest (Department of City Planning 1992).

3. This figure is based on the following calculations: in 1990 there were 32,000 legal Peruvian residents in New York State, of which 75 percent lived in New York City (Bureau of the Census 1993c, 44, 307). The rate of growth of the Peruvian population in New York between 1980 and 1990 was 100 percent (Rodríguez 1995), so assuming the same rate for 1991–95, in 1996 legal Peruvians in New York City would approach 64,000. Based on my interviews, I also estimate that this number should be increased by 25 percent to include undocumented Peruvian immigrants, for a total of 80,000.

4. The data for male employment can be deduced by subtracting female from total figures.

5. Ironically, most government administrations in Peru have not been able to save enough to avoid hemorrhaging deficits.

References

Castles, Stephen, and Mark J. Miller. 1993. *The Age of Migration.* New York: Guilford Press.

Department of City Planning of New York City. 1992. *The Newest New Yorkers: An Analysis of Immigration into New York City During the 1980s.* New York: Department of City Planning.

Golte, Jurgen, and Norma Adams. 1986. *Los Caballos de Troya de los Invasores: Estrategias Campesinas en la Conquista de la Gran Lima.* Lima: Instituto de Estudios Peruanos.

Massey, Douglas S., Jorge Durand, William Kandel, and Emilio A. Parrado. 1996. "International Migration and Development in Mexican Communities." *Demography* 33 (2): 249–64.

Massey, D. S., and E .García España. 1987. "The Social Process of International Migration." *Science* 237:733–38.

Migration News. 1995. Editorial, 2 (10): 2–3.

Monaghan, Jay. 1973. *Chile, Peru, and the California Gold Rush of 1849.* Berkeley: University of California Press.

Portes, Alejandro, ed. 1995. *By-Passing and Trespassing. Explorations in Boundaries and Change.* University of Maryland: Urban Studies and Planning Program.

Portes, Alejandro, and J. Sensenbrenner. 1993. "Embeddedness and Immigration: Notes on the Social Determinants of Economic Action." *American Journal of Sociology* 98:1320–50.

Rodríguez, Orlando, 1995. "Nuestra América en Nueva York: The New Immigrant Hispanic Populations in New York City, 1980–1990." Summary of a report by the Hispanic Research Center, Fordham University, in collaboration with the Institute for Puerto Rican Policy.

Sassen, Saskia. 1988. *The Mobility of Labor and Capital.* New York: Cambridge University Press.

———. 1991. *The Global City.* Princeton: Princeton University Press.

Tilly, Charles, and Chris Tilly. 1994. "Capitalist Work and Labor Markets." Pp. 283–312 in *The*

Handbook of Economic Sociology, edited by Neil J. Smelser and Richard Swedberg. Princeton: Princeton University Press; New York: Russell Sage Foundation.

U.S. Bureau of the Census. 1993a. *1990 Census of Population.* Washington, D.C.: Government Printing Office.

———. 1993b. *1990 Census of Population. Persons of Hispanic Origin in the US.* Washington, D.C.: Government Printing Office.

———. 1993c. *1990 Census of Population. Social and Economic Characteristics.* Washington, D.C.: Government Printing Office.

Waldinger, Roger D. 1995. *Still the Promised City? African-Americans and New Immigrants in Postindustrial New York, 1940–1990.* Cambridge: Harvard University Press.

———. 1994. "The Making of an Immigrant Niche." *International Migration Review* 28:3–30.

Zelizer, Viviana A. 1994. *The Social Meaning of Money.* New York: Basic Books.

CHAPTER 12

Entrepreneurship and Business Development Among African Americans, Koreans, and Jews: Exploring Some Structural Differences

Jennifer Lee

Small businesses are very important. I subscribe to that 100 percent. If you believe in America and what they have done business-wise, you find that in every community, it's run by a group of small businesses. And small businesses are not just the local candy store. It's the fruit stands, the bakery, it's the small store that's making maybe hats. They're all there and they're employing people, and those businesses carry on.

—*African American Merchant in Queens*

During the past few decades, the growth of immigrant entrepreneurs has made a distinct and consequential presence in many large U.S. cities, most notably in the nation's inner cities. Today, Jewish, Korean, and other foreign-born merchants dominate the inner-city retail niche. Large furniture stores that offer everything from washers and dryers to living-room sets and jewelry shops that display heavy gold chains symbolize Jewish enterprise in black communities. Korean retailers make their mark with fruit and vegetable markets, wig stores, urban sportswear stores, and nail salons. Barbershops, beauty salons, and record stores represent African American entrepreneurship. Today's inner-city commercial landscape looks far different from that of several decades past, evoking a tale of ethnic succession. However, it is the Korean immigrants who largely succeeded the Jewish old-timers, not the African Americans.

Jewish merchants dominated the inner-city retail niche until their mass exodus following the urban riots in the late 1960s, which erupted in cities across the nation such as Los Angeles, New York, Detroit, Washington, D.C., and Philadelphia. Old, reaching retirement age, and fearful of violence, few Jewish retailers desired to stay on, showing far more interest in finding prospective buyers for their retail businesses (Center for Community Studies 1970; Mann 1970). In the late sixties, they, along with the Jewish Community Relations Council (JCRC), developed an innovative plan. Together, they created the "Merchants' Program" in which Jewish storeowners "turned over" their businesses to African Americans buyers within the community who had long dreamed of running businesses of their own. JCRC worked in conjunction with the Small Business Administration and local banks to help finance the transition from Jewish to African American ownership. In total, Jewish merchants successfully turned over fifty stores throughout the Philadelphia area alone, but within a few years, the African American merchants closed down these businesses or sold them to other buyers.[1]

Then, in the 1970s, Korean immigrants entered inner-city neighborhoods, bought the stores, and created a profitable niche for themselves. With one-third of Korean families in the United States self-employed (Light and Bonacich 1988), African Americans by contrast are extremely underrepresented, exhibiting a self-employment rate of only 4.5 percent (Borjas and Bronars 1989; La Noue and Sullivan 1998). Clearly, African Americans have not been able to take full advantage of the retail self-employment opportunities in their communities.

This chapter explores the ways in which social structures and processes help explain the greater success in self-employment among Jews and Koreans compared with African Americans. On the basis of interviews of seventy-five merchants from five largely black[2] neighborhoods in New York and Philadelphia, I argue that the limited access to capital—both economic and social—significantly affects the rate and scale of business ownership among ethnic groups. Access to capital gives Jewish and Korean retailers leverage over their African American counterparts—pulling them through a slow business cycle, sustaining them through an unforeseen emergency, and placing them in the optimum business locales. Correlatively, the absence of capital—or access to it—can have severe and permanent consequences for African American business owners, disabling them when emergency strikes, or simply when cash flow is tight.

Immigration and Entrepreneurship

Social scientists argue that certain ethnic groups, particularly when they are immigrants, turn to small business to overcome disadvantages in the American labor market (Lee 1999b; Light 1972; Min 1984; Yoon 1997). A language barrier, unfamiliarity with U.S. customs and culture, the inability to transfer educational and occupational credentials, and discrimination leave immigrants severely disadvantaged to compete with the native-born in the primary labor market. Compared with the native-born, immigrants have fewer "high-priced salable skills" (Light 1972) and therefore turn to self-employment as an alternative to entering the secondary labor market—characterized by low-paying, low status jobs with little room for mobility.

Disadvantages in the labor market alone, however, cannot explain economic organization, since ethnic groups who find themselves similarly disadvantaged do not exhibit equal rates of self-employment. Ethnic groups such as the Chinese (Loewen [1971] 1988; Zhou 1992), Japanese (Bonacich and Modell 1980; Fugita and O'Brien 1991), Jews (Rischin 1962), Koreans (Kim 1981; Light and Bonacich 1988; Min 1996, 1984; Yoon 1997), and Cubans (Morales and Bonilla 1993; Portes and Bach 1985) boast higher rates of self-employment than other ethnic groups. For instance, Laotians, Puerto Ricans, and African Americans, by comparison, reveal low rates of self-employment: 2.6 percent, 4.0 percent, and 4.5 percent, respectively (La Noue and Sullivan 1998).

To explain the disparity in self-employment rates, theorists began with cultural explanations, linking cultural and religious values with entrepreneurialism. Max Weber's *The Protestant Ethic and the Spirit of Capitalism*[3] is the classic example. From the cultural perspective, the high rate of entrepreneurship among ethnic groups is the result of cultural characteristics such as hard work, perseverance, discipline, and thrift. Yet as Roger Waldinger (1986, 9) critically points out, "the bundle of traits, attitudes, and behavioral patterns that are 'cultural' are themselves the product of previous interaction between a group and its original environment." In other words, entrepreneurship and economic organization should be studied in the situational and structural context in which it emerges.

Today, cultural explanations hold little currency in the debates about entrepreneurship. Instead, social scientists have shifted to structural explanations by focusing on the importance of resources—class, ethnic, and social capital—in the development and success of small business ownership among ethnic groups. Class resources (human capital, skills, and wealth) and ethnic resources (aid that is preferentially available to individuals who belong to a certain ethnic group) have been used to explain Cuban and Korean immigrants' prevalence in small business. Sociologists also point to the pivotal role of social capital—the capacity of individuals to command and mobilize resources by virtue of their membership in networks (Portes 1995). Sociologist James Coleman (1988, S98) illustrates the mechanism behind social capital, enabling certain systems to function.

> Social capital is defined by its function. It is not a single entity but a variety of different entities, with two elements in common: they all consist of some aspect of social structures, and they facilitate certain actions of actors—whether persons or corporate actors—within the structure. Like other forms of capital, social capital is productive, making possible the achievement of certain ends that in its absence would not be possible. Like physical and human capital, social capital is not completely fungible but may be specific to certain activities. A given form of social capital that is valuable in facilitating certain actions may be useless or even harmful to others.

Central to Coleman's concept of social capital is the role of closure in the social structure, which facilitates the trust needed to allow actions such as exchange, borrowing, and lending. Also essential to its development is the degree to which the relations are indispensable, or the extent to which members within the social structure depend on one another. Obligation, trust, and expectation are necessary for social capital to operate, the absence of which would not enable systems to function.

Social scientists agree that class, ethnic, and social resources largely explain the prevalence of immigrant entrepreneurship (see Table 12.1), but the low self-employment rate of African Americans remains a puzzle for social scientists, who offer competing explanations (Butler 1991; Caplovitz 1969; Glazer and Moynihan [1963] 1970; Light 1972). For instance, John Butler (1991) argues that segregation severely limited African American business development by prohibiting merchants from operating in an open market—a fundamental difference between African American and immigrant entrepreneurship. Whereas African Americans were strictly limited to serving coethnics, immigrants were not similarly confined. The Chinese in Mississippi, for example, were able to compete in an open market, serving not only coethnics but also the white and black communities alike (Loewen [1971] 1988).

In contrast, Ivan Light (1972) highlights the importance of rotating credit associations, which African Americans lack, while Nathan Glazer and Daniel Patrick Moynihan ([1963] 1970) point to coethnic advantages such as the ability to capitalize on distinctive immigrant and ethnic consumer needs that only fellow ethnics can provide. Positing that African Americans have few distinctive needs upon which African American entrepreneurs can capitalize, Glazer and Moynihan argue that African Americans do not have a specific ethnic niche that they are able to exploit. Consequently, the growth of African American–owned businesses was confined to service niches that are ignored by other ethnic groups such as barbering, hair styling, and restaurants (Butler 1991). However, African Americans do have distinct ethnic consumer needs that immigrant retailers—not African American merchants—supply, such as wigs, ethnic beauty supplies, and ethnic urban sportswear (Lee 1999a).

I argue that the lack of capital—both economic and social—remains the key variable in explaining the relatively low rate of retail self-employment among African

TABLE 12.1. Class and Ethnic Resources and Social Capital

	Class Resources	Ethnic Resources	Social Capital
Definition	Private property in the means of production or distribution, personal wealth, and investments in human capital	Forms of aid preferentially available from one's own ethnic group	The capacity of individuals to command resources by virtue of their membership in networks or broader social structures
Examples	• College education • Economic capital • Skills and work experience	• Loans from coethnic friends and family • Better prices from coethnic suppliers • Coethnic credit	• Kye • Access to business information and market tips

Americans. Economic and social capital determines which retailers can pull through a slow business period or withstand an unforeseen emergency such as a fire, flood, or robbery. Finally, capital determines which merchants will secure the prime business locations, attracting the most customer traffic. These structural advantages are cumulative, ultimately determining which retailers have a better chance of business survival and economic success.

Research Design and Methods

I located five largely black neighborhoods, three of which are low-income and have median household incomes under $20,000 and two middle-income with median household incomes slightly over $35,000. The three low-income neighborhoods are East Harlem, N.Y., West Harlem, N.Y., and West Philadelphia, and the two middle-income neighborhoods are Jamaica, Queens, and East Mount Airy, Philadelphia. Each of these neighborhoods has major commercial strips lined with a variety of retail and service-oriented businesses, much of which is geared specifically for an ethnic clientele, offering fresh fruit, vegetables, and fish, as well as large appliances, sneakers, and wigs. Each commercial strip is located near mass transit stops, thereby attracting a constant flow of customer traffic. The customers are primarily black, and the merchants, a mixed lot—including Jews, Koreans, Middle Easterners, Asian Indians, Latinos, West Indians, and African Americans.

I conducted in-depth interviews of storeowners between March 1996 and May 1997 and interviewed fifteen merchants from each site, totaling seventy-five merchant interviews overall. I interviewed twenty-nine Korean, twenty-five Jewish, and twenty-one African American merchants from the five research sites.[4] I asked the merchants why they decided to open their business, the resources they employed for business purposes, and the obstacles they faced and continue to face in business. On average, the interviews lasted between 1.5 and 2 hours and were tape-recorded and then transcribed verbatim.

Setting Up Shop

Jewish Merchants

Today's Jewish entrepreneurs in black neighborhoods are primarily second- and third-generation European immigrants who have taken over the retail shops from the first generation. Over half of the Jewish retailers in the sample bought their business from their parents or other family members, making Jewish-owned stores the longest lived in black communities, averaging a tenure of forty-two years. While the majority of Jewish-owned shops were simply passed down from family members, another quarter was purchased from non-family coethnics with their personal savings. Finally, 16 percent benefited from coethnic "training systems" (Bailey and Waldinger 1991), buying out the previous coethnic owner for whom they once worked. In this case, buyers and sellers normally worked out a monthly payment plan over a period of many years instead of providing an enormous initial lump sum payment (see Table 12.2).

None of the first-, second-, or third-generation Jewish storeowners received bank or government agency loans to start their businesses, instead reducing their families' ability to set up shop to a simple formula of "hard work," "frugality," and "family participation." For example, a second-generation Jewish storeowner of a large and profitable furniture business in East Harlem explains that his parents immigrated to the United States penniless, yet through hard work, delayed gratification, and perseverance, they succeeded in opening and maintaining a successful business.

> My parents came to this country penniless. They worked hard, and they didn't spend because of the insecurity of knowing what it's like to be poor. When they worked hard and put money in the bank, that gave them happiness. My father started the business with two uncles and then my father bought them out. It was a family business. Everybody would work here. My family was very frugal. My father was such a hard worker. My mother saved and saved, and she wanted to buy the building someday from the landlady. Would you believe the landlady lived until she was 99? My parents were very hard working. My mother was a simple woman, she wasn't frivolous. She never bought anything really fancy.

When asked whether his parents received a business loan, the Jewish storeowner immediately barked at the possibility, reiterating the formula of "hard work" and "innovation," pointing to today's Korean immigrants who have followed suit.

> No loans, my God! It was just hard work and savings. My father used to go and knock on people's doors when they didn't pay for their furniture like they said they would. And then some people would say that they couldn't pay for everything now, but they promised to pay him, and he just had an instinct about them. My father worked so hard, just like the Koreans now. They're hard working people. You see them in the winter, in the cold, with nothing but plastic to protect them in the cold. I would say that you have to be innovative, not lazy. If they really wanted to, they could do it too, but in time. You have to build it slowly, and show people that you're not a fly-by-night business. You have to be here all the time.

Similarly, when asked whether he received a bank or government loan for his businesses, a Jewish clothing storeowner on Jamaica Avenue quickly became defensive and retorted:

TABLE 12.2. Resources Jewish Merchants Used in Starting Their Businesses

Means of Establishing Business Ownership	Number of Businesses	Percentage
Bought from family member	15	60
Bought from coethnics with personal savings	6	24
Bought from previous owner for whom they once worked	4	16
TOTAL	25	100

Ridiculous! Ludicrous! Absolutely moronic! That's ridiculous! That's stupid. It's a fantasy. Everybody knows how a Korean starts a business. They borrow money from their family or their friends and they don't spend any of the money they make. They wear sandals and eat rice. They do things the way people did things long ago, just like the original people [Jewish immigrants] did long ago. So just the way the original people did it many, many years ago, the Koreans are doing when they came along.

The ethnic succession from Jewish to Korean ownership leads many of the Jewish merchants to note striking parallels between the Jewish and Korean immigrant experience. Jewish merchants underscore the belief that every individual—regardless of ethnicity—has the opportunity to open a business if he or she so chooses. Implicit in statements such as "You have to be innovative, not lazy," "If they really wanted to, they could do it too," and "Don't spend money that you make" is that were African Americans simply not lazy, more ambitious, and willing to delay gratification, they too could be just as successful. Jewish merchants are not unique in this regard. Korean retailers, too, often subscribe to the ideology behind the American dream and equality of opportunity—that in essence, all it takes to succeed in small business is hard work, grit, and frugality.

Korean Merchants

Korean immigrants are largely middle class and were motivated to emigrate because of limited opportunities for social and economic mobility in South Korea. Because the supply of college graduates in South Korea far exceeds the demand for such a highly educated work force, the average rate of unemployment for male college graduates is 30 percent (Yoon 1997). Korean professionals who are fortunate enough to secure employment in the Korean economy must endure fierce competition, delayed promotion, underemployment, and job insecurity. In addition, favoritism in the workplace based on kinship, region of origin, and school ties makes mobility nearly impossible for those who are not immersed in these networks. Compared with their limited prospects for advancement in South Korea, middle-class Koreans view migration to the United States as a means of mobility in an open-opportunity structure not only for themselves but also for their children.

Korean merchants, the majority of whom are first-generation immigrants, choose self-employment as a quick route to upward mobility. Their relatively poor English-language skills, inability to transfer their educational credentials, and unfamiliarity with the U.S. corporate culture and customs lead Korean merchants to choose self-employment as the most lucrative option. The Korean merchants in the sample have been in the United States for an average of eighteen years and in business for an average tenure of eight years.

Korean merchants use a variety of class and ethnic resources to set up shop, such as drawing upon loans from kin and coethnic friends and turning to ethnic newspapers to locate businesses for sale. However, unlike the previous literature that stresses the reliance on rotating credit associations (*kye*) (Light 1972; Light and Bonacich 1988), my research indicates that few Korean immigrant merchants use this ethnic resource at the start-up phase. In fact, only 7 percent acquired capital to open their business through funds from a rotating credit association. The majority relied on a combination of their other resources: personal savings, loans from family members, and credit from the previous coethnic storeowner.[5] The remaining 17 percent bought their business from a family member—usually a brother, sister, or in-laws—who immigrated to the United States several years before them (see Table 12.3).

When Jews and Koreans buy from fellow ethnics, instead of going through a third financial party such as a bank, the buyer will normally pay the previous owner one-third of the value of the business as a down-payment and the remaining two-thirds in monthly payments over a period of a few years. Koreans use this debt source more frequently than do other groups because they are likely to purchase retail firms that are already in operation rather than starting from ground zero (Bates 1994).

Although the use of rotating credit associations may not be as prevalent at the start-up phase, this resource is highly utilized at the later stages of business. Rotating credit associations range in both membership size and value, with participation extending from only a few people to over thirty, and the value ranging from $100 to over $100,000. Korean merchants report that the average kye ranges from ten to twenty people, with each member contributing between $1,000 and $2,000 into a pot totaling $10,000 to $40,000. Every member contributes to the fund, and each receives his or her share according to a predetermined schedule. For example, if a rotating credit association has twenty members and each contributes $2,700 a month, the first to receive the pot gets $51,300 ($2,700 × 19). After receiving the pool of money, the individual must thereafter contribute $3,100 until the rotation is complete. Hence, an individual who receives the pot first gets only $51,300 while the one who receives the pot at the tail end of the rotation is rewarded with $58,900—the surplus accounting for interest and appreciation. Coleman (1988) offers the rotating credit association as a prime example of the manifestation of social capital because it is based on a high degree of mutual trust, obligation, and expectation among its members.

Unlike previous research that underscores the importance of rotating credit associations at the start-up phase, my research finds that the use of rotating credit associations is far less important at the beginning and, instead, considerably more important after Korean merchants have already established their businesses. Koreans use the capital for purposes such as buying new merchandise or equipment, remodeling, pur-

TABLE 12.3. Resources Korean Merchants Used in Starting Their Businesses

Means of Establishing Business Ownership	Number of Businesses	Percentage
Savings + loans from family/friends + credit from previous coethnic storeowner	22	76
Bought from a family member	5	17
Rotating credit association (kye)	2	7
TOTAL	29	100

chasing seasonal merchandise in bulk, and pulling them though a slow business cycle. Even though the use of kye varies among Korean merchants, all have admitted that the rotating credit association is a resource they could draw upon if they needed to accumulate capital quickly. The facility with which Korean immigrants can tap into financial resources attests to their easy access to social and economic capital.

However, it must be pointed out that without a high degree of economic capital, social capital would not be nearly as beneficial for an ethnic group. For example, Carol Stack (1974) and Elliot Liebow (1967) illustrate that informal networks of exchange exist among poor African Americans in urban communities, but they "swap" resources that are significantly smaller in scale, such as food stamps, a few dollars, appliances, food, and child care. They immerse themselves in a circle of kin and nonkin alike who help one another by "swapping" goods and services day-to-day. The poor respond to the pressures of exchange so readily because poverty demands that they not turn anyone away. The one whom you help today may be the one who, in turn, helps you tomorrow. Through this intricate web of affiliations the poor are able to meet their daily expenses. However, it is precisely the high degree of social capital coupled with their economic capital that gives immigrant entrepreneurs a distinct advantage over the native-born.

Koreans are not the only ethnic group to benefit from social capital. In fact, not only the African American poor but also first-generation immigrants of many ethnic backgrounds—such as West Indians, Asian Indians, and the Vietnamese—draw upon their versions of rotating credit associations (Kibria 1993). Dense coethnic ties based on shared immigrant experience, common language, lifestyle, and involvement in coethnic institutions provide a firm basis for intraethnic cooperation (Gold 1994). But as these groups acculturate into the U.S. social structure, they utilize this resource far less frequently. For example, whereas first-generation Jewish immigrant entrepreneurs used mutual loan associations (Ellison and Jaffe 1994; Katz and Bender 1976; Morawska 1996), latter generations have long since discarded this tradition. Furthermore, second-generation Korean immigrants, like the second- and third-generation Jewish immigrants before them, have already abandoned this practice.

Korean merchants explain that the benefit of using kye over more traditional means of financing—such as bank or government agency loans—is the facility and guarantee of the kye system. For instance, a Korean sportswear merchant in Harlem explains why Koreans prefer using rotating credit associations over institutional loans:

> I looked into it, but from a Korean's standpoint, it's such a hassle. So much paperwork. You have to give them two years' financial records. You have to give them a business plan of what you want to do for the next three to four years. You have to give them business projections. And it's a lot of things that Koreans don't want to hassle with because there are other avenues to get money, other avenues that are 100 percent guaranteed that you get it instead of going through the Small Business Administration. There's number one, a language barrier, and number two, you lack the expertise in getting the proper information to them. I've looked into them. Next year, we'll qualify to enter into some of their programs. It's a resource that people need to utilize more, but they don't know about it. And if they do, it's too much of a hassle, and they don't want to do it.

In addition, because small business is generally a cash-based business, entrepreneurs often underreport their income, thereby making their businesses appear less profitable, and consequently diminishing the probability that they will receive a bank loan.

Yet some Korean merchants are now wary of using rotating credit associations because they realize the inordinate amount of trust involved for such a system to operate. Many recall recent kye failures where one person took the lump sum of money and left the country. A Korean merchant who has used kye a few times illustrates the risks involved and the difficulty in holding someone legally responsible for defaulting.

> Some people, they don't do kye because no matter what they don't trust because it could happen too. When a guy gets $40,000, after a couple of months, you don't see him anymore. Then where are you going to go get him? You cannot tell anybody what happened. It's no protection. Let's say even you bounced [your check]. So let's say you owe a big company, you don't pay enough on your credit card. They're going to send you a thousand letters. They going to send you [to a] collection [agency], but those big companies can afford it, but a lot of people, you want to get $10,000 from that guy who run away. You want to hire a lawyer, you want to go to court, this and that, time and money, headache. Forget about it. They know what is the risk, so they don't even want to involved.

Although Korean merchants explain that there are no legal ramifications for defaulting, since the members do not sign written contracts, the social sanctions—such as loss of standing in the immigrant community and exclusion from it—are strong enough to prevent losses regularly. The risk is certainly one problem, but another is the costly interest payments, which can be as high as 30 percent, surpassing the legal limit in New York state, for instance, which must be under 25 percent. Although rotating credit associations may help those who need to acquire cash very quickly, they also function as financial investments for the affluent, who benefit from exploiting fellow ethnics with exorbitant interest payments.

Although not all Korean merchants have participated in kye, all have admitted to borrowing funds from their family or coethnic friends, either at the start-up phase or during business when cash flow is tight. Self-employed Koreans have accepted tens of thousands of dollars in loans from kin and coethnic friends. The high degree of social and economic capital remains the most valuable resource for these immigrant entrepreneurs. The importance of these resources cannot be overemphasized, because the availability of cash resources can determine whether a business will be able to withstand emergencies such as break-ins or slow periods when cash flow is tight.

African American Merchants

Unlike Jewish merchants, who rely primarily on family resources, and Korean merchants, who turn to loans from fellow ethnics, African Americans use a combination of resources to accumulate sufficient capital to start their business. Thirty-three percent started their business with their personal savings, and 14 percent purchased their business using a combination of personal savings and borrowed capital from their retirement or insurance plans. Finally, 14 percent started their business with a partner, and 19 percent received a bank or government agency loan from the Small Business Administration. Another 14 percent did not need start-up capital because their businesses are based on consignment—meaning that they sell used furniture, clothing, or appliances without having to purchase the merchandise beforehand. In some cases, people donated merchandise, such as clothing and appliances, to these storeowners and expected no profit in return. Others, who gave furniture or antique pieces, expected to split the profits with the owner after the merchandise was sold (see Table 12.4).

African Americans are more likely than Jews or Koreans to look toward external resources such as bank loans to help finance their businesses. By contrast, the foreign-born rarely rely on external loans—particularly at the start-up phase—because they entail lengthy, bureaucratic processes. Also and perhaps more important, for the foreign-born, there exist immediate, guaranteed alternatives within their coethnic networks. For African Americans, this option is closed because their coethnic networks tend to be far less affluent, consequently directing them to outside channels for capitalization.

For African American merchants, self-employment is not simply a means to an end—achieving upward mobility—but the end in itself. African American business owners often refer to owning one's business as their "passion" or "dream." Others take a more political stance, subscribing to the ideology behind African American economic autonomy. Moreover, whereas Jewish and Korean storeowners would not like their children to follow in their footsteps, African Americans view retail self-employment as an attractive career option for the next generation.

For instance, an African American storeowner in Queens purports that small businesses are the "backbone" of our economy, giving individuals the opportunity for economic growth and upward mobility.

> I believe that Mom and Pop stores are the backbone that keeps American society going. One of the guys I graduated with, this Italian fellow, I asked him, I'll never forget, "What are you going to do?" He said, "I'm going to work for my father's cleaners. I'm going to

TABLE 12.4. Resources African American Merchants Used in Starting Their Businesses

Means of establishing business ownership	Number of Businesses	Percentage
Own savings	7	33
SBA loan, bank loan, or government agency loan	4	19
Savings + funds from insurance, pension, or 401K	3	14
Did not need capital (consignment)	3	14
Bought business from previous Jewish owner	1	5
TOTAL	21	100

run that business." And he's walking out of school with a degree, and they were telling black people that they should take that degree and try to get a job in corporate, and go into a lower level and work your way up. And this is different thinking. Hey this guy is going to work for his father's cleaners, and eventually he can have a chain of cleaners.

Small businesses are very important. I subscribe to that 100 percent. If you believe in America and what they have done business-wise, you find that in every community, it's run by a group of small businesses. And small businesses are not just the local candy store. It's the fruit stands, the bakery, it's the small store that's making maybe hats. They're all there and they're employing people, and those businesses carry on. As I was saying about the gentleman that graduated from college with me, he went into the cleaning business. He takes that onto another level. Before you know it, not only does he have a cleaners, he has two cleaners, and he owns the building that the cleaners are in, so now he's into real estate.

Booker T. Washington and W.E.B. Du Bois extolled self-employment for African Americans as an economic means to developing wealth and power in the early 1900s. Historically, the African American self-employment rate has remained low, especially compared with the rate for immigrant groups, but there are two interrelated reasons for the underrepresentation. First, African Americans' networks have led them into different occupational niches, primarily in the public sector. Second, African Americans are less likely to have access to adequate social and economic capital to open and maintain their businesses.

The majority of the African American merchants in the sample are the pioneers among their families and friends to set up shop. In fact, only two of the twenty-one African American business owners had ties to friends or family members who are also self-employed. By far, the majority established their businesses with no guidance from fellow ethnics. For instance, an African American beauty salon owner in Mount Airy explains why African Americans are much less likely to choose self-employment:

A lot of them [other ethnic groups] had stores, or relatives that owned maybe candy stores or furniture stores, or some type of small businesses. Whereas in an African American community, it was very rare, so I didn't have like an uncle or a grandfather to pass it down from generation, just that mentality of being an owner.

African American business owners reveal that while they were growing up, their families never guided them into self-employment but instead directed them toward securing jobs in the public sector, where job security and decent pay make this niche an attractive option. For example, an African American retailer in Mount Airy explains:

You know when I was coming up, the safe thing was to get a government job. My father's a mailman, a postal worker. Or get a city job, you'd have job security. But we were always taught, you have to work for someone. I never heard around the house, you can do your own thing. I never heard that!

But if you talk to a little Jewish child, you ask them what they want to be, they'll tell you, doctor, lawyer, or I want to own my business like Daddy because they see it in the home, they hear it.

Ethnic social structures create networks that have a "fateful effect" and pull ethnic groups into different occupational niches. Waldinger (1996) describes how separate ethnic networks among African Americans and immigrant groups lead to disparate occupational outcomes. For example, whereas immigrant groups have turned to self-employment, African Americans' search for opportunity led them into the public sector. "Once African-American networks become implanted in government jobs, those networks transmitted signals that led other black New Yorkers to converge on public employment. By contrast, burgeoning business activity among groups like Koreans or Chinese sends out a different type of signal, suggesting to newcomers that they set up shop on their own" (256).

The second main reason behind the low levels of self-employment for African Americans is that they are significantly less likely to be able to draw upon ethnic resources, such as loans from family or friends, both because of their relatively low degree of social capital and because of the lack of economic capital in their social networks. African American business owners are middle-class and American-born, not immigrants, and therefore do not readily utilize social capital. Social capital, like other forms of capital, is unequally distributed among ethnic groups, the consequences of which are serious and permanent.

By illustration, an African American book-store owner explains that unlike other ethnic groups who rely extensively on mutual financial support, he was unable to exercise this option. Critical of his own, he explains the paradox that African Americans are more reluctant to lend to each other compared to other groups.

> One of my sisters was very cooperative. She would lend me some money. But other members of my family were very, I hate to use the word conservative, but you know, "How am I going to get my money back? I don't want to do this," and all that. My brother was like that, and a lot of guys are like that. . . . [Other groups borrow from each other] because they can do it. And the reason they can do it is because other groups understand the importance of that.

Furthermore, he explains that African Americans would rather invest their money "outside of the community," trusting whites over their own.

> We've been poisoned against each other. That is not good. I'll give you an example. You take somebody outside of the community, outside of the black community, to come in with a program, a scheme, an MTM, multi-level marketing. And they can come in and say, "Hey, I'm going to show you guys how to make money." You give them that whole pyramid scheme bit, and you're going to make X number of dollars. And if they work for the city, they will go and borrow three, four, or five thousand dollars from their pension or from their Credit Union and they will put it into that multi-level marketing program, thinking that there's some kind of a pot at the end of the rainbow.
>
> Then you go them and say, "Listen, I'm starting this business, it's going to be in the community. I need about $500, $1,000 short-term." Then they'll say, "I don't know." It's this thing that if somebody white tells you, it's okay, but you have no credibility with someone black, whether it's your family or not.

Moreover, when asked whether she would turn to her family if she needed money for her business, an African American coffee-shop owner responds, "No, not my style, because I've learned from experience, both in the business world and my private life, the family should be a last resort. I try to keep my business, business, and my personal, personal."

Similarly, an African American pharmacist in Mount Airy also admits that African Americans do not utilize social capital to the extent that they could, especially when it comes to business. She candidly criticizes fellow ethnics, using the metaphor of "crabs in a basket" to depict African American non-cooperation.

> It's like this mentality that I'm afraid to let you get a little more than me. Somebody used an analogy that blacks are like crabs in a basket. When one's trying to crawl up to come out, there's one down there in the basket trying to pull him back down. Now I've heard it, and since I've been in business I've been hearing that so much. But if we all work together, we can all get out. I think we're afraid you're going to get a little more than me. There's enough room out here for all of us. If you help me, I can help you.

African Americans regretfully reveal that, as a group, they have not mobilized their business resources to work together. An African American consignment-shop owner in West Philadelphia similarly attests that of the black ethnic and religious groups, African Americans are the least willing to work together, "The Muslims and Jamaicans are tight. The blacks are the least together. Historically there hasn't been anything to bring blacks together." More than a century ago, W.E.B. Du Bois noted this problem in his classic, *The Philadelphia Negro* ([1899] 1967, 123): "Negroes are unused to co-operation with their own people and the process of learning it is long and tedious . . . ; they are just beginning to realize that within their own group there is a vast field for development in economic activity." African Americans have not been able to develop traditions of lending and mutual exchange as have other immigrant ethnic groups, the consequences of which still affect business owners today. Therefore, coethnic resources that play a crucial role in the formation and development of immigrant-owned business do not exist for middle-class African Americans, leaving them severely disadvantaged to compete with the foreign-born.

But it must be pointed out that immigrants take advantage of social capital more easily than the native-born of all types because they are not yet acculturated to the long-standing tradition of middle-class individualism in American society. For the notion that one must depend on and extend help to others in order to succeed stands in stark contrast to models that posit an atomistic person, piloting his or her way with only human capital as the controlling feature. As Katherine Newman (1988, 125) points out, even when white, middle-class families face the prospect of downward mobility, turning to kin for financial assistance creates tension on all sides: "Nothing queers family relationships faster. . . . Confusion and embarrassment can intensify over whether material help is a loan, a gift, or a right—self-abasement or a statement of love and sharing." Therefore, not only middle-class African Americans but also middle-class whites evince low levels of social capital; they too are reluctant to draw upon resources from kin, even in the most dire of circumstances. Social capital among immigrant communities, by contrast, posits that dependable reciprocal relations are critical for survival.

The absence of social capital leaves African American merchants at a disadvantage compared with their immigrant counterparts, but the absence of economic capital poses even greater consequences. Since African Americans tend to have less affluent kin and coethnic friends, their networks cannot supply them with the large sums of financial resources often needed in business. For instance, when asked whether he could borrow money from his family for his business, an African American hair-salon owner in Mount Airy replied: "My family, I have kind of a middle-class, working family, and we don't really have large incomes. Everyone is mainly just trying to maintain their own homes. Maybe I could have gotten $500 here, but not really more than that." By contrast, Jewish and Korean storeowners often borrow as much as tens of thousands of dollars from family or fellow ethnics for business purposes. Hence, the option that Korean and Jewish storeowners regularly utilize is closed to African Americans, severing even the potential for the employment of social capital.

The Importance of Capital in Small Business

The importance of economic and social capital in small business should be underscored. Capital is needed to make renovations, to buy new equipment, to order seasonal merchandise, or to respond to unforeseen emergencies. As a Jewish pawn-shop owner in West Philadelphia explains, "If you're undercapitalized and you're in business, you can't stand a slow period because you have to pay your suppliers. If you don't pay your suppliers, you can't get merchandise." Access to capital is also essential during emergencies, such as robberies and break-ins, which are not uncommon in low-income neighborhoods like Harlem and West Philadelphia. In such cases, Jewish and Korean merchants often turn to coethnics for loans, but African Americans are unable to tap into this ethnic resource.

By illustration, a Jewish, Korean, and African American storeowner each explain the importance of capital in coping with emergencies such as fires or break-ins. All three merchants were able to keep their businesses afloat after the crises, but each turned to different sources, thereby producing very disparate outcomes.

After a fire that ravaged a large Jewish-owned variety store in West Harlem over ten years ago, the merchant drew upon his own capital and a bank loan to quickly rebuild the business. He explains:

> The bank that we used at that time gave us some money but that was based on our own long-term relationship with them and based on collateral, and it wasn't a tremendous amount of money. A lot came strictly out of cash flow. We were way underinsured because in the late seventies when things were a little tough, insurance was very hard to get up in Harlem, and very, very expensive. So we weren't insured for everything that we had so there was a little bit of insurance money that kicked in, but it was a lot of hard work.

The combination of his savings, money from insurance, and a bank loan enabled him to go back into business within a few months after the fire.

A Korean storeowner in Queens also experienced a fire that ruined his business. Prior to setting up shop on Jamaica Avenue, he owned an ethnic beauty supplies business in Brooklyn. When the business adjacent to his caught on fire, his store also became ablaze. After the fire, with the money that he acquired from a kye, the Korean storeowner opened his second business on Jamaica Avenue. Although he stressed the enormous difficulty in keeping up with the monthly kye payments while running a newly formed business, he was able to keep his business afloat and avoid bankruptcy because of his access to financial resources within his coethnic network. In other words, he was able to draw upon his social capital.

Unfortunately, many retailers in low-income black neighborhoods go uninsured because they cannot afford the exorbitantly high rates that insurance companies demand from businesses located in "high-risk" zones. Weighing the high rates against the probability of an accident, many storeowners choose to take the gamble and remain uninsured. Others explain that they choose not to carry insurance because companies will cover only a small fraction of the overall value, making insurance an unappealing option.

In contrast to the Jewish and Korean storeowners who turned to coethnics and loans from financial institutions to rescue themselves from financial disaster, an African American merchant in West Harlem explains how his inability to access capital created a web of misfortune. After a few minor break-ins, his insurance company cancelled their policy at the contract's end. While the owner was searching for another insurance company, robbers broke into his store once again, yet this time, they stole the entire inventory. The robbery snowballed into an even larger financial catastrophe. Since the owner could not secure capital from family, friends, or a financial institution, his only alternative was to avoid paying his business taxes. Consequently, because he failed to pay his taxes, he was immediately disqualified from all types of government or bank loans.

> They came in through the roof, and they cleaned out the store and stole everything. No insurance because they cancelled the policy. No way to really get credit because we were mostly on a cash basis with our suppliers, and we were in a very bad condition. We tried all the lending agencies and none of them wanted to lend. So as a result, what we did is we didn't pay our sales tax. We hadn't paid the IRS. We borrowed money from them, but borrowing from the government is like borrowing from a criminal. Number one, they penalize you for taking their money. And for argument's sake, if you borrow $5,000 from them, with interest and penalties, you owe them $10,000. So as a result, I got behind very badly on my taxes, I didn't pay the taxes and the IRS.

> And it's extremely hard trying to get back together because I wasn't able to get funded. If I were able to get funded, I would have been able to put the store back together and go on with my business making money and paying back the bills. But trying to do it little by little, you're always a pound short and a day late with the merchandise coming in. You're late with so many things that as a result, cash flow is bad. Whenever cash flow is bad, you

can't make money. So anyway I have agreements with the IRS, the state, and I pay back a certain amount of money monthly.

The African American retailer adds that "minority businesses" often struggle with this "tax problem," creating an "awful circle" of disadvantage.

I have tried everything, and the biggest problem most minority businesses have is the tax problem, and the tax problem is not always of their making. That tax problem can materialize from many different acts, like my situation, and as a result when you apply for a loan, the tax looks like a red flag, and they're not going to give it to you. A lot of times, development and money that's supposed to be coming to our community, small people like myself do not even see any of that money because we don't fit the criteria because we have a tax problem. You see, they're not going to lend you city money if you owe the city money. And they're not going to lend you government money if you owe government money. It's an awful circle. So in other words, you're actually forced to stay in the position you are because to be able to break the circle, to get out of the position, that's not made available for you.

In contrast to the Korean storeowner who immediately acquired capital through coethnics, the African American merchant found himself desperately searching for funding from a variety of sources and coming up empty handed. The different routes and outcomes of these merchants in dealing with dire situations reflect the disparity in social and economic capital between Jews and Koreans on one hand and African Americans on the other.

As early as 1969, David Caplovitz noted *in The Merchants of Harlem* that 40 percent of African American entrepreneurs reported that raising capital for their business is a major problem. And even earlier, St. Clair Drake and Horace Cayton ([1945] 1993, 437) noted that African American businessmen face five main problems: difficulty in procuring capital, difficulty in getting adequate training, an inability to secure prime business locations, a lack of sufficient patronage, and finally, an inability to organize for cooperative effort. These disadvantages have made it historically difficult for African American entrepreneurs to compete successfully with other entrepreneurs, native- and foreign-born, in terms of price and quality of their goods. This, in turn, reinforces the negative stereotype that African Americans are not good business people. In essence, although capital is important at the start-up phase, it is just as significant in the maintenance of a business. Entrepreneurs who can access capital more readily than others have an enormous advantage over those whose channels are limited.

It's All in the Location

Drake and Cayton ([1945] 1993) noted more than half a century ago that African American business owners have been unable to secure prime business locations on the main streets of the commercial strips. This disadvantage still holds today. Jewish- and Korean-owned businesses on these shopping strips are more centrally located along the avenues and closer to mass transit stops, attracting a greater flow of customer traffic. With a few exceptions, African American–owned businesses are located on the ends of the commercial strips or tucked away on side streets, as an African American music-store owner in West Harlem observes:

> We own a lot of businesses in Harlem, but most of them are not on 125th Street [the main commercial thoroughfare of Harlem]. They're on the side streets, Lenox Avenue, Eighth Avenue, St. Nicholas Avenue, Amsterdam, you know, places like that, 145th Street, Upper Broadway, that kind of thing. They're not necessarily on 125th Street itself.

Location is not the only disadvantage; size also matters. Jewish-owned businesses tend to be far larger than either Korean or African American–owned stores, and this difference is reflected in the cost of the rent.[6] Although most Jewish merchants own the buildings in which they operate their businesses, the Jewish storeowners who rent their space pay as much as $10,000 a month in pricey New York's Harlem to secure the prime sites. The average rent for Korean storeowners in New York City is $7,000, and in Philadelphia, $1,250. African Americans pay significantly less than their Jewish or Korean counterparts, averaging only about $2,500 a month in New York City and $500 a month in Philadelphia.

Exorbitant rent prices on these shopping strips constrain many African Americans from attaining the best locations for business. Storeowners acknowledge that a large part of business survival is location. As a Korean merchant barbershop owner readily admits, "It's all in the location." Businesses centered on the main avenues and near transit stops are likely to draw a wider customer base than those on the side streets or the ends of avenues. Hence, Jewish and Korean merchants whose businesses are located in prime locations have a distinct advantage over African American storeowners whose businesses are less visible, and consequently less frequented.

Conclusion

Immigrant entrepreneurs have made distinct inroads in many large U.S. cities. Approximately one-third of today's Korean families are engaged in small business, a figure that parallels the rate of self-employment of Jewish immigrants in the early twentieth century. Touted as "model minorities," Jews and Koreans are symbols that the American dream works—if an individual works hard, perseveres, and delays gratification, he or she can make it too (Hochschild 1995). While Jews and Koreans boast high rates of self-employment, African Americans lag far behind—exhibiting a self-employment rate of only 4.5 percent. Business ownership has historically played an important role in the upward mobility of some of America's immigrant groups—including Italians, Jews, Koreans, and Middle Easterners—which is one main reason why the low rate for African Americans is cause for concern. As early as 1963, Glazer and Moynihan recognized that small business ownership holds significance that goes far beyond the dollars that these businesses generate. Business ownership offers the potential for the accumulation of wealth, political influence, and upward mobility.

The small shopkeepers and manufacturers are important to a group for more than the greater income they bring in. Very often, as a matter of fact, the Italian or Jewish shop-keeper made less than the skilled worker. But as against the worker, each businessman had the possibility, slim though it was, of achieving influence and perhaps wealth. The small businessman generally has access to that special world of credit and finance and per-haps develops skills that are of value in a complex economy. He learns too about the world of local politics, and although he is generally its victim, he may also learn how to influ-ence it, for mean and unimportant ends, perhaps, but this knowledge may be valuable for an entire community. (Glazer and Moynihan [1963] 1970, 30–31)

Jews and Koreans have different motivations for engaging in self-employment than do African Americans. For Jews and Koreans, self-employment is simply a means to achieving the goal of upward mobility, but for African Americans, self-employment is the goal in and of itself—the realization of their passion and dream. However, the underrepresentation of African American self-employment should be understood as the result of their employment networks that pull them into the public sector and their lack of economic and social capital. The differing access to capital has severe conse-quences, particularly in the light of unforeseen emergencies or when cash flow is tight. Jews and Koreans can easily access capital in the form of loans from coethnics, family, and rotating credit associations that are unavailable to African American entrepreneurs—both because their networks are not as resource rich, and because African Americans have not mobilized their business resources to work together. In essence, unlike the foreign-born, African American retailers exhibit low social capi-tal. Economic capital, social capital, and coethnic resources play crucial roles in the formation, development, and success of Jewish- and Korean-owned businesses, giv-ing them a distinct advantage over their African American counterparts.

Notes

Acknowledgments: I would like to thank the International Migration Program of the Social Sci-ence Research Council, the Andrew W. Mellon Foundation, the National Science Foundation (SBR-9633345), and the University of California's President's Office for support of the research on which this chapter is based. For comments and suggestions, I thank Herbert Gans, Kathryn Neckerman, Katherine Newman, John Skrentny, Roger Waldinger, and the editors of this vol-ume.

1. Data about the "Merchant's Program" can be found in the JCRC archives, held at the Balch Institute for Ethnic Studies in Philadelphia.

2. Black is a generic category that includes African Americans, West Indians, and Africans.

3. In *The Protestant Ethnic and the Spirit of Capitalism,* Weber ([1958] 1976) notes, "The fact that business leaders and owners of capital, as well as the higher grades of skilled labour, and even more the higher technically and commercially trained personnel of modern enterprises, are overwhelmingly Protestant." Weber argues that differences in entrepreneurial rates stemmed from differences in religious values by positing a relationship between the "spirit of capital-ism" and the ideas of Protestant thinkers such as Luther and Calvin. Their willingness to take

risks, work hard, and enter the capitalist economy derived from the intrinsic character of religious beliefs.

4. My original goal was to interview an equal number of African American, Jewish, and Korean merchants, but some of the neighborhoods had very few African American merchants. Therefore, there is an underrepresentation of African American entrepreneurs in the sample.

5. When I asked Korean merchants about their funding sources, I made certain to ask them to differentiate between funds obtained through a rotating credit association and loans from family members or friends.

6. Although most of the Jewish storeowners own the buildings in which they operate their business, some did not and therefore paid rent. All of the Jewish merchants in Philadelphia own the buildings in which they do business. In fact, Jewish, Korean, and African Americans merchants in Philadelphia are more likely to own the buildings in which they do business because real estate prices are considerably cheaper there than in New York City.

References

Bailey, Thomas, and Roger Waldinger. 1991. "Primary, Secondary, and Enclave Labor Markets: A Training Systems Approach." *American Sociological Review* 56:432–45.

Bates, Timothy. 1994. "An Analysis of Korean-Immigrant-Owned Small-Business Start-ups with Comparisons to African-American- and Non-Minority-Owned Firms." *Urban Affairs Quarterly* 30:227–48.

Bonacich, Edna, and John Modell. 1980. *The Economic Basis of Ethnic Solidarity.* Berkeley: University of California Press.

Borjas, George J., and Stephen G. Bronars. 1989. "Consumer Discrimination and Self Employment." *Journal of Political Economy* 97:581–605.

Butler, John Sibley. 1991. *Entrepreneurship and Self-Help Among Black Americans.* Albany: State University of New York Press.

Caplovitz, David. 1969. *The Merchants of Harlem.* New York: Columbia University, Bureau of Applied Social Research.

Center for Community Studies of Temple University and Jewish Community Relations Council of Greater Philadelphia. 1969. "Survey of Jewish Businessmen Operating in Selected Inner-City Areas of Philadelphia." Unpublished study.

Coleman, James S. 1988. "Social Capital in the Creation of Human Capital." *American Journal of Sociology* 94:S95–S121.

Drake, St. Clair, and Horace R. Cayton. [1945] 1993. *Black Metropolis.* Chicago: University of Chicago Press.

Du Bois, W.E.B. [1899] 1967. *The Philadelphia Negro.* New York: Schocken Books.

Ellison, Elaine Krasnow, and Elaine Mark Jaffe. 1994. *Voices from Marshall Street.* Philadelphia: Camino Books.

Fugita, Stephen S., and David J. O'Brien. 1991. *Japanese American Ethnicity.* Seattle: University of Washington Press.

Glazer, Nathan, and Daniel Patrick Moynihan. [1963] 1970. *Beyond the Melting Pot.* Cambridge: MIT Press.

Gold, Steve. 1994. "Patterns of Economic Cooperation Among Israeli Immigrants in Los Angeles." *International Migration Review* 28:114–35

Hochschild, Jennifer L. 1995. *Facing Up to the American Dream.* Princeton: Princeton University Press.

Katz, Alfred H., and Eugene I. Bender. 1976. *The Strength in Us.* New York: New Viewpoints.

Kibria, Nazli. 1993. *Family Tightrope.* Princeton: Princeton University Press.

Kim, Illsoo. 1981. *The New Urban Immigrants: The Korean Community in New York.* Princeton: Princeton University Press.

La Noue, George R., and John C. Sullivan. 1998. "Deconstructing the Affirmative Action Categories." *American Behavioral Scientist* 41:913–26.

Lee, Jennifer. 1999a. "Retail Niche Domination among African American, Jewish, and Korean Entrepreneurs: Competition, Coethnic Advantage and Disadvantage." *American Behavioral Scientist* 42:1398–416.

———. 1999b. "Striving for the American Dream: Struggle, Success, and Intergroup Conflict Among Korean Immigrant Entrepreneurs." Pp. 278–94 in *Contemporary Asian America,* edited by Min Zhou and James V. Gatewood. New York: New York University Press.

Liebow, Elliot. 1967. *Tally's Corner.* Boston: Little, Brown and Company.

Light, Ivan. 1972. *Ethnic Enterprise in America.* Berkeley: University of California Press.

Light, Ivan, and Edna Bonacich. 1988. *Immigrant Entrepreneurs.* Berkeley: University of California Press.

Loewen, James. [1971] 1988. *The Mississippi Chinese.* Prospect Heights, Ill.: Waveland Press.

Mann, Theodore R. 1970. "Jews in the Inner City." Paper presented to the National Jewish Community Advisory Council, Cleveland, Ohio.

Min, Pyong Gap. 1996. *Caught in the Middle.* Berkeley: University of California Press.

———. 1984. "From White-Collar Occupations to Small Business: Korean Immigrants' Occupational Adjustment." *Sociological Quarterly* 25:333–52.

Morales, Rebecca, and Frank Bonilla. 1993. *Latinos in a Changing U.S. Economy.* Newbury Park, Calif.: Sage

Morawska, Ewa. 1996. *Insecure Prosperity.* Princeton: Princeton University Press.

Newman, Katherine S. 1988. *Falling from Grace.* New York: Vintage Books.

Portes, Alejandro, ed. 1995. *The Economic Sociology of Immigration.* New York: Russell Sage Foundation.

Portes, Alejandro, and Robert L. Bach. 1985. *Latin Journey.* Berkeley: University of California Press.

Rischin, Moses. 1962. *The Promised City, New York Jews 1870–1914.* Cambridge: Harvard University Press.

Stack, Carol B. 1974. *All Our Kin.* New York: Harper and Row.

Waldinger, Roger. 1986. *Through the Eye of the Needle.* New York: New York University Press.

———. 1996. *Still the Promised City?* Cambridge: Harvard University Press.

Weber, Max. [1958] 1976. *The Protestant Ethic and the Spirit of Capitalism.* New York: Charles Scribner's Sons.

Yoon, In-Jin. 1997. *On My Own.* Chicago: University of Chicago Press.

Zhou, Min. 1992. *Chinatown.* Philadelphia: Temple University Press.

CHAPTER 13

When Coethnic Assets Become Liabilities: Mexican, Ecuadorian, and Chinese Garment Workers in New York City

Margaret M. Chin

The first place I worked, my sister-in-law helped me find the job. She was already working there when I arrived [in this country], and within the week after I arrived I was off working in this shop. She brought me there and introduced me to the others. I never sewed before, so I learned to sew in this shop. I learned watching my sister-in-law sew. It took me a while, but the boss never cared. You can sew slow or fast, but you only get paid what you can make—so it doesn't matter [to the boss]. It took me a while to learn. It was no surprise.

—A Chinese woman in her thirties

No, I have never brought a friend to the shops. Many people ask me to bring them to the shop, but I don't. I'm afraid I will lose my job. There was a woman who worked there [in the shop] for seven years and was making $7.00 an hour. She brought a friend to the shop. The friend wasn't experienced, so the owner gave her a job paying $3.00 an hour. The next day the owner fired the experienced worker.

—An Ecuadorian woman in her thirties

Embeddedness in coethnic relations has a great influence on all aspects of the migration process. Immigrants come to New York City in response to information from social or family contacts. The undocumented as well as documented depend on this type of informal information by which they learn in advance where to go, where to live, and what to do. Immigration laws reinforce this type of communication among legal immigrants.

The wish of all of my interviewees is to come here to earn and to save money to be able to provide a better life for themselves and future generations—whether for family here in New York City or back in their home country.[1] Therefore, the procedure of finding a job is an important step in the migration process.

In this chapter, I examine how getting a job is affected by the social contacts who assisted in the departure and arrival. Contrary to expectations, embeddedness in social networks sometimes inhibits coethnics' ability to assist one another. Outside factors circumscribe the effective use of social networks. Thus, embeddedness in social networks is not the only crucial element in immigrant economic adaptation.

Embeddedness and Getting a Job

The concept of embeddedness refers to the fact that economic transactions of the most diverse sorts are inserted in social structures that affect their form and outcomes (Polanyi [1944] 1957). Mark Granovetter (1985) summarizes several research findings indicating how social expectation modified and even subverted the original intent of the transactions. He distinguishes between "relational" embeddedness, referring to economic actors' personal relations with one another, and structural embeddedness, referring to the broader network of social relations to which these actors belong.

Social networks are among the most important types of structure in which economic transactions are embedded. They are sets of recurrent associations between groups of people linked by occupational, familial, cultural, or affective ties. People communicate and exchange within such structures to acquire scarce means, such as capital and information. Social networks are also important in economic life because they simultaneously impose constraints on the unrestricted pursuit of personal gain.

In relational embeddedness, expectations of reciprocity are based exclusively on past knowledge of other actors and the ability of each individual to withhold resources or apply sanctions if expectations are not satisfied. In a broader network of relationships, economic transfers can proceed on the assumption that others will fulfill their obligations lest they be subjected to collective sanctions. For example, in a Chinese-owned garment shop, if a worker is not rewarded for her efforts in recruiting and training a new worker, other potential sponsors will be reluctant to offer their services. The garment-shop owner will have to resort to other means to hire if additional workers are needed. Moreover, the owner himself will be responsible for training the new person.

According to Alejandro Portes (1995), immigrants need to be viewed as members of groups and participants in broader social structures (including social networks) that affect in multiple ways their economic mobility, and not simply as individuals who come clutching a bundle of personal skills. The limits and possibilities offered by the society at large can be interpreted as the structural embeddedness of the process of immigrant settlement. The assistance and constraints offered by the coethnic community are usually mediated through social networks. They can also be defined as relational embeddedness.

Studies supporting these ideas have shown that the Chinese in New York City's Chinatown have been successful in garment and other industries because of their ability to exploit social networks based on ethnic and cultural resources (Bao 1991; Kinkead 1992; Kwong 1987; Waldinger 1986; Wong 1987; Zhou 1992). For example, Min Zhou (1992) has shown that Chinese employers' use of family and ethnic resources is a function of the social embeddedness of these places of work in ethnic neighborhoods.

Moreover, authors such as Roger Waldinger (1995, 1996) and Charles Tilly (2000) have also stressed how coethnic social networks can keep non-coethnics out of jobs. As Waldinger stresses, the other side of embeddedness is that non-coethnics are clearly limited from the same opportunities that are offered to coethnics. In effect, Waldinger discusses how a group can collectively discriminate against another in the job market. Still, his theory points to the positive effects for coethnics.

Embeddedness in coethnic social networks should also help one get a job, assuming that there are jobs and that one's network has access. This system should work in much the same way when coethnics assist one another in entrepreneurship. Enclaves, middleman minorities, and ethnic occupational niches all use ethnic networks as key sources for startup capital and employment opportunities. Likewise, coethnics could use similar contacts to seek job information and therefore facilitate finding a job.

Thomas Bailey and Roger Waldinger (1991) found that Chinese employers facilitated the recruitment and training of coethnics easily through "the web of social relationships that linked the small contractor to his or her immigrant or ethnic community" (440). Employers took advantage of their networks to gain additional information for hiring. Likewise, Anna Karpathakis (1993) found the same among Greek coethnics. Thus, social ties not only facilitated capital but also provided necessary employees for employers.

Coethnic employee-only networks can also work in a similar positive way by helping to spread job information. Robert Smith (1994) and Dae Young Kim (1996) found that Mexicans who worked in Korean-owned restaurants and green grocers frequently recommended their coethnic friends and kin to be co-workers. They also found that Korean employers often treated their Mexican employees like "fictive kin," training and helping them move into better jobs. However, Smith's more recent work indicates that differences between Greek and Korean employers and the restaurant and grocery industries can also hinder reciprocal relationships between the employee and employer and thus limit how much coethnic employees can help one another (1997).

Likewise, differences show up in a comparison of the garment industry with the restaurant and grocery industry (Chin 1998). Garment industry work organization is much more formal than in groceries and restaurants.[2] Garment shops also hire far more skilled workers, requiring a more selective hiring process. Some employers would rather choose workers themselves than be subject to hiring poor workers referred by coethnics. Thus, given specific conditions, coethnic employees cannot help one another.

While it is true that embeddedness in coethnic networks has positive features or assets for immigrant adaptation such as the Chinese in the garment industry, a comparative analysis of the Koreans who hire Mexicans and Ecuadorians and the Chinese who hire coethnics has led me to conclude that mediating factors, such as immigration status, lack of coethnic obligation on the part of non-coethnic employers, Korean reasoning that unconnected Mexican and Ecuadorians demand less on the job, and requirements for a somewhat skilled work force, hamper the use of coethnic employee–only social networks in the Korean sector. The pay system, work organization, and training systems in their respective sectors of the garment industry reinforce the benefits accorded to the level of social embeddedness. Thus, Mexican and Ecuadorian workers devise ways to circumvent the weaknesses of being deeply embedded in social networks because of their negative effect, while the Chinese seek ways to take advantage of their social connections.

This chapter emphasizes that a negative side also exists when coethnic employees cannot use their social embeddedness to their economic advantage. It also tries to specify what conditions constrain the use of coethnic social ties. Coethnic assets and liabilities may explain the differential outcomes of economic incorporation among the various immigrant groups. Those groups who have coethnic liabilities are clearly limited by their inability to use one of the most important and least expensive support systems.

Data and Methodology

This chapter is part of a larger study and is based on interviews conducted from 1994 to 1996, with fifty-five Chinese workers, fifty-five Latino workers, five Chinese employers, and five Korean employers and informal discussions and job-site observations at the Chinese- and Korean-owned garment shops. The Latino workers are mainly from Mexico and Ecuador. The Chinese workers are mainly from the Taisan/Guangdong area of China and Hong Kong. The Chinese workers are overwhelmingly female. Latinos are 61 percent female. All but one of the Koreans owned shops were in the New York City midtown garment district.

Workers were recruited from English as a Second Language (ESL) classes, midtown "for hire" corners, and garment shops, as well as referrals from other interviewees and business associations. I conducted interviews in Chinese and English, and a Spanish translator assisted me in interviewing the Mexican and Ecuadorian workers.

The Garment Industry Today

This next section provides background information on the industry and the workers and some historical information on the New York City garment industry.

Globalization and Unionization

In New York City Chinatown there are about five hundred Chinese sewing shops. In the past ten years, two hundred sewing shops run by Korean owners employing a majority of Latino workers opened in midtown Manhattan (Sassen 1991a, b). These three racial-ethnic groups are the dominant groups in garment production, holding thirty thousand jobs with a majority female work force.[3]

The return of the garment shops has to be understood within the context of the globalization of apparel production and the rise of a postindustrial New York. Within this formulation the continuing presence of garment factories in industrialized nations such as the United States—in which immigrant women figure prominently— is the result of direct competition with low-cost female labor in the Third World. It is reasonable to see a relationship between the recruitment of women into manufacturing in the Caribbean and Asian countries and the employment of immigrant women in industrialized countries, particularly in cities that have undergone the shift to the service economy.

This global perspective—which includes post-industrial New York, helps to explain not only why these garment shops have emerged but also why they have taken their current form where garment shops that hire undocumented workers are side-by-side with those that are unionized hiring legal immigrant workers. Better manufacturers who want both a "Made in the USA" and a union label contract work out to the unionized shops. The other shops sew for manufacturers who want just a "Made in the USA" label (Petras 1992). Industry relocation to the Third World has weakened U.S. manufacturing capacity, sapping the strength of the domestic labor movement and stripping government of its will and capacity to enforce labor standards. Thus, today, many small garment-manufacturers are returning from overseas manufacturing and capitalizing on these weaknesses and realizing the profits from a "Made in the USA" label.

The Chinese and Korean sectors discussed are distinguished by different ethnic makeup as well as by unionization. Korean shops who hire Mexican and Ecuadorian workers are non-unionized and the coethnic Chinese are unionized. It is not clear which sector is a downgraded sector. Some better manufacturers do not want a union label and prefer to have their work made in the Korean-owned shops. In addition, Mexican and Ecuadorian workers, many of whom are undocumented, seem to be paid a little more. For example, on average, they take home a higher wage than the Chinese. For a fifty-five-hour work week, they earn $220–$275 a week, whereas the Chinese, who get paid piece-rate wages, make on average $200 a week. On the other hand, 95 percent of the Ecuadorian and Mexican workers are paid in cash, with no deductions taken out. Furthermore, they have little job security; about 80 percent of them are undocumented. In contrast, over 80 percent of the Chinese are members of the union receiving relatively good benefits, including health insurance.

The Workers: Migration, Family Structure, and Gendered Nature of Work

Evidence from other immigration studies indicates that migration is a first step in the process of developing ties that assist with finding work and settling in. The interviews indicate that family circumstances in the home country and information from undocumented migrants and documented immigrants already in New York City are influential in helping any new migrant come to New York City. Information about job availability according to documentation status influences migrants' immediate and future family structure in New York City. For example, if a Chinese family uses current immigration laws to emigrate, they are most likely to come as a family with children. Whereas those without legal means, such as Mexicans and Ecuadorians, will choose to leave children behind.[4] Ultimately this decision affects family structure; and immigrant families who come with children have different work and living needs than those without children.

The family configuration with which a group migrates or immigrates and the type of family structure with which they settle affects gender work roles in the United States. These gender work roles, largely determined by the ease of men getting jobs in the garment industry and women's lack of child-care responsibilities, have implications for the gendered nature of work. When there are no children or when children are cared for by someone else in another country, men and women have fewer gender expectations both at home and at work in New York City. The data from the Chinese and Latino worker interviewees indicate that having children puts tremendous pressure on families to conform to gender roles that are essential to supporting children, both economically and socially.

For example, Latino men and women both describe themselves as money earners. Most do not have children in New York City even though their spouses are here with them. Therefore, it matters little to these Latinas when there is no child care or there are no household accommodations at the workplace. Moreover, for Latino wage earners the most important aspect of migration is to find a well-paying job, and jobs in the garment industry tend to pay well and to offer a better mobility ladder than those in the grocery and delicatessen industries. Thus Mexican and Ecuadorian men enter the garment industry because these jobs are available to them. Moreover, there is no stigma attached to working in the industry among Latinos because their conception of the job comes from pure economic need. Latinos can get well-paying jobs in the industry and thus they enter the industry. For these reasons the Korean-owned sector of the industry has not been labeled woman friendly and has not been dominated by women workers. In contrast, in the Chinese community, there is a gendered division of labor according to which garment work is stereotyped as women's work.

Nonetheless, garment work can be performed by either men or women. The work has been characterized as "fine," requiring the handiwork of women, but also as "heavy," requiring the strength of men. The implications of these characterizations are that a gendered nature of work is created by the workers and the employers themselves. As workers enter the industry, the men and women and even the garment-shops owners create meanings justifying why men or women are in the industry. As more Latino workers join the industry, they begin to use language to characterize it as more masculine, requiring the strength and speed of male workers. For example, men call the garment shop a "*factoria*" and not just a sewing shop.

The industry, historically, has been flexible enough to change and has been dominated alternately by men and by women. In the early twentieth century, for example, skilled men dominated the New York City garment industry. However, as the division of labor increased, less skilled women entered the industry, and the gendered image of the industry changed along with the gender of the workers. Thus, garment work is not gendered as expected; instead, the work can take on different gendered meanings given the structures and the needs of the different groups of women and men who enter the industry.

Coethnic Assets and Liabilities

Findings

The Chinese Workers

We were the only family [mother and sister also worked in the same factory] but everybody knew someone else. Someone always brought someone there to work. It's too hard if they get a job without knowing anyone else, because the workers make fun of them or give them a hard time. If there is no one else in the factory to help you out, the workers would all scramble and take the best work. The new person just gets hassled all the time. I wouldn't want to join a factory without knowing others there

—*A Chinese woman in her twenties*

For the Chinese workers, coethnic relations support the processes associated with getting a job, where relative old timers help those who are just a little bit newer. Not only does this process work for brand new immigrants looking for jobs; it works for those who are seeking a new job. Coethnic workers share information about potential job openings where current workers can transfer. Only a few people I interviewed got jobs by walking in off the street in response to an advertisement in a newspaper or on a sign posted on the street. For the majority of the workers, someone lets them know when there are "open seats" to be filled in the shop and takes them in. Unless it is a brand new shop where all seats are open, a worker really needs relatives or friends to offer that information. For the Chinese immigrant who is a first-time job seeker or is looking for another job (i.e., his or her nth job), the same procedure applies.

In my sample over one-half of the workers are first-time job seekers. The worker is typically a female immigrant who just arrived in New York. She needs a job and asks everyone, both friends and family, about potential openings at garment factories. Rarely does she turn down the first one who offers to take her to a shop. Such an offer usually comes within the first month of her arrival. Thus, she is the instigator of a chain of events that will lead her to a job on a shop floor with training and social support.

When we first came, my mother and I were both looking for jobs in the garment factories. My aunt knew this and took us to work with her. In her factory there was only one seat available. My mother and I both wanted to learn how to sew. My mother and I shared the seat. If my mother practiced sewing and learning on the machine I would try to piece together the garment for her to sew. My aunt taught us how to run the machine, and showed us how to do pieces. I learned quicker than my mother, so I ended up working there on the machine. My mother didn't want to go to a strange place by herself so my aunt asked if she could stay to "cut threads" [do finishing work].

—*A Chinese woman in her twenties*

The one looking for her nth job also relies on this method. But because these seekers are working, they are much more selective and will wait for a better opportunity. If a shop seems appropriate and the kinds of work do not seem too difficult for the pay given, these workers will ask their friends to take them to the shops. Although they will receive less training from the friend, they will receive similar social support in terms of getting familiar with the shop practices.

I worked in over ten shops in the years that I've been here. I've been to so many that I forgot how many. I've worked in Manhattan and Brooklyn. All for Chinese. In Manhattan, I've worked for big shops, new ones and old ones. The one where I work now is a new shop, opened for only a year. If I look for a job, I always ask around to see what kind of job I can get. I know a lot about the different factories. Even in this building there is a factory above us and another below. I wouldn't work for the one below us because I know they always pay late. I hear the women talking about it. I know enough people to find out which factory is doing well. I'll ask them to keep an eye out for me and to let me know when there is a seat and to bring me in. I like to have a friend who can tell me what the boss likes or doesn't.

—*A Chinese woman in her forties*

Occasionally, it is not the potential worker that inquires about jobs but employers may ask workers to act as brokers to bring in new workers. According to Margaret Grieco (1987), employee referral is the cheapest method of obtaining labor and employee referrals provide an efficient screening mechanism. Experienced workers acting as brokers deliberately link potential workers with employers. Owners reward brokers who are able to bring in new people. Owners often give brokers easier work, by letting them sew the smaller-sized garments that can be finished faster (i.e., because they are smaller, they take less time to sew), thus they can sew more pieces in a given day and earn more money.

The good fast workers, I pay them some money, even on days when I get a little work. I don't want them going to another factory. I really want them to know that they are important. I can always get them to bring in workers when we get a big job. It really works. I give them some easier work and if I can, I give them a *hung bao* [bonus money in a red envelope] at the [Chinese] New Year.

—*A Chinese owner in his thirties*

Moreover, workers who bring in new workers are recognized as "elders," big sisters," or sponsors on the shop floor who are willing to help both workers and owners out. Thus, these workers get compensated. Furthermore, they are expected to assist in the training and acculturation of the new person. In these small ways, those that make an extra effort to recruit and to train other workers get recognition.

Workers are willing to be sponsors and brokers because garment work in a Chinese-owned factory is organized in such a way that new workers (even experienced new workers) are not competitors who are considered lower-waged replacements of the current workers. Piecework sewing is more individualistic and workers are more likely to push themselves to make more than to compete with the person next to them.

The shopowners and the new worker both expect the experienced worker—whether she played a broker's role or not, to take responsibility for the new person by training, by accompanying, and by helping him or her adjust to the factory's rhythms and routines. Because experienced workers take on the extra duty of training a new person, they are given respect as the factory "elder" or sponsor and they are given easier work.[5]

Inside recruitment is nothing new.[6] Other than facilitating the social links that bring together potential employers, the most important factor is that inside recruitment reduces risk on the part of the employer. For the owner, having a referenced employee is significant because it frees up the suspicions that the employer might have of workers' causing trouble (Holzer 1996; Neckerman and Kirschenman 1991). Furthermore, possible troublemakers can be restrained by the ones who brought them to the job.

> We really like workers bringing friends to work here. We don't have to watch them as much. They don't ask us as many questions. Their friends help them and they learn faster. They understand if we have to pay them late because they are learning. I know that the worker will get better. Sometimes the ones that walk in are just looking for any job and have never been able to learn to sew. They just go from place to place. They are the one that friends and family are not willing to sponsor or teach. Workers like that waste time. They are just looking for a shop that is sewing something easy. We don't have easy work all the time. They leave when the work gets hard.
>
> —*A Chinese owner in his fifties*

> I like hiring through friends. They have done well here, and they take care of each other. That, I like.
>
> —*A Chinese owner in her forties*

The Latino Workers
The personal and informal hiring and training scenario that characterizes the Chinese sector is not wholly appropriate to the Korean sector of the garment industry. Even though some of the Mexicans and Ecuadorians I interviewed did bring friends and relatives to their garment shops, the majority of them did not. The few that do bring friends express that it is their personal preference that they do so.

> I found my job in the Spanish newspaper over ten years ago. They only had three machines. Now they have over sixty machines. When it was a small shop, they had no problems with payment, but as they expanded it became harder and harder for them to pay weekly. I have brought friends to work there. I was one of the first workers when the shop opened, and I like to help when I can. I know many women who need jobs. The owner knows me well and doesn't mind when I bring others in. I came to the U.S. twenty-five years ago with four children to join my husband who was already here. After living with

him for one year we separated. Fifteen years ago I married a Dominican man who is a citizen.

—An Ecuadorian woman in her forties

The workers that bring others tend to be better skilled, more confident, and secure both with their jobs and their lives in general. Moreover, they admit that they want to be acknowledged as the ones that are helping others. One Mexican woman told me that she likes being recognized for her efforts by the others on the shop floor. More often than not, workers are afraid of what will happen to them if new workers do not work out or if new workers are selected to replace them.

I only tell people the address. I never introduce them to the owner. I don't like it when they [the owner] start asking me about them. The owners just need to know if we can sew—nothing else.

—A Mexican woman in her thirties

I don't feel comfortable introducing a worker to the owner. What happens if they get the job, and it doesn't work out? It would be a bad reflection on me. I help only by telling them where they could go to find a job.

—A Mexican woman in her twenties

The most typical scenario is that Mexicans and Ecuadorians send workers to shops other than their own, where there might be openings. Various difficulties hinder the workers' job searches, such as their undocumented status and the lack of coethnic employers. They do not rely on informal employer and employee personal connections as do the Chinese. Rather, keenly aware of possible exploitation, both workers and prospective workers take measures to limit their use of personal ties to get jobs. Potential workers still inquire about possible jobs but very few receive the personal treatment that the Chinese workers get.

Newcomers may indicate to friends and kin that they are searching for a job and ask for help. In return, friends and kin may mention that they know of openings in certain factories. The addresses may be exchanged, and the prospective worker is sent, on her or his own, to make an inquiry about the opening. Very often, experienced workers send new workers to shops other than their own because of fear of being identified. Other times, a prospective worker may be told about the area in midtown where the shops are located, and he or she may investigate potential jobs by himself or herself.

At my first job, a friend of mine told me where to go. He didn't introduce me to the owner or anything. I just came in and asked to see if they had a job.

—A Mexican woman in her twenties

In the spring I went to look for a job and came down to this neighborhood because friends told me there were many factories here. I came looking for a job. I was standing in front of the building. Then I saw someone put up a sign across the street and it was a job posting for this factory. I came up to the factory and asked the man if I could have a job. He told me to talk to M [his wife]. M asked me what I could do and asked if I could use a mer-

row machine that had two bobbins. I said no, I never did that. I worked with better mer-
row machines that had five or six bobbins. I was overqualified.

—A Central American woman in her twenties

Latino workers prefer to be anonymous, out of fear of immigration authorities. Having relatives and friends in the factory only adds to the possibility that someone may
leak information about them. Rarely did any of the workers have close friends or kin
in the same factory. The majority of the Latino workers had friends or kin elsewhere,
in nearby factories.

I am friendly with everyone. It doesn't matter where they come from, but I don't have too
many friends from the factories. I don't trust them because when it comes time to fire people, I don't want to be the one fired. I don't have papers. Someone can find this out and
use it against you. The owner can go fire someone and then the worker can say to the
owner why not fire her instead, she doesn't have any papers. I've seen this happen. People don't help each other as much as they should.

—A Mexican woman in her forties

Thus, the way Mexicans and Ecuadorians find work is impersonal. While they rely on
social contacts for getting ideas of which factories may have openings or even where
these prospective factories are located, they do not go the extra step of asking friends
and kin to give a personal reference for them. Workers fear that other workers' knowing too much about them may lead to misuse of the information. Furthermore, a personal reference may not help one get the job.

Korean owners in the garment industry prefer to hire those workers with fewer ties
because they assume such workers are newer immigrants and thus know little about
what an acceptable wage is and have less support than do more experienced workers
who have been in the United States longer. Newer immigrants are more vulnerable and
therefore more attractive to the employer. For one thing, the employer can offer him or
her lower wages.[7] Often new workers are willing to accept lower wages for a first job
to gain experience and then quickly leave when they hear of a better opportunity.

They do pay three dollars an hour. I just got here and was looking for a job. I went to the
factory, and the Korean man just said to me in Spanish, I'll give you three dollars an hour
to help bag the clothing. I took the job. I worked there for three months. Later on, other
workers started telling me that they pay me too little. I'm supposed to get four dollars. I
left after that and found another job.

—A Mexican woman in her twenties

Moreover, since Korean employers do not appreciate or feel any obligation toward
workers who bring in fellow Latinos, there is little benefit in stressing interpersonal
connections. Twenty-nine of the fifty-five Latinos interviewed have experienced or
seen others fired and replaced by the newly arrived who may be given lower wages.
Ten of the twenty-nine reported that the experienced worker was replaced by friends
or kin. Thus, many Latino workers are reluctant to help these newer immigrants. Here
coethnic assets become liabilities.

I had experience sewing in Mexico. I came to New York City because my mother was here. She helped me get my first job by taking me to her factory. I worked there for eleven months until the factory went bankrupt.

Where is your mother now?

At that first factory, they fired my mother two months after I started. I sewed better than she. My mother and I have different ways. I don't know what she is doing now. I don't keep in contact with her.

—A Mexican woman, age twenty-four

In my factory, the owner wants everyone to be experienced. It doesn't matter if you bring someone who is a good sewer to this factory. It doesn't matter if you do extra things when you are finished with your work. The owner only cares if he can have everything finished quickly so he can start another order. All the workers know that they can be fired if they are slow or are slowing everything down. We also know he wants to squeeze as much as he can for the pay he gives. If he can pay a worker less than another, and get the same or more work, he'll do it.

—An Ecuadorian man, age thirty-five

As a result, workers and employers have resorted to a very casual system of looking for work and workers. When I started this project, workers would look for posters placed on poles throughout the garment district. As the district became more upscale by attracting higher quality designers, and better maintained as a result of becoming a New York City Business Improvement District, a central posting site was organized that later evolved into the "for hire" corner.[8] Workers gather at a street corner in the center of the garment industry, with men on the south side of the corner and women on the north, every morning waiting for employers to recruit them.

I haven't worked for three weeks now. But I come every day to try to look for a job. I found out about this corner by accident. I just asked the people there why they were there. They told me they were looking for jobs. So I started to come around as well. I've made some acquaintances with the people on the corner.

At one time there were posters put up on the bulletin board—but the police took them all down. They were notices that advertised for jobs at this corner. Even after the posters were taken off, people still gathered here.

People do find work from the corner. Usually it is the younger women who know how to sew with the Singer machines that get jobs. Once I saw a man come and take people's home numbers of people with documents. He wanted to pay everyone by check. I can't do that, I have no papers.

Right now, only five older women are looking for jobs. Most of those women with experience are younger and can work the Singer machines. Whenever I see a younger woman here, I tell them that they should learn the Singer machine. There is an academy right here on Eighth Avenue on the third floor that you can go to learn. It costs three hundred dollars to learn the machine for three weeks.

—An Ecuadorian woman in her forties

Sector differences

Not only is the ethnic composition of these two sectors of the garment industry different but the pay system, work organization, and training are all different and all reinforce the actions corresponding to the two types of coethnic relationship.

Pay System and Work Organization

You see every factory at full capacity can have close to fifty people sewing in it. But most of the time, there are only thirty or so people. There's always room to try a new person. It's no loss to the owner when he already has the room to have a new person come in. In all the shops I've been, there are always people coming in to work all the time. There's no contract so the women come and go all the time.

—A Chinese woman in her twenties

In the Chinese shops, workers earn money by piece rates, and usually they sew whole garments. Therefore, any one worker—whether she works fast or slow—does not interfere with any other worker. Factories have a cadre of experienced career workers who do the bulk of the sewing, which has to be fast enough to meet the manufacturer's deadline and quality requirements. Few factories have all experienced workers. Seasonal fluctuations, leaves, and vacations all contribute to the worker fluidity in the shops.

I think I work well with them [Chinese workers]. I let them know when they have a lot of work to do and I let them know when I have little to do. They can schedule themselves [to work late or come in on Saturdays and Sundays]. I pay them whatever the rates that come from the manufacturers. For new workers, I want them to learn. I don't want them to just occupy the seat. They have to sew to practice. They can ask questions. They have to work and I will pay them for what they do.

—A Chinese owner in his forties

New, inexperienced workers can join the shop floor without affecting the profitability of the shop. Any number of pieces of clothing a new worker makes, however small, will earn the garment-factory owner profits, though the worker-in-training will receive only minute wages. If this new worker makes mistakes, she is expected to learn from them by going back and correcting them. Therefore, as long as the factory can complete its orders, whether the seats are all filled with experienced workers does not matter. Sometimes, though rarely, a Chinese owner will keep the factory open all night to complete its orders and insist that workers stay and make money. It is more likely, however, that the shop will be open every week, including weekends so that orders can be completed.

In contrast, in the Korean shops, wages are paid at an hourly rate and workers are assigned to sew portions of a garment. And if any group of workers is brand new, inexperienced, and extremely slow, then the whole production process is slowed down. Therefore any new, inexperienced worker can greatly affect the yield. In these shops, experienced workers are preferred over inexperienced ones.

> I have only section work. My workers only do one part of a garment and they do it fast. For example, a group will only do collars, or only sleeves. Most Koreans are set up to do section work. They don't do piece-rate work like the Chinese. The Chinese do pieces like that. But many [workers] leave for long lunches, leave early. I can't have that, this is team work and if one operator is missing, the work gets messed up. If any of them have trouble for not coming in, I want them to tell me the day before or even two days before. That way I can move another worker to replace them. I can rearrange it so that my output is still high. The Chinese don't do that. They just keep their shops open all the time [have long hours until the orders are completed].[9]
>
> —*A Korean shop owner in his forties*

Labor Supply

What is the explanation for the development of these two forms of work organization? One can hypothesize that a partial explanation is that ethnicity and the ease of obtaining resources from coethnics is an organizing rule behind the development of a particular form of work organization.

Chinese immigrants are much more heterogeneous than Korean immigrants. There tends to be enough Chinese both who want to be employers and who want to be employees in the garment industry, and there seems to be enough women who are able to work in the industry to make it a successful ethnic niche. But the situation is different for the Koreans. Korean men and women, on average, are more highly educated than the Chinese. Korean women who also want to be entrepreneurs look elsewhere for jobs and, in general, have been able to find a better-paying niche in the nail salon business as both owners and workers. Garment-shop owners without an adequate supply of coethnic workers must turn to another low-wage population. In this instance they turn to the immigrant Mexican and Ecuadorian population in New York City.

> Mainly Spanish—speaking from Mexico on down. We get a variety, a lot from Mexico. They want to work in these jobs. So many of them know that we need workers that they just come and knock on our doors.
>
> —*A Korean owner in his forties*

With these differences in labor supply, the work organization on the shop floor in each sector has to be arranged to accommodate the workers. For Chinese-owned factories, the Chinese woman is the target employee. After 1965 and the liberalization of the immigration laws, New York City saw a huge influx of Chinese immigrant families with adults who wanted to be both garment-shop entrepreneurs and garment-shop workers. Chinese immigrant women quickly learned that a single income brought home by the men from their work in restaurants was not sufficient to support the family. In addition, men's work in Chinatown most often did not include any health insurance. Thus, women looked for jobs to make up the difference. Moreover, women in the Chinese community constituted the only surplus labor available. To be able to keep the women, the work organization needed to accommodate their home responsibilities and family needs.

> My husband works in the restaurants in Chinatown. He's been working in different restaurants for the past ten years Right now he makes thirteen hundred dollars a month, which is good. I'm not working now but I still have Blue Cross [health coverage from the union]. He never had any union. I work enough to get Blue Cross. Next month I have to look for another [unionized] job.
>
> —*A Chinese woman in her forties (in an ESL class and on unemployment insurance)*

> My husband came first, he came as a specialty cook for a restaurant in the suburbs. He worked and ate there. When we came he looked for work in Chinatown. In Chinatown, he didn't make enough for all of us. We didn't have enough money to get a bigger apartment. The five of us lived in a one-bedroom apartment on Mott Street. When I started working, we started to save money for a house in Brooklyn.
>
> I could only work because back then my children could come to the factory after school. I would take them to school and get to work by nine-thirty, and I would pick them all up. I had them do their homework in the factory. Later, I sent them to Chinese School after school and I would pick them up afterwards to go home for dinner. After dinner my oldest daughter would watch if I had to go back to the factory. Now it is different. Many people have the grandparents to take care of their kids.
>
> —*A Chinese woman in her fifties*

> I don't know how to sew too well. I don't make that much money, but I make enough to help out. I only make about one hundred dollars a week. That pays for the groceries. I qualify for Blue Cross [health insurance]. My husband doesn't make that much. He's just a bus boy. He's waiting for an opening to be a waiter at the restaurant. I think he can make more, if he starts getting tips.
>
> —*A Chinese woman, age twenty-eight*

The piecework–whole garment system is the most flexible that is available in garment work, allowing the woman to determine how fast and at what time she can work. Therefore, while this system pays only for pieces that are completed, the woman can be flexible about her working hours on the job. The system allows her to complete her work at more convenient times when she does not have to be caring for the children or doing other household duties. For example, a Chinese garment worker can go to work after she drops off her children at school, go buy groceries at lunchtime, go back to work, pick up her children at three and take them to a relative to care for them, and then go back to work till nine in the evening.

> I was a forelady for a while, but that's not the kind of job I like. There are too many headaches. I don't like having to open and close the shop. The owner and I are always trying to predict if an order can be finished by a certain time. We can't ever predict it unless we rush everyone. The workers are always going in and out, especially the ones with children.

Sometime, I have to let them bring their children to the shop in the evening. The inspectors rarely come in the evenings to check. Other times, I have to give them a *hung bao* to get them to do extra work.

—*A Chinese woman in her forties*

The owner or forelady of the shop keeps the shop open longer hours, so that this kind of flexibility is allowed. In the end, even though the worker may show up for work at 9:00 a.m., and not leave till 9:00 p.m., she may have only put in eight hours of work. This particular system is flexible because the women are being paid for whole garments and not by the hours they have put in at the shop. If the owner needs to rush out goods, those that are there will be told to work faster, and owners can request that workers return quickly from errands to do work. Twenty of the Chinese workers have stressed that flexibility was one of the attractions of working in this industry.

I live in Brooklyn, so I can't go pick up my children from school, but I take them to school before I come to work. I don't get here till nine-thirty or I work till six and then get home by seven. My mother picks up my children. I do the shopping here in Chinatown. Two or three times a week I buy cooked meat like a chicken or roast pork to bring home. Then I have less to cook. It's convenient to work in Chinatown, especially to buy groceries. My bank is here, and I pay my gas and electric here at the bank too.

—*A Chinese woman in her thirties*

For the Korean employers, a piecework–whole garment system does not seem suitable for a population that was made up of undocumented Mexican and Ecuadorian men and women. These men and women often come to the United States without children and are much less likely than Chinese or Koreans to be permanent immigrants.

My husband came first. I came after him. I have two children, one four and the other five. They are in Mexico being taken cared of by my mother. I just work here. I don't waste any time [taking care of the kids].

—*A Mexican woman in her twenties*

I pay them by the hour here, and I pay them well. Many of the workers don't want piecework. I wanted to give them piecework rates for each seam they sewed, but many workers wanted to leave. If I paid piecework, it wouldn't be like the Chinese piecework where they got dollars for each whole dress, but I would pay a few cents or a dime for a seam. The workers didn't like that. Almost all the Korean factories pay by the hour. I can't be different, I would lose all the workers.

—*A Korean owner in his forties*

Thus, the flexibility afforded by the piecework system in the Chinese shops is not crucial in attracting these workers. Korean owners and the workers in the shops would have to be willing to work longer hours to make up for the flexibility. Moreover, the piecework–whole garment system would also require highly trained workers or the implementation of a training system to teach workers how to put together and sew a whole garment. Again, this did not seem to fit the characteristics of the labor supply that the Koreans owners faced. A piecework pay system is effective only in paying first-time workers. According to these Korean owners, if they pay piece-rate wages, workers will stay only until they learn that they can get hourly wages for the same work.

> I worked at one place that gave me piece rates. When you work piece rate, you take breaks whenever you want. It's all right when you work by the hour. You go to work at 8:00, you get a break at about 10:00 a.m., then half an hour lunch, then another break at 4:00 p.m. and get out of work at 6:00 p.m. You don't get paid during your half hour lunch break. . . . In this shop, when you first start you make piece rates. Then when you get faster you can get hourly wages. They pay people both piece rates and hourly wages.
> —*An Ecuadorian woman in her thirties*

The Koreans needed a system in which they could control the workers and moreover accomplish the work necessary in the requisite amount of time. A section-work system with hourly wages, which is an assembly line, affords the employer the most control. Each minute item of work can be split off so that less-experienced workers can do it. Any worker who is familiar with the sewing machines can replace another quickly on the line if necessary. Moreover, the wages are determined solely by the employer. A faster worker could conceivably get paid the same hourly wages as a slower worker, whereas in piecework the one who can sew more pieces will automatically get higher wages. Thus, the assembly line gives the owners considerable control over the workers.

These two types of work organizations and pay systems have different implications in terms of hiring and training. In the Chinese piece rate–whole garment, long hours system, speed is not crucial, and therefore new people can be accommodated and trained as long as there is room for them and as long as there are enough trained people to complete the necessary work. The more experienced are counted on to do the bulk of the work, while the new workers learn and earn meager wages. Moreover, the coethnic personalized hiring system allows workers to monitor one another. New workers rely on the sponsor workers to train, and in turn the owners reward these sponsor workers for their training. Sponsor workers also encourage new workers to learn quickly to increase the overall expertise in the factory.

For the Koreans to maintain the section–hourly rate system, it is crucial that the they hire someone who is semi-trained or at least able to manage the sewing machine. An absolutely untrained person cannot be productive, but one with minimal machine experience can. The person also need not be a professional garment worker but must be proficient enough to work a machine. With this kind of system, the owner wants to decide personally who can join the assembly line and what wages he or she will receive.

Training

Considering the pay systems and the work organizations of each of these types of shop, it is understandable why Korean shops would rather not train people. If there is an easy job—such as sewing a straight seam—then new sewers are hired to take that job. But, otherwise, a Korean-owned factory is not organized to accommodate absolute beginners. Very little training takes place in these factories. If young women want to learn, there are schools that have been organized to provide this type of training. Absolute newcomers are not often given a chance to sew. Instead they are given floor work—which is to hang, cut threads, and package the sewn items.

The Korean shop itself is not set up to train new workers: most of the time all the machines are used to manage the minute sections of work that have to be completed, and so there are no extra machines to be used for training . Moreover, there really is no one who can train new people. Owners, foremen, and forewomen are required to manage the workers and see that production is proceeding according to schedule.

> I think my shop is very organized. I give the workers lots of room to do their work. I try not to have too many things around them. It makes them work faster. I don't like empty machines. They learn as they sew. I can't teach them. They have to be smart to learn when I show them what they are sewing. I try to have someone who has some experience at all of my machines. Someone who is very good has to be at every section.
>
> —*A Korean owner in his forties*

In section work, the owner arranges his shop so that the machines are in a particular order to be most efficient at producing garments. Workers are required to work at a certain speed. Workers are assigned to making different pieces of clothing according to the speed at which they work and the necessary tempo of the assembly line. Thus, it is very difficult for experienced workers to stop their work to assist a newer worker. In fact, stopping would mean slowing down the whole line or whole production process.

> I've gone knocking on doors, and I've stood here waiting for people to come hire me. It's the same either way. The owner asks what you can do, and you tell them. I can sew fast. They have never asked me for papers, just what I can do. They take you over to your job. At the end of the day, or week, they tell you how much you'll be making. If you can't do the job, then you're fired.
>
> —*A Mexican woman in her twenties*

Consequently, if a Korean owner hires an employee's friend or kin who cannot sew, he or she risks slowing down the production process. A friend's recommendation in this case does not guarantee a sufficiently experienced sewer for the Korean employer. Thus, the Korean owners are more wary and more selective. They want to be able to test and see the worker in action for themselves before they offer a position. The Korean employer does not want to owe anything to the other worker either, such as feeling obligated to offer a job to this new person, without making an informed decision. Workers get paid only for the hours they sew. If workers come in and there is very little sewing to do, or if there is no work for the day, they receive only part of their daily wages or they are not paid at all. Thus, when there are many such days in a row, workers frequently go off to find another job.

Moreover, Korean owners know that the majority of the Mexican and Ecuadorian workers are undocumented and thus are unwilling to stay in New York City for an extended period. The Korean garment employers do not see the benefit in doing favors for these immigrants. Consequently, by not offering any kind of incentive for finding workers, they also discourage any type of coethnic support among the workers.

In contrast, the Chinese shops expect experienced workers to train the new, inexperienced workers, especially kin and friends. This expectation is seen as a favor in return for the owner's "hiring" the kin or friend. As long as there is a seat, experienced workers are allowed to bring in kin and friends, and thus, there are always new Chinese workers being trained to be garment workers.

Conclusion

Ethnic ties and the resources that can be shared across social ties regarding work are useful only when employers see benefits for themselves. They are useful for Chinese immigrants looking for work in Chinese-owned garment factories, but they are of no use for Mexican and Ecuadorian immigrants looking for work in Korean-owned garment factories.

Close ties are especially helpful in the Chinese community; there the information that is shared among Chinese coethnics is valued by Chinese employers because it gives them some modicum of control. And the benefit is reciprocated. For example, employers give bonuses, including easier jobs, to employees who use their close ties to other workers to train them and monitor their work.

Close ties and information shared among coethnics is not useful, however, if employers prefer to discriminate or choose workers based on their own criteria rather than on recommendations from others. For example, this study found that while Mexicans and Ecuadorians shared information with close friends and kin, they could not use the job information they received from one another to the fullest extent, because Korean employers were not interested in hiring those who knew others on the shop floor or those, in general, who knew much about the New York garment industry. They were interested only in those who had experience in their home country and had little information about the Korean shops in New York City. Moreover, some workers have seen how their relatives and friends who shared information lost jobs. Thus, sometimes greater information sharing between coethnics becomes a liability.

Notes

1. Even though some of the undocumented Mexicans and Ecuadorians want to return to their homeland in the future, all of them want to find jobs to earn money to provide for their own as well as their families' futures. Most Mexican and Ecuadorian workers I interviewed intended to return to their home countries within five years

2. A grocery or restaurant usually hires only five to ten workers to do manual labor. In a gar-

ment factory, there are on average thirty-five to forty workers, and the majority need to be skilled in working a machine.

3. These are estimates from the Union of Needletrades Industrial and Textile Employees (UNITE) Organizing department formerly two separate unions, the International Ladies Garment Worker's Union, and the Amalgamated Clothing and Textile Worker's Union that voted to merge at a joint convention in July 1995.

4. Even though Mexicans and Ecuadorians come undocumented and leave children in their home country, they are closer in geographical distance than the Chinese to their families and their homes.

5. Bailey and Waldinger 1991 offers insight into this process.

6. Granovetter's *Getting a Job* (1974) and Waldinger's *Still a Promised City* (1996) are but two works in this large area.

7. In the late nineteenth and the early twentieth century, German Jewish manufacturers felt the same way about the new Russian Jewish immigrants. "I want no experienced girls, they know the pay to get . . . but these greenhorns . . . cannot speak English and they don't know where to go and they just come from the old country and I let them work hard, like the devil, for less wages" (Seidman 1942).

8. The owner of the building, where the posting site was, protested this use of his building wall. Eventually this location, the West side of 37th Street and 8th Avenue, just evolved into the "for hire" corner, where workers and owners would frequent to look for work and workers.

9. The Korean owner is referring to why Chinese shops are open till late at night. It is especially true that all of the Chinese workers make up for the slower ones by working extra hours. However, some of the experienced sewers also take time off during the day to attend to childcare and household duties.

References

Bailey, Thomas, and Roger Waldinger. 1991. "Primary, Secondary, and Enclave Labor Markets: A Training Systems Approach." *American Sociological Review* 56:432–45.

Bao, Xiaolan. 1991. " 'Holding Up More Than Half the Sky': A History of Women Garment Workers in New York's Chinatown, 1948–1991." Ph.D. diss., New York University.

Chin, Margaret May. 1998. "Sewing Women: Immigrants and the New York City Garment Industry." Ph.D. diss., Columbia University.

Granovetter, Mark. 1974. *Getting a Job*. Cambridge: Harvard University Press.

———. 1985. "Economic Action and Social Structure: The Problem of Embeddedness." *American Journal of Sociology* 91:481–510.

Grieco, Margaret. 1987. *Keeping It in the Family: Social Networks and Employment Chance*. London and New York: Tavistock.

Holzer, Harry J. 1996. *What Employers Want: Job Prospects for Less Educated Workers*. New York: Russell Sage Foundation.

Karpathakis, Anna. 1993. "Greek Sojourners." Ph.D. diss., Columbia University.

Kim, Dae Young. 1996. "The Limits of Ethnic Solidarity: Mexican and Ecuadorian Employment in Korean-owned Businesses in New York City." Paper presented at the annual meeting of the American Sociological Association, New York, August.

Kinkead, Gwen. 1992. *Chinatown: A Portrait of a Closed Society*. New York: HarperCollins.

WHEN COETHNIC ASSETS BECOME LIABILITIES   299

Kwong, Peter. 1987. *The New Chinatown*. American Century. New York: Noonday Press.

Neckerman, Kathryn, and Joleen Kirschenman. 1991. "Hiring Strategies, Racial Bias, and Inner-City Workers." *Social Problems* 38:433–47.

Petras, Elizabeth Mclean. 1992. "The Shirt on Your Back: Immigrant Workers and the Reorganization of the Garment Industry." *Social Justice* 19 (1): 76–114.

Polanyi, Karl. [1944] 1957. *The Great Transformation*. Boston: Beacon Press.

Portes, Alejandro. 1995. "Economic Sociology and the Sociology of Immigration: A Conceptual Overview." In *The Economic Sociology of Immigration*, edited by Alejandro Portes.

Sassen, Saskia. 1991a. *The Global City*. Princeton: Princeton University Press.

———. 1991b. "The Informal Economy." In *Dual City*, edited by John H. Mollenkopf and Manuel Castells. New York: Russell Sage.

Seidman, Joel. 1942. *The Needle Trades*. New York: Farrar and Rinehart.

Smith, Robert C. 1994. "Doubly Bounded Solidarity: Race and Social Location in the Incorporation of Mexicans into New York City." Unpublished paper.

———. 1997. "Racial and Ethnic Hierarchies and the Incorporation of Mexicans in New York City: Transnational Communities and Labor Market Niches." Paper presented at Transnationalism, Migration, and Political Economy conference, New York, February.

Tilly, Charles. 2000. "Chain Migration and Opportunity Hoarding." In *The Governance of Cultural Diversity*, edited Janina Dacyl and Charles Westin. Paris: UNESCO.

Waldinger, Roger. 1986. *Through the Eye of the Needle: Immigrants and Enterprise in New York's Garment Trades*. New York: New York University Press.

———. 1995. "The 'Other Side' of Embeddedness: A Case Study of the Interplay of Economy and Ethnicity." *Ethnic and Racial Studies* 18 (3): 555–80.

———. 1996. *Still the Promised City: African Americans and New Immigrants in Postindustrial New York*. Cambridge: Harvard University Press.

Wong, Bernard. 1987. "The Chinese: New Immigrants in New York's Chinatown." Pp. 243–72 in *New Immigrants in New York*, edited by Nancy Foner. New York: Columbia University Press.

Zhou, Min. 1992. *Chinatown: The Socioeconomic Potential of an Urban Enclave*. Philadelphia: Temple University Press.

About the Contributors

ADRIAN BAILEY is currently Senior Lecturer in Geography at the University of Leeds, England. His research interests include the space-time relations of transnationalism and gendered migration.

VILNA BASHI BOBB, an Assistant Professor of Sociology at Rutgers University, is interested in research that analyzes how group membership affects the life chances of its members, particularly as groups are incorporated into local and global labor markets and other socioeconomic structures. Her background in economics, international studies, and sociology and demography enables her to use both qualitative and quantitative methods in her ongoing studies of race, immigration, and labor markets. She is currently writing a book about West Indian migration to New York and London.

MARGARET M. CHIN is Project Director for the Working Poor Under Welfare Reform project. She is currently revising her book *Sewing Women*, about Chinese, Koreans, Mexicans, and Ecuadorians in the garment industry. Her research interests include immigration, work, race and ethnicity, urban communities, and the working poor. She received her Ph.D. from Columbia University and will join Hunter College's Sociology Department in 2001.

DENNIS CONWAY received a B.A. and an M.A. from Cambridge University, a Dip. Ed. from Oxford University, and an M.A. and Ph.D. from the University of Texas at Austin. Currently he is Professor of Geography and Latin American and Caribbean Studies at Indiana University, Bloomington. His most recent book (co-authored with Robert Potter) deals with Caribbean housing problems. He has contributed several chapters to books on Caribbean migration and development issues and is pursuing research on migration and development relations in the contemporary Caribbean and Central America, specifically remittance impacts on households in Trinidad, Belize, and Nicaragua.

HÉCTOR R. CORDERO-GUZMÁN received his Ph.D. from the University of Chicago and is an Assistant Professor at the Robert J. Milano Graduate School of Management and Urban Policy at the New School University in New York City, where he teaches courses in quantitative research methods, urban demographic, economic and fiscal change, and immigration policy. He is currently completing a book that analyzes the role of community-based organizations in the adaptation and incorporation of immigrants and is directing a project that examines the impacts of changes in immigration and welfare laws on immigrants and community based social service providers.

MARK ELLIS is an Associate Professor of Geography at the University of Washington in Seattle. His research concerns the racial, ethnic, and employment consequences of immigration in U.S. cities.

NANCY FONER is Professor of Anthropology at the State University of New York, Purchase. She is the author or editor of seven books, the latest being *From Ellis Island to JFK: New York's Two Great Waves of Immigration* (2000) and *Immigration Research for a New Century: Multidisciplinary Perspectives,* edited with Rubén Rumbaut and Steven Gold (2000).

GEORGES E. FOURON is an Associate Professor of Social Sciences at SUNY–Stony Brook and a Haitian transmigrant. His research is on Haitian bilingualism, transnational social fields and national identities, and the connection between race, blood, and nation. He is the co-author of *Georges Woke Up Laughing: Long Distance Nationalism and the Apparent State* (forthcoming).

PAMELA M. GRAHAM is the Latin American and Iberian Studies Librarian at Columbia University. She holds a Ph.D. in Political Science from the University of North Carolina at Chapel Hill and her ongoing research focuses on Caribbean migration, politics, and the impact of new communications technologies on the social and political organization of migrants.

RAMÓN GROSFOGUEL is a Professor in the Sociology Department at Boston College. He is a Research Associate of the Fernand Braudel Center at SUNY-Binghamton and of the Maison des Sciences de l'Homme in Paris. He has written on Caribbean migration to Western Europe and the United States and on Latin American/Caribbean development. His book *Modern Coloniality and Colonial Subjects: Puerto Rico and Puerto Ricans in a Global/Comparative Perspective* is forthcoming from the University of California Press.

ALEX JULCA is a twin born in Huanuco, Peru, the same place where the composer of "El Condor Pasa," Daniel Alomia Robles, was born and where most of his family comes from. He has a Ph.D. in Economics from the New School for Social Research and works as a consultant for the United Nations in New York City.

PHILIP KASINITZ is Professor of Sociology at Hunter College and the Graduate Center of the City University of New York. He is the author of *Caribbean New York: Black Im-*

migrants and the Politics of Race (1992), editor of *Metropolis* (1995), and co-editor of *The Handbook of International Migration* (1999).

JENNIFER LEE is an Assistant Professor in the Department of Sociology at the University of California, Irvine. Her recent articles focus on race and ethnic relations, black/immigrant competition, employers' hiring practices, and immigrant entrepreneurship. She has completed a book, tentatively titled *Negotiating Race in Urban America: Blacks, Jews, and Koreans,* which is forthcoming from Harvard University Press.

JOHANNA LESSINGER is an anthropologist who has studied the issues of informal sector employment and gender roles in India. In addition she has followed the evolution of the Indian immigrant community in the United States for over fifteen years and is the author of the ethnography *From the Ganges to the Hudson: Indian Immigrants in New York City.* She currently teaches in the Department of Anthropology at the University of New Hampshire.

ZAI LIANG is an Associate Professor of Sociology at City University of New York–Queens College. His major research interests are in migration and race and ethnic relations. His current research projects include internal migration in China and international migration from China to the United States.

SARAH J. MAHLER is an Associate Professor of Anthropology at Florida International University in Miami. She received her undergraduate degree from Amherst College and her graduate degrees from Columbia University. Her research and publications focus primarily on Latin American and Caribbean migration to the United States and the development of transnational ties between migrants and their home communities. She is the author of *American Dreaming: Immigrant Life on the Margins* (1995).

NINA GLICK SCHILLER is an Associate Professor of Anthropology at the University of New Hampshire and Editor of *Identities: Global Studies in Culture and Power.* She co-edited *Towards a Transnational Perspective on Migration* (1992) and co-authored *Nations Unbound: Transnational Projects, Postcolonial Predicaments, and Deterritorialized Nation-States* (1994) and *Georges Woke Up Laughing: Long Distance Nationalism and the Apparent State* (forthcoming). She has also written on the connection between race and nation and the relationship between past and present transnational migrations and nation-states.

ROBERT C. SMITH is an Assistant Professor in the Department of Sociology and a member of the Barnard Project on Migration and Diasporas at Barnard College. He has received research or postdoctoral grants from the National Science Foundation, Social Science Research Council, Oral History Research Office at Columbia University, and the Spencer Foundation, National Academy of Education. He is currently finishing a book manuscript entitled *Migration, Settlement, and Transnational Life.* He is co-authoring another book, *Comparing Migration Systems,* with Aristide Zolberg. His current work focuses on second-generation school and work mobility and gender.

MILTON VICKERMAN is an Associate Professor of Sociology at the University of Virginia and conducts research on immigration and issues pertaining to race. He has conducted extensive fieldwork among West Indian immigrants in New York City and among blacks in Prince William County, Virginia. His publications include *Crosscurrents: West Indian Immigrants and Race* (1999) and other chapters and articles dealing with West Indian immigrants in the United States.